1 MONTH OF
FREE
READING

at
www.ForgottenBooks.com

By purchasing this book you are eligible for one month membership to ForgottenBooks.com, giving you unlimited access to our entire collection of over 1,000,000 titles via our web site and mobile apps.

To claim your free month visit:
www.forgottenbooks.com/free609591

ISBN 978-0-484-58418-0
PIBN 10609591

THE NORTH CAROLINA TEACHE

VOL. IX. RALEIGH, SEPTEMBER, 1891.

EUGENE G. HARRELL, = = = =]

THE SCHOOL MARM.

Oh, School Marm!
Thou who teachest the young ideas
How to shoot, and spankest the erstwhile
Festive small boy with a hand that taketh the trick
Who also lameth him with a hickory switch,
And crowneth him by laying the weight
Of a ruler upon his shoulders,

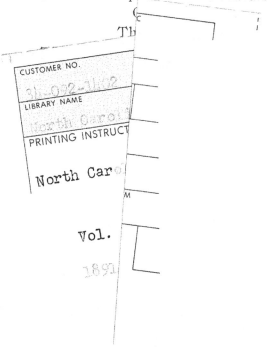

SPECIAL INSTRUCTIONS

TR M   COVER SIZE   X

JOB NO.

COVER NO

COV. TRIM

THE NORTH CAROLINA TEACHER.

VOL. IX.   RALEIGH, SEPTEMBER, 1891.   NO. 1.

EUGENE G. HARRELL, - ■ ■ - Editor.

THE SCHOOL MARM.

—

Oh, School Marm!
Thou who teachest the young ideas
How to shoot, and spankest the erstwhile
Festive small boy with a hand that taketh the trick;
Who also lameth him with a hickory switch,
And crowneth him by laying the weight
Of a ruler upon his shoulders,
        Oh!
     Thou art a daisy;
Thou makest him the National emblem —
Red, white and blue —
Thou furnisheth the stripes,
And he seeth the stars.
     Oh, School Marm!
We couldn't do without thee,
And we don't want to try;
Thou art lovely and accomplished
Above all women, and if thou art
Not married it is because thou art
Too smart to be caught that way!
All school marms are women,
But all women are not school marms
And angels pedagogic;
That's where thou hast the bulge on thy sisters.

Oh, School Marm !
Thou mayest not get much pay here below,
But cheap education is a national specialty,
And thou wilt get thy reward in heaven;
The only drawback being that thou stayest there
When thou goest after it, and we,
Who remain here below for our reward,
Miss you like thunder.
School Marm, if there is anything we can do for you,
        Call on us:
Apply early and avoid the rush;
Office hours from 8 A. M. to 5 P. M.;
Wé were a school-boy ourself once,
And can show the marks of it.

WHAT YOU DO WHEN YOU BLUSH.

When Dr. T. C. Minor was asked just what a blush
was, and how it was caused physiologically, he laid aside
his cigar, pondered deeply for a moment and spoke these
wise words:

"A blush is a temporary erythema and calorific efful-
gence of the physiognomy ætiologized by the perceptive-
ness of the censorium when in a predicament of unequi-
librity from a sense of shame, anger, or other cause, event-
uating in a paresis of the vaso-motor nervous filaments of
the facial capillaries, whereby, being divested of their
elasticity, are suffused with radiant, aerated, compound
nutritive circulating liquid, emanating from an intimidated
præcordia."

When the doctor finished a sigh of relief was heard from
his audience, and they only recovered their equipoise when
the doctor asked them to go over to the Grand Hotel and
hear him make a speech.

North Carolina Teachers Abroad:

A SUMMER JAUNT

IN

ENGLAND, SCOTLAND, IRELAND AND FRANCE.

CHAPTER XXI.

PARIS BY SUNLIGHT AND BY GASLIGHT.

A RESTLESS PEOPLE — OUR GUIDE WITH THE "CLEVELAND HAT" — RABBIT OR CAT? — THE CHAMPS ELYSEE — ARC DE TRIOMPHE — BADLY LEFT — HONOR TO THE AMERICAN FLAG — TOMB OF NAPOLEON — "BE REVERENT" — THE LOUVRE GALLERIES — FRENCH LOVE OF THE NUDE IN ART — RELICS OF PHARAOH — A THEOLOGICAL PROBLEM — THE LUXEMBOURG MUSEUM — IN A FRENCH RESTAURANT — PALAIS ROYAL — ENGLISH SPOKEN HERE — AN EMBARRASSING SITUATION — "QUEL JOLIE FILLE" — NOTRE DAME CATHEDRAL — SOME RARE RELICS — DOUBTING NORTH CAROLINIANS — CHURCHES OF ST. SULPICE AND ST. ETIENNE DU MONT — ST. GENEVIEVE'S BLESSING — A BUSINESS BOOM — AVENUE L'OPERA — GRAND OPERA — PARIS BY GASLIGHT — PRESIDENT CARNOT'S RECEPTION — MEISSONNIER, THE GREAT ARTIST.

HE more we see of this splendid city of Paris the more we realize the extent of the political unrest which exists here among the masses of the people. There is every evidence that the government is on the eve of a great change, but in what manner this change is to come is yet unknown. It may be war, and if so, the very thought of the murder and destruction which will attend it causes us to shudder; and this Republic may be transformed into an Empire in a day upon the fiat of the *vox populi* as expressed at the ballot-box; then there may be seen a "Revolution of Peace'' throughout this fair land, and all other nations will be filled with wonder, and history will record the birth of the new Empire without dipping the pen in blood. We cannot suppress a sigh for the political fate of ''La Belle France.''

Having arranged with our friends, Messrs. Henry Gaze & Son, for a pleasant and systematic tour of this gay capital, we found four handsome excursion carriages at the door of our hotel waiting for us as we left the breakfast-table on the next morning after our arrival, and the twenty magnificent iron-gray horses were prancing with their impatience to be off.

Our guide and interpreter for the sight-seeing tour was an exceedingly clever and intelligent man of English parentage named Gallop. To prevent his being lost to us in a crowd his large round head was ornamented by a tall white ''plug,'' well known in America as the ''Cleveland hat.'' All we had to do, when the party became separated in the vast throngs of people visiting the public places, was, at a signal from a whistle, to ''rally on that Cleveland hat.''

The breakfast was excellent and our appetites were in good order and we greatly enjoyed the French dishes, many of which were unknown to us.

''How I enjoyed that very savory rabbit which we had for breakfast!'' exclaimed one of our girls, as she climbed into the carriage.

''Yes, indeed you did, Sue; and so did I,'' answered her neighbor. ''It was so fine that I had the waiter to serve me twice with the rabbit.''

''Young ladies,'' said Mr. Braswell, ''did you notice what a number of cats there were creating a disturbance in the hotel court last night after we had retired?''

''O yes, I remember that fearful catawauling last night,'' replied several of the girls.

"Well, doesn't it strike you as a singular coincidence that not a single one of those cats has been seen or heard this morning — and we had *rabbit* in abundance for breakfast?"

"Oh! you horrid man!" came in startled tones from every part of the carriages, as our horses dashed away over the pavement while the sparks glistened under the wheels.

On the faces of some of our girls there came during the day expressions of profound meditation, but they most emphatically denied that it was the reflection of their thoughts while trying to solve the suggestion of a mysterious relation between the facts that they had heard and seen cats in the evening and had been served with rabbit for breakfast in the same hotel next morning. We couldn't keep from hoping that rabbit would be again served to us, mainly as an object-lesson in natural history, but it was a dish that never came to us again.

Just two blocks from the hotel our carriages dashed into the Champs Elysées, the most beautiful street in the world. As we entered that celebrated thoroughfare we glanced along its entire length feasting our eyes upon the harmonious beauty of a wide street, smoothly paved, fine rows of shady, green trees, sparkling fountains at pleasant intervals, whose falling waters caressed most tenderly exquisite groups of marble and bronze statuary; while away to our right, about half a mile distant, in the very centre of the great boulevard, stood the famous Arch of Triumph, towering in sullen and majestic grandeur far above the surrounding buildings, as some grim sentinel of the ages silently proclaiming the conquests of Napoleon Bonaparte.

The Arc de Triomphe de l'Etoile being our first point of visitation the carriages halted by the side of it, and after a long climb of one hundred and sixty feet up a winding stairway in one of the four columns there were a hundred North Carolinians cooling themselves on the top of the pile, while enjoying the charming landscape spread out before them along the twelve fine avenues which radiate from that point.

This is the finest triumphal arch in existence, and it is situated upon an eminence so that it can be seen from almost every point of the city. On the gigantic proportions of the Arch, carved in high relief, are immense groups of statuary representing various victories of Napoleon. The Arch was thirty years in building and cost over two million dollars.

When the city was captured by the Prussians in 1871, the German army marched into Paris through this Arch of Triumph for the purpose of humiliating the French people as much as possible. And they succeeded. With the hope of restoring to the clever people of Paris their natural pride in so celebrated a structure we waved from the summit of the Arch our beautiful American flag, the emblem of "the land of the free and the home of the brave." The flag was cheered by friends walking on the pavement below us and we felt that our mission of restoration was accomplished.

There was a large crowd of visitors upon the roof of the Arch besides our party, and in the fascination of the scene the time was forgotten until suddenly the Secretary found that the party had descended to the carriages and had taken their departure, leaving him with Misses Helen Fowle and Mabel Upchurch alone upon the Arch. We knew, however, that the next point of destination was the Hotel des Invalides, and taking a convenient cab we were soon at this place awaiting the arrival of our party.

From whatever point you may stand in Paris if you look towards the Seine you will see a beautiful gilded dome towering three hundred and forty feet high and glittering in the sunlight, while its bright rays seem to flash forth the martial glories of France. "What is that magnificent structure?" we ask, and the answer comes to us in the low tones of reverence and adoration, "Under that gilded dome is the tomb of the great Napoleon!"

Having rejoined our party at the gate and safely run the gauntlet of the companies, battalions and regiments of dealers in photographs, views, and other souvenirs of various kinds, which formed a line of battle in front of the building, we finally stand beside the tomb of Napoleon. The tomb is very magnificent and imposing, and we look down upon it over a circular railing.   There we see the sarcophagus, made of a single block of granite weighing over sixty-seven tons, which contains the mortal remains of Napoleon, a man who conquered the greater part of Europe.   This single block of reddish, polished granite was brought from Lake Ladoga in Finland, and cost near thirty thousand dollars.

While gazing with reverence and awe upon the lovely mosaic pavement which represents a wreath of laurels, we read the inscription, in French, which is taken from the conqueror's will and inscribed over the entrance to the vault :

> "I DESIRE THAT MY ASHES MAY REST UPON THE BANKS OF THE SEINE, IN THE MIDST OF THE FRENCH PEOPLE, WHOM I HAVE SO WELL LOVED."

The body rests in an open circular crypt, twenty feet in depth and thirty-six feet in diameter, and the walls are adorned by relief in marble by Simart.   Surrounding the crypt are twelve colossal figures in marble by Pradier, emblematic of the famous victories gained by the great Emperor.   French soldiers are always on guard about the tomb, and they seem to have learned two words in all languages.   They never speak except when there is evidence of levity or boisterousness on the part of some thoughtless visitor, and then, in the native tongue of the visitor, he is reprimanded by the guard in the most solemn manner to "Be reverent!"

Having duly paid our respects to the ashes of the "child and grave-digger of the French Revolution," we return to our carriages and drive rapidly to the great palace of the Louvre. This immense palace, with its courts and buildings, covers some twenty acres, and has been the residence of Kings, Queens and Princes. It is now converted into a vast museum for the people, and its miles of grand halls and galleries are filled with paintings, statuary, and other rare works of art, from all parts of the world. It would take a daily visit of several hours for a whole year to give even one look at every painting and statue in the Louvre.

Here are finest works of art by the most famous painters and sculptors of the world, and while wandering through these never-ending galleries and looking through these miles and miles of paintings, we become as familiar with the names of Raphael, Titian, Leonardo de Vinci, Lorraine, Murillo, Vernet, Correggio, Vandyke, Rubens, and other noted artists, as we are with the cognomens of Smith, Brown and Jones in America. What a rare pleasure it is to gaze upon the priceless original pictures, copies of which we have loved for many years. There are paintings and statuary here to see which alone is worth a visit to Paris, even if we saw nothing else.

First among the prominent objects to attract our attention and admiration is that famous statue, the original Venus de Milo, which is perhaps one of the chiefest and rarest gems in the marvelous collection in the Louvre. This, the loveliest of all the beautiful forms of Venus which the noted sculptors of the world have chiseled from the marble, is on a pedestal standing alone in the centre of a hall on the first floor, and a strong iron railing is built around the figure just far enough away to prevent the thousands of admiring visitors from touching the celebrated stone.

The Egyptian Museum greatly interested us. The collection of relics of that noted country are so numerous and varied that we can here study the history of Egypt almost as well as if we were in that land itself. Here is a large stone Sphinx which once belonged to Pharaoh, and the inscriptions upon it show that it must have been a very old stone when he owned it. Here are also three life-size figures, in stone, which are portraits of distinguished individuals who·flourished before the great pyramids were built, about four thousand years before the Christian era!

As we contemplate these strange things preserved from the earliest centuries, we wonder why it is that not a relic or even the vestige of a genuine relic or picture has been preserved, and is anywhere on earth to be seen, of Christ, Paul, Peter, Stephen, Matthew, Mark, Luke, John, or of any other person or persons in anyway connected with the Saviour, or with His coming into the world to establish a new religion, which fact has been for eighteen centuries conceded to have been the most important event in the world's history. It is quite evident that we must accept the Gospel of Christianity solely by *faith*, certainly not upon any *visible* testimony that now exists.

In the vast picture galleries we find that it is impossible to give even a passing glance to each of the myriads of beautiful paintings, therefore our study is given to the best known and most celebrated works. Among these are "Madonna and Child with Angels," by Perugino; "Holy Family," by Rembrandt; "Immaculate Conception," by Murillo; "St. Michael and the Dragon," by Raphael; "Marriage at Cana," by Veronese; "Jupiter and Antiope," by Titian; "Virgin in the Sepulchre," by Leonardo de Vinci.

In all these great galleries of the Louvre the visitor has abundant evidence of the wonderful love of the French people for the charms displayed by the highly-colored and naked female forms gracefully posing upon the canvas and in the white marble. In the Rubens Gallery the eyes of the visitor are surfeited by the vast sea of fat, red, undraped women among the clouds, surrounded by puffy little cherubs — even the pink-tinted flesh, usually so beautiful in a painting, absolutely becomes tiresome. There are many amateur artists in the principal salons with easel, brush and crayon, making copies of some favorite painting or statue, and as we glance over their shoulders we see that, in almost every instance, the object selected for the model is a lovely nude female figure, or a particularly striking piece of undraped statuary. All of these amateur artists were French women, except one solitary negro man who was on a vacation trip to Paris from a government clerkship in Washington City.

In the Louvre are a number of most interesting relics, and we were specially attracted by a little, worn shoe belonging once to Marie Antoinette, and an old gray coat of the first Emperor of France.

We left the fascinating Louvre with reluctance and a promise to visit it again during our stay in Paris, and then drove to the palace of Luxembourg, which now contains another collection of paintings and statuary, and all are the works of living French artists. Many of the subjects here shown are of a high character, but the collection is constantly changed by the removal from time to time of the works of dead artists to the Louvre, and admittance of new paintings. The gardens about the palace are very extensive and very beautiful, and they contain many fine fountains and statues.

We are now thoroughly tired of looking at paintings and statuary for the present, and of course we were hungry, that seeming to be the chronic state of our party at all times, so we made our way to the Palais Royal for lunch.

A French restaurant is a thing to not only interest the hungry visitor but also to excite his wonder. Everything that he makes use of in disposing of his meal is charged separately on his bill. The plate, knife and fork, glass of water, salt, bread, butter, napkin, chair, pepper, vinegar, mustard, tooth-picks, are each charged for separately, and when the servant brings, at the end of the meal, a bill about a foot long, the guest is horrified until he glances at the bottom and finds that the entire outfit for the dinner amounts to but fifty or sixty cents. The charges are generally reasonable for the usual course.

The Secretary once, during a sudden attack of recklessness, ordered, in a French restaurant, half of a chicken, but the shock occasioned by the receipt of a bill for the chicken amounting to *two dollars*, effectually cured him permanently of all future attacks of such recklessness. We give this prescription without any charge for the benefit of our friends who contemplate a visit to Paris.

The Palais Royal represents the history of France for two centuries and a half. It was built by Cardinal Richelieu in 1629, and has been in turn occupied as a royal residence by Anne of Austria, Louis XIV and two generations of the family of Orleans. The grandson of Philip of Orleans having exhausted his means by riotous living, built the arcades to the palace and rented them to shop-keepers, and they exist to this day and are used for the same purpose.

In one of the Cafés of this building the destruction of the Bastile was organized by Camille Desmoulins, just one hundred years ago, in 1789. In the Revolution of 1848 the Royal Apartments were wrecked by the mob, and most of the elegant and valuable paintings were destroyed. In 1871 the Communists again raided the Royal Apartments,

and destroyed the south wing by fire.   The Palace is now
completely restored and is used by the Council of State.

The arcades of the Palais Royal are well known to tourists who want to buy presents for friends at home.   Most
of the shops are specially devoted to the sale of jewelry and
photographs.

Copies of all the celebrated paintings and statues may
be obtained here; besides, there are exhibited a great many
photographs from life which will shock the modesty of
the average American in the highest degree; and such an
exhibit as those show windows present would not be permitted for even an hour in New York, or in any other city
west of the Atlantic.   Yet, in Paris there is always a crowd
of men, women, and even little children, standing before
those immense show-windows of the Palais Royal which
display such lively contents of the diminutive shops behind
them.

All the articles for sale in the arcades of the Palais Royal
are at very reasonable prices, except in those shops whose
windows bear the tempting inscription, "English spoken
here." It seems that the average French shop-keeper labors
under the delusion that an American is perfectly delighted
at the privilege of paying about three prices for an article
if he can only conduct the transaction in his beloved
"English" language.   Therefore, the aforesaid deluded
shop-keeper nurses a conscience as clear as sunlight, while
he "murders the Queen's English" and robs Uncle Sam's
subjects.   As you value the "dollars of our daddies" be-
ware the seductive suggestion *"Anglais parlez ici."*

The visitor to a foreign country, where a language is
spoken different from his own, is constantly impressed by
the feeling that all the people he meets other than his companions are deaf and dumb.   Influenced by this strange
idea, he is often tempted to an unusual boldness and reck-

lessness in his observations upon persons about him. As the Secretary and several members of our party were admiring the beautiful display in one of the windows of the Palais Royal, several other persons also stopped to enjoy the sight and were conversing in French.

Turning to one of his friends, the Secretary said: "What an exceedingly lovely French girl that is standing by my side!"

Before his companion could reply the supposed "French girl" answered, in English: "While I thank you for the compliment I must confess that the sudden candor with which you Americans express your opinions is somewhat startling."

The Secretary couldn't apologise — it was not exactly the thing to do. The situation was certainly embarrassing, but the customary "*Excusé moi, s'il vous plait*" seemed to be satisfactory to the lady, while the Secretary has not yet ceased to thank his good luck which made him happen to compliment instead of criticise the stranger. We met that young English lady again; it was in the Cemetery Perè la Chaise, and, encouraged by our former experience with her and inspired by the grave surroundings, we formed a very pleasant acquaintance; and perhaps we thus prevented a possible declaration of war between England and the United States.

But the French people are very susceptible to compliments. We have often stood among a crowd of people in Paris and would say to our companions, just loud enough to be well overheard, "*Quel jolie fille!*" (what a pretty girl). Instantly a number of charming French maidens would appropriate the description unto herself, and would smilingly bow her acknowledgment of the off-hand compliment, replying in the sweetest of French "*Je vous remercie, monsieur.*"

Having sufficiently indulged our curiosity among the arcades of the Palais Royal were turned to our carriages, and, after an interesting drive along Rue de Rivoli by the magnificent Garden of the Tuileries, then down the splendid Boulevard Saint Germain, we crossed the river Seine and reined up in front of the famous Notre Dame Cathedral, which stands on the Isle de Cité.

This noted building is the most interesting church in Paris, and it is also one of the most celebrated in the world. The present Notre Dame Cathedral was founded in 1163, on the site of a church which was built in the fourth century. The interior of the building consists of a nave, with double aisles crossed by a transept, and the general effect is of a highly æsthetic character. Specially beautiful are the many large stained glass windows, some of which are exceedingly ancient. In the centre of the second story is a magnificent rose window forty-two feet in diameter. Within the building is a series of niches containing statues of twenty-eight French kings. The original statues were all destroyed during the Revolution, but have since been restored.

In the centre portal is a very fine carving, representing "The Last Judgment," and on the left portal is a relief, representing the "Burial of the Virgin," which is lovely beyond description. The great bell of Notre Dame, mentioned by Victor Hugo, is one of the largest in Europe, weighing sixteen tons, and the clapper alone weighs one thousand pounds. The Cathedral seats twenty thousand persons.

We paid half a franc each and were admitted to the treasury, where are a number of "sacred relics," which are shown to us with great ceremony and devotion. Among the curiosities is a piece of the cross upon which the Saviour was nailed, and one of the nails which were driven through his hands, also fragments of the crown of thorns which the Jews placed on the head of Christ. Tradition says that these relics were purchased by St. Louis from Jean de Brienne, King of Jerusalem, for $600,000. The sight of the sacred mementoes did not inspire us to a very high degree of devotion, as we knew that several dozen more of the "original nails" and two or three more cords of wood from the "true cross" are exhibited in other places throughout Europe. We kindly informed the guard of the sacred treasures of Notre Dame of this fact and he didn't seem to appreciate the information, but promptly denounced all of the relics in other Roman Catholic Churches as impositions. We accepted his statement without question as we had likewise done when the keepers of the sacred relics in the other churches enlightened us concerning similar treasures in the Notre Dame.

We concluded that as we were now somewhat specially interested in studying ecclesiastical things and architecture we would visit some of the other noted churches of Paris before returning to our hotel for dinner, therefore the guide was instructed to drive to the church of St. Sulpice. This is a very large building, and the architecture is of the eighteenth century. It has two immense towers which are not of uniform design. This grand and beautiful church was very piously erected almost entirely from the proceeds of lotteries! It has one of the finest organs in Paris, which contains six rows of keys, one hundred and eighteen stops and seven thousand pipes.

The church of St. Etienne du Mont next interested us. It is a Gothic edifice of the fifteenth century style, and the interior is the finest in France. The first chapel contains the remains of Saint Genevieve, the patron saint of Paris. It is a beautiful gilded tomb, upon which tapers are always burning. You may buy a taper from a little table standing near, for a franc, and it will be lighted and placed upon the tomb to burn a prayer for you. There were no purchases, as most of the party said they needed the franc more than they did the prayer.

In one of the recesses of the nave was a sleepy looking old woman offering for sale a great variety of little trinkets, at prices from five cents to twenty-five cents. There were crucifixes, hearts, anchors, and other neat designs. Our party examined them but without buying anything, and we were about to move on when a member of the party whispered to one of our chaperons that there was a strange tradition connected with that particular booth for the sale of trinkets.

"What is it?" she asked with much interest.

"It is said," he replied, "that St. Genevieve pronounces a special blessing upon all who purchase from that old woman, and every unmarried person who wears one of those trinkets will be happily married within a year after purchasing it."

This information was by some means soon circulated, and the spirit of pious investment seemed to suddenly possess that party in a most alarming degree. The old woman was startled by such an unparalleled rush of business, and she was compelled to call to her assistance two other women, equally old and ugly, to wait upon her eager customers. We found it impossible to move the party from that niche until each person was supplied with at least a crucifix, which was at once suspended from the neck or watch-chain in the most orthodox manner.

Our guide with the "Cleveland hat" was greatly astonished at the tremendous impulse of trade which had struck the crowd, and when he learned the cause of it, some hour or two afterwards, he said: "Well! well! that was the meanest joke ever played on a party." It was lucky for the man who started it that we never found him out.

The Secretary still has in his possession about a dozen little silver crucifixes with the blessing of St. Genevieve attached, for which he has been offered fabulous sums, but nothing can induce him to part with them.

Returning to our hotel, the route lay through the splendid Avenue l'Opera. This is said to be the finest thoroughfare in the world. The avenue is three-quarters of a mile in length, and before its construction the ground was covered with a perfect network of dark and gloomy streets. There are no trees along the magnificent avenue it being thought that they would obstruct the view of the Grand Opera-House to which this boulevard leads.

The Frenchman is as fond of amusement as he is of broad and beautiful streets, extensive parks and playing fountains. No city in the world but Paris would have erected such a building for amusement as the Grand Opera-House which graces the head of the Avenue l'Opera. This is the finest and largest theatre on earth, and in its construction over five hundred houses were demolished for a site, which cost $2,100,000. The building was commenced in 1861 and finished in 1874, at a cost of over seven million five hundred thousand dollars. Thus the entire cost of that single building is as great as the combined total valuation of all the property in three of North Carolina's largest cities as appearing on the assessor's books, or nearly as much as North Carolina levied for State, school and county taxes during the past ten years! The building covers about three acres and nothing can equal the magnificence of the materials with which the interior is lavishly decorated. The Government appropriates near two hundred thousand dollars annually for the support of this opera.

After an enjoyable dinner at our hotel most of the party formed small companies for a visit to the opera and other places of amusement, or to stroll down the lovely Champs Elysées and the gorgeously lighted boulevards of the city. Surely there can be no more beautiful sight than these great thoroughfares at night, which are so profusely and artistically lighted by the myriads of gas-lamps that the

2

stranger is inclined to believe that the city is conducting a grand illumination specially for some celebrated occasion.

Paris only becomes really gay and glittering after the sun has disappeared and the soft twilight takes possession of the city. Then the air is filled with the notes of lively music in every direction, the laughing and shouting of thousands of happy children and merry maidens; the rumbling of the vast brigade of cabs and victorias, all occupied by some jolly sight-seers; the clatter of the dancing and the warblings of the singers from numbers of concert halls and dancing saloons representing every degree of sensational abandon; the importunate appeals of the peddler of small wares of various kinds; the discordant voice of the street minstrel, accompanied by a still more tuneless accordeon or a heart-rending violin; and all these sights and sounds and scenes continue entirely through the night only to cease with the dawn of another day.

Just half a block from our hotél is the Palais de l'Elysée, the official residence of President Carnot, the chief magistrate of the Republic of France. During the reign of Louis XV this mansion was the residence of the noted Madame de Pompadour and it was purchased from her heirs as a residence for foreign embassadors. The building has in turn been occupied by the Duchesse of Bourbon, Murat, Napoleon I, Louis Bonaparte, King of Holland and his queen Hortense, Emperor Alexander I of Russia, the Duc de Berry, and Napoleon III as President of the French Republic.

On this evening President Carnot was holding a magnificent royal reception in honor of the Shah of Persia, to which all the visiting nobles and prominent persons of Paris were invited.

As we returned from our ramble over Paris by gaslight the gates of the Palace were opened and the distinguished guests were taking their leave.

On either side of the entrance was a line of mounted guards, gorgeously attired, while between them drove the open carriages bearing the royal guests. A vast crowd of people had gathered about the entrance to see such an array of nobility and of course we joined the throng, and, as usual, soon occupied "reserved seats on the front row."

Under brilliant gas and electric lights each person could be plainly seen as he rode through the gates, and among the guests were kings, princes, emperors, embassadors and rulers of countries of every degree of nobility. The crowd of spectators kept perfect silence as one after another of these magnates rode by; there was no cheering or demonstration of any kind. At length there came a carriage with only one occupant, a fine looking man whose hair and long beard were perfectly white with age, and as the people caught sight of him there arose such a mighty burst of applause and cheers as almost deafened us; hats and canes were waved in the air, and mingled with the torrent of enthusiasm every voice was shouting the beloved name "Meissonnier!" "Meissonnier!"

Yes, it was indeed the great artist Meissonnier, and this storm of demonstrations of joy and love told us in unmistakable words that the supreme love of the French people is for Art.

[For The North Carolina Teacher.]
WHISPERING.

BY MISS CLAUDE L. GRIER, CONCORD, N. C.

Can whispering be suppressed in an ungraded country public school? I answer, "Yes." "How do you prove it?" some weary worker in a crowded school-room faintly asks. "How would you prove that our globe *can* be circumnavigated?"

Required on the part of the teacher courage, firmness, courteous bearing toward pupils, and above all a double portion of that spirit which must animate the true teacher, that of helpfulness to those under his care. With this feeling in his heart let him lose no time in bringing his pupils to this view of his relation to them. Let both get rid of the idea of guard and substitute that of guide.

With this idea clearly in my own mind on the morning of the opening of my school I chatted familiarly with the boys and girls who had gathered in the little low house to begin a term of four months school in a district where a part of the committee were opposed to employing a lady teacher, because it took a man to manage *those* children! "Those children" arrived slowly, but noticing that the hands of my tiny clock pointed to 9:15 I rapped for order (there was no bell), and all took their seats on the long benches extending across the room.

I then busied myself in examining the books of my new pupils, and assigned work of some sort for each one immediately, remarking as I did so, that, as our school term was so short, we could not afford to lose any time in getting down to regular work. Then standing there among them, looking fairly into the expectant faces turned toward me, I said, in substance: "Boys and girls I am here to help you make the very best use of the time we spend together; we must have *work* but we will all try to make it pleasant work. But to have good school work we must have *quiet*. In a little more than an hour we will have a few minutes recess, and until that time I must ask you to speak to no one except myself (surprised glances exchanged.) When I am not hearing a recitation or busy at the blackboard I will be glad to give you any help you need if you will raise your hand and come quietly to me." Pausing a moment I noticed smiles of almost incredulity on some faces. Turning to a pleasant faced girl of eleven, I said,

"Ida, you seem surprised at what I have said." "Don't you 'low any talking?" she asked. "No," I said, "I do not." "Well, I never saw a teacher that did not allow any speaking at all in school." "How much did your other teachers allow you to talk?" "O, we could always talk about our *lessons*." "Ah! and of course you never spoke about anything else?" A general laugh, in which I joined, was sufficient answer. "Now," I resumed, "don't think about how long it will be till four o'clock this afternoon. You have only to keep busy, and I'll see that you have plenty to do until half past ten, then after a little rest, till half after twelve, we will have a long hour to tell each other all the good things we've thought of this morning. Now, Harvey, bring your First Reader and we will go to the board."

Thus we started, and thus we kept on. By no means was all the work done the first day. Persevering effort was required to carry out the principles laid down in my "Inaugural," and some discouragements arose as the number increased and the novelty of the proceedings wore off, but gratifying success crowned my efforts, and visitors to the school-room expressed astonishment at the almost perfect order maintained. This, too, when of the twenty-eight attending, quite a number, both of boys and girls, were larger and older than their teacher, though she claimed one hundred and thirty avoirdupois, and twenty years' residence on this sublunary sphere.

Before each recess and the close of school I called for reports, as I found it better to keep things straight *two hours at a time* than to leave all until an accumulation of six hours' struggles and failures would tempt to deception. When any had spoken without permission the offender was told to go on with studies while the others went to play. Recesses are highly prized where a school is working well. I sometimes add a task to the keeping in, but not as a rule.

It is likely we will meet with incorrigibles sometimes who require sterner treatment than I have outlined above. In such cases I would not hesitate to resort to the birch when all else fails. It is frequently wise, as well as kind, to separate a boy who has a persistently communicative disposition from his companions; give him a seat by the teacher's desk, or on the platform with his back to the school. Tell him he can return to his own seat when he thinks he can be trusted among other boys.

Let us avoid treating whispering as a high crime. It is not. Some good and studious pupils have been known to indulge in it; but if time is wasted and others are interrupted reparation must be made as far as possible, whether the offender be idle or diligent.

IN AFTER YEARS.

And now the sweet girl graduate,
  In pride and brand-new gown,
Comes forth in crowds to agitate
  Each quaint old college town.
She knows she's just the sweetest thing
  Of this season of the year,
And expects to make the whole world ring
  With "Woman and Her Sphere."
But let us forward look, perchance
  Five years — that ought to do —
She's cutting down dear Willie's pants
  To fit the other two.

NORTH CAROLINA expects to cover herself with glory by her educational exhibit in the Inter-States Exposition at Raleigh this fall. Your school must be represented.

TO BE A GOOD TEACHER.

BY CAROLINE B. LE ROW.

The following from *The Ladies' Home Journal* so closely applies to the teaching of music that we give it entire:

"Good health is particularly necessary for the teacher, as the labors of the school-room draw so constantly and heavily on the vocal, mental, and nervous forces. Teachers need to be continually on their guard against anything which can interfere with their physical well-being. This precaution has also a moral significance and importance.

"Of couse, the more liberal and thorough the education, the better the foundation on which the teacher's work is based; but there have been many great scholars who have proved very poor teachers, for the possession of knowledge by no means implies the ability to impart it. It is safe to assume that natural talent in this direction is the best possible test of the 'born teacher.' In addition to what is usually included in a liberal education, a knowledge of the comparatively modern science of psychology is indispensable, familiarity with the laws which control the development of the mind, the material upon which the teacher exclusively works. If she succeeds in her work without this knowledge, her success will result 'more from good luck than good looking to,' or be the outcome of a happy intuition which, unfortunately, few possess. This branch of science has but lately been accorded its proper place in our curriculum, but every day strengthens its claim to be considered the corner-stone of every educational structure.

"Martin Luther asserted in his cast-iron style of rhetoric, 'Unless a schoolmaster knows how to sing, I think him of no account.' Such a test would materially decrease the number of pedagogues; nevertheless, it is true that such

ability is of the greatest service to the teacher.   The physical benefit resulting from singing is sufficient reason for its
use, even if no other existed; but is peculiarly valuable as
a source of enjoyment to children, and a great aid in the
preservation of order.   Even a little knowledge of drawing
places a mighty power in the hand of the teacher.   Nothing so much helps to make instruction clear and impres-
sive as simple and rapid illustration, particularly in the
primary grades.   At present these two accomplishments —
improperly so termed, for they are really essentials — are
required in most schools.   The children of to-day, who are
the teachers of to-morrow, are receiving thorough instruction in these two matters, and experience proves that it is
almost as instinctive for them to sing and draw as for a
bird to fly.''

[For The North Carolina Teacher.]

THE NEW METHODS IN COUNTRY SCHOOLS.

BY JOHN C. HOLDER, PLUCKEMIN, NEW JERSEY.

A large number of the pupils in the public schools of
this State belong to the rural districts, and are therefore in
the ungraded schools.   This fact alone makes it of importance to consider the ''New Methods'' in relation to these
schools.

By the term ''new methods'' we understand the use of
such means in primary education as tend to lay the foundation for the harmonious education of the *whole* child — his
physical, mental and moral being.

In the graded schools this can be more effectually accomplished because the work can be planned with reference to
the future.   There the work is more systematic, and hence
more thorough, because each year's work builds the foundation for the succeeding year, or, in other words, each

year's work is dependent upon the one just finished. It is also more thoroughly done, because the greater number of the teachers in the primary departments of the graded schools are specially trained for it.

But this is *not* the case with the greater number of the country schools. These schools are ungraded, and for this reason the work cannot be so aptly arranged as to produce definite results within a definite time. Another obstacle in the way is the absence of a practical knowledge on the part of the teachers themselves.

A large number of the country school-teachers have no special training in the use of the new methods, and many do not take the time and care to inform themselves. Considering what is required of the country school-teacher in this era of our public schools there is also a lack of time. No matter how well or skillfully the teacher may manage there is just so much to be done in a limited time.

The number of classes to each teacher in the ungraded schools is greater, and each class must receive, as nearly as possible, a just and proportionate share of the teacher's time and attention.

What is done in a period for recitation by the teacher in the graded school, with ample time and under favorable surroundings, would have to be done by the teacher in the ungraded school within perhaps less than one-half the time and under the most *unfavorable* surroundings.

Again, there is the lack of material or the proper apparatus. In some of the country schools there would be a lack of the proper kind of coöperation with the teachers, and this, if not judiciously dealt with, would be liable to grow into positive and aggressive opposition on the part of parents, guardians and district school boards.

We have here briefly stated what we consider the most serious obstacles in the way of an effective use of the new methods in the country schools. They do not form an objection to the methods themselves but to their *feasibility*, and these objections are perhaps not so formidable as they appear at first sight.

1. The lack of time might, to some extent, be obviated by the teacher securing the help of his older and more advanced pupils, not as *teachers* but as *helpers*.

2. The want of special training on the part of teachers themselves by reading up on the subject.

3. The enthusiastic and ingenious teacher can furnish much of the material for himself, with but little expense except the time and labor in making it.

4. Our farmers in the rural districts judge new methods much as they do improved machinery on their farms. If better results follow they will give their approval and support.

We have but hinted at the benefits that may arise from a closer study and application of the so-called *new methods*, and to the progressive teacher a hint is sufficient.

SMALL PAY FOR TEACHERS.

Teaching does not seem to be a profitable employment in Germany, according to the statements of the Mecklenburg *School Gazette*.

Near Grabow lives an invalid educator seventy-nine years old. He has worked fifty years for an annual salary of $160, and as he has saved nothing is compelled to totter daily to his task. August Weiss, of Butzow, gets $60 a year. He is nearly eighty, and has been in the harness half a century. Another poor old fellow, who lost his place after sixty years of toil at teaching, has gone to work as a day laborer.

Steps are being taken to provide these aged martyrs of learning with small pensions.

PROFESSOR CHARLES D. McIVER.

It has often been the pleasure of THE TEACHER to present to its readers excellent portraits of prominent North Carolina educators, and each cut is engraved by the finest workmen in the country expressly for THE TEACHER.

With this number we are glad to present the familiar face of Professor CHARLES D. McIVER, the sixth President of the North Carolina Teachers' Assembly, and first President of the "North Carolina Normal and Industrial School for Young Women."

Mr. Charles D. McIver was born in Moore County, September 27, 1860, of good Scotch parentage, and was reared on a farm.

He was mainly prepared for college by Prof. John E. Kelly, then principal of Union Home School in Moore County. He entered the University in 1877 and remained there until graduation, paying his own expenses while there. He took the degree of A. B. with the class of '81 — the largest class graduated at the University since the war. He received the medal as the best Greek scholar and other class distinctions.

He began teaching in August, 1881, as assistant in the Durham Male Academy, of which he became principal in January, 1882. In September of the same year he became assistant superintendent of the Durham Graded School and principal of the high school department. In February, 1884, greatly to the regret of the people of Durham who were strongly attached to him, he accepted a similar position, at increased salary, in the graded school of Winston, whose building was then approaching completion and was soon to be opened for the reception of pupils.

He remained in Winston two and a half years, and in September, 1886, he accepted, at increased salary, a position at Peace Institute, Raleigh, N. C., as Professor of Latin and Mathematics.

While in Winston he married Miss Lula V. Martin, who was teacher in the primary department of the Winston Graded School.

He has had much experience in normal school and Institute work. He was secretary and instructor in the Winston Normal School in 1885 and in 1886. He was superintendent of the Sparta Normal School in 1887, and again in 1888. In 1888 he was also principal of the Wilson Normal School. He has conducted Institutes in various counties in the State during the past five summers. This experience will be especially valuable to him as a State Institute Instructor, in which work he is now engaged. In his Institute work Mr. McIver has been greatly aided by his estimable wife.

Besides this, he has had a wide range in teaching, having taught in both public and private schools. At first he taught boys only, then girls and boys together, and then girls only. While he was at Peace Institute he conducted a normal department in that school — the first school of similar grade in the State to establish such a department.

Mr. McIver is an earnest advocate of female education, and during the Legislature of 1889 made strenuous efforts as chairman of the committee appointed by the Teachers' Assembly to secure the passage of the bill to establish a teachers' training-school. The proposition failed, as it had failed before, but its passage by the Senate and its large vote in the House was largely the result of Mr. McIver's earnest and convincing presentation of the question. The Legislature of 1891, in response to the demands of the times, voted an appropriation for the establishment of the long desired Normal and Industrial School for Young

Women, and to Mr. McIver is due much credit for its organization.

Recognizing his position as a progressive educator the General Assembly elected him a Trustee of his venerable Alma Mater. Young—now only thirty-one—progressive, thoroughly in earnest, strong in advocacy of whatever he believes in, a successful teacher, an accurate scholar, and fully in love with his work, Mr. McIver will accomplish great things for public education in the State.

He was appointed one of the Conductors of State Teachers' Institutes under the Act of Assembly of 1889, and during the two years which he has given exclusively to this work he has held very successful Institutes in most of the counties of the State, and his work and public addresses have done much towards creating a greater interest in popular education within our borders. Mr. McIver is a strong speaker on his favorite theme, "Popular Education." He is forcible and logical in argument and never fails to favorbly impress an audience.

At the seventh session of the North Carolina Teachers' Assembly, at Morehead City, in June, 1890, he was unanimously chosen president of that great organization, which is the highest educational honor that can be conferred in this State.

At the meeting of the Trustees of the State Normal and Industrial School for Young Women, after it had been located, Mr. McIver was unanimously chosen the first president of that institution. It was a wise selection and meets the heartiest approval and endorsement of the people of North Carolina. His earnestness, enthusiasm, zeal, experience and ability will bring to the school the greatest success and popularity, and under his excellent management this pet institution will at once take its proper place in the front rank among the educational institutions of our country.

IN THE SCHOOL-ROOM.

BEFORE AND AFTER TAKING.

FOR RECITATION.

Picnic morning,
  Bright and fair,
Golden sunshine,
  Balmy air.
What a pleasure
  Thus to go
Where the woodland
  Breezes b'ow.
Happy hours,
  Free from care,
Joy and beauty
  Everywhere.
Through the leafy
  Woods we'll stray,
Gracious gladsome
  Picnic day.

Picnic evening,
  What a plight!
Rained from ten
  O'clock till night.
Flossy garments,
  Once so nice,
Filled with mud
  And beggars' lice.
Dinner ruined,
  Pies and cakes
Food for ants
  And garden snakes,
Full of doleful
  Dank dismay,
Dirty, drizzly
  Picnic day.

DON'T TELL people all you know the first time you meet them. Half of friendship is curiosity.—*Atchison Globe.*

————✕————

DON'T TALK.

It doesn't pay to do much talking when you're mad enough
    to choke,
Because the word that stings the deepest is the one that's
    never spoke;
Let the other fellow wrangle till the storm has blown away,
Then he'll do a heap of thinking 'bout the things you
    didn't say.

————✕————

WHEN THE hour of trouble comes to the mind or the body, or when the hour of death comes, that comes to high and low, then it is not what we have done for ourselves, but what we have done for others, that we think on most pleasantly.

————✕————

A BEAUTIFUL face wins instant admiration, but a beautiful mind and heart and soul retains and holds the friendship.

————✕————

WHAT IS GOOD.

"What is the real good,"
I asked in musing mood.

"Order," said the law court;
"Knowledge," said the school;
"Truth," said the wise man;
"Pleasure," said the fool;
"Love," said the maiden;
"Beauty," said the page;

"Freedom," said the dreamer;.
"Home," said the sage;
"Fame," said the soldier;
"Equity," the seer.

Spake my heart full sadly:
"The answer is not here."

Then within my bosom
Softly this I heard:
"Each heart holds the secret;
'Kindness' is tl e word."

—John Boyle O'Reilly.

——⋊——

DON'TS.

MISS ALICE M. BURNEY.

Don't scold continually, or for every little trifling offence; "familiarity breeds contempt," and your pupils will soon come to think that scolding is your forte and you do it for fun. Thus its effect upon them when deserved is lost.

Don't attempt to teach by comparison until you weigh well that the minds of children are easily confused, and in your care to teach the correct, by showing the incorrect, you run the risk of impressing upon them the very thing you seek to eradicate.

Don't try to have your pupils learn too many things, or spend your strength in advancing them too rapidly. You might as well "pour water through a sieve."

Don't forget that your pupils are rational beings, and that they have a code of rights that should be respected as sacredly as the rights of their elders.

Don't forget the time when you were a soldier in the battle of child-life; try to have your pupils feel that your own childish trials and discomforts are still fresh in memory.

Don't forget that your pupils are the men and women of to-morrow; that they are essentially what they are made, either by precept or example; that to primary pupils example is of more value than precept.

Don't think that order consists in the quiet of the tomb, or fancy that the air of an Egyptian mummy is creditable in a child.

Finally, don't forget to look and be your brightest, sweetest, and prettiest, when in the presence of your pupils. Don't forget to know and do that which is best.

————✕————

EDUCATIONAL GENERALS.

What we want at the heads of our schools and colleges, as what we want at the head of our army divisions, is generals. And that State is the most thrifty which searches for this power wherever it can be found, and placing it at the head of its educational institutions, pays for it whatever it may demand, as it pours out its treasure at the feet of its successful army generals.

————✕————

NEATNESS IN GIRLS.

Neatness is a good thing for a girl, and if she does not learn it when she is young she never will. It takes a great deal more neatness to make a girl look well than it does to make a boy look passable. Not because a boy, to start with, is better looking than a girl, but his clothes are of a different sort, not so many colors in them; and people don't expect a boy to look so pretty as a girl. A girl that is not neatly dressed is called a sloven, and no one likes to look at her. Her face may be pretty, and her eyes bright, but if there is a spot of dirt on her cheek, and her finger ends are black with ink, and her shoes are not laced or buttoned up, and her apron is dirty, and her collar is not buttoned,

and her skirt is torn, she cannot be liked. Learn to be
neat, and when you have learned it it will almost take care
of itself.— *Christian at Work.*

——————※——————

A LITTLE GENTLEMAN.

It is well to teach children at an early age how to shake
hands and to speak distinctly the names of the older persons they may have to greet. Some children when
addressed by their parents' friends look up frankly and
give an honest little paw to be clasped in the bigger hand
as though it was a pleasure to be recognized, while others
shyly hang their heads and stretch out a limp apology for
a hand in return. Which form of a greeting is the more
attractive need not be pointed out. "I know a bright
little chap," says a writer, "an only child, whom it is a
pleasure to meet, because he always shakes hands as
though he really meant it, and he felt you were as much
his friend as though eight years old like himself. But his
name is Paul, and who ever heard of a Paul who was not
frank and what the world calls a little gentleman?"—
Boston Herald.

——————※——————

"EDUCATION IS ALL RIGHT," says the *Galveston News*,
"so that it does not leave the victim too smart to work and
not smart enough to get along without work."

——————※——————

THE DOLLAR SIGN.

The dollar sign ($) is not, as some suppose, a corruption
of the monogram "U. S.," but is a relic of the times when
the transfer from the old Spanish to the more modern
monetary system was made and accounts were, for a while,
kept equally in dollars and reals. One dollar equaled eight
reals, and amounts were written: One dollar ‖ eight reals.

Later on the 8 was placed between the parallels |8|, and afterwards the perpendicular lines crossed the 8. Then, with a little changing, the present sign ($) was evolved.

ENCOURAGE YOUR PUPILS to greet you before the bell rings; to take your hand and wish you "good morning." Talk with them when you have five minutes to spare — waiting for the class to change — of the meaning of the common greeting. Does it really mean that you wish the morning to be good?

"I SHOULD SMILE!"

One is sometimes inclined to believe that the maiden of the fairy tale, from whose red lips issued toads and lizards instead of pearls and diamonds, still lives and walks among us. Says the *Youth's Companion:*

" The winter sunset was glowing in the south-western sky, and the lady who was walking toward it seemed to see in it once more the Spanish castle of her youth, and the faces that long ago looked out at her from its windows. She began to hear far-off voices sound, and to dream the old dreams over again. Suddenly a very different voice close behind her broke the spell.

" ' Sing for nothing? Well, I should smile! I get paid for it when I sing, and don't you forget it.'

"The lady cast a hasty glance over her shoulder, and saw the speaker — a girl of perhaps twenty, well-dressed, with a quick, buoyant step, and a pretty face. Yes, it really was a very pretty face; and the simple yet good toilet like a lady's choice; but her speech detrayed her. Slang is not the language of well-bred maidenhood. When you hear a girl finish her sentence with an interrogative, 'See?' you need search no further for indications of what she is. 'Well, I should smile!' is as comprehensive as a biography."

North Carolina Teachers' Assembly.

ORGANIZATION FOR 1891–'92.

OFFICERS:

Hugh Morson (Raleigh Male Academy), President, . . Raleigh.
Eugene G. Harrell (Editor Teacher), Sec. and Treas., . . Raleigh.

VICE-PRESIDENTS:

1. J. J. Blair (Supt. Graded Schools), ... Winston.
2. J. E. Kelly (Model Male School), ... Charlotte.
3. Miss Catharine Fulghum (Graded School), . . Goldsboro.
4. W. J. Ferrell (Wakefield Academy), . . . Wakefield.
5. Miss Lizzie Lindsay (Graded School), ... Greensboro.
6. P. M. Pearsall (County Superintendent), . . Trenton.
7. Miss Lina McDonald (Graded School) . . . Winston.
8. T. J. Drewry (Horner Military School), . . . Oxford.
9. Mrs. S. Montgomery Funk (Chowan Bap. Fem. Inst.), Murfreesboro.

EXECUTIVE COMMITTEE:

Hugh Morson, *ex officio*, President, ... Raleigh.
E. G. Harrell, *ex officio*, Secretary, ... Raleigh.
Eben Alexander (University North Carolina), . . Chapel Hill.
W. L. Poteat (Wake Forest College), ... Wake Forest.
James Dinwiddie (President Peace Institute), . . Raleigh.
Charles D. McIver (President Normal and Industrial School
for Women), ... Greensboro.
J. Y. Joyner (Superintendent Graded School), . . Goldsboro.
A. C. Davis (Superintendent Military School), . . Winston.
E. E. Britton (Principal High School), ... Mount Olive.

·ASSEMBLY NOTES.

There will be a beautiful solid gold watch, lady's size, awarded in the Instrumental Music Contest at the next Assembly. The rules relating to performers will be the same as before, and it is expected that there will be at least twenty entries for the contest. Seven names have already been given to the Secretary.

SEVERAL PROMINENT members of the Southern Educational Association, and among the most prominent educators in the South, have promised to attend the next session of our Assembly.

WHEN YOUR schools commence the fall term keep in mind the fact that you want to be represented in the Educational Exposition at the Teachers' Assembly next summer, and begin at once to get ready for it. The exhibits at Morehead City this summer were very fine and attracted great attention, and they will prove of much benefit to the schools represented. We want the next display to be much larger and more complete, and you cannot afford to have your school unrepresented.

DO YOU KNOW that over half as many people attended the eighth annual session of the North Carolina Teachers' Assembly as were present at the meeting of the National Educational Association at Toronto in July? The same ratio of growth will in a few more years make our Assembly the biggest educational meeting in America, as it is now the largest in the South! Not more than one in ten of those attending the National Educational Association are actual teachers, and the other nine persons are merely sight hunters.

WE KNOW THAT the teachers of North Carolina will be gratified to know that the Executive Committee has been so fortunate as to secure an engagement with "Frank Beard," the most celebrated and skillful chalk artist in America, for three days' work at the next session of the Assembly. His work will include two public evening entertainments, with special private instruction to the teachers on "The Marvelous Power of Rapid Drawing in the School-room, and How to Use the Crayon." The work by Frank Beard will alone be worth to a teacher many times more than the expense of attending the Assembly.

EDITORIAL.

THE TEACHERS' ASSEMBLY WORK.

THE NORTH CAROLINA Teachers' Assembly is doing exactly the work that it set out to do, and it is being done in precisely the same manner that its originators contemplated, and we have never heard a North Carolina teacher express a desire to have the plans and work of the Assembly changed in the slightest manner. It is the biggest educational success to be found in the United States, and it is entirely unnecessary that any suddenly awakened friend (?), who possibly has been hoping to attend its funeral ere this, should at this late day propose to be its nurse. The child is now too strong and healthy and vigorous and popular to need any other nurse or diet than that which it has so successfully had and thrived upon from its birth.

The Assembly is not by any means a normal school, nor did it ever intend to be, nor does it now propose to be a normal school. It was originated at a time when the normal schools in the State were under full headway, and with the expressed intention of being an entirely different thing from the normals. If the *Southern Educator* knows what the Teachers' Assembly should be so much better than the teachers know what they want it to be it is a great pity that the editor did not give to the teachers of Virginia, his own State, the benefit of his experience (?) and wisdom by organizing for them a similar association, as it is well known that they have been trying to effect a State organization for several years but without success. We did not intend to have anything to say on this line but for the fact that a number of criticisms of the Assembly, of very doubtful friendship, with slurs upon its work and management, have recently appeared in the *Southern Educator*. We might say a great deal more upon this subject but will resist the temptation to do so at present. The Teachers' Assembly is the special pet of THE NORTH CAROLINA TEACHER and we propose to guard it with jealous care. It is the habit of some people who are unable to originate anything, to labor under the constant delusion that they can vastly improve somebody else's work, ideas and plans.

MARK THE prediction! Within five years the doors of every college in North Carolina which desires to prosper in its work will be opened to girls on the same terms as to boys. It doesn't matter what may be our views as to co-education, the demand for this system of education is growing and the colleges and the University will not be able to resist it much longer.

WE HAVE BEEN highly gratified at the great number of renewals of subscriptions to THE TEACHER with the beginning of the new volume. The magazine now enters upon its ninth volume, and it is more firmly established in the good will of the teachers of North Carolina than any other educational journal that has ever been published in North Carolina. The main reason for this love which the teachers of this State cherish for THE TEACHER is because it is strictly a *North Carolina* journal of education whose efforts are wholly given to the upbuilding of our native State and for the success of North Carolina teachers.

THE WHOLE State truly sympathizes with Trinity College in the wreck of its elegant new college building at Durham on the 8th of August. The structure was nearing completion for the opening of the fall term of the College in September, and the entire tower, one hundred feet high, with its foundation walls, fell to the earth with a terrible crash. The cause of the damage is mainly assigned to faulty

architecture and imperfect material.   The damage is estimated. at $15,000, and the work of repairing will begin at
once.   It is hoped that the session will not be delayed
longer than the first of December.   In the meantime, the fall
term will begin at the usual time in the old buildings at
Trinity College.

THE VERY first thing that should be taught to a child,
as the foundation of its education, is the English Alphabet,
and this should be taught thoroughly so that it may be
repeated backward or forward or in any other direction.   It
is well known that the alphabet is not only the thing most
used in acquiring an education, but it is in constant service
during a business or literary life and therefore every person should be thoroughly familiar with the order in which
the letters are fixed, as many books and all ledgers, dic-
tionaries, catalogues, and other works of reference are
arranged on the alphabetical plan.   This is not the
"alphabet method," but it is the *alphabet*.

IF YOU WOULD like to join a select party of fifty persons
on a delightful fifteen-day visit to Cuba, to leave on December 29th, 1891, please write to the editor of THE TEACHER
about it as soon as possible.   The entire actual expenses
of the trip will not be over $75.   It is proposed to spend a
week in Havana and about four days in the mountains of
Cuba where the sugar plantations are and "where the
Havana cigars grow."   The route has not yet been fully
decided upon, and we will give further information in
regard to the tour in a few weeks.   The party is positively
limited to fifty persons.   Cuba is the most charming
country on the globe to visit in mid-winter, it being a land
of perpetual summer where fires and stoves are unknown;
the fan is always in order, and the overcoat is eternally at
a discount; where every variety of fruit and vegetable is in
season all the year round, and the lovely senorita "is
always on deck."

ABOUT OUR TEACHERS AND SCHOOLS.

MISS IDA ASHWORTH is teaching at Chimney Rock.

MISS ELLEN KISER is teaching at Dallas, Gaston county.

MISS BELLE JARRETT is teaching at Hayesville, Clay county.

MR. J. O. BLALOCK is Principal of a school at Kings Mountain.

MISS BETTIE WEBSTER has a school at Henderson, Vance county.

MISS SALLIE BULLOCK is teaching at Williamsboro, Vance county.

MISS BETTIE BURGESS is teaching at Wade's Point, Beaufort county.

MISS FLORENCE HARGROVE, of Chatham county, is teaching at Merry Oaks.

MR. JOHN F. BRADLEY is teaching a large public school near Gastonia.

MISS MARY V. HOPPER has a good school at Leaksville, Rockingham county.

MR. J. W. JOHNSTON has a good school at Haw River, Alamance county.

MR. S. T. ANDREWS is teaching at Mt. Vernon Springs in Chatham county.

MR. R. L. McIVER, of Winston, is assistant teacher in Sanford High School.

MR. J. LEE MIDDLETON is Principal of the Baptist Female School at Durham.

MR. W. S. WILKINSON is Principal of the Male and Female Academy at Battleboro.

STATESVILLE HAS recently voted $10,000 for the establishment of a graded school.

REV. T. C. BUCHANAN has taken charge of the Academy at Globe, Caldwell county.

MISS LIZZIE ALLEN, of Virginia, has been elected a teacher in the Graded School of Shelby.

MR. W. J. HELMS, of Albemarle, has been elected Principal of Hayesville Academy, Clay county.

TARBORO and Henderson have recently voted an extra tax for the support of their Graded Schools.

MR. W. H RAGSDALE, of Granville county, is Principal of the Male Academy at Greenville, Pitt county.

CAPTAIN JOHN DUCKETT, of Greenville, has taken charge of the High School at Hamilton, Martin county.

MESSRS. E. M. KOONCE and A. H. White are Principals of the High School at Polloksville, Jones county.

MR. J. B. SPARGER is Principal of the High School at Westfield, Surry county, and the school is flourishing.

MR. F. A. FETTER, of Washington, has been elected Principal of the Academy at Kernersville, Forsyth county.

MRS. JOHN A. MCDONALD and her daughter, Miss Lina, have accepted positions as teachers in the Winston Graded School.

MR. J. B. BLANTON is Principal of Mooresboro High School, and the fall term began on August 20th with flattering prospects.

MISS ROSEDNA SLEDGE, who has been teaching in Franklin, Macon county, will teach at her home this fall at Hendersonville.

MR. G. T. HEAFNER, of Lincolnton, is in charge of the Academy at Fallston. Over sixty pupils are enrolled for the fall term.

MR. Z. D. MCWHORTER, of Jonesboro, has accepted the principalship of the Male and Female Institute, at Greenville, Pitt county.

MR. J. T. ALDERMAN, County Superintendent of Davie, has accepted the position of Principal of the Graded Schools of Reidsville.

THE FARMERS' ALLIANCE had a most enjoyable educational pic-nic at Chatham High School House, Williams' Mill, on August 7th.

MISS CARRIE HARDING, late of Missouri, has returned to her home to engage in teaching with her sisters, the Misses Patrick, at Kinston.

MR. E. E. BRITTON, Principal of Mount Olive High School, attended the Encampment at Wrightsvllle as a member of the Goldsboro Rifles.

MR. W. J. MATTHEWS has resigned the principalship of Greenville Male Academy to assume charge of the Academy at Wadesboro, Anson county.

MISS KATE EDMUNDSON and Miss Bettie Young, both of Peace Institute, have a flourishing school for boys and girls at Leachburg, Johnston county.

MR. B. D. BARKER, who has been teaching at Williams' Mill, Chatham county, for several years, has taken charge of the High School at Apex, Wake county.

THERE IS TO be a first-class military school opened at Scotland Neck under the superintendency of Mr. W. C. Allen, former principal of Vine Hill Academy.

MR. CHAS. J. PARKER, formerly Superintendent of Tarboro Graded School, has resigned to accept the superintendency of the Graded Schools of Shelby.

MR. E. B. PHILLIPS, of Wilson county, is Principal of Hibriten Mountain Academy, Caldwell county. The school opened August 3d, and near fifty pupils are enrolled.

MR. LOGAN D. HOWELL, of Goldsboro, has been elected Superintendent of the Graded Schools at Tarboro. Mr. Howell is a graduate of the University and a fine teacher.

PROF. KARL P. HARRINGTON, of Wesleyan University, Middletown, Conn., was elected on August 7th by the trustees, as Professor of Latin in the University of North Carolina.

MR. HERBERT SCHOLTZ (Elon College), has been elected Principal of Chatham High School, at Williams' Mill, Chatham county. Miss Havens Cherry, of Greenville, is teacher of music.

MISS GOULDMAN, a graduate of the Western Female High School, Baltimore, has been added to the Faculty of Wilkinson Female Institute, Tarboro, as teacher of English and Elocution.

MR. A. L. RUCKER, of Rutherfordton, will shortly remove to Piedmont. We sympathize with him in the loss of his excellent horse, which was killed by lightning on August 12th.

MISS ANNIE MCDONALD, of Picton, Nova Scotia, has been added to the faculty of Louisburg Female College as Music Teacher. She is a graduate of the New England Conservatory of Music.

MISS MATTIE WHITAKER (Peabody Institute, Baltimore), of Enfield, has accepted the position of Teacher of Music and Stenography in La Grange Collegiate Institute, Lenoir county. Prof. George W. B. Hadley is Principal of the Institute.

MR. J. F. BROWER is Principal of the Boys School at Salem, and the school is flourishing. The enrollment has more than doubled in two years, and the outlook is most encouraging. His assistants are Miss Mary Lewis and Rev. J. F. McCuiston.

MISS BESSIE KRIDER, who won the medal in the Teachers' Assembly Musical Contest, at Morehead City, on June 26th, was immediately offered a situation as teacher in a high grade school at Searcy, Arkansas, at a salary of $600 per year and all expenses.

PROF. D. MATT THOMPSON has been elected Superintendent of the Graded Schools at Statesville, which position he has decided to accept. Statesville people are to be congratulated on their choice. As a superintendent of schools Prof. Thompson has few equals.

THE HEIRS OF the late Hon. Paul C. Cameron have established at the University in his memory ten "Cameron Scholarships," to be given to deserving young men. This is a noble and lasting memorial to Mr. Cameron, who was for over half a century a warm friend and benefactor of the University.

MR. F. M. HARPER, Principal of the Centennial Graded School of this city, has resigned to accept the superintendency of schools in Dawson, Ga. The successor of Mr. Harper will be elected before the opening of the school, 18th September. Applicants can address T. H. Briggs, Secretary School Committee, Raleigh, N. C.

THE TRUSTEES of the University have elected as Professor of Biology Dr. Henry V. Wilson, director in charge of the U. S. Fish Station at Wood's Hall, Mass. Dr. Wilson is a native of Baltimore, a graduate of Johns Hopkins University, both as A. B. and Ph. D., a gentleman of fine ability, of extraordinary culture, of large experience in biological work, and of national reputation as a scientist.

PEACE INSTITUTE, Raleigh, will begin the fall term on September 5th, and the outlook is for the most successful term in the history of this popular institution. Prof. James Dinwiddie has greatly strengthened the already excellent faculty by the addition of Misses Manly and · Clements, from Florida. The buildings are in splendid condition for the hundred boarding pupils who will soon occupy them.

THE UNIVERSITY ALUMNI have established a large number of scholarships at the University. Young men of talent and character who need help in getting an education, and who can give references as to their financial needs and merits, may obtain assistance by applying to President Winston, at Chapel Hill. The University also offers free tuition to all young men intending to preach, and to the sons of preachers of all denominations.

THE NORTH CAROLINA COLLEGE OF AGRICULTURE AND MECHANIC ARTS, Raleigh, begins its third session on the third of next September. This College is taking a high rank among the institutions of the State, and is doing thorough and honest work. The Board of Trustees is adding largely to the plant of the College, and will, this summer, put up two new buildings, and in addition add such new equipment as is needed in the development of the work of the College.

AT THE examination for Teachers' State Certificate, at the Teachers' Institute held in Concord, Miss Nettie Anderson, a young lady of Concord, undertook the examination just for the benefit. In the spelling examination she spelled ninety-eight words out of the one hundred given. This is the best record made anywhere in the State. Miss Nettie is very bright, and by her laudable ambition she is accomplishing no little for herself, and reflects credit on her teachers.

JUDSON FEMALE COLLEGE, Hendersonville, Henderson county, enters upon the fall term, September 28th. Dr. R. H. Lewis, one of North Carolina's most eminent and beloved educators, is meeting with most gratifying success as President of this institution. The College was established by the Baptists in 1858, specially for the girls of Western North Carolina. It is, however, drawing a liberal patronage from other portions of North Carolina and from the adjoining States.

CAPTAIN C. B. DENSON, one of the principals of the Raleigh Male Academy, has been nominated recently as a Fellow of the Society of Science, Arts and Letters, of London. This society has for its officers such men as Sir Valentine Goold, who is President; Count De Lesseps, the Duke of Argyle, the Duke of Teck and others.   After consideration Captain Denson has accepted, with a view to presenting a series of papers giving the truth in regard to the social condition of the South, and with a view to correcting misrepresentations which have been published in the Encyclopedia Britannica and other authorities.   THE TEACHER rejoices in the conferring of this honor upon one of the most distinguished scholars and teachers of North Carolina.

SAINT MARY'S SCHOOL, Raleigh, N. C., one of the oldest and most popular educational institutions for girls in the South, begins the fall term on September 24th.   This is the fiftieth annual session of this school, it having been established in 1842.   The outlook for the coming term is exceedingly bright for even a larger attendance than in several years.   Rev. Bennett Smedes, D. D., is the accomplished rector of the institution.

CUPID AMONG OUR TEACHERS.

'Tis said that "figures never lie,"
    That one and one are always TWO;
But Cupid proves, with wor so sly,
    Some wondrous things that figures do.
And when he claims a teacher's hand
    All rules of figures then are done,
Though TWO before the preacher stand
This one and one are ALWAYS ONE.

PROFESSOR L. L. LOHR, of the Faculty of Gaston College, Dallas, N. C., married MISS JESSIE ZINN, of Gettysburg, Pa., on July 15, 1891.

THE INFANT CLASS.

" A lovely being, scarcely formed or moulded,
    A rose with all its sweetest leaves yet folded.'

DONALD ELLIS, son of Mr. D. L. Ellis, President of Fairview College, Buncombe county, was born at Shelby in July.

HARRY BARNETT GRIMSLEY, son of Mr. George A. Grimsley, Superintendent of Graded Schools at Greensboro, was born at Kinston on July 16, 1891.

IN MEMORIAM.

"Death hath made no breach
In love and sympathy, in hope and trust.
No outward sign or sound our ears can reach,
But there's an inward, spiritual speech
That greets us still, though mortal tongues be dust.
It bids us do the work that they laid down—
Take up the song where they broke off the strain;
So, journeying till we reach the heavenly town,
Where are laid up our treasure and our crown,
And our lost, loved ones will be found again."

MRS. W. E. YOUNG (*nee* Miss Verlester Rhodes), a member of the Teachers' European Party, died at her home in East Durham on May 20th, 1891. Her infant daughter survived her but fifteen days. Mrs. Young had been, since her marriage, assisting her husband in the management of the Academy at East Durham.

AT RECESS.

The books and slates now put away,
And let us laugh a little while;
For those who work there should be play,
The leisure moments to beguile.

ANSWERED.

"Can you tell me, you stupid,"
The cross teacher said,
"What S double E spells?"
The boy shook his head.

"What do I do?" said she,
"Look here! with my eye?"
The boy's face grew brighter,
"Squint," was the reply.

———※———

AT THE table of a well known school teacher, the subject of widows was under discussion, when one of the sons inquired: "What is a grass-widow?" "Why, Harry," responded the other, "don't you know? A grass widow is a woman whose husband died of hay-fever."

"I GUESS WE have so many things to learn at our school that we don't have any room to understand them in," said a little girl, pathetically.

TEACHER—"Johnny, what was there remarkable about the Battle of Lookout?" Johnny (at the foot of the class)—"It caused bangs on the brow of a mountain.

TEACHER (in Sunday-school)—' Why is it you do not learn your lesson as well on Sunday as on week days?" Bad Little Tommy—"'Cause you can't lick a feller at Sunday-school."

SUNDAY-SCHOOL SUPERINTENDENT (trying to inspire patriotism on Sunday morning after a big Fourth of July celebration the day before)—"Now, children, what day was it yesterday?" Young America—"Saturday, sir." Superintendent—"The lecture on patriotism is indefinitely postponed."

———※———

A BOY'S COMPOSITION.

The kokonuts is a native to the tropik. It grows onto trees and is good to eat. Billy Brown's oncle is a vessil kaptain, and one time he fetched Bill a hole lot of Kokonuts from West Ingines. Hit tuck us a hole week to eat 'em up. Wot Billy and me wants to no is how dos the milk git inside the kokonut. Does the kokonut grow round the milk or does the milk leke in from the outside, if so, wot fur? Kokonut py is my favorite, but Billy likes kokonut candy best. Kokonuts is pulled off the trees by munkys, which throws 'em at peple like bas ball. I wish I was a mun—no; a koko—no; I mean a pepel, so I cud git kokonuts 'thout payin' for 'em.

TEACHERS' BUREAU.

TEACHERS WANTED.

1. A MALE Principal for the High School at Mount Olive, N. C. Salary from $700 to $900 per year. The building is in first-class order. Write to R. J. Southerland, Chairman, Mount Olive, N. C.

2. A FIRST-CLASS male teacher who can build up a high school. Material in abundance to build up and maintain a fine school for years. A teacher with family desiring to locate here can purchase a good home at very reasonable prices. This is certainly a fine opening for a successful school. Write to J. A. Younts, Pineville, N. C.

3. AN EXPERIENCED male teacher (unmarried) to take charge of the High School at Scull's Store, Northampton county. Guaranteed salary $40 per month. Address, with testimonials, A. Grant, Rehoboth, N. C.

ARE YOU A TEACHER?

YES.

THEN THIS IS WRITTEN TO YOU!

We want every teacher in this State to be a subscriber to THE NORTH CAROLINA TEACHER for the year 1891.

The subscription price is only **one dollar** for the year. We are perfectly willing to credit all teachers until they have a dollar to spare, but we want your names on our books **now.**

To each person who sends a dollar with the name we will give a copy of that remarkable teacher's book, "Evolution of Dodd," or six pieces of vocal or instrumental music. Besides, if, at the end of the year, you feel that you have not been helped very greatly by reading THE TEACHER you need not pay for it, or, if you have already done so, we will return the money or extend your subscription another year and let you try the magazine again.

THE TEACHER is a *live* journal of education, and we believe it will encourage you to do more thinking in your work. The teachers who think most do the best work and get the best pay. We do not require you to agree with us in regard to any method of teaching that we suggest or in any criticisms we may make upon some methods now being used; we only ask you to read THE TEACHER and then do just as the editor does — *think for yourself.*

THE TEACHER believes thoroughly in **the Old North State and her teachers**; it will try to be your best friend and defender at all times, and from all misrepresentations or slurs, no matter from whomsoever they may come. THE TEACHER shapes its own policy and line of thought; is most thoroughly independent, but by no means neutral; is mainly original, and will try to be generally right.

If you carry THE TEACHER to school with you in the morning it will be easy for you to do better teaching that day than you did the day before.

THE TEACHER is now regularly read by over seven thousand people in North Carolina and the Southern States. We want to have ten thousand readers before the end of 1891. If *you* are not now one of that number we want you to be. If you are already a subscriber to other educational ournals, so much the better. Don't cut off any one of them, but *be sure* to add THE TEACHER to your list, for it will tell you things that will interest you and which cannot be found anywhere else.

The principal work of THE NORTH CAROLINA TEACHER is to secure a good school for every teacher and a good teacher for every school. We want you at all times to feel free to write to us for anything you want relating to professional work, and we will do our level best to aid you.

EUGENE G. HARRELL, Editor.

ALFRED WILLIAMS & CO., PUBLISHERS.

OFFICE OF

STATE SUPERINTENDENT PUBLIC INSTRUCTION.

RALEIGH, N. C., Aug. 10, 1891.

The Constitution of North Carolina requires the public schools to be kept open at least four months per annum. If the tax is not sufficient to do this, it should be supplemented in every neighborhood by private subscription. Surely the patrons of every school can add enough to have a school at least four months.

The following *course* of *study* is intended to guide the teachers not so much as to *how much* should be accomplished in this general system of public schools, but more especially to guide them as to the *order* in which the different books on our State list should be taken up.

The course supposes that the child enters school at six years of age and attends regularly four months each year. If he has ordinary capacity and good teaching, and especially if he is encouraged to read and study at home during the long vacations—at least enough to hold progress already made—this course can be fairly well accomplished as laid down.

Every teacher should strive earnestly to have the pupils become interested in completing the steps year by year, and to secure such co-operation by parents as will induce them to buy for their children not only the text-books as they are indicated by the course, but to get also for them other entertaining books that will induce them to read. This reading will not only give them information which they ought to have, but it will give them a vocabulary and an ability to understand the language in which their text-books and other books are written, and so enable them the better to accomplish the course. If children do not advance as rapidly as they should, their parents may be as much at fault as the teacher.

The age of the children will not always indicate what branches are to be taken. Some children will be found less advanced than others who are younger, and will have to take studies according to advancement rather than age. But still the course of study will indicate what branches ought ordinarily to be pursued at the same time as parallel studies. Other children will be found who are advanced proportionally more in one branch than in another, and the course will, perhaps, not show what branches they ought to take as parallel studies. Under such conditions there is opportunity for the exercise of the common sense of the teacher, without which success is impossible.

If the teachers will carefully note what is specially intended, they will the more easily be able to classify the pupils and advance them.

1. An earnest effort is to be made to get the children to read understandingly at as early an age as possible. Hence the stress laid upon the use of the Readers and Harrington's Speller in such thorough and systematic way as necessarily to give the children the meaning and use of the words. In the early stages of the course, this meaning is not to be learned from *definitions*, but by actual use of the words in sentences.

2. The four fundamental rules in arithmetic are to be thoroughly learned before the pupils are allowed to pass beyond them. At first the children will not be able to read well enough to use an arithmetic, and so the teacher will have to devise means to teach them something about figures without the book in their hands.

As a rule, perhaps Sanford's Primary Arithmetic may be placed in their hands when they begin the Third Reader. Of course, along with this practice in the four fundamental rules the pupils must have some practical examples. These can be made up by the teacher or be taken from the books. It is, perhaps, needless to say that blackboards are indispensable.

3. Penmanship is to be incidentally taught at the very

beginning of the course by the use of slate and pencil. Later it should be taught to all the pupils by the use of pen and ink and copy-books.

' In what has been said so far, attention to reading, writing and elementary arithmetic has been emphasized. The three R's are of first importance, and every teacher should give special attention to the instruction of the smaller children in these fundamentals. It too often happens that the smaller children in our ungraded county schools are neglected. In the multiplicity of the work which the teacher has to do, he rather inclines to bestow undue attention upon the more advanced pupils. They ought to be more able to help themselves than those less advanced. A determined effort ought to be made by all teachers to advance the smaller children, so that at as early a day as possible they may be able to use the text-books intelligently and profitably. This accomplished, the books on the different subjects should be put into their hands and lessons assigned. At regular times (not necessarily every day in each study), these lessons should be "heard" and thoroughly explained and enlarged upon by the teacher.

---

4. Geography and history, in this course, occupy a prominent place. All will at once see the reason for this. Certainly everyone should know what kind of a world he lives in; what kind of people have lived in it, and what kind now live in it; what they have made out of it, and what they have done. One of the greatest mistakes some people make is to lay little stress upon these branches as studies to be pursued *in the schools*.

Our law do·s not specially contemplate the use of text-books in the natural sciences. All through the course, however, from the very beginning to the end, the teachers should give instruction about Nature—all objects which surround the children in such great numbers. While the study of geography is pursued there is excellent opportunity for this line of work. Teach the children to go through the world with their eyes open, seeing everything and enquiring about everything.

5. As to English grammar, two mistakes are made:

(*a*). A disposition to neglect it, if not entirely to eliminate it from the school course; and

(*b*). An effort to place books on technical grammar in the hands of children before they can comprehend the language in which they are written.

This course of study indicates what is considered a proper place for this very important study. Perhaps there is no branch that is more difficult to teach and that requires more effort on the part of the teacher. But surely it has a place in a course, the main object of which should be to give to every pupil the intelligent and fluent use of his own language—the language in which he reads and conducts his ordinary business orally and by letter-writing. It is conceded that much can be done in this direction by language lessons, such as we have in our readers, speller, and other books, but at the proper time the grammars must be studied.

6. Instruction is to be given to all children orally, or from lessons assigned them from text-books when far enough advanced to use them, relative to the preservation of health and the effects of alcoholic drinks and narcotics. The course indicates a plan for this instruction, and every teacher must give due attention to it.

7. The course is not laid down beyond 16 years of age. At that age the pupil is supposed to have gone over the branches usually studied in the common school course. If pupils desire to pursue other studies, such as usually belong to a high-school course, the committees have authority to arrange for them to be taught. They can charge tuition for such branches—all not specially named in the Public School Law.

Our system is weak from lack of money, and it is suggested

that at least enough tuition be charged to employ sufficient assistance to insure due attention to all pupils in the lower branches.

8. Last, but not least, every teacher must set an example of good manners and good morals, and must continually seek to instruct all the children in this direction. We have no text-book on our State list on this subject, but every teacher is supposed to be informed on the subject of ethics, and no better book on morals has ever been written, or ever will be, than the Bible. This is a Christian country, and the morality required by our law to be inculcated by all teachers is Christian morality without sectarianism. The teacher must never lose sight of the fact that by *example* and by *precept* he is to build the characters of his pupils, and that example is much more effective than precept.

COURSE OF. STUDY.

FIRST YEAR.

(Suppose that the child enters school at six years of age, and has no knowledge of books).

McGuffey's Primer, with slate; writing words on slate; making figures; counting, etc.

[*Note.*—The teacher in teaching reading should not confine himself to any one method. A combination of the different methods is best, especially of the *word method* and the *alphabetic method.* Begin with the word method, but as soon as possible have the child write in script the letters and words, and spell orally, using the names of the letters. When the child has advanced far enough he should be taught all the diacritical marks and the different powers of the letters, but there is danger of attempting too much of this in the first years of the course.]

SUPPLEMENT.

SECOND YEAR.

Holmes' First Reader; Harrington's Speller, first twelve pages; writing on slate; addition and subtraction of numbers to ten, with some simple examples given by the teacher, as time may allow.

THIRD YEAR.

Holmes' Second Reader; Harrington's Speller, from page 13 to page 26; addition and subtraction, not using numbers so large that the children cannot readily comprehend them.

FOURTH YEAR.

Holmes' Third Reader; Harrington's Speller, from page 27 to page 50; Sanford's Primary Arithmetic; the multiplication table perfectly learned.

FIFTH YEAR.

Holmes' Fourth Reader; Harrington's Speller, from page 51 to 78; Sanford's Primary Arithmetic — long division specially taught.

[*Note.*—It is presumed that the teachers will spend six hours in actual work each day. At least half of this time should be given to the course as laid down for the first five years. If this is done the pupils will have opportunity to lay a good foundation, and the work of the teacher in the course beyond the fifth year will be not so much one of hearing recitations as of assigning lessons and seeing that each pupil devotes a reasonable amount of time each day in diligent study of each branch. The teacher should always be ready to help him over the rough places, and he should hear at least two or three recitations each week by each class. No teacher need fear results if he succeeds in enlisting earnest effort on the part of his pupils.]

SIXTH YEAR.

Mrs. Spencer's First Steps in History; Sanford's Intermediate Arithmetic to multiplication of fractions; Maury's Elementary Geography to page 62; Harrington's Speller, part second, first twenty pages.

[*Note.*—It is to be presumed that during all the years that precede this year the teacher has taught orally the first principles of geography. At this stage in the course every pupil should have a dictionary and be taught how to use it, and during the whole of the remainder of the course the dictionary should be freely consulted.]

SEVENTH YEAR.

Maury's Elementary Geography, from page 62 to end; Harrington's Speller, second part, from page 21 to page 40; Sanford's Intermediate Arithmetic, from multiplication of fractions to the end.

EIGHTH YEAR.

Holmes' U. S. History; Sanford's Common-school Arithmetic to page 156; Harrington's Speller, second part, from page 41 to page 65.

[*Note.*—In studying history some geography should always be at hand as reference book.]

NINTH YEAR.

Sanford's Common-school Arithmetic, from 156 to page 279; Harrington's Speller, second part, from page 65 to page 88; Harvey's Elementary Grammar to False Syntax.

TENTH YEAR.

Harvey's Elementary Grammar completed; Sanford's Common-school Arithmetic reviewed and completed; Maury's Manual of Geography to British America; Moore's N. C. History.

ELEVENTH YEAR.

Harvey's English Grammar, revised edition, to Syntax; Steele's Physiology and Hygiene; Maury's Manual of Geography, completed; Higher Arithmetic or Algebra.

"Good Health for Children" taught orally, two lessons per week, to classes in Fourth Reader and to all children below Fourth Reader.

"Health Lessons for Beginners," until completed, in the hands of all pupils above Fourth Reader, two lessons per week.

Besides the writing that the pupils will do on the slates and with lead pencils, which should all the time be encouraged, the teacher should have systematic work in penmanship for the whole school at least twice a week.

Every teacher will take note of the fact that this course is not intended to be rigidly adhered to, and it is not considered absolutely necessary that every pupil thoroughly complete any step before he can take the next, and no child should be kept from advancing to a higher branch of study because others of his grade are not considered ready to go with him. It is often best to let pupils take a step that is somewhat too high rather than discourage them by keeping them back too long.

While it is certain that a very large proportion of the children will not be able to go to school long enough to complete this course, it is believed that it is best to have something definite to work at—certain books named and the order fixed in which they should be studied. It is hoped that very many children will be stimulated to an effort to possess and study all the books out of school as well as during the session.

Every teacher is earnestly requested to leave on record in his register the branches pursued at the preceding session by every pupil, so that his successor may have the desired information in organizing the school.   S. M. FINGER,
Superintendent Public Instruction.

[*Note.*—To the end that not only every pupil but every parent may have a copy, I will be very thankful if the newspapers will print not only the course of study, but the whole paper.]

THE NORTH CAROLINA TEACHER.

VOL. IX. RALEIGH, OCTOBER, 1891. No. 2.

EUGENE G. HARRELL, = = = = Editor.

AT SCHOOL.

BESSIE CHANDLER.

We are all at school in this world of ours,
  And our lessons lie plain before us ;
But we will not learn, and the flying hours
  And the days and the years pass o'er us.

And then we grumble and mourn, and say
  That our school is so tiresome and weary,
And we ask for a long bright holiday
  That will banish our lessons dreary.

But what is it God is trying to teach ?
  Is it patience, or faith, or kindness ?
Is the lesson really beyond our reach,
  Or made hard through our willful blindness ?

If we were in earnest and tried to learn,
  If our listless study we mended,
Who knows but our holidays we would earn
  And our school-days be gladly ended ?

Who knows but we make our lessons long
  And hinder their meaning from reaching
The hearts that would be full of joyous song
  If we knew what our God was teaching ?

Then let us study His will while we may;
  There's a warning for us in the rule
That the scholar who will not learn all day
  Is the one that is kept after school.

North Carolina Teachers Abroad:

A SUMMER JAUNT

IN

England, Scotland, Ireland and France.

CHAPTER XXII.

THE GREAT EXPOSITION OF 1889.

Shopping—The Famous Parisian Stores—Some Special Prices—
Tariff and the Currency Questions—The Great Eiffel
Tower—Sensations of the Ascent—A Memorable Scene—Up
in a Balloon—Capt. Goddard, the Celebrated Aeronaut—A
View of France from the Clouds.

OON after we reached Paris the girls
of our party suggested that they
must have a day exclusively for shopping, therefore the second day of our
stay in the French capital was what
we considered an "off-day," or a day
wholly in the interest of the shop-
keepers of Paris, and the aforesaid
shopkeepers must have considered the
day a decided success, if we are to
judge from the number of sight drafts
on friends at home which the Secretary
negotiated with the bankers, and the
immense pile of boxes and bundles which reached the
hotel about 6 o'clock P. M. addressed to various members of the North Carolina party. Some of these drafts
did not reach North Carolina for collection until after we
had been at home at least a month.

.Although we were among a people speaking a language
unknown to us, our ladies did not seem to experience
the slightest difficulty in quickly finding the best places

for making purchases. Almost before we were comfortably located in Paris our girls were as familiar with the Bon Marche and Magasin du Louvre as if they had been residents of France for several years.

The Bon Marche is one of the largest and most wonderful stores in the world, and is one of the most interesting sights of Paris. It is truly a town within itself, with its immense floors, endless galleries and an army of employees numbering thirty-five hundred. One of the special advantages of this great emporium is that a visitor can go anywhere about the building and inspect the goods without being solicited to buy at every step. We also discovered a special *disadvantage*, so far as concerned our party: The building was so large and so packed with goods and people that our whole party was quickly lost from one another, and never got together again until we met around the dinner-table at 6 o'clock P. M.

The Magasin du Louvre possesses a rare attraction for children, from the custom of the proprietors every day at 12 o'clock to give a beautiful inflated balloon to every child in the building, each balloon bearing the name "Louvre" clearly printed on it. Both of these establishments have a host of guides and interpreters for visitors, speaking English, German, Italian, Spanish, Chinese and other languages of Europe.

There are several business houses in Paris which confine their trade to specialties and they have a world-wide reputation. Of course such houses increase their prices in proportion as they have been able to establish a reputation. These places of business are almost entirely confined to the Rue de la Paix, and among them is Worth, the great costumer, who charges $125 for his cheapest dresses and from this price up to $12,000 ; Mdme Virot gets twenty-five dollars for the simplest little bonnet about the size of a bird's nest ; Mdme Leoty will not make a lady's corset for less than twelve dollars and the price for her best work is $150. We visited all these shops but do not think the party made many investments there.

A great many articles are remarkably cheap in Paris. A nice quality of kid glove may be bought for twenty-five cents and a much better grade for thirty-five cents. If these are bought in a regular glove shop a beautiful little French maiden carefully fits a sample pair to your hand, and it is marvelous how quickly and charmingly she can smooth the glove over your fingers and hand and have it buttoned, and, laughing at the sensation she has produced, stand ready to take your order for the number of pairs you desire. Some of the gentlemen of our party have enough gloves to supply all their sisters and cousins and aunts for a life-time, as they never passed a glove shop without having one fitted and buying at least a dozen pairs.

All articles made of silk are also cheap in Paris. A very neat black silk dress of good quality may be purchased and fitted to order for twenty dollars, such as would perhaps cost fifty dollars in the United States. Silk handkerchiefs cost forty cents, such as we pay one dollar for at home, and the finest of silk neckties and scarfs are sold for twenty-five cents.

If an American girl buys from $300 to $400 worth of clothes for the winter she can go to Paris to make her purchases and save enough in difference of prices between those here and what she would have to pay at home to meet all the expense of her summer trip to Europe. The iniquitous so-called "protective tariff" of the United States is driving thousands of our people to Europe every year to purchase their supplies of clothing and fancy articles for the household.

A high tariff between nations is just about as absurd as would be a tariff between the States of our country upon their various articles of manufacture and produce.

Free trade with the whole world is the only true and just policy of nations which consider the interest of their people instead of the pockets of their capitalists and monopolists, and the traveler in Europe becomes daily more convinced of this fact.

It was very gratifying to us to realize that the currency of the United States, either gold or paper, is worth one hundred cents on the dollar in any civilized country, and therefore we hate to know that Congress is tinkering with our currency in a way that will soon cause depreciation in some one of our "legal tenders" at home and abroad. Our silver dollar would also be worth one hundred cents if it contained one hundred cents worth of silver. Our Congress cannot swindle foreign countries with this coin as it has done our own country.

Having spent as much time and money in the fascinating shops as we desired, or, rather, could afford, we decided that the day following should be devoted exclusively to an examination of the great International Exposition which was exciting the admiration and wonder of the world. Our hotel was also fortunately located as to convenience to the Exposition, it being so near that we did not have need to use the cab or other public conveyance to reach it, simply a short walk down the Rue Montaigne for four blocks and we were at the main entrance to the Champs de Mars, in which spacious grounds the Exposition is held. The price of admission is twenty-five cents at the gates, but we soon learned that tickets were sold at every street corner throughout the city by men, women and children for only ten cents. Our sympathies for the laboring masses of course compelled us to buy our tickets exclusively of them.

The Exposition is far too big a thing for any ordinary person to comprehend or describe, even in the course of an extended stay, therefore we cannot undertake to write a guide-book of the exhibits, or tell of even a tenth of the beautiful and wonderful things that we saw. All that the most observant visitor can do in such an immense place is to impress upon his mind the most memorable and interesting objects that meet his eye. As for all the rest there remains simply a bewildering and confused recollection which it is impossible to ever straighten out so as to tell anyone about it in detail. Therefore we wisely concluded to waste as little time as possible with the things that did not specially interest us, but to search out the best exhibits and concentrate our attention upon these.

Of course the correct thing for us to do first was to ascend the famous Eiffel Tower, or *Tour Eiffel*, as it is known in Paris. This marvelous iron spire is the feature of the Exposition and the new landmark of Paris. It is an airy, graceful shaft of filagree, making its own peculiar contribution to the unique attractions of one of the most beautiful cities in the world. Unlike all other monuments it is visible from almost every part of Paris, while from its summit you obtain a great panoramic view of the heart of France. In the daytime the flag flutters at the masthead, but at night, as from some sky-piled Pharos, streams over the great city the electric light which represents the transmitted energy of engines of 500-horse power.

They say that the beacon on the Eiffel Tower is visible at a distance of forty miles, and that by the rays of its lamps you may read a newspaper in the street of St. Germain— at least seven miles "as the crow flies." The electric light at the summit of the tower blazes at times through red and white and blue glasses, the idea being that the Tower should flaunt the tricolor of France on the loftiest flagstaff in the world.

The crowd is so vast about the Tower waiting for a chance to begin the ascent that we had to take our turn like everybody else, and although we arrived at the opening at one of the feet of the tower at 9 o'clock A. M. we did not reach the top until near 1 o'clock P. M.! The sensation in ascending is novel. It presents the semblance without the reality of danger. It is as safe as going upstairs in your own house, and a great deal easier if you care to go up in the elevators. Four elevators start from the base of the Tower, one from each of the colossal feet upon which the giant whose head is in the clouds steadies himself on earth. You get into a room large enough to hold one hundred persons, adjust yourself comfortably, and before you fairly realize that you are off you are landed on the first floor.

Then you mount to the second floor, where you change cars. The second elevator runs to the top of the tower at about the rate of six miles an hour. The hoist contains seventy-five persons, and you are landed at the summit in less than ten minutes. You leave the hoist at the top just as if you were in a hotel, and step out upon a perfectly secure platform from which you cannot fall even if you try. After you have enjoyed the sensation of being mast-headed at an altitude to equal which the tallest pine in North Carolina would stretch its length in vain you come down again by the same safe and simple method. Their maximum lifting capacity is said to be 2,350 persons per hour to the second floor, and 750 an hour, or twelve journeys to the summit.

Standing under the Tower it impresses you by its combination of solidity and of grace. The great arches springing from the four bases meet overhead at a height which is greater than the summit of Washington Monument. Half way up the Tower stand the cannon whose brazen throats thunder forth the hour of opening and closing the great show.

The Tower stands four-square on feet of solid masonry, to which it is bolted by anchor rods four inches in diameter, an arrangement which more than doubles its power of facing the winds. Even if it stood loose on its stone pedestal, it would not blow over under pressure of anything less than a hurricane concentrated on its summit. It sways slowly and almost imperceptibly in a strong gale.

To put it up complete cost from first to last about $1,300,000. If it had been built of stone it would have cost $4,000,000.

The loftiest stone monument in the world, the Washington Monument, is only 554 feet high, but it weighs 45,500 tons. By using iron M. Eiffell got, at one-sixth of the weight, 430 feet nearer the sky.

The honor belongs to the rivet. The Tower is the work of the riveter. The whole structure is held together by the rivet and nothing but the rivet. Next to the imposing altitude and audacious sweep of the immense span, the first thing which impresses the imagination is the number of rivets. Two millions and a half rivets have been employed in its construction. Every one of these was heated white hot on the Tower and hammered into position there. But the holes for the rivets were all cut at the works of M. Eiffel at Levallois-Perret, from which the 12,000 separate girders, beams, joists, and other descriptions of iron work were sent to Paris punctured with no fewer than seven million holes.

Forty draughtsmen and calculators were employed constantly for two years in preparing the 500 engineers' drawings and 2,500 working plans, by the aid of which every hole was punched in the right place before a girder left the works. The Tower as it stands is a great monument to the absolute accuracy and scientific precision with which the modern engineer can manipulate his material.

When the second floor was being laid it was discovered that the two western piles were about a fifth of an inch higher than the two eastern. Only a fifth of an inch in the rearing of the four sides of the gigantic pyramid which

overtopped the towers of Notre Dame!   But that was not
allowed to pass without immediate rectification.   One-fifth
of an inch on the first floor would have thrown all the
rivets out of place in the upper part of the Tower.   The
hydraulic screw press that is fitted in the shoe, so to speak,
of each of the four feet of the Tower was brought to bear.
The western piles were lowered and adjusted and the work
went on without interruption.

The weight resting on each of the four uprights, which
together form each foot of the Tower, is nearly 500 tons.
Each of these uprights terminates in a steel hat fitting into
an iron socket sunk in masonry.   Within this socket the
hydraulic ram is introduced to raise or depress the superstructure at will.

There is a certain massive simplicity about the Tower
which exists side by side with a sense of the bewildering
intricacy of innumerable girders, tie-beams, and interlacing
iron work.   Over and above all else the memory carries
away an abiding impression of the great span and the great
spine.   Span and spine alike are four-fold.   The Tower
stands four-square to all the winds that blow.   North and
south, east and west, you are confronted always by one
span and one spine.   The span is the great arch that sup-
ports the first floor.   The spine is the iron upright which
runs outside the Tower from the second floor to the summit, straight, flexible and strong.   There is something
living and personal about the Tower, with its four feet, its
lofty head, and its erect, graceful spine.   It somewhat
reminds you of a giraffe, but a giraffe chained.

Under the central arch there is a fountain placed which
is a great rendezvous now that the Exhibition is open.
"Meet me at the fountain under the Eiffel Tower!"   What
romances will not be begun, and, alas! sometimes ended,
at that trysting place!   The fountain itself is allegorical of
the hemispheres and the continents.   Female figures, more

or less boldly designed and scantily attired, represent all the uttermost ends of the earth gathered together to celebrate the centennial of the French Revolution. The Tower is to be a permanent structure, so they say, although permanence when iron work is concerned is by no means an eternity. If it stands for twenty years it will probably pay its expenses.

On each of the three floors of the Tower are a number of shops, restaurants and newspaper offices. On the second floor the *Figaro* has a small printing office, and publishes a daily edition at a height of four hundred and sixty feet above the earth! When you reach the third floor you may purchase an international postal card, write it and mail it while overlooking the city of Paris at an altitude of nine hundred feet. Eight hundred persons can stand in the hall at the summit of the Tower, and ten thousand persons can be on the Tower at one time without crowding at all. The price of ascending this giddy iron pile is one dollar. The sensation of making this ascent is so peculiar that we want to try to tell you about it.

In ascending the first portion of the Tower you get a better view of the massive network of iron girders, angle irons and tie-beams than of anything else. At last we came out on the platform that surrounds the first floor. We were at the height of the tower of Notre Dame and Paris lay stretched as on a carpet at our feet. For seeing Paris we think the first floor is better than a higher elevation. You are high enough up to see the whole city lying below you. It does not help you to climb higher into the clouds unless you wish to see beyond the city. In that case it is necessary to choose a clear day.

Looking across the city you notice first and foremost before everything else the natural and unchanging features of the landscape, the Seine, which winds like a silver ribbon at your feet, and the heights of Mont Martre in the north. . Until the Eiffel Tower was built Mont Martre was the highest point in Paris, with the possible exception of the gilded dome of the Invalides. Long after the Eiffel Tower has rusted into red oxide Mont Martre will remain the centre of the tragedy of Paris. It was there where St. Dennis was martyred in the early centuries, there where the avenging Russian and Prussian crushed the last spark out of the First Empire, and there in our own times were planted the cannon of the Commune which first roared defiance of the Versaillese, and then being captured by these Versaillese impartially shelled the Communists out of Père La Chaise.

A grim acclivity, scarred with the wounds of centuries of strife and destined mayhap once more to echo with cannon thunder in the troublous time to come, Mont Martre revives reminiscences of Edinburgh Castle. It is the only hill near enough to dominate Paris. Mont Valêrien lies westward, fort-crowned and formidable, although from its bastions the smoke of artillery fire no longer tells how in the last great war its defenders stood sentinel to the last against the Prussian at Versailles.

All round the Tower on these crowded streets the German shells dropped thickly during the bombardment. Just over the river are the ruins of St. Cloud, and further away to the westward, not visible on the horizon, stands Versailles, the lordly pleasure-house of the Grand Monarque, which, by the irony of history, was to witness in our own time the proclamation of the King of Prussia as Emperor of Germany.

The landmarks of Paris are easily picked out from the Tower. Looking northward across the Seine, leaving the Bois de Boulogne on your left, the first noted point is the somewhat unrecognizable side view of the Arc de Triomphe de l'Etoile, with its proud array of thirty French victories and one hundred and forty-two battles, which, with its twelve radiating avenues, forms the centre of the Star of Western Paris. The great glass roof visible through the trees is the Palais de l'Industrie in the Champs Elysees. Further down the river stands the imposing pile of the Louvre—beyond the Tuileries Gardens. Even the ruins of the Tuileries have now vanished forever.

The Madeleine lies a little to the north, still more to the northward the church of St. Augustin, and then farther eastward you can see the great mass of the Opera House. Coming back to the Seine, you can indistinctly see beyond the Louvre the Hotel de Ville and the Tour St. Jacques. Crossing the river, the two towers of Notre Dame direct your thoughts to the glories of the past, while the great dome of the Pantheon recalls you to the profanation of the present. The towers of St. Sulpice lie nearer to you, and nearer still the great gilded dome of the Invalides which covers the sarcophagus of the First Napoleon. It is a wonderful panorama, over which you can gaze meditating for hours. How much of the history, of the romance, of the world had this as its theatre, and what strange tragic drama will not be enacted before the dwellers in these streets have said their last word to their kind?

As a matter of fact you feel much less giddy the higher you ascend. Whether it is that the attraction of the earth diminishes as you ascend, or whether it is that you become acclimatized, we do not know, but after you get past the four hundred feet you feel quite at home in the high latitudes.

The scene now becomes more inspiring as we move towards the third story. The steamboats that crawled along the Seine far below seemed little larger than bits of black stick floating in the stream. Mont Martre, Mont Valerien, the Invalides, the Pantheon, stand out in clearer relief. We were now far above them all, higher than we had ever been on steeple or tower before, and we imagine how sublime it is to be on the very summit of the lofty Tower when the lightning plays round and the thunder crashes as it were in your very ear. Since Jove sped his bolts from the top of Olympus could any situation be more sublime? The Tower is said to be not only the safest place in the world during a thunder-storm, as it is nothing but one gigantic lightning conductor but it is a protection against lightning for all the surrounding buildings.

While standing as far towards the top of the Tower as visitors are allowed to ascend, nine hundred and ten feet above the earth, one of our charming girls assisted the Secretary in waving our compliments to the city with the Stars and Stripes, and we then descended to the earth again by the lifts, feeling that we had honored ourselves by contributing so much time to the most wonderful modern achievement of scientific engineering.

"There is a strange fascination in ascending to great heights," remarked Miss Sells, as we descended to the first floor of the Tower, "and," she continued, "I always feel like remaining longer at such an altitude as that from which we have just descended."

"If you really enjoy such heights," returned the Secretary, "suppose we make a journey in the great Goddard Balloon which you see just over the river making regular trips among the clouds."

"I would be delighted to do so," replied the lady bravely, much to our surprise, as we know that most persons, men and women, are afraid to leave the earth very far.

"Then let us go at once," he said, "before it is too late to make the ascent, and we will soon have the pleasure of flying our American flag over the city of Paris at an altitude of two thousand feet above the earth and a thousand feet higher than the Eiffel Tower!"

Quickly calling a cab we were soon within the enclosure

where from a vast pit in the ground the great balloon takes its flight towards the skies.

It was a wonderful air-ship. The basket was circular, twelve feet in diameter, open in the centre, and it would hold eleven passengers. The immense bag was ninety feet high and thirty feet in diameter, and as it impatiently swayed in the breeze it seemed like some huge bird eager to be on the wing. From the opening in the centre of the basket was suspended a gauge to which was attached a large rope two thousand feet long coiled around a windlass which was operated by a steam engine.

Having paid the fare, two dollars for each person, we stepped into the light willow car with the great French aeronaut, Capt. Louis Goddard, and in a moment, almost before we realized it, the balloon began to ascend. Slowly we rise above the houses, then the trees seem to grow shorter and there comes over us a feeling of loneliness. Looking over the sides of the car we see the city spread out beneath us as some little town which the children make for their dolls. The street cars and omnibuses look like baby carriages, and a man walking appears to be only a hat moving along the ground without any visible means of locomotion.

There is a gentle, yielding motion to the car which assures us that we are still climbing into the clouds, and as the sudden gusts of wind strike the balloon it careens far to the side and we have a sensation something like that experienced in a boat when riding the waves.

"This is indeed grand!" exclaimed Miss Sells in enthusiasm, "and I never imagined what the sensation would be when soaring above the earth in a balloon."

"Yes, it is truly grand so long as the rope holds," replied the Secretary. "And only look below," he added, "and you will see that the breeze has carried us a long way from the little engine that holds the other end of this rope which appears to be no larger than a spider's thread before it reaches the earth.''

The view was truly one of surpassing loveliness. The whole of France from the English Channel to the Mediterranean sea lay spread out beneath us like a map. The air was as clear as crystal and the distance at which we could see with distinctness was something incredible. The ocean, the mountains and the beautiful valleys were combined in one magnificent landscape, the scene dotted here and there with cities and towns, moving trains and steamboats.

The wind was now blowing with considerable force and the balloon had a swaying motion of about a quarter of a mile and the rope was chafing considerably on the edges of the car.

''How much strain will this rope bear?'' we asked of Captain Goddard with some degree of interest.

'' Three thousand pounds,'' he replied.

Then looking at the gauge we saw that each gust of wind would cause the needle of the gauge to spin around to *twenty-seven hundred pounds!* Only three hundred pounds more of strain and the rope will break! We were not at all frightened, but the situation was somewhat interesting and the wind was increasing rapidly in power.

''The wind is too strong for us,'' said the Captain, ''and we will descend.''

We knew that when the engine began to wind in that rope the strain would be much greater, and we almost thought that it was much safer to remain in the clouds as we then were than to take the risk of having the rope to snap.

The situation was growing in interest.

''Now, Miss Effa,'' said the Secretary, ''if you will please hold one corner of our little flag we will soon have the Stars and Stripes proudly floating over La Belle France a thousand feet nearer the heavens than that French tricolor which is flying beneath us from the top of the Eiffel Tower."

As the Star Spangled Banner unfolded to the breeze Captain Goddard took off his hat out of respect to that famous emblem of freedom and bravery, and exclaimed " *Vive la Republique Amerique !*"

We gratefully acknowledged the compliment and Miss Sells replied, "*Pour notre contree, nous vous remercie, Monsieur.*"

The balloon gradually yielded to the rope and, like a spoiled child, reluctantly began to descend, and in a short while, just as the sun was setting, it was again safely anchored in its port and we stepped from the car upon the ground greatly pleased with our first experience "up in a balloon." We had been among the clouds about an hour.

There is a wonderful fascination about a balloon and we desire to make another trip skyward. We want to take our dinners and spend the day up among the birds.

When we reached the hotel it was almost impossible to make our party believe our thrilling account of the balloon trip with the statement that we had just been looking down upon our hotel from an altitude of over a third of a mile. We produced our tickets for the ascent and a souvenir card of the trip signed by Monsieur Goddard as evidence and the question was settled.

In our dreams that night we visited in a gigantic balloon all the countries of the earth, under the earth and above the earth ; fell out of the sky-scraper a dozen or more times ; dropped into the sea, and was impaled upon the North Pole ; was flattened out upon the dome of the Eiffel Tower, and suspended by our heels among the trees ; waved. the Stars and Stripes at the spirits in the air, and sailed through storm and tempest amid the lightning's lurid glare.

But we returned to the earth and awoke just in time for breakfast.

THE VALUE OF SCHOOL WORK.

A very observing correspondent thinks that the value of an education depends upon the use to which it can be put in serving the ends of life. Upon this condition alone depends its utility or its uselessness. The fact is easily proven by the variety of special schools that are springing up in so many parts of the country.

Not many years ago they were confined almost wholly to law, medicine and theology. Now they include civil and mining engineering, architecture, dentistry, pharmacy, nursing, agriculture, mechanic arts, manual training, commercial education, etc.

The more important of professional pursuits are successfully followed only when a liberal education precedes the one that specializes; but it is not always possible for a majority of our young men to enjoy such extended advantages. For them there should be courses in the grammar or high schools tending to special preparation.

The fact that such instruction cannot be had in many of these schools prompts a large number of pupils to withdraw from them before graduation. Many seek positions in business houses and others enter schools that teach special branches. In one city whose high schools enrolls 1,399 pupils, over 400 of them gave up a course the cost of which is nothing and pay from $75 to $150 a year for tuition in the several business colleges in that city.

This seems to indicate that the education they get in these schools will be of more use to them than would be the course of study they give up. Would it not be fair if the schools that furnish a free preparation for college would also furnish free tuition in special subjects for those who cannot go to college?—*School Journal, New York.*

2

MUSIC IN PUBLIC SCHOOLS.

The schools of North Carolina are advancing. Every day we hear of music being adopted in public schools where it was never taught before. Educators and school officers are opening their eyes slowly, but surely, in this direction.

The city of 5,000 inhabitants that has no music lessons in its schools is behind the times, and if they care to draw comparisons they will find that their public schools without music must be placed at the tail end of the procession.

It is easily understood now by those who have music taught in their schools how the singing lesson helps the other lessons. It is restful, healthful and invigorating to all the children who engage in it. There is no better lung exercise in the world for children than singing. Then it lightens their hearts and softens the harsher elements in their nature.

Every school committee ought to arrange with some competent singing teacher to visit his schools two or three times a week and give them lessons in the rudiments of music and singing. Money spent in this way would be well invested. Every teacher should give music some attention. It is sure to be a regular branch of learning in the public schools.

Music is greatly needed in all the schools, under the guidance and instruction of competent persons. We shall be glad to hear from school teachers and others on this subject. Our pages are at your disposal.

Do not fail to have a class in North Carolina history for this term of your school. The boys and girls will be delighted with the study.

HOW I FOUND TIME.

How one is to get time to perform all the work laid out for him by Institute conductors and superintendents is a question which has troubled many a conscientious country teacher already burdened with multitudinous daily tasks. The writer once felt the pressure of this great load, and made up his mind that he would see what could be done. On carefully going over the ground he found that he could gain time in the following ways :

1. By being thoroughly prepared for every lesson of the day, so that no time should be wasted in considering what to say or do.

2. By talking less and right to the point, making explanations concise and clear, rather than verbose.

3. By having pupils come to the recitation with examples, maps, etc., on slates or paper, fully prepared for the proper work of the period.

4. By reducing the number of classes to the lowest feasible limit and having several advanced classes recite every other day, giving twenty-five minutes to a recitation instead of fifteen every day.

5. By not repeating questions himself or permitting pupils to do so.

6. By having a place for everything needed to carry on the day's work ; training classes to move promptly, not hastily, and insisting on distinct utterance.

7. By having good blackboards and plenty of them, so that work could be prepared in advance of the recitation, or held over if needed for further reference. Blackboards and globes are the most indispensable parts of school furniture.

8. By refusing to solve examples for pupils while a class is waiting.—*School Education.*

A GROWING EVIL.

Our witty friend, Editor Bardeen, replies to his critics who take him to task for an essay read before the late National Convention of Superintendents, that the other fellows used up the time and he made no essay, but talked a few minutes on another subject.

Our educational conventions are fast getting into the chronic abomination of political meetings. They advertise everybody, and if half the notabilities come, each having prepared himself, as he has a right to do if he is to travel five hundred miles at his own expense, to read a paper to the assembled wisdom of the nation, the inevitable result is that everybody's "piece" must be "docked," everybody is "mad" and the audience maddest of all, that it is compelled to listen to extracts from what may be a profitable discourse.

The same nuisance breaks out in the Institute. It is the horror of the Chatauqua Assembly; the misery even of the weekly Teachers' Association. The writer of this, for two meetings of the teachers of a city of seventy thousand inhabitants, in succession, found himself in the pleasing position of being invited, as a visiting stranger, to deliver a lecture of the usual length. Of course he cheerfully assented to the proposition that his address should follow a "very short paper" by one of the home teachers. Whereupon, a clever little lady presented an elaborate essay that covered the entire session, and a learned brother pedagogue repeated the same entertainment, on the second trial.

Now, nobody was to blame. The home teachers had prepared a paper, to the best of their ability, and took the occasion to present it in full to their associates. The superintendent trusted in human nature to suppress itself, with the same admirable faith which has swamped a thousand managers of public meetings. The real trouble was the persistent habit of trying to attract people by a lying programme, which would bury an audience in an avalanche if it were carried out; and, in any event, winds up with the exasperation of the speakers and the disgust of the crowd.—*Popular Educator.*

[For The North Carolina Teacher.]
QUESTIONING.

BY JOHN C. HOLDER, PLUCKEMIN, NEW JERSEY.

Thorough teaching depends largely upon the teacher's mastery of the art of questioning, and since questioning is in some way connected with all the work of the school-room the teacher should make it a subject of close study.

The fact that there is a *science* as well as an *art* in teaching should be kept in mind by the teacher, if he would succeed in maintaining that logical order in the application of the principles that underlie the art of questioning.

As a *science* it is founded upon psychological laws, especially those laws which govern the development of mind in the child.

As an *art* it is founded upon the logical relation of truths to each other in connection with these laws of mind. No series of questions should be used in the school-room without due regard to the pupils questioned, the kind of instruction to be given, and those laws of mind which govern memory and thought.

Hence, in order to secure perfection in this art, each question should be clearly stated; should have its proper place in the series, and should not do violence to the laws of mind. If this be done, the teacher will know not only *how* questions should be stated, but also *why* one form of statement is better than another.

His questions should be conditioned on the extent of the child's previous knowledge, age, mental powers, home influences, habits and all environing circumstances which influence or affect the powers of the child's mind; and these very conditions themselves the teacher will be able to comprehend if he is an intelligent and skillful questioner.

We quote the following statements of the *uses* and rules for questioning as given in his *Westminster Normal Outlines* by Rev. J. A. Worden:

QUESTIONING AND USES.

1. Probes the scholar.
2. Fixes attention.
3. Makes the mind receptive.
4. Stimulates the memory.
5. Quickens thought.
6. Guides thought.
7. Arouses the effort to express thought.

RULES FOR QUESTIONING.

1. Begin with easy questions, thence pass to difficult ones.
2. Proceed in logical order.
3. Ask for explanations of terms and ideas.
4. Often ask questions of review and recapitulation.
5. Lead scholars to apply the lessons.
6. Give questions of ellipsis.
7. First ask the question, then name the scholar to answer the question.
8. Ask questions of the whole class.
9. Sometimes ask very hard questions, to be studied and answered at the next recitation.

WHAT TO AVOID.

1. Ambiguous or indefinite questions.
2. Leading questions, *i. e.*, questions which give or suggest the answers.
3. Very difficult questions.
4. Foolish, useless questions.
5. Asking questions in rotation to pupils as placed in class.
6. Repeating questions for the *inattentive*.
7. Staring at the pupil while answering.
8. Uncivil treatment of honest answers.

Some of the other and more apparent advantages gained by skill in this art are these:

1. It leads the teacher to a clearer and more correct knowledge of himself, for no teacher can ask questions judiciously or logically upon any subject which he himself does not clearly understand; and if during the course of his questionings he discovers his deficiencies he has gained a great point in thus being enabled to know what to add to his fund of knowledge.

2. It aids him by giving system to his work, and as a natural result becomes both time saving and labor saving.

3. It excites and fixes the attention of pupils during the periods of study, diverts their minds from what might otherwise produce disorder or confusion in the school-room, and by that means reduces the discipline of the school to a minimum.

Our public schools would be greatly improved in both quantity and quality of good results, if teachers in general would make the *art of questioning* a subject of close, earnest study and systematic practice.

Especially in preliminary work there is a great amount of time lost as well as effort wasted on the part of teachers because they do not by judicious questioning ascertain what their pupils *know*, what they do *not* know, or what misconceptions they may have.

A great deal depends upon the kind of *beginning* the teacher makes in his work. A correct beginning is more than half the accomplishment of the end, and a bad beginning will make all the work of a school year unsatisfactory.

By questioning properly the teacher knows *how* and *where* to begin, by having pointed out to him the obstacles to be met and the means needed to remove them, and hence can intelligently lay a firm foundation upon which to erect that "noble structure," THE EDUCATED MAN.

SOME DEFECTS IN OUR PUBLIC SCHOOL SYSTEM.

BY E. H. CANFIELD, LUVERNE, MINN.

The first defect in our school system that I note is the lack of personal interest in the schools. Both morally and legally it is the duty of the parent to actively and personally co-operate with the teacher in educating the child. Whoever fails in that is not a good citizen. Any parent is sadly derelict in his duty who, without question, commits the education of his child to strangers about whose moral and mental fitness he knows nothing. We must have more personal interest in the schools, and the live and enthusiastic teacher will mingle with the parents and seek to arouse that interest.

On account of this lack of personal interest there naturally follows a lack of moral supervision. I am not one of those who believe that the public school-room is the place for religious instruction, but I do believe that one of the greatest dangers to our public school system is the immoral influences that find their way into the school-room.

One child who has been born and reared in vice, or who later has become morally corrupted, will poison an entire community of children when brought together in the school-room. One rotten apple will spoil a whole bin full of good ones. It is doubtful if, in any village school, there are not children who ought to be in the reform school. One intelligent teacher of my acquaintance says that, if she had children, she would do almost anything rather than permit them to attend the public schools on account of certain vicious tendencies to be found there. A child given to the use of obscene language is a dry rot in the school-room, and under our present system he is largely protected in his vice. The teacher does not hear it, and the innocent child is afraid to communicate it to the stranger teacher. The parent pays no attention to it, until some morning he wakes up to find that his child, once pure, has been saturated with corrupt thoughts.

We want better school-houses and more attractive surroundings. Beautiful pictures should be hung upon the walls. An opportunity should be given the children to cultivate flower gardens in the summer, and gaming devices should be furnished the children just as much as wall maps and globes. By so doing going to school would become a pleasure, and the intervals of work would be no more dreaded than the task of climbing the hill when coasting.

We want a public school system that pays more attention to the individual needs of the scholar. Our present system aims to deal out to each and every pupil the same intellectual food, all cut, dried, and baked in the same oven, without regard to the taste of the boarders. It aims to send out young people as the brick machine turns out brick—all of the same length, breadth and thickness. The tendency is to bring every pupil to the same common level of mediocrity. The strong points of a child ought to be studied and given an opportunity to develop. Our schools afford but little encouragement for an Edison. The system is often inconsistent. It deals too much with the abstract, and not enough with the concrete. Children are made to bend over desks and study the theories of physiology and hygiene, while so doing they may be violating the simplest laws of health of which a bug-eating Digger Indian would not be guilty.

Children are taught to find the hypothenuse of a right angle triangle who cannot measure a cord of wood or a potato patch. In the town and city schools too much effort is made to develop the mental faculties at the expense of the nervous system. Prizes are offered for the greatest mental feats regardless of the effect on the child's health, while the less precocious one is left behind discouraged in the race. The child's nervous system and vitality are wasted before he reaches maturity, when he the most needs them.

Besides offering prizes to the scholar who will master the most of grammar or history, I would also give one to the boy who can run the fastest, jump the farthest or wrestle the best. I prefer a vigorous ignoramus to a consumptive Latin scholar. I have but little faith in the mere study of books on physiology and hygiene. A treatise on swimming will never enable a boy to swim, and to read a cook-book to a starving man will not appease his hunger.

Our present school system has led to another serious condition. There is a tendency among boys to undertake the work of the man before the work of the boy has been completed. He is impatient to prepare for his life work. If he has decided to become a carpenter he can see little use in the study of grammar. He is eager to grasp the square and plane. After that his attendance at school is a forced one. He may be bodily present in the school-room, but his mind is absent building imaginary castles. He fails in his lessons and thus passes as a dull scholar. Why should not the school furnish manual training—that training that the boy so much needs for his life work.

I would make the boy a skillful carpenter as well as a skillful mathematician. This I would do in the public school-room. By uniting this work I would lead him to see that he cannot become a first-class mechanic without becoming a first-class scholar, and thus I would make of him a good citizen, capable of self support. By so doing the schools would become attractive for the boys, the school-house better filled, the army of tramps and educated fools diminished. The money and labor annually expended in supporting little two-by-four sectarian schools, the principal work of which is the propagation of some one's pet "'ism," would go a great way toward making our schools what they ought to be.

Let patriotic Americans unite in lifting up the public schools of their country. Let not the bigotry of party politics or of sectarianism enter in. Let them keep pace with advancing civilization, for in the maintenance of our public schools is the guaranty of freedom and of popular government.—*School Educator* (Minnesota).

INSULT TO INJURY.

A wise professor loved a pretty maid;
Calling the cause of science to his aid,
　　'Twas thus he wooed her:—
"My life work on the Prehistoric Human
Has need of your bright wits, as I'm a true man,
Oh, share my toil and fame, most lovely woman!"
　　'Twas thus he sued her.

The mercenary girl made answer trite:
"I really fear I must, sir, in that light
　　Decline to view you;
Although you cause me pride and great elation,
I cannot wed above my mental station,
But I'll become, for a consideration
　　Assister to you."
　　　　　　　　—*Harvard Lampoon.*

A WOMAN may possess a face and form as beautiful as that of an angel, but if she has a sarcastic tongue it will be an effectual protection to her from matrimony and its cares.

IN THE SCHOOL-ROOM.

THE REASON WHY.

[To be Recited by a Little Girl.]

"When I was at the party,"
  Said Betty (aged just four),
"A little girl fell off her chair,
  Right down upon the floor;
And all the other little girls
  Began to laugh, but me—
I didn't laugh a single bit,"
  Said Betty, seriously.

"Why not?" her mother asked her,
  Full of delight to find
That Betty—bless her little heart!—
  Had been so sweetly kind.
"Why didn't *you* laugh, darling?
  Or don't you like to tell?"
"I didn't laugh," said Betty,
  "'Cause it was me that fell!"
          —*Mary E. Bradley, in St. Nicholas.*

A SHORT, EXCELLENT SERMON.

Here is a short sermon by a woman. It is a good one, and is pretty sure to hit you somewhere, whatever may be your age and circumstances: "The best thing to give to your enemy is forgiveness; to an opponent, tolerance; to a friend, your heart; to a child, good example; to your father, deference; to your mother, conduct that will make her proud of you; to yourself, respect; to all men, charity."

A BIT OF PHYSIOLOGY.

1 bone in each thigh.
1 bone at the root of the tongue.

2 bones in the lower leg.
2 bones in the fore arm.

3 bones in each finger.
3 bones in each small toe.

4 bones in each ear.
4 vocal chords.

5 bones in the middle of the foot.
5 bones in the palm of the hand.

6 salivary glands.
6 muscles to move the eye.

7 bones in each ankle.
7 true ribs on each side.

8 bones in each wrist.
8 bones in the skull.

—Popular Educator.

WHICH IS CORRECT?

Will the editor of THE NORTH CAROLINA TEACHER please inform his readers if he would say "The new Union passenger *deepo, dippo, daypo* or *deppo?*" M. S. T.

RALEIGH, N. C., Sept. 1, 1891.

[The editor of THE NORTH CAROLINA TEACHER would say, if he wanted to be correct, "The new Union Passenger *Station*." A "depot" is a place of deposit for the storing of goods; a warehouse; a storehouse. A building or place where passengers assemble to board a train is a station and in no sense a depot. The word depot should be pronounced *daypo* by a Frenchman in France, but an American or Englishman should pronounce it only as *deepo* unless he is wiser than Noah Webster.—EDITOR.]

WHAT A BARREL OF WHISKEY CONTAINS.

A barrel of whiskey contains a good deal more than any other barrel of the same size; for, in addition to the regular forty-two gallons, it also contains:

A barrel of headaches, of heartaches, of woes;
A barrel of curses, a barrel of blows,
A barrel of tears from a world-weary wife,
A barrel of sorrows, a barrel of strife;
A barrel of all unavailing regret;
A barrel of cares and a barrel of debt;
A barrel of hunger, of poison, of pain;
A barrel of hopes ever blasted and vain;
A barrel of falsehood, a barrel of cries,
That fall from the maniac's lips as he dies;
A barrel of poverty, ruin and blight;
A barrel of terrors that grow with the night;
A barrel of crime, and a barrel of groans;
A barrel of orphan's most pitiful moans;
A barrel of serpents that hiss as they pass,
From the head of the liquor that glows in the glass.

—*Selected.*

ORIGIN OF MATHEMATICAL SIGNS.

The radical sign was derived from the initial letter of the word "radix."

The sign of equality was first used in 1557 by a sharp mathematician, who substituted it to avoid repeating "equal to."

The multiplication sign was obtained by changing the plus sign into the letter X. This was done because multiplication is but a shorter form of addition.

Division was formerly indicated by placing the dividend above a horizontal line and divisor below. In order to save space in printing, the dividend was placed to the left and the divisor to the right, with a simple dot in place of each.

The sign of subtraction was derived from the word "minus." The word was first contracted into m n s, with a horizontal line above to indicate the contraction, then at last the letters were omitted altogether, leaving the short line —.

The sign of addition is derived from the initial letter of the word "plus." In making the capital letter it was made more and more carelessly until the top part of the p was placed near the center, hence the plus sign was finally reached.

[For The North Carolina Teacher.]

THE MODEL PUPIL.

BY S. M. S. ROLINSON, HATTERAS, N. C.

There's a young and pretty maiden
  Every morning comes to school,
And the best of lessons has she;
  And she never breaks a rule.

Yes, her face is always pleasant,
  And her smile is bright and sweet,
While the roses are not equal
  To the bloom upon her cheek.

Every word and every action
  Show her good as she is fair;
Crowned is she with gentle manners
  Which are jewels rich and rare.

May Life's sweetest flowers open
On her pathway day by day,
Chasing every care and sorrow
From her bright young life away.

POINTS FOR GIRLS.

Your mother is your best friend.

Have nothing to do with girls who snub their parents.

Tell the pleasantest things you know when at meals.

Do not expect your brother to be as dainty as a girl.

Exercise, and never try to look as if you were in delicate health.

Introduce every new acquaintance to your mother as soon as possible.

Don't think it necessary to get married. There is plenty of room for old maids, and they are often happier than wives.

Enjoy the pleasures provided for you by your parents to the fullest extent. They will like that as a reward better than any other.

Take care of your teeth at any cost of time or trouble, and do without new dresses rather than neglect a needed visit to the dentist.

Most fathers are inclined to over-indulge their daughters. Make it impossible for your father to spoil you, by fairly returning his devotion and affection.

Never think you can afford to be dowdy at home. Cleanliness, hair well-dressed and a smile will make a calico look like silks and satins to a father or brother.

Do not quarrel with your brother; do not preach at him, and do not coddle him. Make him your friend, and do not expect him to be your servant, nor let him expect you to be his.—*Drake's Magazine.*

THE MAIN THING.

It makes little difference what educational creed we profess. The important point to settle is, what creed do we follow. Am I an old fogy hearer of recitations or am I a teacher? Many are just now more anxious to settle their educational standing than their educational practice. They read Pestalozzi, but follow the schoolmen. They preach reform, but practice conservatism.

The thing for us to remember is, that there are tens of thousands of pupils this autumn who are starving on the food they get. It is educational bran bread; the brain can not hold and digest enough of it to nourish the system. But these teachers insist on cramming their pupils with the miserable stuff.

One teacher just now, in order to better facilitate this cramming process, has rhymefied the whole of English history, and is filling the mouths of his pupils with it. Poor, hungry, starving souls, they are dying for want of mental food, and don't know where to get it, and their teachers don't know enough to tell them; and so in the midst of abounding plenty they starve!

Isn't it pitiable that the children who are crying for the bread of living, nourishing thought, should be given the indigestible stones of meaningless vocables.—*Oregon School Journal.*

EVERY EXPLANATION, every particle of showing, every bit of the pupil's work that the teacher does—whenever, in brief, she does anything for him that he can do for himself—she has not only robbed him of an opportunity to discover, to think, or to do, but she is building up a habit that will result in making him that drone in the world's hive, and that unhappy nuisance in society — a helpless, despondent man or woman.—*Quincy Methods.*

TO NORTH CAROLINA BOYS AND GIRLS.

The editor of THE NORTH CAROLINA TEACHER will give a handsome, cloth-bound set of DICKENS, THACKERAY or ELLIOTT'S works, large print, library edition, to the boy or girl in a North Carolina school who will write the best account of "The Battle of Alamance and the causes which led to it," the facts to be as stated either in Mrs. Spencer's "First Steps in North Carolina History" or Moore's "School History of North Carolina."

The article must not be less than two nor more than four pages of foolscap paper, and it should be mailed to THE TEACHER by October 15th, 1891.

A competent committee will examine all papers, and the one that is considered best will be published in THE TEACHER for December.

Write with ink and only on one side of the paper. Sign your name on a separate slip of paper and pin it to the article so that it can be removed before the sketches are given to the examining committee.

There are thousands of bright boys and girls in North Carolina who can do this little piece of literary work well, and we hope that many of them will undertake it, as the effort will be of very great pleasure and benefit to all, even to those who may not win the prize.

THE UNSELFISH man or boy should be undemonstrative and unobtrusive, and almost secretive, in his acts of self-denial and self-sacrifice. Whether you spend the pocket-money which would otherwise have gone in sweets or toys in buying a book for your sister, or whether you save a life at the risk of your own, let no hint or suggestion of yours remind either the person obliged or the world at large of what you have done. There is no such modest man as your real hero; it is the Ancient Pistol that blazons his own great deeds.—*Selected.*

North Carolina Teachers' Assembly.

ORGANIZATION FOR 1891–'92.

OFFICERS:

Hugh Morson (Raleigh Male Academy), President, . . Raleigh.
Eugene G. Harrell (Editor Teacher), Sec. and Treas., . Raleigh.

VICE-PRESIDENTS:

1. J. J. Blair (Supt. Graded Schools), ... Winston.
2. J. E. Kelly (Model Male School), ... Charlotte.
3. Miss Catherine Fulghum (Graded School), . . Goldsboro.
4. W. J. Ferrell (Wakefield Academy), . . . Wakefield.
5. Miss Lizzie Lindsay (Graded School), . . . Greensboro.
6. P. M. Pearsall (County Superintendent), . . Trenton.
7. Miss Lina McDonald (Graded School), . . . Winston.
8. T. J. Drewry (Horner Military School), . . . Oxford
9. Mrs. S. Montgomery Funk (Chowan Bap. Fem. Inst.), Murfreesboro.

EXECUTIVE COMMITTEE:

Hugh Morson, *ex officio*, President, ... Raleigh.
E. G. Harrell, *ex officio*, Secretary, ... Raleigh.
Eben Alexander (University of North Carolina), . . Chapel Hill.
W. L. Poteat (Wake Forest College), ... Wake Forest.
James Dinwiddie (President Peace Institute), . . . Raleigh.
Charles D. McIver (Pres't Normal and Industrial School
    for Women), ... Greensboro.
J. Y. Joyner (Superintendent Graded School), . . Goldsboro.
A. C. Davis (Superintendent Military School), . . Winston.
E. E. Britton (Principal High School), ... Roxboro.
Ninth Annual Session—June 21 to July 2, 1892.

ASSEMBLY NOTES.

The Teachers' Assembly has appointed the following committee: J. J. Blair, Winston; Josephus Daniels, Raleigh; E. A. Alderman, Chapel Hill; S. M. Finger, Raleigh; J. Y. Joyner, Goldsboro, to solicit subscriptions for the purpose of erecting a monument, to be placed in Capitol Square, Raleigh, to the memory of Archibald D. Mur-

PHEY, the originator and earnest advocate of popular education in North Carolina. The *first* subscription, twenty-five
dollars, has been sent to the committee by the editor of THE
NORTH CAROLINA TEACHER. The public graded schools
of Raleigh, Charlotte, Wilmington, Goldsboro, Greensboro, Durham, Asheville, Salisbury, New Bern, Shelby,
Reidsville, Tarboro, Wilson, Henderson, Statesville, and at
other points in the State as they may be organized, are
requested to make special solicitations for this purpose.
Two or three hundred dollars from each of these schools,
with the individual subscriptions expected, will erect a
"Murphey Monument" such as will be creditable to our
State. Subscriptions may be sent to any member of the
committee. The Teachers' Assembly intends to make a
liberal contribution to this fund.

THE TEACHERS' ASSEMBLY building at Morehead City
has been very popular with various organizations this sum-
mer as a meeting-place for their sessions. On July 8th the
State Pharmaceutical Association met in our hall, the
Tobacco Association held a session there on July 17th, the
Southern Dental Association held their annual session and
Exhibition of Dental Supplies there on August 13th.
The State Farmers' Alliance would also have met in the
Teachers' building but for the fact that its officers did not
notify the Secretary of the Assembly as to the time of
their meeting, and in the meantime the Dental Association
had given the usual notice and engaged the building for a
date which happened to be the same as that upon which
the Farmers' Alliance was to meet. The Teachers were
anxious to have the Farmers meet in their convenient
building, and regret that they neglected to give the Secretary the absolutely necessary information as to date. Of
course when some other organization had, some time before,
secured the building on a date when it was to be wanted by
the Farmers' Alliance, the Secretary of the Assembly could

not break faith with a previous engagement. The Teachers' Assembly has always been pleased to give any reputable organization the use of its building without any charge whatever for rent, and it only asks that organizations desiring the use of the building for their sessions will give the Secretary the customary notice that he may avoid any conflict of dates with other bodies. However, in order that the farmers should not be disappointed in a meeting-place, the Secretary of the Assembly went to Morehead City and secured the Bell Hall at that place, located very convenient to the Atlantic Hotel, had a platform built and moved into the hall a sufficient number of the Teachers' Assembly settees to comfortably seat the Alliance during its daily sessions. We make this statement for the benefit of some members of the Farmers' Alliance who have been disposed to say unpleasant things by way of criticism of the Assembly, because they did not have the use of the Assembly building, when they did not know the facts in the case.

It was specially gratifying to have such a great number of our friends of education at the Assembly this summer. The object of the organization is to bring not only the teachers but *the people* together in these annual gatherings, and we hope to see the number of those attending who are not teachers largely increased. The Executive Committee tries to make the programme of exercises of so general a character that it will interest everybody.

The Teachers' Assembly will be represented by a fine exhibit in the Exposition at Raleigh. It will include life-size portraits of all the Presidents of the Assembly, with photographs of the teachers on their various trips to New York, Washington City, Canada and Europe. There will also be a printed tablet setting forth a brief history of the Assembly and the splendid work which it has accomplished for education in North Carolina.

EDITORIAL.

OUR FOUR MONTHS' PUBLIC-SCHOOL COURSE.

The proposition which was discussed at the past session of the Teachers' Assembly providing for a regular course of study for four months' public schools in the country to be prepared by the State Board of Education has been received with heartiest approval by the teachers of the State. The outline course which had been arranged by our State Superintendent, Major S. M. Finger, and which was submitted by him as merely suggestive of what he was working to accomplish, created a very great interest in the scheme. He has since the Assembly carefully revised and improved his course, and it has now been officially issued by him for the guidance of the teachers in our country public schools for the fall terms of school. This course of study has been most thoroughly and thoughtfully planned by Major Finger, and it is the longest step forward towards promoting the efficiency of our public schools that has ever been taken by a Southern State. We rejoice that North Carolina is the first State of the South to perfect the idea and officially promulgate it, thus placing our beloved State again at the head of the column as a grand leader in progressive education. We hope that every public-school teacher will at once adopt the four months' course. If there is not sufficient public money in your district to pay for a four months' school, have a meeting of your committee and go with them to every person in the district and solicit enough individual aid from them to supplement your public school fund so that it *will* pay for a continuous school for four months this winter. We do not believe there is a district in this State where this help cannot be easily secured upon a proper canvas. Then four very desirable things will have been accomplished: 1. The people of the district will be aroused to a greater interest in education and particularly in their school. 2. The teacher will be encouraged to do more correct and satisfactory work, having in view some definite goal to be reached. 3. The active and energetic canvas will bring into the school many children who have been staying at home, as the parents will know that they are to have a longer and better school than ever before. 4. The pupils will be stimulated to work harder with their studies so as to complete the required course and be ready for advancement at the beginning of the next term.. If the teachers and the school committees will now cordially co-operate in this great advance movement, as we believe they will do, it will not be long before we shall see what we have long desired to see, a good four months' public school in every district in North Carolina.

PLEASE send to us a brief note of every educational event occurring in your section.

Now is a good time to re-organize your Teachers' Council for the fall educational campaign. Invite the public to your meetings, hold them at some convenient place, have a telling address by some popular invited guest, intersperse the exercises with some good songs and recitations by teachers, and your Council will be a most gratifying success and a pleasure to the teachers and their friends in your community. We will send upon application plans and hints for organizing Teachers' Councils to any persons interested in the work. The circulars cost you nothing but the postal card upon which you write for them.

THE NORTH CAROLINA TEACHER is published only ten months in the year. During the months of July and August THE TEACHER takes a vacation like all·other good teachers.

THE *fourth* edition of Mrs. Spencer's "First Steps in North Carolina History," the *tenth* edition of Moore's "School History of North Carolina," the *eighteenth* edition of Alfred Williams & Co.'s "North Carolina Copy Books" are just from the press. The large and frequent editions of these books which are sold speak their praise and success in strongest terms.

THE OFFICE OF THE NORTH CAROLINA TEACHER is in Alfred Williams & Co's Book-store and Publishing House. When you visit Raleigh, during the Exposition or at any other time, you are cordially invited to call at our office and make yourself perfectly at home. We have on exhibition all the latest school text-books and other publications, and you will enjoy an examination of them.

A LARGE number of "educational picnics" have been held this fall throughout the State under the auspices of the Farmers' Alliance, and they have resulted in much good to the cause of education in the various communities, and the interest awakened will increase the attendance upon the schools above what it has been in several years. When the people meet pleasantly together and talk about education they will then make some sacrifices, if necessary, in order to keep their children in the schools.

WE do not believe that the people of North Carolina will consent to write the name of our beautiful Elm City as "Newbern," notwithstanding the recent action of the Post-office Department. We propose to write it correctly, · "New Bern," as heretofore. The action of the Post-office Department is as nonsensical as if they had ordered the following as correct: Newyork, Newjersey, Newhampshire,

Newengland, Westvirginia, Northcarolina, Newhaven, Newlondon! How absurd! We hope that the people of North Carolina will "stand by" our lovely city of "New Bern." The editor of THE TEACHER assisted our lamented Col. W. L. Saunders, Secretary of State, in a long search of the old records for the correct orthography of this name and we found it to be, beyond all possible doubt, "New Bern," and in this manner we expect always to spell it.

CAPT. C. B. DENSON, Associate Principal of Raleigh Male Academy, has been appointed general manager of the Educational Exhibit in the Exposition. Every leading school in North Carolina, graded school, high school, seminary, college and the University should be represented in this exhibit, and teachers are requested to notify Captain Denson at once as to what amount of space they desire for their displays. Let us show to the thousands of visitors what North Carolina schools are doing and can do.

THE NORTH CAROLINA TEACHER submits the following needed words for adoption by the teachers and the public generally : *Typewriter*, a machine for typewriting ; *Typograph*, the paper that is written on the typewriter ; *Typographist*, the person who operates the typewriter. A general use of these words, with definitions accepted as here given, will save much confusion in our uses of a very popular and necessary aid in the modern methods of conducting business.

THE NORTH CAROLINA TEACHER is a North Carolina journal of education for North Carolina teachers, and it is of more value to the teachers of our State than are all the journals published beyond our borders. That it has done more for the teachers of North Carolina and for the general cause of education in the State than any other educational publication in or out of the State is a fact well known and established beyond all contradiction. That it is the only journal of education that has ever shown an interest in North Carolina teachers towards helping them to better schools, better salaries, better recognition and better appreciation is a fact likewise admitted and is beyond dispute. That THE TEACHER intends to always remain true to its original policy, "North Carolina for North Carolinians," is also a fact not to be doubted.

THE EXPOSITION authorities have designated October 19 to 24 as "Educational Week." You can come to Raleigh for a rate of only one cent a mile on all railroads in this country, and there ought to be an attendance of ten thousand teachers and pupils on that occasion.. Can't you afford to suspend your school for a week at that time so that you may come to the Exposition and bring a good number of your pupils. A visit to this Exposition, the largest inter-states display ever made in the South, will be worth as much to you and your scholars in the matter of instruction as will be a week's work in school. Come!

THE recent death of the eminent scholar and poet, James Russell Lowell, leads us to inquire "Where are the men and women of our time to take the places of these noted literary people who are passing away?" And in surveying the field we are forced to admit that this present generation has no such poets, authors and statesmen as Longfellow, Bryant, Tennyson, Whittier, Lowell, Byron, Moore, Hemans, Browning, Dickens, Emerson, Hawthorne, Thackeray, Scott, Elliott, Bulwer, Webster, Clay, Calhoun, Davis, Vance, Ransom and hundreds of others equally great in letters and in politics. Is it the fault of our modern system of education? If the race is not mentally degenerating, and no one will admit that, then there must be some defect in the training of the present generation. There is too much machine education, and machine education has not made, never will, and cannot make, eminent

scholars, thinkers or statesmen. The so-called " new education " has been at work for thirty years, about a generation, and it has not yet produced even *one* great literary
or eminent man or woman. Isn't it about time to investigate the new method of education ?

THE NORTH CAROLINA TEACHERS' ASSEMBLY specially
desires to have every friend of education in the State to
meet with the teachers in their delightful annual sessions.
The editor of the *Southern Educator* objects to this. That
is because he doesn't know anything about educational
meetings. He did not go to the meeting of the Southern
Educational Association when it was organized in his
present home State; he was not present at the second session of the Southern Educational Association at Chattanooga, Tennessee, in July, nor did he attend any session
of the North Carolina Teachers' Assembly so long as he
felt that he could afford to stay away. Surely the editor of
the *Southern Educator* has proven himself to be no "friend
of education." He objects to the public attending the State
Institutes "because they are meetings for teachers,"
although our esteemed Superintendent of Public Education
and the Institute Conductors very wisely *invite* the public
and insist upon their attending the Teachers' Institutes.
They want the North Carolina public informed upon educational matters interesting our State, and so does the
Teachers' Assembly and everybody else who is in sympathy with progressive education in North Carolina. The
editor of the *Southern Educator* wants to have "paid lecturers" at the Assembly. We have yet to hear of a State
Teachers' Association in America that pays the speakers
who are on its programme. The Assembly does not want
anything of the kind, as there are plenty of true, competent and devoted teachers in North Carolina who are
enough interested in the State to do all the regular lecturing that the Assembly wants. Besides, the Assembly does

not want any "lecturers," paid or unpaid, but enthusiastic
and helpful *speakers* such as we have in North Carolina.
Perhaps the *Southern Educator* would like to be paid to
afflict the Assembly with his pet scheme "Outline of
Rhetoric," of which samples have been given in that
journal. If necessary, the Assembly could well afford to
pay handsomely to be excused from suffering an affliction
of all such useless and impractical theorizing. We think
that those who speak or give papers at the National Educational Association get no pay, and yet tney ride from one
hundred to a thousand miles, paying their fares and also
the expenses of their board at the hotels. So this generation is not wholly devoid of teachers who love their work
and delight in meeting with and speaking to their
co-laborers in great conventions. North Carolina, we are
proud to say, is yet full of such faithful and conscientious
teachers, who, like all the officers of the Assembly, are
willing to work for their Assembly without pay just as the
teachers in other States work for their State Associations—
with a much higher motive than the reward of a few
dollars. Under the wise management of the editor of the
Southern Educator no doubt the Teachers' Assembly would
soon be as eminently successful and well known as are
his "Southern Association of City Superintendents" and
"Education Club of the South," of which mythical
organizations that enterprising journal professed to be the
official organ! It might be well for him to try his
experienced hand in organizing a Teachers' Association in
his own county of Durham!

ONE OF THE most useless and nonsensical things ever
undertaken by an educational assemblage is the so-called
"Dress Reform Club" which was organized by a few Boston women at the New York Chautauqua this summer. If
the reform (?) is to dispense with the corset as a part of
female apparel, and all "dress reformers" seem to have

this sole object in view, then the crusade should be against the *abuse* of the corset and not the *use* of this much discussed and maligned garment. A woman's dress must have some regard for neatness, comfort, happiness, convenience and decency, and this does not by any means include a tightly laced corset; but the woman·who is so indifferent to her personal appearance as to appear habitually in public without a corset would be as much out of place as a man would be without a coat, or a collar, or shoes and stockings. They might consider themselves well and properly attired because of the imaginary comfort and health induced by that style of dress (particularly in hot weather), but it is quite certain that both would be very quickly repudiated in polite and refined society—and justly, too. The corset is a neat, comfortable and useful garment, and it can be worn with safety and without the slightest injury to health; but if it is to be dispensed with entirely because some women draw the laces too tight, then the same argument would abandon shoes because some men and women wear them too small, and we would all have to return to the toga and the sandals of the dark ages! Those fanatical Boston females may, if they desire, appear on the public streets of "The Hub" in a "Mother Hubbard" and woolen pantalettes and without a corset, but we think it will be far in the future before any sensible North Carolina woman will adopt such a style of "dress reform."

ABOUT OUR TEACHERS AND SCHOOLS.

Miss Amanda Winecoff is teaching at Concord.

Miss Claudia Bullock has a school near Fayetteville.

Miss S. E. Bridgers has a private school at Mooresboro.

Mr. G. W. Guilford is teaching at Clayton, Johnston County.

Mr. M. F. Little has a school at Bost's Mill, Cabarrus County.

Mr. George H. Haigler is teaching at Hayesville, Clay County.

Miss Irene Wood is teaching at Swepsonville, Alamance County.

MISS MITTIE CRAWFORD is teaching at Troy, Montgomery County.

MR. F. J. PUGH has a good public school at Topia, Alleghany County.

MISS ACOREE C. FOUNTAIN has a school at Richlands, Onslow County.

KINSTON COLLEGE opened on September 1st with a hundred pupils.

MR. P. A. SCOTT is Principal of Bethel Academy, Sonoma, Haywood County.

MR. CHARLES H. HAMILTON is teaching at Coddle Creek, Cabarrus County.

MISS M. A. BLAIR has a very prosperous school at Lilesville, Anson County.

MISS LIBBY ALLEY, of Staunton, Va., has opened a select school in Clinton.

MISS LUCIE G. FREEMAN has a good school near Youngsville, Franklin County.

MISS LUCIE O. WILLIAMS is teaching a public school at Windsor, Bertie County.

MISSES PATRICK'S school at Kinston opened with forty-six pupils on September 1.

MR. J. P. LEITNER is Principal of the High School at Menola, Hertford County.

MISS GERTRUDE BAGBY, of Kinston, is teaching at Vandemore, Pamlico County.

MR. B. M. C. MORROW has charge of a school at Forest City, Rutherford County.

MR. M. S. COLONNA, JR., is Principal of the Academy at Hertford, Perquimans County.

MISS EMMA VAUGHAN, of Rocky Mount, is teaching at Scotland Neck, Halifax County.

MISS H. A. CHAMPION has a flourishing private school at 261 Chestnut street, Asheville.

MISS ELLA BERRY is in charge of the school at Connelly's Springs. This is her third term.

MR. P. WRIGHT has a fine school at Enochville, with one hundred and thirty-eight pupils enrolled.

MISSES MAY BARNES and Lottie Dancy have been elected·teachers in the Tarboro Graded School.

MISS CORINNA BRILES is conducting a successful school at the Davidson Academy in Hannersville.

MISS MARY LOU BROWN is teaching a school in the Masonic Building at Clinton, Sampson County.

MISS CLARA QUEERY, of Charlotte, is Principal of the graded school in the northern portion of Winston.

MISS LIZZIE PORTER, of Tarboro, an accomplished musician, is teaching music in Asheville Female College.

MISS MATTIE DAVIS of Yadkin College, has charge of the Academic Department in the school at Swepsonville.

MISS LIZZIE S. HOLDEN is in charge of Poplar Grove School near Hillsboro. Forty-nine pupils are enrolled.

REV. S. R. TRAWICK is teaching at Wilkesboro. His school building is being furnished with new patent desks.

REV. B. S. BRONSON is master of the Home School at Warrenton· He is one of the best teachers in the State.

REV. J. R. JONES, of Salisbury, has been elected Principal of the Female Academy at Milton, Caswell County.

MISS MAMIE WHITEHURST has a select school for boys and girls at Tarboro. The third session began August 3i.

MISS NANNIE SPEIGHT, of Tarboro, has been chosen as a teacher in Claremont College at Hickory, Catawba County.

MR. P. R. BOGGS, Principal, and Mrs. M. F. Gillam, Assistant, have charge of the Academy at Windsor, Bertie County.

MISS CAPITOLA GRAINGER, of Kinston, has accepted the position of music teacher in the Female College at Greensboro.

PEACE INSTITUTE opened the fall term on September 3d with near a hundred boarding pupils at the table for the first meal.

MR. JOHN F. BRADLEY is Principal of Pisgah Public School near All Healing, Gaston County. Fifty-four pupils are enrolled.

MR. W. R. GENTRY is Principal of the Institute at Laurel Springs, Alleghany County. The fall term opens very encouragingly.

MR. WILLIAM MCDOWELL (Trinity College), of Tarboro, has accepted a position as Assistant Professor in Mathematics in Trinity College.

MR. BREVARD NIXON is Principal of the High School for boys and girls at the growing little town of Mount Holly, in Gaston County.

THE PEOPLE of Greenville, Pitt County, are making an effort to establish a high grade school specially for girls in that charming little town.

RUTHERFORD MILITARY INSTITUTE began its second year on September 3d with seventy-five students. Capt. W. T. R. Bell is Superintendent.

MR. T. S. ANDREWS is Principal of the Mount Vernon Springs Academy, near Ore Hill, Chatham County, and the school opens prosperously.

Mr. J. E. Smith (Wake Forest), of Raleigh, has been elected by the Trustees as Principal of the High School at Mount Olive, Wayne County.

Miss Katharine Yingling, of Virginia, has charge of the Music Department in Captain John Duckett's school at Hamilton, Martin County.

Miss Sallie Newlin, who has been teaching at Fallston, in Cleveland County, has entered Greensboro Female College to complete her education.

Mr. W. H. Pope (University of N. C.), of Chatham County, has been elected Principal of the High School for boys and girls at Selma, Johnston County.

Mr. Chas. J. Parker has resigned the superintendency of Shelby Graded Schools to accept the principalship of the Centennial Graded School at Raleigh.

Mr. A. L. Crutchfield is Principal of the Pinnacle Academy at Culler, Stokes County. Mrs. Emma Gwaltney Crutchfield, his wife, has charge of the Music Department.

Miss Lizzie Guthrie has secured the handsome new building of J. H. Wood at Rutherfordton, and will open a first-class boarding and day school for girls on October 1.

Miss Bessie Worthington, of Rocky Mount, has accepted a very pleasant and remunerative position as music teacher in a large school for girls in Charlottesville, Virginia.

Mr. A. A. F. Seawell, of Jonesboro, and Mr. A. M. Scales, Jr., of Greensboro, are assistant teachers in Cape Fear Academy at Wilmington; Mr. Washington Catlett is Principal.

Wake Forest College had about two hundred students present on opening day, September 3d. New students arriving on every train, so our correspondent writes on September 8th.

Miss Truletta Kreth, of Raleigh, a graduate of Peace Institute and the Raleigh Business College, will be a teacher of typewriting and stenography at Peace Institute this term.

Lexington Seminary began a very successful fall term on August 24th. Mr. W. J. Scroggs, A. M., is Principal, and Mrs. S. Jordan Puckett and Mrs. M. K. Crawford are his assistants.

York's English Grammars, well known in this State as the "Blind Man's Grammars," have been sold to Mr. F. P. Julien, of Peoria, Ill., a former pupil of Dr. York, the author of the grammars.

Mr. Willie H. Clendenin is Principal of the High School at Plain View, Robeson County, N. C., and he reports one hundred and seventy pupils enrolled, the best opening in the history of the school.

THE SHELBY GRADED SCHOOL, among its first good work, adopted Mrs. Spencer's "First Steps in North Carolina History" and Alfred Williams & Co.'s "North Carolina Writing Books" for use in the school.

ALL THE schools of Raleigh are certainly "on a boom." Every train is bringing in girls and boys for the various schools, and there will be a larger number of students in the Raleigh schools from a distance than ever before.

THE State Agricultural and Mechanical College opened with an unusually fine attendance on September 3d. The enrollment will almost double that of any previous year. Near a hundred students on the first day.

MR. THOMAS C. DANIELS (Trinity College), of New Bern, has been spending the summer at the Harvard and Springfield Gymnasium, preparing to take his position in Trinity College this fall as Director in Physical Culture.

MR. W. H. WILLS, an A. B. graduate of the University, opened Wilson Male Academy August 31st. He is a young man of brilliant parts and comes highly endorsed, bringing recommendations of undoubted worth.

THE UNIVERSITY opened September 3d with two hundred and thirty boys, of which number there were a hundred new students. The enrollment will no doubt reach three hundred during this the first term under Dr. Winston, the new President.

YADKIN NORMAL SCHOOL, Mr. Zeno H. Dixon, A. B., Principal, opened with fifty students on August 30th; Miss Lizzie Petty, of Ashboro, is in charge of the Music Department. The commodious new buildings will be completed by October 1st.

THE RALEIGH BUSINESS COLLEGE is enjoying a season of prosperity, and well it should, for not a single graduate of the institution has ever failed to secure a pleasant and paying position. This fact speaks in unmistakable terms the high character of the college.

MR. E. E. BRITTON has resigned the principalship of Mount Olive High School to accept a like position in Roxboro High School, Person County. He made a good reputation at Mount Olive. He and his accomplished wife will be a valuable addition to the progressive town of Roxboro.

THE TEACHERS' COUNCIL of Northampton County is one of the livest in the State. At a recent meeting the Council had a public address from the distinguished orator, Hon. Frank D. Winston, which was greatly enjoyed. Mr. Andrew J. Connor, the County Superintendent, is President, and Miss Annie Parker is Secretary.

4

ELON COLLEGE is one of the most successful institutions in North Carolina. The new term opens with a large enrollment and new students are arriving daily. This is a "co-education college," and no person can doubt the success of this feature. Patrons and friends alike are gratified at the splendid condition of the institution.

THE COLLEGIATE INSTITUTE at Enfield began a prosperous term on August 24th. Mr. O. L. Sapp, Ph. B. (University N. C.), is Principal of the institution; Miss Sue M. Whitaker is assistant in Academic Department; Miss Minnie F. Whitaker (Peabody Institute, Baltimore,) is teacher of Music and Stenography; Mr. F. L. Pippen is instructor in Telegraphy.

BERTIE COUNTY has a flourishing Teachers' Council, with Mr. Percy R. Boggs as President. At the meeting on August 14, at Ross' Church, Miss Oliyia Taylor presented an excellent paper on "School Management." Mr. A. J. Cobb discussed "The Advantages of a School Teacher's Life," and Hon. F. D. Winston delivered a charming address upon the subject "The Educated Citizen."

SUPERINTENDENTS Hughes of Reidsville, and Graham of Charlotte, had a very successful Teachers' Institute at Gastonia, July 27—31. Over fifty teachers were enrolled, including every public school teacher in the county. Many friends of education attended the daily sessions. The teachers express themselves as greatly pleased with the work, also encouraged by the pleasant meeting and acquaintance with one another.

THE RALEIGH MALE ACADEMY, Messrs. Morson and Denson principals, sends about twelve students to the University and the colleges this term, yet notwithstanding this the fall session of the Academy began on September 1st with ninety boys the first week, which is eleven more than ever before on the first day of school. This is one of the best and most prosperous preparatory schools for boys in the State. Mr. Morson is one of the finest classical teachers in the South, and it is hard to find Captain Denson's equal as a literary scholar.

THE TEACHERS' INSTITUTE of Davidson County convened in Lexington, August 10, and closed August 14, Profs. Alex. Graham and E. L. Hughes, conductors. It was the largest and most enthusiastic gathering of teachers that ever assembled in the county. Two years ago our Institute numbered only forty or fifty. One year ago ninety-four. This year the teachers came from all parts of the county, and one hundred and seventeen were enrolled. Professors Graham and Hughes are energetic, progressive instructors, and are well up with the times. The teachers received information that will enable them to do more effective work than has heretofore been done in the schools of our county. Six young men received State certificates. Friday, the last day of the Institute, was set apart for public speaking. At ten o'clock, sharp, the bell was rung, and the teachers, with quite a number of visitors, promptly assembled. The County Superintendent submitted a few practical remarks, directed especially to the teachers, on the line of their work the coming winter, and then introduced Professor Hughes, who was followed by Professor Graham. The addresses of Professors Graham and Hughes were strong appeals for education, and for longer terms and more effective work in the public schools. The better class of teachers in Davidson County are coming to the front, and the educational outlook is encouraging. P. L. LEDFORD,

County Supt., Davidson County.

CUPID AMONG OUR TEACHERS.

'Tis said that " figures never lie,"
That one and one are always TWO ;
But Cupid proves, with wor so sly,
Some wondrous things that figures do.
And when he claims a teacher's hand
All rules of figures then are done,
Though TWO before the preacher stand
This one and one are ALWAYS ONE.

MISS LILLIE GAY, of Wilson, an accomplished teacher of vocal and instrumental music-and a member of the Teachers' Assembly, was married to MR. WILLIAM T. SHAW, of Weldon, on September 2d, 1891. Rev. J. H. Cordon, D. D., of Raleigh, performed the ceremony.

AT RECESS.

The books and slates now put away,
And let us laugh a little while;
For those who work there should be play,
The leisure moments to beguile.

A BOY, kept in after school for bad orthography, excused himself to his parents by saying that he was *spellbound.*

TEACHER—"Tommy, man has been called the 'laughing animal.' Can you mention some other attribute that raises him above the mere brute?" Tommy Figg—"Yes'm. He—knows how to spit."

A STREET CAR PONY.—Boston School Boys (jumping on front platform)—"Hello, McDonald!" Car Driver—"Mornin', gents." School Boy—"Here, Jack, you take the reins; grab the brake, Ginger. Now, driver, just run over this page in the Anabasis for us before we get down to the high school."

NO YELL AT VASSAR.—First Vassar Student—Say, girls, there's one thing we've forgotten. We haven't any college yell. All colleges have yells, you know. Second Student—Why, of course, strange we never thought of it. Let's have one. Third Student—But I don't see how we can yell without taking the gum out of our mouths. Fourth Student—Let's let the yell go. It isn't very lady-like anyhow.

ATLANTIC COAST LINE.

Wilmington & Weldon R. R.

AND BRANCHES.

CONDENSED SCHEDULE.

TRAINS GOING SOUTH.

Dated Sept. 1, 1891.	No. 23. Daily.	No. 27. Fast Mail. Daily.	No. 41. Daily Except Sunday.
Leave Weldon	12 30 p. m.	5 43 p. m.	6 20 a. m.
Arrive Rocky Mount	1 40 p. m.		7 24 a. m.
Arrive Tarboro	*2 18 p. m.		
Leave Tarboro	10 .35 a. m.		
Arrive Wilson	2 18 p. m.	7 00 p. m.	7 53 a. m.
Leave Wilson	†2 30 p. m.		
Arrive Selma	3 30 p. m.		
Arrive Fayetteville	5 30 p. m.		
Leave Goldsboro	3 15 p. m.	7 42 p. m.	8 40 a. m.
Leave Warsaw	4 14 p. m.		9 34 a. m.
Leave Magnolia	4 27 p. m.	8 40 p. m.	9 49 a. m.
Arrive Wilmington	6 00 p. m.	9 55 p. m.	11 20 a. m.

TRAINS GOING NORTH.

	No. 14. Daily.	No. 78. Daily.	No 40. Daily Except Sunday.
Leave Wilmington	12 35 a. m.	9 15 a. m.	4 24 p. m.
Leave Magnolia		10 57 a. m.	6 10 p. m.
Leave Warsaw		11 11 a. m.	6 25 p. m.
Arrive Goldsboro	3 05 a. m.	12 05 a. m.	7 30 p. m.
Leave Fayetteville		‡9 10 a. m.	
Arrive Selma		11 08 a. m.	
Arrive Wilson		12 20 p. m.	
Leave Wilson	3 35 a. m.	12 58 p. m.	8 23 p. m.
Arrive Rocky Mount		1 30 p. m.	8 53 p. m.
Arrive Tarboro		*2 17 p. m.	
Leave Tarboro		10 35 a. m.	
Arrive Weldon	5 05 a. m.	2 55 p. m.	10 00 p. m.

*Daily except Sunday.

Trains on Scotland Neck Branch Road leave Weldon 3.30 p. m., Halifax 3 52 p. m., arrive Scotland Neck at 5.00 p. m., Greenville 6.50 p. m., Kinston 7.55 p. m. Returning leaves Kinston 7.00 a. m., Greenville 8 10 a. m., arriving at Halifax 11.00 a. m., Weldon 11.25 a. m., daily except Sunday.

Train leaves Tarboro, N. C., *via* Albemarle & Raleigh Railroad daily except Sunday 4.40 p. m., Sunday 4.40 p. m., arrive Williamston, N. C., 7.18 p. m., 4.20 p. m., Plymouth 8.30 p. m., 5 20 p. m. Returning, leaves Plymouth daily except Sunday 6.20 a. m., Sunday 9 a. m., Williamston, N. C., 7 40 a. m , 9.58 a. m., arrive Tarboro 10.05 a. m., 11.20 a. m.

Train on Midland North Carolina Branch leaves Goldsboro, N. C., daily except Sunday 7 a. m., arrive Smithfield, N. C., 8 30 a. m. Returning leaves Smithfield, N. C., 9 a. m., arrive Goldsboro, N. C , 10.30 a. m.

Train on Nashville Branch leaves Rocky Mount at 3 p. m., arrives Nashville 3.40 p. m. Spring Hope 4.15 p. m. Returning, leaves Spring Hope 10 a. m., Nashville 10.35 a. m., arrives Rocky Mount 11.15 a. m., daily except Sunday.

Train on Clinton Branch leaves Warsaw for Clinton daily except Sunday at 6.30 p. m. and 11.15 a. m. Returning, leaves Clinton at 8.20 a. m. and 3.10 p. m., connecting at Warsaw with Nos. 41, 40, 23 and 78.

South-bound train on Wilson and Fayetteville Branch is No. 51. North-bound is No. 50. *Daily except Sunday.

Train No. 27 South and 14 North will stop only at Rocky Mount, Wilson, Goldsboro and Magnolia.

Train No. 78 makes close connection at Weldon for all points North daily. All-rail *via* Richmond, and daily except Sunday *via* Bay Line.

JOHN F. DIVINE,
General Superintendent.

J. R. KENLY, *Assistant General Manager.*
T. M. EMERSON, *General Passenger Agent.*

THE NORTH CAROLINA TEACHER.

VOL. IX.   RALEIGH, NOVEMBER, 1891.   NO. 3.

EUGENE G. HARRELL,   =   =   =   =   Editor.

MARCHING HOME.

MRS. M..F. BUTTS.

Hark to an army tramping,
　To the beat, beat, beat,
Over the fields and highways,
　Of little children's feet;
Hark to the dancing rhythm,
　As captain and colonel come,
With rank upon rank of soldiers,
　Marching, marching home.

They bring the summer's roses
　Set in the dimpled cheek;
In their eyes the glint of the sunshine
　They marched away to seek;
The sweep of the wild bird's pinion
　In their motions glad and free—
Marching down from the mountain,
　Marching up from the sea.

They have rocked with birds in the tree-tops.
　All over the flowery land;
They have raced on the wild sea-horses
　Across the gleaming sand;
Now, back to books and to duty
　Captain and colonel come,
With all the glad child army,
　Marching, marching home.

—Wide-Awake.

North Carolina Teachers Abroad:

A SUMMER JAUNT

IN

ENGLAND, SCOTLAND, IRELAND AND FRANCE.

CHAPTER XXIII.

ENJOYING THE EXPOSITION

HISTORY OF HUMAN HABITATIONS—THE PICTURE GALLERIES—"LA PREMIÈRE POSE"—THE AMERICAN EXHIBITS—THE EDUCATIONAL DISPLAY—A FAMOUS FRENCH UNIVERSITY—THE DOLL SHOW—VENUS IN CHOCOLATE—OUR CHAPLAINS IN THE BALLOON—ENGAGING A CAB UNDER DIFFICULTIES—THE GRAND ILLUMINATION.

WE had not yet seen enough of the Exposition, therefore we decided to give another day to the great show.

We fully realize, however, that the most important thing to see in Paris is Paris itself. Paris is much more than any Exposition can possibly be. Expositions are all, more or less, modeled after the same pattern, but Paris is unique. There is only one Paris but there are many Expositions, nor is this Exposition by any means the most notable thing in Paris.

This is the biggest Exposition ever held in the world. There are nearly seventy thousand exhibitors, and the cost of the great display is over nine million dollars! There are thirty-eight countries represented in the exhibit, and this includes every civilized nation.

One of the most valuable features to a teacher is the sight of the various peoples of the earth, clad in their own costumes, speaking their native languages, and surrounded by the products of their own countries.

The study of the history of human habitations greatly interested us. One of the novel features of the Exposition is a street illustrating the evolution of human habitations from the cave of our Paleolithic progenitors to the handsome edifices of modern Europe. In this collection we are shown what the domicile of pre-historic man was like.

The picture galleries, after the Tower, are the most popular and attractive feature of the Exposition. There is not only the choicest of the French *salons* for the past ten years, but there are the masterpieces of French art in the hundred years that began with the Revolution. Nearly every foreign country is represented by its best painters. There is no phase of human life, hellish or divine, that is not portrayed on the walls of the Fine Art Gallery, often with wonderful fidelity and startling realism.

Here are the two extremes of beauty and of hideous ugliness, of the noblest heroism and the most hateful pictures of loathsome horror. From Munkacsy's "Christ before Pilate" to the masked nudity which is the crowning shame of the French gallery, there is no note of human aspiration, heavenward or hellward, that is not rendered more or less faithfully in the glowing canvas. The ideas, the emotions, the passions of humanity, not of one nation but of all, are here incarnate in color, radiant in light and instinct with life. And their setting is as various as the countries from whence they come.

Nature in all her caprices, from the glaciers of Norway to the steppes of Russia, from the surf-beaten shore of the Atlantic to the eternal snow of the Alps, from the peaceful vales of Italy to the magnificent thundering Niagara, is here interpreted by the most gifted of her sons. This Fine Art Gallery is truly a whole world in itself, a Universal Exhibition which strikes deeper and appeals more directly and strongly to the popular mind than all the other exhibits in all the other departments of the World's Great Show.

In these galleries, as in all others east of the Atlantic, are many pictures of various degrees of excellence and of shame representing the nude.   Of the artistic side of this question nothing need be said here, but those who regard all questions strictly from the point of view of the human ought, if possible, before coming to a positive conclusion, to visit this vast display of pictures and spend some time before the remarkable painting "La Premiere Pose." Few pictures in all the gallery are more touching.   Even now, as we write of it entirely from memory, some three thousand miles away and near two years after seeing it, the picture is vividly in mind as if we saw it but yesterday.

A young girl, beautiful and innocent, timorous and graceful as a startled fawn, is disrobing for the first time before the artist to whom her mother—a stern woman in the background—has brought her as a model.   The poor child is hesitating before completing her undress, and her expression of shame and confusion is piteous to see.   The tender pathos of the girl's position deepens into tragedy as you turn to the artist's companion, a woman from whom all womanly modesty has long since been painted out, who lolls upon a couch and contemplates the blushing embarrassment of the maiden with cynical enjoyment.   There are two distinct types before you—the one that is and the other that which she will be.   Whether for the sake of all the painted beauties who ever glowed on canvas it is worth while to subject such purity to such shame, is a question which we cannot decide but which each person must settle for himself.   It may be that there are things worthy of a human sacrifice, but do not let us ignore the fact that the sacrifice is exacted.

We were told that this wonderful picture will be sent to the United States to be exhibited in the World's Exposition of 1893.   If so, doubtless thousands of our North Carolina friends will see it.

The Educational Department of the Exposition was particularly attractive to us.   The United States exhibit was in charge of Mr. C. Wellman Parks, of Troy, New York, and our country was well represented. We found many things from North Carolina that were familiar to us, among them were catalogues of Charlotte Female Institute, Chowan Baptist Female Institute at Murfreesboro, Davenport College at Lenoir, Greensboro Female College, St. Mary's School at Raleigh, Trinity College, and the University at Chapel Hill. We were pleased to find conspicuously displayed a complete file of the current volume of THE NORTH CAROLINA TEACHER, and this was the only educational journal from North Carolina in the exhibit or mentioned in the official catalogue.

The colossal globe was indeed another curiosity, as instructive as it was interesting. This is the biggest terrestrial globe ever made. It is in a round special building near the Children's Theatre at the end of the Liberal Arts Palace. It represents the earth a million times reduced, and is over forty feet in diameter. This immense globe is covered with a peculiarly prepared paper resembling metal, on which the continents, seas and countries of the world are indicated just as on an ordinary map. We could easily find North Carolina and see our capital city Raleigh properly located. The globe revolves slowly on its axis. The spectator is hoisted up to the top of the building in an elevator, and then descends by a spiral stair-case which encircles the globe at some distance from it.

The French Educational Exhibit was large and exceedingly fine, and we are inclined to believe that we were just a little envious of the evidences of the very great liberality of that nation to education. One of the institutions of learning in Paris is noted throughout the world.

It is what is usually called "The University of Paris," but what is in reality only an aggregation of several different Faculties and is without doubt the largest educational institution in the world. This year (1889) it has a scholastic population of ten thousand one hundred and seventy-three, which is, however, a decrease of about two hundred compared with the preceding year.

Of this number one thousand eighty-six were foreigners, representing thirty-five different countries. Russia sent the largest contingent, namely, two hundred and ninety-two. Next in order comes North America with one hundred and sixty-seven; but as Mexico is separately reported this must refer chiefly to the United States. There were one hundred and forty-nine Roumanians, ninety-three Turks, and sixty-three Englishmen. The other lands represented fall below fifty, six having but a single representative. The great majority of foreigners—seven hundred and fifty-nine—was in the school of medicine.

The entire number of female students was one hundred and fifty-two. Of this number one hundred and twenty-three were in the medical department; ninety-two were Russians, seventeen French, seven English and but one American. In the department of science there were nineteen women, nine of them Russians and six French. One of the latter received the doctor's degree with the highest possible honors. The co-education feature of the University is immensely popular and successful. The Faculty of Protestant Theology reports twenty-nine regular students. Strangely enough this Faculty is supported by the State, while the Catholic Faculties were disbanded in 1885. The salaries of the French professors vary from $3,250 in Paris to $1,200 in the provincial cities.

We want just such an institution as this in North Carolina, which shall admit on equal terms the boys and girls of our State and furnish education as thorough and extensive as can be secured in any city of Europe.

France has within the last few years undergone a most remarkable educational revival in all departments. It is more heavily burdened with debt than any other European country, yet its appropriations for the cause of education have been increasingly liberal from year to year, almost from the time of the establishment of the present republic.

The Minister of Public Instruction of France claims a whole side of the Educational Gallery for his exhibit, and he presents such a mass of educational appliances belonging to all grades of schools that simply an examination gave us not only a fair idea of the educational system of France, but also many very instructive object-lessons— more than we were able to take away and assimilate. Much of the school machinery shown did not receive the approval of our party, it being but an enlarged plan, both as to extent and objection, of the unsatisfactory method of "shoe-pegs, splints, tooth-picks and peas" with which our country is becoming as disgusted as it is familiar.

The United States is well represented at the Exposition, not only as regards the quality and character of the exhibits, but also in the ability of the Commissioners sent officially in behalf of the Government. Altogether, the United States occupies one hundred thousand square feet, which, after Great Britain, is the largest space alloted to any foreign country. Of this, forty thousand square feet is in the Machinery Hall where there is a grand display of electrical apparatus, the Edison exhibit alone occupying over eight thousand square feet, and the wonderful phonograph is here shown for the first time in Europe. The railway section does not do justice to the American railway system, because of the difficulty of sending the heavy machinery so great a distance. In the art section there are two hundred and fifty American exhibitors and their paintings would do credit to any country. On the Quai d'Orsay there is a fine collection of our agricultural implements. The International Company which lights the Exposition grounds and buildings contains the leading American firms, and one of the devices employed by Edison is to utilize the trees and shrubs for electric lamp posts. The Frenchman thinks that this is a very ingenious "Yankee trick."

While strolling about the main building we noticed in one of the wings far away a great crowd of children seeming to be in ecstacies of joy. As we drew near we quickly discerned the cause of their happiness. It was a splendid exhibit of toys and dolls of every conceivable taste and ingenuity.

Here, under the green trees, walking in a miniature Champs Elysees, is every kind of automaton doll, peasant dolls, baby dolls, nurse dolls, little boy and little girl dolls, grand-lady dolls, papa and mama dolls, soldier dolls, bride and bridegroom dolls, all wonderfully true to life in every detail, except that these little people, judging from appearances, must take a great deal more care of their clothes than do their brothers and sisters in real life. The trees were filled with mechanical birds chirping and singing, while the proud peacock strutted about the miniature lawn displaying all the colors of the rainbow.

This exhibit was a perfect paradise for the children, and we enjoyed it so much that we were willing to admit that it was also a paradise for grown people as well. Our party purchased several of these beautiful automaton figures to delight the little ones at home.

The children were also very much interested in another rare exhibit in a different part of the building. It was an immense statue about fifteen feet high on a pedestal, representing the Venus de Milo, and the figure and the pedestal were made wholly of sweet chocolate by the celebrated manufacturers, Baker & Co. It is presumed that Venus is a sweet creature at any time, but this Venus was literally and peculiarly sweet; yes, irresistibly sweet to the children, for they had bitten her toes, fingers, heels and legs, and, still being intensely in love with the divine creature they had also eaten away the four corners of the pedestal on which she stood! But the temptation to bite that lovely figure was truly irresistible to children and grown people alike, and we noticed that even some of our party yielded and also smacked their lips at the delicious flavor of the brown toes of the chocolate goddess.

To see every department of this immense Exposition it is estimated that the visitor would have to walk over fifty miles. We therefore concluded that, as we had walked something over thirty miles during the two days that we had given to the exhibit, we would try to be content with the millions of curiosities that we had inspected, and leave the remaining twenty miles of show to some other visitors. The subject was not by any means exhausted, but our party was.

For those people, however, who desire to see the entire affair, there are various modes of locomotion about the buildings and grounds. There are rolling chairs pushed by a guide for twenty cents an hour; several railway trains to carry you to the different departments at five cents a trip; a thousand Egyptian donkeys are at your service, each ready saddled and led by a native of the Nile, for twenty-five cents an hour. You may charter a sedan chair, borne by two Arabians, for fifty cents an hour; or you can hire a velocipede and do your own propelling, for ten cents an hour; nothing to do but "pay your money and take your choice."

We had all day missed our chaplains, Dr. Marshall and Dr. Smedes, in our tramping, and many enquiries were made among ourselves as to their probable whereabouts, but without satisfaction. Consequently, our surprise was considerable when, on reaching our hotel, we found these two gentlemen quietly enjoying their dinners.

"Where on earth have you men been all day?" anxiously asked several of our girls at the same time.

"We have been up in the balloon," answered Dr. Marshall, "and enjoyed the novel sensation very much indeed."

"Is that really possible!" exclaimed Miss Slater and Miss Dowd; "it is almost beyond belief."

"Yes," said Dr. Smedes, "I admit that it is hard to believe that the two dignified and honored chaplains of such a cultivated party of teachers as this should spend nearly a day in sailing over the earth in a balloon! But it is a fact, nevertheless, young ladies, for here is the proof"— and he produced a photograph which had been taken by an amateur artist, showing the two reverend gentlemen in the car of the balloon just as it had left the earth on its upward flight.

"Well! well! well! that beats all I ever heard of!" murmured a dozen or more of the girls, as we joined our chaplains at the dinner table and spiritedly discussed the viands and the reckless exploit of our esteemed clergymen.

While we sat at the table the Secretary "passed word down the lines" that we would go to the Exposition at night to see the grand illumination in honor of the Shah of Persia. Accordingly, we were soon engaging cabs for the evening, so that we could ride about the grounds wherever the scene was most beautiful.

" *Cocher!*" called Mrs. Church to a cabman near by, at the same time beckoning for him to come.

" *Oui, madame!*" he quickly replied as he reined up at the curbstone awaiting her orders.

"I want to go to see the illumination," said Mrs. Church to him, but he looked at her in blank amazement.

Mrs. Church did not speak French and the cabman did not understand a word of English, but she tried again to give her order.

"Illumination!" she said.

" *Plait il?*" returned the driver.

"Fire-works!" Another trial.

"*Plait il?*" with a shake of his head.

"Shah of Persia!" she suggested. ·

"*Plait il?*" came again.

"Lights! Red! Green!" More suggestions.

"*Plait il?*" came the inevitable.

Our puzzled chaperon seemed to despair of ever making the cabman understand that she desired to see the fireworks and the Exposition illuminated, but finally a happy idea occurred to her and she exclaimed with a suddenness which nearly threw *cocher* from his box:

"Siz-z-z-z! Fiz-z-z-z! Rip-p-p-p! Shew-w-w-w! Whoop! Boom-m-m-m! Slam!! Bang!!!!" throwing up her arms with the last word as if a thousand rockets had exploded at one time.

We laughed until our sides ached, and *cocher* fully took in the meaning of this lively pantomime.

"*Oui! oui! madame,*" he exclaimed in delight. "*Certainment!*" and he quickly threw open the door of the cab for Mrs. Church and her companions, and they dashed away towards the Champ de Mars.

No wonder that there is an exodus from Paris every night to the Exhibition, or that the grounds are thronged. The spectacle, although two tickets are charged for admission after sunset, even on ordinary nights is one of unparalleled beauty. No other exhibition ever afforded the like of it either for extent or splendor. The Champ de Mars is a veritable fairy-land. During the day people go to the Exhibition partly for instruction; at night they go solely to be entertained and to witness a brilliant spectacle.

When a gun, on the second story of the Tower, gives the signal at six o'clock for the closing of the galleries, the people pour into the gardens. Others have been streaming in through the gates before the price was raised and there they remain crowding the grounds and waiting three and four hours for the last of the illuminations.

The Machinery Hall, the central vestibule and gallery leading to it, and the Sculpture Gallery are still left open, but beyond these and the Tower, entertainments and the restaurants, the gardens are only left to the visitors. The gardens are exceedingly pleasant, and bands play every evening, only there are too few seats—as usual. The area illuminated by electricity alone is three million seven hundred and six thousand square feet, and over three thousand horse-power is required to furnish the supply. Gas is used for illuminating the Trocadéro, the Tower, and the central dome of the Exposition Building.

Standing in the centre of the garden you are encompassed with a blaze of light—a harmonious combination of the brilliant lustre of the arc electric light, the softer splendor of the incandescent lamps, and the quiet yellow hues of the gas. At one end of the axis the great circular frontage of the Trocadéro is picked out with gas, and the cascade underneath resembles terraces of flame. At the other end the magnificent dome shines resplendent, covered with thousands of colored lamps, until the great statue of France overhead gleams like gold. Behind this is seen the graceful roof of the Machinery Hall with the electric light shining through.

Then there is the Tower which looks grander and more beautiful by night than by day, with its gigantic arches rimmed with light, its platforms ablaze with a thousand lamps, while high up above the third story a huge electric light flashes its radiating search-lights over the whole neighborhood—now directing them on the gilded dome, then on the river, next over the city of Paris, or piercing the darkness to a distance of ten miles.

Then in the gardens the mingling of the gas and the electric light has a very pretty effect. The parterres are bordered with rows of incandescent lamps, and small lamps shine out from clumps of rhododendrons and from trees.

These lamps are made of large petals with a stigma of electric light in the centre, and resemble a flower. The sculpture in the Gallery Rapp and the Machinery Hall should be visited at night. It requires eighty-six arc lights of three thousand five hundred candles each to light the Machinery Hall, and this illumination is supplemented by a powerful light-house refraction light in the centre that sends a procession of rays round the building, and by Edison's colossal incandescent lamp.

The colored fountains play every night at ten. A good view of the fountains and of the whole scene may be obtained from the balcony over the central entrance, or from the first floor of the Tower. Above the basin from which rise the jets and colored water is the fountain of Progress, representing the town of Paris as a vessel, with a battering ram as a prow, and surmounted by a figure personifying Progress, surrounded by groups very skillfully executed by M. Coutan.

The colored fountains are a great attraction, and people sit round the basin from six o'clock to ten waiting for the water to be turned on. The illumination is effected very simply. Circular chambers are constructed underneath each basin, the roofs of which are pierced with a number of openings to receive a series of vertical cylinders, each placed below a jet. In each cylinder is arranged a set of thick plates of colored glass, which can be made to move in various directions by means of cords and levers. The rays from a very powerful arc lamp are directed up the cylinders by means of a parabolic reflector mirror and condensers, and as the light must traverse one or more thicknesses of colored glass before it reaches the jet of water, many combinations of colors may be produced.

In illuminating the Eiffel Tower the whole structure, from bottom to top, is filled with a dense smoke by some combustible material, and then this smoke is beautifully and brilliantly lighted in all the colors of the rainbow by calcium reflectors. The effect is as startling as it is magnificent, and the occasion cost the management over fifty thousand dollars. The sight was witnessed and enjoyed by over three hundred thousand persons and the admission receipts were near a hundred thousand dollars! The beauty and splendor of that display we do not believe anything on earth ever before equalled in grandeur, magnitude and brilliancy. The whole scene seemed to be managed by magic hands and every detail of the illumination was perfect. Not an order was heard, not an operator was seen and there was not the slightest delay or confusion in the entire affair.

We reached our hotel about midnight, tired and sleepy from a hard day's work of sight-seeing, but in our visions through the remainder of the night we saw stars and rockets, colored fire and smoke, a perfect storm of flashing meteors and a dazzling ocean of electric light.

DO LEARNED WOMEN MAKE GOOD WIVES?

A young woman received from Columbia College the degree, *cum laude*, of doctor of philosophy. Although she is comparatively young, she has shown remarkable mental maturity. Mathematics is her forte, and the toughest problems are as easy as dancing to her. While at Wellesley College she stood at the head of her class, and after her graduation she refused to become a director of the Observatory of Smith College, and declined a professorship in her *alma mater*.

Two months later there was a wedding in Trinity Church in New York. The party of the second part was Miss Winifred Edgerton, the young woman of whom we have been writing, and the party of the first part was Professor Merrill, a young Columbia professor and graduate.

It is said that Mrs. Edgerton-Merrill is as much at home in the kitchen as in the recitation-room ; that she can sew, wash and iron, and is naturally as domestic as a shy country maiden. It is expected that she will continue her studies, and do more literary work under her new relations than she could have done had she remained simply Miss Edgerton, and that while darning stockings she will still continue reading *Mechanique Celeste.*

A thorough course of training will help any man or woman. Dr. Vincent says : "If I had a boy who expected to be a blacksmith all his life, I should want him to be a college graduate. Every man owes it to himself, his wife and his children to be as much of a man as he can be. When parents are educated enough to take a real interest in the studies and work of their children, it is as easy again to teach the boy. The blacksmith needs an education because he is a citizen. In this country we cannot afford to educate a special class to investigate political subjects and to dictate to the masses how they shall vote. Every man must think and act for himself. Moreover, it is the duty of every man to acquire all the education he can. The thought of immortality ought to be an inspiration to every man."

What Dr. Vincent says of the boy applies equally well to the girl. A wife ought to know as much as the husband. Ignorance in either is sure to be productive of evil. Ignorant wives suit Mohammedans, but average Americans want their wives to know as much as is possible. No sensible North Carolina girl has ever made a mistake in pursuing her studies to graduation in some of our first-class high grade institutions of learning, but she has added greatly to her own happiness and to her usefulness in society, in the home, or in any other walk of life.

THE GIRL AT A BOYS' COLLEGE.

The girl who goes to the University of Michigan to-day, just as when I entered there in 1872, finds her own board-ing-place in one of the quiet homes of the pleasant little city whose interest centers in the 2,500 students scattered within its borders. She makes the business arrangements for her winter's fuel and its storage; she finds her washer-woman or her laundry; she arranges her own hours of exer-cise, of study, and of sleep; she chooses her own society, clubs and church. The advice she gets comes from another girl student of sophomoric dignity, who chances to be in the same house, or possibly from a still more advanced young woman whom she meets on the journey, or sat near in church on her first Sunday. Strong is the comradeship among these ambitious girls, who nurse one another in illness, admonish one another in health, and rival one another in study only less eagerly than they all rival the boys. In my time in college the little group of girls, sud-denly introduced into the army of young men, felt that the fate of our sex hung upon proving that "lady Greek" involved the accents, and that women's minds were particularly absorptive of the calculus and metaphysics. And still in these sections where, with growing experience, the anxieties about co-education have been allayed, a healthy and hearty relationship and honest rivalry between young men and women exists. It is a stimulating atmosphere, and develops in good stock a strength and independent balance which tell in after life.—*Mrs. Alice Freeman Palmer, in The Forum.*

[We do not propose to admit the charge, which some persons who oppose coeducation intimate that North Carolina girls would not behave with perfect propriety in a "mixed college," for we have unbounded confidence in our boys and girls and know that they will conduct themselves as properly in school as in the home or in society.—EDITOR.]

GENTLE GYMNASTICS FOR GIRLS.

Light gymnastics embrace the use of dumb-bells, bar-bells, Indian clubs, wands, hoops, and exercises without anything whatever in the hands. Marching, deep-breathing movements, poising, stretching and equilibrium exercises, all of which have in a great measure grown out of the Delsarte system, also come, says the *Ladies' Home Journal*, under the general term, light gymnastics.

The beneficial results of all these are many and varied. Hardly anyone is too weak for gymnastics. Gentle massage will start the muscles and send the blood into healthy circulation. Then the patient should help herself. One of the advantages of light gymnastics is that the sick and convalescent can make what appear to be trifling efforts, and by them, in time, be restored to active health. If too feeble to be practically able to make but little exertion, try what are known as deep-breathing movements. Lie flat upon the back, take as long and deep breaths as possible, and while the mouth is closed, slowly throw the arms up in front and then at the sides. Rest for ten minutes. Try again the same inhalation and exhalation of air, the latter being pure and fresh. After awhile attempt the same, sitting up. These exercises can safely be taken by the sick one every day several times, and the whole muscular system will be improved, just as if some revivifying tonic had been given, a far better one than any charged with alcohol or some like stimulant.

From this step to the use of light apparatus in the dumb-bells is a short one. But the mistake is too often made in trying to be too muscular, and using bells of too great a weight. Attempt nothing above your strength at the start; it is even better at first to go under it than over it. Above all things be methodical and regular in these exercises.

2

Irregularity in anything—habits, expenditures, diet—brings its uncomfortable reward. Exercise must be constant and systematic to be effective.

If a beginner, purchase wooden dumb-bells of a pound each in weight.

Stand with the heels together, body erect and head up. Place the bells on the shoulders and push up that in the right hand to a count of eight or twelve; then the left; then both together at the same time.

Place the bells on the chest; push the right-hand bell out in front eight times, the left-hand afterward, then both.

Push the bell in the right hand out from the chest to the right, the left the same, and next both.

Put bells under the armpits. Curl them out alternately and at the same time.

With bells on the shoulders roll out as in the movement above described.

Strike the bells quickly over the head and under the right leg; then the left leg; then again behind the back.

With the right-handed bell extended from right side at right angles with the body, strike it as if it were an anvil eight times with the bell in the left hand as a hammer. Do this in the same manner to the left and in front, holding the bell that acts in lieu of anvil on the right and left knees.

These are but simple movements. A teacher in the gymnasium will give you dozens more. But just after the morning bath, in a cool room, before the corset is put on, if tried for five or ten minutes daily, will end in sending a glow through the body and bringing a rich tint to the cheeks. Beauty is not always born; it can be made. Not with cosmetics; try light gymnastic exercises, and you will prove to your own satisfaction that a light step, a bright eye, a clear, good-colored skin, without the faintest tint of rouge or powder, makes a woman truly beautiful, as well as "healthy, wealthy and wise."

Apropos of this last assertion, that a woman can grow wiser, yes, actually know more, from regular gymnastic exercise is an established truth.

The greatest practical result of both light and heavy gymnastics is the fact that the mind grows in proportion to the muscle. The muscles need a will, and a strong one, to control them. The moving to exact time and to music demanded by these exercises when taken in the classes of the gymnasium has its effect on the brain, and it is as important as the resulting physical gain. Dr. W. G. Anderson, the specialist, states that women who, by reason of undeveloped will power, cannot compel this servant to aid them in works they must perform, are greatly benefited by light gymnastic exercises; and that those women who are sensible enough to adopt the methods that make men the stronger, the healthier sex, who expect to be known as the mothers of healthy children, and, above all, women who wish to aid in the realization of the ideal human being, whether mentally, morally or physically, are able to be all that they would be by gymnastic exercise.

It is a constant source of complaint that American women are not graceful. And the dancing-school has been, until recent years, the refuge for the awkward and unbalanced-muscled young or old woman. But much more valuable is the gymnasium in its education of the feet, and of the poise and carriage of the body.

To this end fancy step movements are given, and grace and ease of self results. Then, too, dexterity is a quality the phlegmatic, slow-by-nature girl and woman needs to get on in this busy, work-a-day world, where she who moves the quickest and thinks .the fastest, keeping her mind clear and steady on what she has in hand, puts to rout the moral of that ancient fable of the hare and tortoise, in reaching the goal long before her slower and more deliberate neighbor.

"TOO MUCH OF A GOOD THING."

The Pittsburg *Dispatch* quotes the opinions of many parents and physicians to the effect that much of the teaching of the study of physiology is worse than a waste of time. Has not the matter been practically overdone. Surely there is not so much in the science that it should be required in every school and taught to every grade of pupils, as is required by the usual physiology-hygiene law.

If the law were rigidly complied with we should do little effective teaching in that subject or any other. The intention of the ladies who have been instrumental in framing and advocating the passage of this law in various States has been good, but they have blinded themselves to other school interests of equal or paramount importance, and nothing has saved the schools from a general demoralization of the teachers who have a condition and not a theory confronting them, and they have adapted their practice to the demands of the school.

That the enactment of the law diminishes the evils at which it aims has not yet been proved so far as results go. The tobacco habit among boys, with all our hygienic teaching, is on the increase instead of the reverse. It never has been from a lack of knowledge of the evil effects of both tobacco and intoxicating drink that boys and men have been debased by their use. These evils are like many others, we have sometimes thought, in this that the less they are discussed the less will the innocent be inclined to make a personal trial of them in order to experience their effects.

We believe in teaching the subject of physiology, and we believe in teaching and upholding temperance, but we believe also that the zeal of those on the outside of the school-room walls, may, on this question, overstep the

bounds of prudence and do quite as much harm as good.—
Educational News (*Philadelphia*).

[It seems to THE TEACHER that the subject of "Physiology, Hygiene," etc., etc., is being somewhat "run in
the ground." We are likely to have too much of even a
good thing. We believe that this subject is a most important one, and have always strongly advocated its being
taught in every school. We hold the same opinion yet,
but when this branch of study, or any other one, becomes
"a craze," there is certain to be some harm done and much
of the real merit in the subject will be lost.

The late Legislature of North Carolina passed an act
for teaching Physiology, Hygiene and the effects of Narcotics, Stimulants, &c., in the Public Schools. We have
no doubt that the act was intended for the good of the
people, but when a law compels a teacher in the public
schools to teach physiology and the effects of alcohol to
children *orally before they have even learned to read*, it
seems to us that somebody is responsible for a little fanati-
cism on the subject.

Zeal without proper judgment, even with the best of
people, is to be deplored. We do not see how any good
can be accomplished by talking the science of physiology
and the effects of stimulants to the babies in the school-
room who cannot read.—EDITOR].

TO TEN THOUSAND IN A YEAR.

BY SUPT. J. M. GREENWOOD, KANSAS CITY, MO.

[We heartily commend the following sound and sensible
thoughts to the most careful consideration of every North
Carolina teacher. Professor Greenwood is one of the most

efficient educators in this country, and he is doing a lasting service to the children of the United States by ridiculing out of the school-room much of the shoe-peg nonsense that has been dwarfing the minds of pupils and making mere machines of otherwise good teachers.—EDITOR].

Children are usually not admitted to the public schools before they are five years old; some of the States keep them out until they are six, and a few exclude them, in some cases, till they are seven. In general, a child should not be started to school before the sixth year. At that age the brain has attained about 85 per cent. of its adult size, and the child is able to use it with as much precision as he controls his hands and feet. Without pursuing this remark further I wish to call attention to what an average child from six to eight years of age will do in numbers the first year he attends school, if he has a chance; and it is the chance that I am contending for at this time. If any one's toes are tramped he can obtain ample redress by pitching into me.

I assert that the educational doctors, big-pill, little-pill, foreign, or native, from Missouri, Massachusetts, or the Sandwich Islands, who prescribe "10," or "100," as the maximum dose which the child should take the first year he is in school, should be "bored with a dull gimlet for the simples." Such an educator is a fitter subject to lead a mule to a haystack than to outline number work for little children.

There are crimes of a more virulent nature than others. It is more humane to kill a fellow-creature by one blow with a bludgeon than it is to flay him alive, or to starve him in a noisome dungeon, or to press him to a pulp by a slowly descending heavy mass of wood or iron. But what are these methods of torture compared to the person who sets himself up as a teacher, and then, in the name of education, starves the mind to a mental death? Who will say it is not a more heinous crime? It may lack the element of *intent*, and, therefore, save the culprit from hanging or electrocution, but the effect is the same. If such an instructor should be arrested for mental murder, what plea could he make that would hold good at the *Bar of High Heaven?* Ignorance by appealing to mercy might save him, but outraged justice—never!

How long does it take the average child to learn his letters? How long, reader, were you at that job?

This question was put to one hundred and sixty-five teachers at an Institute in Iowa by the writer, and only one person of that number remembered when he did learn his "a b c's", and yet a noted educator had spent forty-five minutes in showing what an herculean task it is for children to learn their letters. How long will it take for the child to learn from "o to 9?" Should it take more than a day for this job, even if it be let by contract?

In a week a child will read numbers up to 100, if the teacher will first let him learn 10, 20, 30, 40, 50, 60, 70, 80, 90, 100. A little practice each day and the job is complete. If the child cannot count to a hundred have him learn to do so at once. Children at first usually count away from the objects to be counted if they are put to counting them. That is, they like to exercise their imagination in counting as well as in other matters. It is a good thing for them to do so, irrespective of objects or previous conditions of mental, moral, or educational servitude. *Let the fancy caper*, is an excellent motto. The next step is to have them read 11, 21, 31, 41, 51, 61, 71, 81, 91, 101. Only one figure changes at each step. Some fellow from the rural district, or the city percentage district, will hop up and say, "Mr. Speaker, it can't be did!" Hold on, my worthy friend. Where is the child that ever went to school for a week, unless it be a school for the deaf and dumb, that did not learn, "Ten, ten, double-ten, forty-five and fifteen," and have these separate things creep up through his thinking apparatus as fixed forms for all time—eh?

But now let us reconstruct. To destroy the foundation of belief and not to give something better in its place is wrong.

Teachers, one more sacrifice! Throw away all your shoe-pegs, tooth-picks, beans, grains of corn, and seldom or never use them except to illustrate some point. Put your children to working with numbers, if you want them to pull ahead. If you give a concrete example, follow it by an abstract one. If one is to be solved on the slate or blackboard, give the next one as a mental problem to be solved in the head.

I can take a class of average children of the age mentioned, and I will give no more time to numbers than I give to other subjects proportionately, and in one years's time they will write numbers correctly to 1,000,000; add columns of figures up to 100 like a streak of greased lightning; subtract readily, multiply by three or four figures, and divide numbers by any one of the nine digits, and not hurt or strain or tire their thinkers the least bit. Try it.

Some years ago I took charge of a class of a dozen little boys and girls, and I heard them for forty minutes each day recite their number lessons. The first rule was, that no one would ever copy or look at another's work till he had finished his own. All their written work was put on the blackboard during the recitation.

During the year no one ever copied from another. Honest failure was meritorious, and they so regarded it.

This class not only read and wrote numbers to trillions rapidly, but they could work by "long division" as well as by short, and they had learned all the simpler cases of fractions as well as nearly all the tables, by doing them in Reduction.

They neglected no other work, but they were always a little ahead of time in getting into my recitation-room.

Instead of having children copy "nonsense" on their slates and calling it "little stories in numbers," put the children to the blackboard, give problems either to the entire class or to each individual member, or to sections of the class, and put them to work and let them work with a will, not dream and snore, and grow lazy and dull, doing a little very laboriously. We want teachers who know how to get children to do rapid, intelligent, sensible work. Method in general is worth something, but that which cannot be put into practice, and does not charge the pupil with enthusiasm, is not worth raising a disturbance over.

Throw away the things about numbers and let the children work with numbers, if you wish to succeed and quiet your conscience.

This is getting at the subject in downright earnest.— *School Journal (New York).*

A GOOD WAY.

Under date of September 14th Superintendent C. B. Way, of Buncombe, writes THE TEACHER as follows:

I will tell you how we "supplemented" the public school fund in our school district. The committee selected a competent teacher and agreed on the salary. We, the people (a part of them), promised to pay what the school fund lacked of paying it, on condition that the whole term should be free to the whole district. Result: To-day our school opens in charge of Miss Edith F. Smith for a full nine-months' free term! If you think that a good way to "supplement the public fund" you can just tell how it's done in THE TEACHER, and maybe some other districts will agree with you and go and do likewise. I believe zealous, liberal committeemen could double the school term in half the districts in the State if they had a "mind to work. But I would advise them, always, to have the whole term free to all. Not a part free and part "subscription." It will make the public school popular as well as beneficial.

[This is certainly a good way, brother Way; and we would like to see the way of the Buncombe county Way become the "way of the world," or at least of that part of the world within the limits of North Carolina. This is also the right way and is a Way ahead of any other way within our knowledge. We hope that every other school district in Buncombe County will adopt the way of this Way.— EDITOR].

LET US WRITE IT RIGHT.

We have received the following communication from one of our friends at New Bern in regard to the proper orthography of the name of that charming little city:

NEWBERN, N. C., Sept. 21st, 1891.

Editor of the N. C. Teacher:

I noticed an article published a few days past in your journal which says: "The editor of THE TEACHER assisted in a long search of the old records for the correct orthography of this name and we found it to be, beyond all possible doubt, New Bern." I will be obliged if you will inform me where those records are, or give me some extracts from them. If so, I will send them to the authorities at Washington City. Of course I want no *private opinions* about it, I want legal evidence, such as the authorities at Washington City require.

I will look with considerable interest for your journal containing the above and your reply to it.

Very respectfully,

WILLIAM H. OLIVER.

In reply to the above, we will say that when *Moore's School History of North Carolina* was undergoing revision under the auspices of the State Board of Education, the editor of THE TEACHER was assisting in the work, and in order to obtain the correct orthography of the name of this city he, with the Secretary of State, the late Col. William L. Saunders, who had the matter of revision in charge, spent several hours a day for about two weeks in searching the old State records pertaining to the matter in question. Col. Saunders was the highest historical authority in North Carolina, and he never made a statement upon North Carolina history until he was sure that he was correct, and his opinions have been so accepted by the people.

The city was founded by Baron De Graffenried, a Swiss nobleman, in 1709, about fourteen years before the charter of the place was passed by the General Assembly. De Graffenried named the place NEW BERN in honor of his former home the capital of Switzerland. The name was first spelled with a final "e" only in French maps.

In all of De Graffenried's letters, and also in all other official documents, the name is spelled "New Bern." In a few instances the "B" was a small letter, but in no case was the final "e" added to the Bern. The custom of condensing the name into one word is contrary to all precedent in names of this class; the final "e" is a modern innovation without authority for its use, and should not be tolerated.

The act of Assembly which chartered the city in 1723 is not the slightest authority for the spelling of the name, any more than it is for several other words in that same document which were misspelled by the person who wrote the bill. That act was to provide for the details in the charter of a city and was not to fix the spelling of any certain word. In that same session of the Legislature there are many proper names of prominent and well known families in North Carolina incorrectly spelled, but it has not been considered that the act in which the names were mentioned was authority for changing the orthography of the names. Nor can we accept the mere mention of the word "Newbern" in the charter of that city as a reason why the correct spelling of the name of our charming Elm City, as given by its distinguished and intelligent founder, should be so changed and mutilated that the tender and patriotic devotion represented by the word should be lost.

Of course the people of New Bern have a right to change the name of the city or the spelling of the present name if they desire to do so, but if they are seeking to ascertain the original and correct name of the city as was given to it by its devoted founder, the official records and Baron De Graffenried's correspondence show that the name must remain NEW BERN. If, however, the name should be adopted as Newbern it will be a *new* name and it will be no longer the city which De Graffenried named, but it will henceforth be a city which was named by some member of the Legislature of 1723! Both of the school histories of North Carolina will be compelled to adhere to their present spelling, "New Bern," because it was so ordered by the State Board of Education as the original and only correct orthography of the name.

That there may be no further doubt in the matter we append the following extract from "the manuscript of Christopher De Graffenried, copied from the original manuscript in the Public Library at Yuerdon, Switzerland, and translated by Du Four," as preserved in the office of Secretary of State at Raleigh:

"They (the palatines) arrived in the county of Albermarle on the River Chowan at the residence of a rich settler Col. Pollock, of the Council of North Carolina, he took care of them, supplying them with all necessaries, *sed pro pecunia*, for money, and put them into great boats to cross the sound and enter the county of *Bath*, where they were located by the Surveyor-general on a tongue of land between the News' and Trent rivers, called Chatawka, where afterwards was founded the small city of New Bern."

This is an exact copy, following language, punctuation, and italics. The city was never known to De Graffenried, the Surveyor-general, and his settlers, by any other name or style of spelling the name than "New Bern," and thus the name should remain if the memory of its scholarly and distinguished founder is to be perpetuated, as is most truly desired by the people of North Carolina.

IT IS a great point to learn to respect the opinions of others—even of inferiors. The man who has opinions and sticks to them is to be admired ; but the same man is more to be admired if he have sufficient broadness of views to see that there are other opinions to be held.

PATRONS are more likely to give moral support to a teacher who, outside of the school-room as well as in it, sustains her reputation for common sense, and shows herself amenable to the motives common to cultivated people in other vocations.—*A. S. Draper, State Supt. of Schools, New York.*

AN EXCHANGE wisely remarks that a teacher should ever remember that among children—however it may be among adults—*respect* always precedes *attachment.* If he would gain the love of the children he must first be worthy of their respect. He should therefore act deliberately, and always conscientiously. He should be firm, but never petulant. It is very important at the outset that he should be truly courteous and affable.

IN THE SCHOOL-ROOM.

DON'T KICK.

Though the weather be wet,
  And your clothing be mussed,
    Be a brick;
Don't grumble and fret,
  For the rain, don't forget,
    Is laying the dust—
      Don't kick.

Though the weather be hot,
  And boiled be your blood,
    Till 'tis thick;
Be content with your lot,
  For the sunshine is what
    Is drying the mud—
      Don't kick.
        —Detroit Free Press.

DOING NOTHING.

Worthless, wicked boys I've seen,
  Doing nothing;
And they grow up worthless men,
  Doing nothing;
Life to them a pastime proved,
As they spent it all unloved,
  Doing nothing.

MANNERS FOR BOYS.

In the street—Hat lifted when saying "Good by" or "How do you do?" Also when offering a lady a seat or acknowledging a favor.

Keep step with anyone you walk with. Always precede a lady up stairs, but ask if you shall precede her in going through a crowd or public place.

At the street door—Hat off the moment you step in a house or private office.

Let a lady pass first always, unless she asks you to precede her.

In the parlor—Stand till every lady in the room, also older people, are seated.

Rise if a lady enters the room after you are seated, and stand till she takes a seat.

Look people straight in the face when they are speaking to you.

A NEW LANGUAGE.

There is a girl ten years old near Pittsburg, Pennsylvania, who speaks only in a language of her own invention, though she reads and understands English. The only person who can translate the peculiar tongue is an elder sister. A portion of her vocabulary is as follows: "Chy-chy-kyk," a colt; "sota," angry; "phatota," pleasure or fun; "tooky tuba," a strong rope; "meli," mamma; "beloh," papa; "popo tikon," to swing to and fro. Certain philologists are studying this new speech with the hope of discovering some facts as to the origin of language.

DON'T.

Don't pronounce "nephew" as *nev-ue ;* it is *nef-ue ;* only English cockneys say *nev-ue.* Don't pronounce "beneath" as *be-neethe* (th as in bathe) it is *be-neeth.* Be very cautious in giving "a" the broad sound in such words as "half," "calf," "basket," "pastor," "behalf," "casket," "after," for such a pronunciation belongs to a certain system which is not correct or popular among intelligent people in the South ; to be consistent you must use the whole system of pronunciation, which makes "i" long in "neither" and "either."

No other system of pronunciation is so correct or pleasing as that used by the educated people of the Southern. States, and it should be the aim of teachers to keep our pronunciation pure and uncorrupted by Northern or foreign innovations.

PRACTICAL FRENCH.

Two teachers of language were discussing matters and things relative to their profession.

"Do your pupils pay up regularly on the first of each month?" asked one of them.

"No, they do not," was the reply. "I often have to wait for weeks and weeks before I get my pay, and sometimes I don't get it at all. You can't well dun the parents for the money."

"Why don't you do as I do? I always get my money regularly."

"How do you manage it?"

"It is very simple. For instance, I am teaching a boy

French, on the first day of the month his folks don't send the money for his lessons. In this event I give him the following sentences to translate and write out at home: 'I have no money. The month is up. Hast thou got any money? I need money very much. Why hast thou not brought the money this morning? Did thy father not give thee any money?' The next morning that boy brings the money."—*Jewish Messenger.*

A PIECE OF ADVICE.

BY F. G. B.

Children, I'm going to give you all
  A piece of good advice:
Remember, now, each word I say —
  I cannot give it twice.
You've doubtless heard it many a time,
As told in prose and told in rhyme.

Each morning early be at school,
There study well, obey each rule;
Be sure your hands and face are clean,
Your hair well brushed when there you're seen.
At home take care to close each door,
And don't throw things upon the floor.
Follow these rules, and though you're small,
You'll find yourself beloved by all.
         —*School Journal* (*New York*).

ILL-HUMOR arises from an inward consciousness of our own want of merit, from a discontent which ever accompanies that envy which foolish vanity engenders.—*Goethe.*

3

Southern Educational Association.

ORGANIZATION 1891-1892.

SOLOMON PALMER, President, East Lake, Florida.
EUGENE G. HARRELL, Secretary and Treasurer, Raleigh, N. C.
W. T. WATSON, Assistant Secretary, Memphis, Tennessee.

VICE-PRESIDENTS:

1. E. B. Prettyman, Maryland.
2. John E. Massey, Virginia.
3. B. S. Morgan, West Virginia.
4. S. M. Finger, North Carolina.
5. W. D. Mayfield, S. Carolina.
6. S. B. Bradwell, Georgia.
7. A. J. Russell, Florida.
8. J. G. Harris, Alabama.
9. J. R. Preston, Mississippi.
10. W. H. Jack, Louisiana.
11. J. M. Carlisle, Texas.
12. J. H. Shinn, Arkansas.
13. W. R. Garrett, Tennessee.
14. Ed. Porter Thompson, Ky.
15. W. E. Coleman, Missouri.

EXECUTIVE COMMITTEE:

Solomon Palmer, *ex officio* Chairman, East Lake, Alabama.
E. G. Harrell, *ex officio* Secretary, Raleigh, North Carolina.
1. J. H. Phillips, Superintendent City Schools, Birmingham, Ala.
2. W. H. Sutton, Superintendent of Schools, Jackson, Mississippi.
3. Thomas D. Boyd, President State Normal, Natchitoches, La.
4. O. H. Cooper, Superintendent City Schools, Galveston, Texas.
5. J. W. Conger, President Ouachita College, Arkadelphia, Arkansas.
6. J. M. Stewart, Agricultural and Mechanical College, Lake City, Fla.
7. J. M. Greenwood, Superintendent Schools, Kansas City, Missouri.
8. R. N. Roark, State Normal College, Lexington, Kentucky.
9. Frank M. Smith, University of Tennessee, Knoxville, Tennessee.
10. Euler B. Smith, President State Association, LaGrange, Georgia.
11. Edward S. Joynes, University of South Carolina, Columbia, S. C.
12. Hugh Morson, President Teachers' Assembly, Raleigh, N. C.
13. L. H. Vawter, Superintendent Miller Industrial School, Crozet, Va.
14. W. R. White, Superintendent of Schools, Morganton, W. Va.
15. Daniel Gilman, Johns Hopkins University, Baltimore, Maryland.

THIRD ANNUAL SESSION, JULY, 1892.

THE SOCIAL ENJOYMENTS of the grand meeting on Look-out Mountain, Tennessee, in July, have left the most pleas-ant impressions with everyone who was present on that occasion, and the educational reunion next summer will be enjoyed by thousands of Southern teachers. Will you try to be present?

THE SECRETARY has the manuscript copy of the pro-ceedings of the recent session on Lookout Mountain about ready for the press. There are yet three papers to be sent in for publication, and that will complete the work. The volume will be near three hundred pages, and we propose to make it, in mechanical appearance, as it is in literary merit, fully creditable to the Southern Educational Asso-ciation and the eighty thousand teachers of our Southland whom it represents.

HON. JOSIAH H. SHINN, of Arkansas, the first Presi-dent of the Southern Educational Association, attended the National Association at Toronto, Canada. It is said that his response to the address of welcome was the best speech made during the session of that body, and we are fully prepared to believe this, knowing, as we do, that Prof. Shinn is one of the finest orators in the entire South. His eloquence is always intensified by the inspiration of the very strongest Southern devotion and patriotism.

THE NEW PRESIDENT of the Southern Educational Association — Hon. Solomon Palmer — is a distinguished, cultured, courtly and typical Southern gentleman. He has most acceptably served his State (Alabama) as State Superintendent of Public Instruction for several terms, and he is now President of the Atheneum at East Lake, Ala-bama, an educational institution of high grade and most gratifying success. President Palmer will have the heart-iest co-operation of all Southern teachers in his official work during the present fiscal year.

WHAT A FAR-AWAY NORTH CAROLINIAN THINKS OF NORTH CAROLINA.

The writer of the following letter, Mr. D. S. Richardson, is held in tender memory and esteem by the editor of THE TEACHER, and also by many of our readers who were his pupils at Wilson during those dark days of the War for Southern Independence. The letter is a most interesting one, coming to us from the far-off Pacific Slope, and giving pleasant impressions of the wonderful educational progress that North Carolina is now making, and setting forth the proud reputation which North Carolina bears among sister States.

EAST OAKLAND, CAL., Sept. 4, 1891,
Eleventh Avenue and Twenty-fourth St., No. 1679.

MR. EUGENE G. HARRELL,
Editor North Carolina Teacher.

DEAR SIR — I well remember you and your parents at Wilson, and would be glad to hear more of you all. Seven years ago I drifted to the "Golden Gate" — "God's own Country" — and reside here, just across the bay from San Francisco; wife, son and his wife, and the grandchild, all together and happy.

I was seventy years old on the 1st inst., and that terrible old cowboy, Time, has at last rounded me up and branded me "Old Man," though I still remain, as of yore, a "*boy*" — kind Holmes' "gray-haired boy." Of course I live much in the past, through "memory's mellowing glass," and I hardly need say that I cherish, with increasing fondness, the memory of the "Good Old North State forever," where I labored so many years and claim so many dear ex-pupils and friends. It gives me much joy to learn of her prosperity, especially in educational interests. Never has there been a time when I have been slow to "protect

and defend her" from the taunts of flippant "witlings,"
with "Mecklenburg" and General Lee's panegyric and
benediction at Appomattox, when with tears in his eyes he
blessed the "Tar-Heel" boys for having *stuck* to him and
the cause the *closest* of *all;* and latterly with the solid facts
I got from your "TEACHER," telling us that North Carolina pays more to-day, in proportion to her wealth, notwithstanding her utter impoverishment from the war, for the
education of her whites *and blacks*, than either of her more
boastful sister States of New York, Connecticut or Massachusetts.   But who in the North and West sees such statements?
Continue to let them come.   I wish to see a copy of Supt.
Finger's facts and figures on Education in the South.   A
quarter of a century since the war, it is true, but the
"sober second thought" and intelligence of both sections,
North and West, are ready now, thank God, to accept the
"truth of history."   Let the evidences still come from
other Binghams at National Educational Conventions and
from journals like your own   And permit me to congratulate you on the "TEACHER"—so elegantly gotten up, so
well edited and so well supported, I confess to a surprise !
I at once went to comparing it with our old "N. C. Journal of Education," rather antediluvian now and hard doubtless to find a copy of it amid the debris of the war.   It was
born at Salisbury, at an Educational Convention, in 1857,
by "Resolution" of your humble servant, and was at once
adopted by the Association and by Superintendent Wiley
as the official organ, with W. B. Carr, G. W. Brooks and
myself the editorial corps, and we carried it forward into
the first year of the war, upholding the universal cause and
holding up the hands of Supt. C. H. Wiley as our Moses—
"Aaron and Hurr on the right and on the left." And your
late issue well suggests a monument to his honor and other
pioneers in education.   His whole soul and private purse
were in the cause.   Let Minerva, as well as Mars, have her

demi-gods. In front of the State House in Boston stands the marble statue of Horace Mann, side by side with Daniel Webster! May I suggest? Let the "mites" of the school children of the whole State be permitted to meet the necessary "mickle" of contribution, only I would like to add a trifle myself.

This subject brings before me sad reflections—the "giants in those days" are nearly all gone, I see. Their records and their memories should be timely and suitably embalmed by the historians of your Assembly, if only a volume or two, to accompany Wiley's and your more recent History of the State. Heaven forbid that all "the good" due to the faithful, unpretentious "school-master," shall be forever "interred" with his "bones."

But your "Assemblies"—they are immense! perfect ovations to the cause! and supplemented with royal excursions!

"God send Rome one such other sight, and send me there to see."

All these things speak so eloquently for the *esprit du corps* and character of your whole teaching fraternity. Indeed, all things are possible, when each teacher can lay his hand on his heart and say truly, with Jean Paul Richter, "I love God and little children." Have you any malcontents? Not many, I feel assured. Some "offences must need come" from a few pessimists—"born blind," unwitting, unamiable, cynical—but get on all the same, "*itur ad astra*."

I notice that State book publishing is in discussion. Good—at least so far as each State's editing and publishing its own histories. California has been experimenting in this line, but the project is a failure.

In conclusion, I am,

Yours fraternally,

D. S. RICHARDSON,
formerly of the " Wilson Schools," Wilson, N. C.

EDITORIAL.

" For the cause that lacks assistance,
For the wrong that needs resistance,
For the future in the distance,
And the good that we can do."

CONTRACTS SHOULD BE RESPECTED.

The following notice we clipped from the Columbia, S. C., *State*, and we think that it is a strong appeal for reliability, and faithful compliance of contract, on the part of teachers :

A TEACHER WANTED—ONE WHO WILL "STICK" AFTER HE HAS BEEN ELECTED AND ACCEPTED.

The Barnwell Graded School is again without a principal, for the second time this year, before the session opens. Early in the summer the board met and re-elected the principal, Prof. Otis, who kept us waiting for about a month and then accepted. He afterwards got a better offer and resigned. We then advertised for a principal, and out of a dozen or more applicants we elected Mr. C. R. Spencer, who had testimonials from Sumter to Germany. He accepted, but in a week resigned, although he knew his salary, but got a better offer somewhere else.

Now, this is a poor way for teachers to do—apply for anything they see, and accept and resign at their own will, leaving the board of trustees to hunt up another teacher, not knowing then, if elected and accepting, whether he will be here on time or not.

We hope that the Teachers' Institute will have a few lectures on legal and moral obligations during their summer meeting.

We want another teacher at a salary of $75 per month.   A. T. W.
BARNWELL, S. C., Aug. 25th, 1891.

After a teacher has applied for a position, well knowing the salary and all other conditions of the position, and has been elected by the school board, and arrangements completed for opening the school, it is not right for him to accept the situation and then make any change during the term for which he was elected, no matter what may be the inducement to go elsewhere. An honest and faithful com-

pliance with an honest contract is much more expected of
and due from a teacher than from any other person. A
teacher of a school cannot afford to be known as an unre-
liable man or woman. This is not the kind of reputation
that a real teacher wants to make and this is not the example that a teacher should set for pupils to follow.

THE NORTH CAROLINA TEACHER is read not only in the
forty-six States of this Union, but we have subscribers in
England, Canada, Scotland, France, Italy, China, Cuba,
Germany and South America.

WE HAVE had a number of applications by mail for our
"Instructions for Organizing Teachers' Councils," and
several county organizations have been effected during the
past month. Is *your* county organized?

DIDN'T WE tell you that 1891–2 would be the biggest
and best educational year in the history of North Carolina?
The Teachers' Assembly has aroused our State on the subject of education more than ever before in its history.

WE WILL be obliged to limit our Cuban party to fifty
persons, as only that number of berths can be secured on
the steamer at our low special rate. If you desire to join
the party don't delay too long in sending your application
as, the places are being rapidly taken.

SINCEREST THANKS are tendered our friends throughout
the State for sending us so many interesting news items
about our teachers and schools. We will not tempt ourselves into vanity by publishing any of the very kind and
friendly words that come with most of the reports.

THERE HAS never been such an educational revival in
North Carolina as now; every school in the State has more
pupils than ever before and the teachers are doing better
work. The "shoe-pegs, splints and tooth-picks" have
disappeared from all the principal schools and the children
are making rapid and honest progress in their studies.

A MEMBER of the Georgia legislature recently introduced a bill making it a misdemeanor for any teacher in that State to allow the use in his school of a history which refers to the War for Southern Independence "as the war of the rebellion." North Carolina teachers are justly discarding all such books without waiting for a law to prohibit their use.

A NUMBER of teachers have taken advantage of the special reduction to $3.00 for ninety days made by Messrs. Alfred Williams & Co., on their Cobb's "School Map of North Carolina," and have supplied their schools. The map is in size 4x6 feet, is handsomely mounted for the wall, and it is indispensable in every well organized school. Your school committee will purchase a copy for you if you desire it.

THE DATE appointed for "Educational Week" during the Southern Exposition at Raleigh is October 12th to 17th. The Educational committee under the direction of its energetic chairman, Captain C. B. Denson, is working hard to secure a good representative exhibit by all the leading public and private schools in North Carolina. The indications are for an excellent display of school work, and there will be thousands of teachers in Raleigh to see it.

THE NORTH CAROLINA TEACHER received, during the year which closed with the "Assembly Number," *fourteen hundred and sixty new subscriptions*, making an average of near one hundred and twenty-five subscribers each month. Not another word is needed to prove the popularity of THE TEACHER and how heartily it is endorsed by the teachers of North Carolina. This popularity is steadily and rapidly increasing, while the subscription list is likewise growing.

A "NORMAL AND INDUSTRIAL SCHOOL FOR YOUNG WOMEN" fully established; first-class Teachers' Institutes in every county; about sixty Teachers' Councils holding live and enthusiastic meetings each month in as many counties of the State; every school in the State full to overflowing; and over three thousand teachers and friends of education in attendance upon the Teachers' Assembly in June! Indeed, the Old North State is far in the lead and intends to hold that position.

᾿ EVERY SCHOOL in North Carolina should be interested enough in the State and the cause of education as to suspend work during ''Educational Week'' at the Exposition, and let teachers and pupils come to Raleigh to see the biggest display of school work ever made in our State. All public school committees ought to give that week of holiday—*and not deduct anything from the teacher's salary.* The people who pay taxes for schools are liberal and willing enough to *give* ''Educational Week'' to the teachers.

THE *Southern Educator,* of Durham, seems greatly distressed because some teachers, whose names did not even appear on the programme of the Teachers' Assembly, and one or two other persons whose names did appear, were for various unavoidable reasons not present at the session, even after accepting invitations to attend. He forgot to continue his investigation long enough to also ask where was Rev. John W. Crowell, D. D., the owner of the *Southern Educator,* and its editor-in-chief, who, upon his *own special request,* had been given a whole week on the programme for a course of lectures upon ''Political Economy,'' and yet did not put in an appearance, although he was less than a hundred and fifty miles from Morehead City, during the session of the Assembly, while the other absentees mentioned were each several hundred miles distant from the State! It is sometimes better before we undertake to criticise other people to first look around our own homes, if we want to keep ourselves from appearing ridiculous to those who happen to be posted.

THERE ARE yet a few text-books on Geography which persist in telling the children of the United States that "North Carolina is noted for tar, pitch and turpentine." This statement is a falsehood "from the whole cloth," and all authors of Geographies who are so ignorant as not yet to know that the great staples of North Carolina are cotton, corn, tobacco, wheat, rice, oats, and that the State has nearly all the valuable metals and minerals, and woods and timbers that are to be found in America, is unworthy of belief in any statements they make, and their so-called text-books should be used by no North Carolina teacher. It is well known to everybody, except a few yet benighted Geography makers, that North Carolina fills more of the blanks in the United States census reports than any other State in the Union, and we propose to shortly give the readers of THE TEACHER the names of all authors of Geographies who have never taken the trouble to enquire what are the chief products of North Carolina so as to tell the children of our schools the truth in this matter.

THE TEACHERS in some of our colleges and seminaries complain that many of the students coming from the public graded schools are deficient in English and in spelling. This shows the result of not giving more attention and study to the grammar and spelling book. We have stated many times before that while "language lessons" and "dictation exercises" were good in their place, they could not do the indispensable work of the grammar and spelling book. The teacher who thinks he is teaching a child to spell without requiring it to thoroughly memorize daily lessons from some regular spelling book, is wasting time and the child finds it out when it enters college. A man or woman may know all about Latin, Greek and the sciences, but if they cannot spell correctly and write easily and clearly they are not educated, but are sadly deficient in the foundation of all learning. "Though they speak with the tongues of men and of angels," and have not a thorough knowledge of English grammar and spelling, they are as nothing among educated people, but "are as sounding brass or a tinkling cymbal."

A NORTH CAROLINA teacher, male or female, is wanted as stenographic secretary for the next session of the Assembly. An expert stenographer and typographist will be required, but the work will be light and the remuneration will be good. Of course the papers and written addresses are not to be reported in short-hand, only the discussions and *ex tempore* speeches. A teacher is preferred for the work, but if no teacher desires the position it will be given to some pupil in a North Carolina school. Applications should be sent to the Secretary.

IT IS NOT the mission of THE TEACHER to criticise any school books, but it is our special work to "protect and defend North Carolina" and correct so-called history of the State wherever found. A book for schools has been recently published entitled "Montgomery's Leading Facts. in American History," and the author is so ignorant of history or full of sectional prejudice that not even a single line or word is mentioned concerning the "Mecklenburg Declaration of Independence" or the "Battle of Alamance" two of the most important leading facts in American history. The book would more correctly bear the title "Leading Facts (or supposed facts) in Massachusetts History," for the author gives many pages to painting the Revolutionary history of Boston in most brilliant hues, and his New England enthusiasm runs away with his veracity so far as to cause him to make the most astounding statement that "Massachusetts declared for independence in 1772!" North Carolina schools have no use for such a so-called history of "leading facts." There are other important omissions and inaccuracies in connection with this reputed history which concern the South sufficient to fill a volume.

DR, GEO. T. WINSTON, will be formally inaugurated as President of the University at Chapel Hill on October 14th. We hope that it will be a grand occasion and largely attended.

WHEN The Southern Educational Association was organized at Morehead City in 1890, it had one bitter enemy in what purports to be *The Southern Educator* of Durham. The "Southron" editor of that journal was "not in it" as he delights to express it; but the Southern Educational Association is marching on to grand achievements just the same, while Mr. Sheppe, his spiteful antagonism and his little monthly are scarcely heard of beyond the corporation of the city of his present abode.

IF THE TEACHERS of North Carolina do not think it worth their while to subscribe for your *Southern Educator*, brother Sheppe, don't get into a snarl and denounce the teachers and their great and delightful Assembly under the guise of "friendly criticism." The teachers have made their Assembly just what they want it to be, and it will be well for you to let them manage their own business as they think proper. If you or a few of your allies do not like the Teachers' Assembly and its management, you are at perfect liberty to be absent when thousands of the leading teachers of North Carolina meet in their grand annual gatherings. You have no fees to pay whether you are present or absent, and "you never will be missed." Perhaps you and your two or three associate growlers can spend your time more profitably and pleasantly during the summers with your "Southern Association of City Superintendents" and "Education Club of the South," which mythical bodies are more congenial to your ideas of what an educational organization should be—exist only in name and in the imagination of the F. F. V. editor of the *Southern Educator*, their reputed organ.

The Durham *Southern Educator* seems to esteem The North Carolina Teacher very highly, as it has not only tried to imitate this journal as near as possible in style and departments, but the ingenious editor of the *Educator* has made up almost the entire department of "North State Notes" in his September number from the personal pages of a previous number of The North Carolina Teacher!

> "He who would honestly edit
> Should always be willing to "credit";
> But to clip without end,
> And no credit append,
> Is not the fair thing,—we have said it."

In the September number of the *Educator* there are fifty-six news items and forty-three of them are taken from The Teacher, and the astute editor did not have caution enough to keep from following some changes that we had made in the items which were sent direct to us purposely to recognize them again!

The North Carolina Teacher most cordially welcomes to this State worthy strangers and teachers from all other States and lands, and does all in its power to make their residence with us both pleasant and profitable, and we are proud to say that there are many such teachers in our State. But the educational "foreigner" who "knows it all;" wants to reorganize in order to destroy our most successful Teachers' Assembly; tries to rechristen our country as "The New South;" scarcely knows the State well enough to find his way to the capital; hardly "knows the alphabet both ways;" writes the "Queries" for his journal in his office, from imaginary correspondents, and answers them from a book; never sees anything good in North Carolina without trying to prove that a like thing is much better in some other State; tries earnestly to belittle North Carolina and all her enterprises; depreciates the faithfulness of our teachers; and whose whole conduct shows that he cares nothing for our State except what he can make out of it—from all such afflictions "Good Lord deliver us."

WHEN A MAN tries to accomplish some particular thing and realizes that he is devoid of the brain force necessary to success, he is always envious and jealous of any other person who is successful in similar undertakings. The F. F. V. editor, Mr. Edwin S. Sheppe, of the *Southern Educator alias* the *Winston School Teacher*, tried to organize and keep alive a "Southern Association of City Superintendents" and an "Education Club of the South," but failed to secure even a single meeting, consequently he hates most cordially the North Carolina Teachers' Assembly which has been holding such grand and enthusiastic meetings for eight years, bringing together annually thousands of the most prominent teachers of this and other States and their friends, increasing in popularity and attendance at each session until its roll for the meeting this summer shows over three thousand persons present. And yet, this famous (!) organizer of "Superintendents Associations" and "Educational Clubs" asserts that such educational leaders as Winston, Burwell, Hume, Dinwiddie, Dr. Lewis, Poteat, Morson, Smith, Moses, Finger, Davis, Joynes, Claxton, Noble, Alderman, Howell, McIver, Holt, Blair, and other members of the Executive Committees of the Teachers' Assembly do not know how to manage the affairs of the Assembly! The celebrated "cheek of the government mule" would glitter as celestial modesty when compared with this brazen effrontery. The Executive Committees of the Teachers' Assembly have entire charge of the programmes, and engagements with Dr. Talmage and every other special lecturer are made by order of the Executive Committees. Mr. Sheppe's "friendly criticism" disguise is an enmity dodge as old as the serpent which invented it in the Garden of Eden, and North Carolina teachers are fully aware that it is only a silly effort to lessen the benefits of the Teachers' Assembly, devised by the jealousy of the sojourning editor of the *Southern Educator*.

WILL SOMEBODY who happens to be near enough, please gently pat on the head the little *Southern Educator* of Durham and its excited Virginia editor, Mr. Edwin S. Sheppe, and persuade "Sheppie" to let his "furrin" blood cool down. He is too hot to tell the truth even about his native State, Virginia, and of course we cannot expect him to do any better for North Carolina, where he is at present sojourning. But he is only following the well known habit of every other envious Virginian who has written about North Carolina. They have claimed Virginia Dare, declared that Virginia made the first Declaration of Independence, have tried to rob us of the immortal glory won by our gallant Pettigrew at Gettysburg, and now this more modern migratory F. F. V. editor of the *Educator* wants to remodel the North Carolina Teachers' Assembly, with the hope that he may destroy it as he has done two nominal educational organizations that were in his hands! It is very strange that Mr. Sheppe had to leave his home, Virginia, where he says there are so much larger schools and more school money than in North Carolina, to come into the Old North State for a support! Perhaps his rare rhetoric and marvelous organizing skill were not fully realized and appreciated by those who knew him; and we are not surprised at this when we see in the September number of the *Southern Educator* such elegant editorial headlines as "Northampton Gets There," "Davidson to the Fore," and "They All Are In It," and remember the fate of the so-called organizations of which his journal professed to be the official organ.

ABOUT OUR TEACHERS AND SCHOOLS.

Miss M. E. Ellison is teaching at Fayetteville.

Miss Laura Holton is teaching at Yadkinville.

Miss Amelia Eaton is teaching at Cana, Davie County.

Miss Bettie Graves, of Wilson, is teaching at Asheville

Mr. P. E. Johnson is teaching at Rome, Johnston County.

Miss Fannie Thompson has a crowded school at Pittsboro.

Mr. Moses Morgan is teaching at Light, Davidson County.

Miss Ella Morris has a school at Coleraine, Bertie County.

Miss Josie Pierson is teaching at Walnut Cove, Stokes County.

Miss Jennie O. Grady is Principal of the High School at Halifax.

Miss Lula Gay, of Wilson, is teaching at Spring Hope, Nash County.

R. L. Fritz is Professor of Mathematics in Highland College, Hickory.

Miss Hattie Lee Atwater is teaching at Rialto, Chatham County.

Miss Annie Patterson has a school at Mangum, Richmond County.

Mr. J. H. Quinn is principal of the High School at Boiling Springs, N. C.

Miss Kate Clendennin, of Graham, has taken a school at Franklinton.

Miss Annie C. Lee, of Vanceboro, is teaching at Ernul, Craven County.

Miss Sallie Maynard, of Graham, is teaching at Corbett, Alamance County.

Miss Sallie McCracken has a good school at Crusoe, Haywood County.

Miss Anna Merritt has a fine Music School at Pittsboro, Chatham County.

Mr. D. McBryde is Principal of the High School at Faison, Duplin County.

Miss Janie M. Hicks is now in charge of a school at Cherokee, South Carolina.

Miss Fannie Cobb has been elected a teacher in the. Graded Schools at Raleigh.

Greenville Institute opens with 154 pupils. Mr. W. H. Ragsdale is Principal.

Miss Irene Carroll, of Sampson, is teaching at New Hope Academy near Clinton.

4

MR. D. T. WILSON, of Sampson County, is teaching at Beaufort, Carteret County.

MISS LUCIE BRINKLEY is teaching at "South End," near Manteo, Dare County.

MISS CHLOE PARKER, of Raleigh, has taken a school at Belcross, Camden County.

MISS MATTIE E. ROUSE has a very successful Art School at Washington, Beaufort County.

MR. W. P. WHITE and wife have charge of Cross-Roads Academy at Cape, Randolph County.

MR. LEON CASH, of Farmington, has been elected County Superintendent of Davie County.

MISS CHARLOTTE BUSH has charge of a class in Physical Culture at Pittsboro, Chatham County.

THE Public Graded Schools of Raleigh opened on September 18th with a very fine attendance.

MISS FLORENCE WHITLOCK has charge of the music department of the Graded Schools of Asheville.

REV. J. B. NEWTON, of Bertie County, has taken charge of the Academy at Fork Church, Davie County.

MISS VIRGINIA MURPHY, of Winston, has been elected a teacher in the Graded Schools at that place.

MISS CORA CONRAD, of Lewisville, is teacher of Art in the Baptist College for Girls at Danville, Va.

MISS VIOLA BODDIE, of Nashville, has accepted a position as teacher in the Asheville Graded Schools.

THE DURHAM GRADED SCHOOL bonds have all been sold, and work on the building will begin at once.

THERE are more pupils in the schools of Raleigh than in the schools of any other city of North Carolina.

MR. E. L. CROCKER (Wake Forest College) has charge of the Academy at Williamston, Martin County.

MISS HELEN MCVEA has opened a school for little boys and girls at her home on Halifax street in Raleigh.

MISS ADA BARWICK, of Grifton, has taken charge of Alexander's Academy at Edwards' Mill, Beaufort County.

MISSES ELLA HOUSTON AND ONA PATTERSON are Principals of the High School at Waco, Cleveland County.

MR. HOLLAND M. THOMPSON, of Lincolnton, has taken a position as teacher in the Charlotte Graded Schools.

Mr. W. O. Riddick (Wake Forest College) has been elected Principal of the High School at Franklin, Macon County.

Mr. G. E. Barnett (Randolph-Macon), of Dailsville, Md., is Principal of the Academy at Mocksville, Davie County.

There are one hundred and forty students at Davidson College, the largest number since its foundation fifty-four years ago.

Mr. Perrin Busbee (University of N. C.), of Raleigh, has accepted a position as assistant teacher in the Raleigh Male Academy.

Mr. Hunter Harris (University of N. C.), of Raleigh, has been appointed Assistant Professor in Mineralogy at the University.

Mr. W. H. Cralle (Virginia Military Institute), of Blackstone, Va., has been elected Principal of the Graded Schools at Goldsboro.

The Davis Military School at Winston is preparing to bring a large battalion of soldier boys to the Exposition at Raleigh in October.

Mrs. J. M. Barbee, formerly a teacher in the Raleigh Graded Schools, has again accepted the position, much to the delight of the little folks.

Mr. H. F. Ketron has a school of seventy-five pupils at Mt. Carmel, Buncombe County. He is assisted by Miss Eula Campbell, of Asheville.

Mr. M. L. John, who has been for the past two years Principal of the Academy at Mocksville, is now taking the law course of the University.

Stokes County Teachers' Council is prospering under the management of Capt. S. B. Taylor as President, and Miss Mildred Hill as Secretary.

Mr. Edgar G. Wingfield, of Virginia, a graduate of the University of Virginia, has been elected Superintendent of the City Graded Schools of Shelby.

The Excellent Graded Schools at Goldsboro, Mr. J. Y. Joyner Superintendent, opened September 21st with the largest attendance in their history.

Mr. A. C. Hottenstein is Principal of Piedmont Seminary at Lexington, and Miss Mattie McLean is assistant. Prospects for a successful term are good.

Mr. John A. Oates (Wake Forest College) is Principal of the South River Baptist Institute at Autryville, Sampson County. Miss Annie Clute is Music Teacher.

Greensboro Female College, Rev. B. F. Dixon, D. D., President, began the fall term with one hundred and twenty-five charming young ladies as boarding pupils.

Mr. John B. Spillman (Wake Forest), of Weldon, who was recently assistant teacher in the Raleigh Male Academy, is in charge of a large school at Starrville, Texas.

THE RALEIGH GRADED SCHOOLS began the fall work on September 17th with eight hundred and ten white children and about five hundred Negro children in attendance.

ST. MARY'S SCHOOL, Raleigh, began its fiftieth term on September 24th. Near a hundred and fifty pupils in attendance, a larger number than ever before at the opening.

REV. GEORGE W. GREENE, Professor of Latin, Wake Forest College, has sailed with his family to China as a missionary, under the auspices of the Southern Baptist Convention.

MR. J. D. BARDEN, of Wilson, has been elected Superintendent of Schools for Wilson County, in place of Mr. W. S. Barnes, who resigned to accept the secretaryship of the Farmers' Alliance.

MR. W. H. CLENDENNIN is Principal of the High School at Plainview, Robeson County. Miss Sallie Sinclair is assistant and Miss Virginia Coble is Music Teacher. Eighty-five pupils are enrolled.

THE "WESTERN NORTH CAROLINA TEACHERS' ASSOCIATION" will hold a working session at Bryson City, October 28–30, 1891. A fine programme has been arranged and a good crowd is expected.

MISS M. H. BAIN, who was a teacher at the Oxford Female Seminary for several years, has taken charge of the Portsmouth (Va.) Seminary, a long-established and popular English and Classical School for young ladies.

DR. R. H. LEWIS the excellent President of Judson College at Hendersonville, is increasing the patronage of the institution very much. He is assisted by Miss Katharine Lewis, Miss E. H Draughan and Miss Kate Johnson.

REV. J. R. JONES is Principal of the Seminary for Girls at Milton, Caswell County. His assistants are Miss Corinne Jeffress, of Chase City, Va.; Miss Anna C. Ott, of Spottswood, Va., and Miss Mamie Dodson, of Milton, N. C.

MR. D. MICHAEL, Professor in "Lillo de Costa Rica" at San Jose, Costa Rica, South America, sends a subscription to the TEACHER. We hope to give our readers some notes upon South American Schools from Mr. Michael ere long.

MISS MAMIE WEBB, of Richmond, Va., is in charge of the Primary Department of Carolina Male and Female Institute at Nashville. Miss Lee Parker, of Wilson, is Music Teacher, and Mr. W. O. Dunn, of Nash County, is Principal of the Institute.

FAIRVIEW ACADEMY, W. T. Whitsett, A. M. Superintendent, Gibsonville, has opened with more students than ever before. Over sixty are already present from fifteen counties and four States, and others are entering almost daily. The school was founded in 1884.

MISS LAURA P. MOORE, of Kenansville, N. C., who taught in Dillon, S. C., last year, has returned, and is assisting Prof. Joseph Clay Blanton, of Hampden-Sidney College, Va., in the High School at Dillon, S. C.

THE EXECUTIVE COMMITTEE of the "Western North Carolina Teachers' Association" have called a meeting of the teachers of that portion of our State to be held at Bryson City, Swain County, on October 28 and 30. THE TEACHER wishes them a pleasant and successful session.

THE MANY people who have sons to educate, and who have wished to enjoy the society, the coolness and healthfulness of Chapel Hill, will be glad to know that a Classical High School for boys began there August 31st, with Mr. Caswell Ellis, of Louisburg, as head master. Mr. Ellis is a University graduate, and a man of scholarship, character and experience in teaching. The Faculty endorses him very highly.

APEX HIGH SCHOOL, under the leadership of Mr. B. D. Barker (Wake Forest College), with Miss Emma Parker, Morrisville, N. C., as assistant, and Mrs. Dr. Rogers, Apex, N. C., as Music Teacher, is progressing finely. The number of pupils is flattering already, and still they come. On the evening of the 9th of October, 1891, Prof. C. E. Brewer, of Wake Forest, N. C., is to make his *debut* as a lecturer before this school. We anticipate for him a large audience.

BUNCOMBE COUNTY teachers organized an Association at Asheville, N. C., on the 19th of September. About fifty members were enrolled. The following officers for 1891–'2 were elected: Supt. C. B. Way, President; Mr. James Cooper, Secretary; Miss Lola S. Stanley, Treasurer. A regular programme of work will be arranged at every meeting, and much good will doubtless be done. This is the second of the thirteen counties west of the Blue Ridge to organize as an auxiliary of the "Western North Carolina Teachers' Association."

THE TRUSTEES of the Graded Schools at Wilson very properly and wisely decided that only the regular common school course as prepared by the State should be taught at the expense of public taxation. This is the true basis of public education, and if all public schools would do this same right and proper thing it would remove much of the antagonism which now exists toward the public schools. People are willing to pay taxes for the education of the masses, but not for teaching Latin, French and Higher Mathematics to a favored few in a public school.

FAIRVIEW COLLEGE, twelve miles from Asheville, has opened in primary and intermediate work with fifty pupils. The Normal and Collegiate Departments open November 2. The following teachers are engaged in the work: Mr. D. L. Ellis, President; Mrs. D. L. Ellis, Music; Miss Lola S. Stanley, Latin, Greek and Higher Mathematics; Miss M. May Ellis, Art and History; Miss Mary F. McDonald, Kindergarten Department. A prosperous year is looked for, and, with the opening of the college work proper, it is probable that one hundred and fifty students will be enrolled by December.

PROFESSORS HUGHES AND GRAHAM say that the Montgomery County Institute was the best one they had in the State. Nearly all the teachers of the county were present, and an enthusiastic Teachers' Council was organized, with Mr. T. C. Hoyle as President. The School Committeemen also organized an association for the purpose of creating more interest among the people in behalf of the schools. Many high compliments were paid to the efficient County Superintendent Mr. R. H. Skeen for his excellent work, which had done so much for the teachers and schools of his county.

THE SCHEME for a Baptist University for Girls to be located in Raleigh seems to have failed for the present. The following principal causes have been assigned : 1. The Trustees did not plan for the establishment of such a high grade institution as was expected and as had been promised to the Baptists, and therefore many Raleigh subscribers withdrew and the whole city became indifferent in the matter. 2. The site selected by the Trustees was too small (being less than three acres) and not at all suitable for such an institution of learning. The price demanded was beyond all proportion to the market value of the property and would have consumed the entire fund without establishing the school. 3. The course of study authorized for the institution was only an average seminary course, and would have brought the school into competition with other Baptist schools of similar grade in the State, and the denomination did not desire to do this. If the plan of the institution is reorganized, and a suitable site selected, the people of Raleigh will contribute promptly and liberally to the cause, and the University will be quickly established. The Trustees did not take enough interest in the matter to give a quorum of attendance to a very important meeting on August 31st, when the life of the University was to be considered.

CUPID AMONG OUR TEACHERS.

'Tis said that " figures never lie,"
That one and one are always TWO ;
But Cupid proves, with work so sly,
  Some wondrous things that figures do.
And when he claims a teacher's hand
  All rules of figures then are done,
Though TWO before the preacher stand
  This one and one are ALWAYS ONE.

PROF. CHARLES L. WILSON, of Raleigh, a teacher of vocal music, married Miss VIRGINIA MAYES, of Staunton, Va., on September 17th. Rev. D. K. McFarland, D. D., pastor of the First Presbyterian Church at Staunton, performed the ceremony.

IN MEMORIAM.

"Death hath made no breach
In love and sympathy, in hope and trust.
No outward sign or sound our ears can reach,
But there's an inward, spiritual speech
That greets us still, though mortal tongues be dust.
It bids us do the work that they laid down—
Take up the song where they broke off the strain ;
So, journeying till we reach the heavenly town,
Where are laid up our treasure and our crown,
And our lost, loved ones will be found again."

ON THURSDAY, September, 10th, Mr. H. W. Spinks, Principal of Monroe High School, died at his home in that place. He was for a long time the faithful County Superintendent of Stanly County.

MRS. VARINA S. CLAXTON, wife of Mr. P. P. Claxton, Superintendent of the Asheville Graded Schools, died at her home, on September 14th, after a brief illness, aged twenty-six years. Her remains were interred in Goldsboro, her former home. She leaves one child.

AT RECESS.

The books and slates now put away,
And let us laugh a little while ;
For those who work there should be play,
The leisure moments to beguile.

BILLIE (who snapped school yesterday)—"I gave the fish a big surprise yesterday." Harry—"Did you? Catching 'em?" Billie—"No! I fell in."

TEACHER—"You must not come to school any more, Tommy, until your mother has recovered from the small-pox."

Tommy—"There ain't a bit of danger. She ain't going to give me the small-pox."

Teacher—"Why, how is that?"

Tommy—"She's my stepmother. She never gives me anything."

TEACHER—"You may answer, Tommy Jones. Why do birds fly?"

Tommy Jones—"Cause they ain't such fools as to walk when they don't hev ter."

TEACHER—"What would the Prince of Wales be if the Queen of England should die?"..."A orphan, ma'am."

FUNNY WAYS OF CONJUGATING VERBS.—Children have funny ways of conjugating their verbs, as was illustrated by a little boy of a writer's acquaintance told about in *Wide Awake*. This little man had been out with his sled and came in saying eagerly: "Oh, mamma! I have been out with my sled and I slud clear to the foot of the hill, while Johnny Laurence only slod half way. It's such good fun to slide!"

APEARANCE WAS DECEITFUL.—A beautiful young school girl, dressed in the height of fashion, was leaning over the gate when a smitten young man approached her.

"Good evening, miss. Will you kindly inform me if you have noticed a stray dog pass here?"

She unclosed the rosy portals of speech and answered quickly—

"No. . I ain't saw any other dorg this evenin'."

And another cherished ideal was smashed to smithereens.

"SASSING" HIS EMPLOYER.—Sampson (just from the public school) was a clerk for one day only at the mammoth establishment of William Bobson, in Dallas, Texas. Bobson, although very wealthy is also very illiterate. He was writing a letter, when he looked up and asked Sampson Jennings, who was at the next desk :

"How do you spell inducement—with a '*c*' or an '*s*'?"

"Dunno," responded the new clerk.

"All the clerks I ever had except you knew how to spell."

"So did all the bosses I ever had," replied Jennings.

The *entente cordiale* was spilled over the floor, and a new man stands at the desk formerly occupied by Sampson Jennings.

NEW SCHOLARS.

FRANK PRESTON and CHARLES MANNING, sons of Prof. F. P. Venable, Professor of Chemistry in the University, were born at Chapel Hill on Monday morning, September 3d, 1891.

EVVIE SIMPSON, daughter of Prof. John A. Simpson, teacher of music in the Institute for the Deaf and Dumb and the Blind at Raleigh, was born on September 5th, 1891.

GEORGE EDGAR MILLER, son of Mr. John P. Haskett and wife, was born on September 19, 1891. Mr. Haskett was a member of the Teachers' European Party, and his wife is teacher of music in Misses Patrick's school at Kinston.

Professor—"WHY IS IT, MISS CARRIE, THAT YOUR HAIR IS SO WAVY THIS MORNING AFTER BEING SO STRAIGHT ON YESTERDAY? IF THE LORD HAD WANTED YOUR HAIR TO CURL HE WOULD HAVE MADE IT SO."

Miss Carrie—"HE DID MAKE IT CURL FOR ME WHEN I WAS LITTLE, BUT HE THINKS I AM NOW OLD ENOUGH TO CURL IT FOR MYSELF, SIR."

THE NORTH CAROLINA TEACHER.

VOL. IX.   RALEIGH, DECEMBER, 1891.   NO. 4.

EUGENE G. HARRELL,   =   =   =   =   Editor.

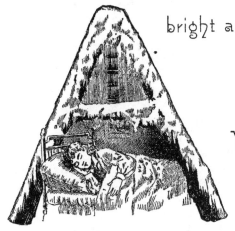 bright and blessed Christ-

mas Day,

With echoes of the

angels' song,

And peace that cannot pass away,

And holy gladness calm and strong,

And sweet heart-carols glowing free!

This is our Christmas wish to thee!

—*Frances R. Havergal.*

North Carolina Teachers Abroad:

A SUMMER JAUNT

IN

ENGLAND, SCOTLAND, IRELAND AND FRANCE.

CHAPTER XXIV.

FAMOUS PLACES IN PARIS.

THE WANDERING MINSTRELS—SOMETHING ABOUT GUIDES—A FRENCH
DAIRY—THE CONCIERGERIE—THE PANTHEON—FAMOUS HIS-
TORICAL LOCALITIES—THE GOBELIN TAPESTRY WORKS—CEME-
TERY PERE LA CHAISE—THE STOCK EXCHANGE—THE NORTH
CAROLINA TEACHERS CAPTURE THE EXCHANGE—HONOR TO THE
AMERICAN FLAG—THE MORGUE AND ITS OCCUPANTS.

OW strange a sight it is to an
American — the vast number of
wandering street minstrels and
flower girls which seem to exist
throughout France !

While waiting for our breakfast
this morning we were amused by
the songs and antics of a very
pretty girl and a man who seemed
to be her father, dancing, playing
and begging in front of our hotel.
Their frantic efforts to sing ''Yankee Doodle'' as a special
compliment ''to the American party'' were indeed amusing
and we ''rewarded them for *effort* and not for *results.''*

We were tired with walking for the present so we again
chartered the comfortable and handsome excursion carriages
of our friends Gaze & Sons.

We made it a condition of the charter that our incomparable guide with the Cleveland hat, Mr. Gallop, should accompany us.

As a general rule, when travelling in a strange country, the less your guide knows the more you will learn about that country because he will not be able to talk so continuously, and thus you will have more time and opportunity for observation and investigation. The principal use of a guide is to put your enquiries of the people about you into their native tongue and translate the answers for you. You will therefore ask only the things you want to know without having to waste valuable time in listening, or appearing to listen, to a guide reciting his lesson like a talking-machine fully wound up never to run down.

The French people are realizing that their language is fast losing its hold upon the world as the international language and that English is taking its place. They are, however, doggedly resisting this change, and they resort to every possible scheme to prevent the speaking of English by their people.

There are thirty thousand cabmen in Paris who receive a large portion of their patronage from the English and Americans and yet they will not learn even a single word of English, although it might add greatly to their business. Just fourteen miles of water separate France from England, and yet there is less English spoken in France than in any other foreign country on the globe.

But as the English-speaking people are to-day ruling the world so their language is destined to be the universal tongue, and the sooner this fact is learned by the French, as by all other foreign nations, the better it will be for them.

When we gathered in the breakfast-room this morning the *chef*, or head waiter as he was better known to us, with many courtesies and Chesterfieldan manners informed us that for some cause "ze meelk for ze cafe have not arreeve zis mornin'." However, while we were eating there was a great tinkling of bells on the street by our windows and the waiter exclaimed "Ze meelk!" Looking out of the window we saw a man with a bell and a tin bucket surrounded by a herd of about fifty goats. This was the "milk man and his dairy." He drives the herd from house to house and milks direct from the goats into his pail whatever quantity of milk may be needed, and thus it goes at once to the table. Some of our habitual milk-drinkers seemed to suddenly lose their appetite for this class of nourishment after the interesting dairy performance that we had just witnessed.

It isn't always well to know too much when you are away from home.

After taking our seats in the carriages the guide informed us that we would begin the day by a visit to the Pantheon, the "Westminster Abbey of Paris." Before reaching the Pantheon we spent a few moments in the outer court of the Conciergerie, the most famous prison in Europe — a prison from which a century ago delivery was but to the guillotine, and whose walls have contained the Royalty of France. Almost side by side are the cells of Marie Antoinette and Robespierre.

It was just outside these walls where in 1793 there surged a howling mob of men and women more cruel and blood-thirsty than even the guillotine, whose frenzy was not appeased until they had most foully murdered and mutilated over a thousand prisoners of the Conciergerie. We looked up at the little barred window of the cell in which the beautiful Marie Antoinette proved herself greater and nobler in chains than when she sparkled with diamonds and sat on the glittering throne of France.

From the gate of the Conciergerie is seen, only a short distance away, the dome of the Pantheon towering above the surrounding buildings. This cathedral is erected upon the site of the tomb of St. Genevieve, the patron saint of Paris, who died in the year 512.

As we enter the massive stone gateway of this famous structure we realize that we stand within a Christian church which is devoted to the glorification of men. The altar is gone and the building is thoroughly secularized. It is now dedicated not to St. Genevieve, who still implores, in marble, Attilla the Hun to spare the city of Paris, but to the great men of France. Victor Hugo is sleeping here, Voltaire, Rousseau, Mirabeau, and Marat rested in the vaults for a time, but they, too, have shared the fate of the exiled saints and their ashes have been removed to resting-places now unknown.

The walls of this great cathedral of emptiness glow with imposing paintings of the miraculous Middle Age. Saint Dennis is pictured as he walks with his head in his hand after it was decapitated; Saint Louis is administering justice; Charlemagne is displayed in all his glory, and Saint Genevieve is everywhere, but the color is only on the walls.

The colossal building is still full of emptiness, hollow as a stone balloon, when Heine saw it cold and chilly and bare.

Yet the Pantheon is not without its memories. In June, 1848, the insurgents had their headquarters here, and in 1871 it was occupied as the central citadel in the worst of a network of barricades by the men of the Commune. But they were driven out like a swarm of angry wasps, not without powder, and smoke, and tumult, and bloodshed, now barely audible; and so hurried was their departure that they did not have even time to fire the powder with which they had stored the vaults beneath, the parting tribute that they proposed to render to the great men of the country to whose memory the Pantheon is now dedicated.

We followed our guide into the vaults where is the tomb of Victor Hugo covered with flowers and wreaths. Somebody in authority, with remarkable bad taste, has caused elaborate monuments to Rousseau and Voltaire, the famous infidels, to be erected beside the tomb of Hugo! In the vaults there is also a most interesting whispering gallery.

From the Pantheon we drove eastward to the fatal spot where the Bastille stood and where the Bastille ceased to stand just a century since. The outlines of the famous old fortress are still to be seen traced in the square from the centre of which springs the Column of July, commemorating yet another revolution.

The Bastille itself has been rebuilt in fac-simile lath and plaster and is one of the adjuncts to the exhibition in the Champ de Mars. But better than the lath and plaster fac-simile to enable you to realize the great siege is the " Panorama of the taking of the Bastille" which stands near at hand, and where you see rendered in realistic paint the features of that ever-memorable assault upon the grim old prison by the populace of Paris. It is like the unfolding of Carlyle's dithyrambs on colored canvas, the pictured death agony of the old régime. It is a hundred years since the passionate populace precipitated itself thus upon the Bastille, believing that they were in their headlong way going to inaugurate the millennium.

The destruction of that hated fortress, and the liberation of its seven prisoners — only seven within the whole gloomy walls — how it seemed, even to Americans like Wordsworth and Coleridge, the rising of the day-star of liberty, heralding the new day! A century has passed, and all those who raged so fiercely then have long since ceased their raging. The children of that day are now old men. There have been many more revolutions — two empires and two Monarchies have come and gone; we have now the third Republic, and behind it the shadow of yet another Emperor. The millennium is still far off, and France, this "poet of the nations," has even ceased to dream of the hopes so oft deferred.

The July Column marks the site of the famous fortress. The plan of the Bastille is traced in lines of white granite on the west side of the square. Many fiercer fights have taken place on the site of the demolished prison than that which led to its demolition. The July Column itself commemorates not the destruction of the Bastille but the Revolution of July, 1830, when Louis Philippe was seated on the throne from which the elder branch of the Bourbons had just been driven. Eighteen years later, the throne of Louis Philippe was publicly burned at the base of the column erected in honor of the Revolution which made him King. A great barricade was thrown up in June, 1848, on the east of the Place fronting the Rue du Fraubourg St. Antoine which required much pounding with heavy artillery before it was captured, and in the fight Archbishop Affre was shot dead even while pleading with the insurgents for peace.

That was on June 25, 1848. On May 25 — twenty-three years afterwards — the Communists made a stout resistance behind their barricades, which, however, only retarded for a time the advance of the Versaillese. As the victors cleared out the "wasps' nest," an attempt was made to blow up the Column and overwhelm the district in one mighty explosion. The vaults beneath the Column were crammed with powder, but in the confusion the match did not go off, and St. Antoine was saved once more. De Launay also, a hundred years ago, threatened a mighty explosion, but it did not come off.

From the Column of the Bastille we drove westward along the Boulevards. Battle of the fierce insurrectionary order has often waged along these stately streets. Nor is it only insurrection. At a little house, No. 42 of the Boulevard du Temple, Fiesché launched his infernal machine in 1835 at Louis Philippe, missing his mark but killing fifteen people, a Marshal of France included.

At Porte St. Martin, a triumphal arch erected in honor of victories of the seventeenth century witnessed the entry of the German and Russian armies, who in 1814 actually arrived at Paris to restore the old régime. They had started more than twenty years before, but it took them all that time before they arrived. If they had foreseen the vicissitudes of the journey they would probably never have started. Here also and at the other triumphal arch, the Porte St. Denis, barricades were thrown up and fierce fighting took place in 1830, 1848, and 1871. Another famous barricade, alike in February, 1848, and in May, 1871, closed the Boulevard end of the Rue du Fraubourg Montmartre.

Between the Hotel de Ville and the Boulevards lay the district in which the insurrectionary forces always barricaded themselves in all times of disturbances. The most famous barricade of the Coup d'Etat was not in the Boulevards, but in the Rue St. Marguerite, where Baudin fell, shot through the head by a battalion of the line as he was endeavoring to assert the supremacy of the law and of the Constitution.

The Boulevards, from the Rue du Sentier to the Madeleine, witnessed much bloodier work when, on the 4th of December, 16,000 soldiers were drawn up in the carriageway in subdivisions at quarter distance, pending the anticipated attack on the great barricade at Rue St. Denis. Suddenly, at three o'clock in the afternoon, with or without pretext of the abortive shot fired from a window in the Rue du Sentier, the troops shot down in cold blood, without warning, the men, women and children who crowded the pavement and were gazing from the windows on the military display. . For a quarter of an hour or twenty minutes the soldiers fired volley after volley upon an unarmed and peaceful crowd of sightseers. The Boulevard seems busy and delightful now, but then ——! Thirty-seven corpses lay heaped in the Cité Bergère: men, women and children dead in groups or singly all along the foot pavement, and around each of the hollows about the trees blood lay coagulating in little pools. Inside the houses helpless people were hunted from room to room and massacred in cold blood. At the barricades no quarter was given. By night peace reigned in Paris, and Louis Napoleon was established on the throne, from which nothing but Sedan could shake him off.

Passing these scenes of sanguinary crime, we come to the Madeleine, the great church which Napoleon intended to be a Temple of Glory, but which has been completed as a temple of the Magdalen—Christ and the Magdalen. The building has none of the historic charm of Notre Dame. It is not so old as the Revolution, but it also has its memories. It was in this church that the Communists rallied when the Commune was sinking in the flames of Paris, and it was here, before the altar of the God of Pity, that three hundred of the wretched Communists were butchered like rats in a pit by their Versaillese conquerors. Not in the first great Revolution, not in the worst days of the Terror, were such wholesale massacres accomplished as those which took place only eighteen years ago, under the eyes of Europe, and without a single protesting cry of indignation and of shame. Such an outrage could not occur in America.

The pavement, which then ran red with human blood, is clean enough to-day. The silent worshipers bow in prayer before the altar on which the great sacrifice is being represented, all heedless of that holocaust of 1871. And high above all forms divine and human in the great church soars aloft the sublime figure of the Magdalen, supported by the angels who, above the high altar, are bearing her into Paradise. Christianity was worth inventing, snarls the cynic, if only to raise high above all the saints and the angels in the most fashionable church in Paris that eternal

exemplar of trampled womanhood.   They worship her in
the Madeleine.   Outside they thrust her into St. Lazare,
and torment her with the *police des mœurs*.

From the Madeleine we went southward toward the
Seine, crossing the Rue St. Honoré, along which there,
all gay with tricolor, came the death scene of the Queen
Marie Antoinette.

Turning down the Champs Elysées is the Place de la
Concorde, formerly the Place de la Révolution, best known
for all time as the Place of the Guillotine.   It is a spacious
square of bloody memory.   All round the great palace sit
the statues of the cities of France.   That of Strasbourg is
half buried beneath the wreaths of unavailing regret.   The
great fountains splash up their water ceaselessly in the sunlight, and the Obelisk of Luxor stands as a silent warden
over the spot where a century since the guillotine made
France a hissing, a bye-word and a reproach among all
nations of the earth.

The knife that struck off the heads of so many Frenchmen and women whose names live in history, stood a little
to one side of the Obelisk.   Louis XVI was the first to be
beheaded here, on the site of the statue of Louis XV, which
had been melted down into penny pieces.   It went always
for two years, nor did it cease until 2,800 heads had fallen
to the basket.   Louis the Unfortunate was only thirty-
eight when the axe fell.   The spectres of the guillotined
must often hold sombre tryst round the Obelisk of Egypt.
Louis is there, and his Queen, and his sister, and with them
the fair executioner of the foul Marat.   Danton and St.
Just, Robespierre and Camille Desmoulins, Philippe Egalité
and Anarchist Clootz, with a vast throng of nearly 3,000
more, a gruesome company, headless as St. Denis, but less
blessed.   Would that they could speak and tell us what
they think of it all after a hundred years!

Turning from the Place de la Concorde and its headless ghosts, we enter the Tuilleries Gardens.   It was out of this gate that some three hundred Swiss poured, when the order reached them to cease firing, on August 10, 1792, and were butchered to a man.   Inside the gardens it was that they stood like a granite mass, pelting with deadly bullets the ''glittering steel tide'' which submerged the Tuilleries, and slaying some 1,200 men before they were abandoned by their King.   It was a pitiful massacre—the last death struggle of the old régime, rendered abortive by the King himself.   How different it was when authority was vested not in the son of sixty kings, but in a born ruler of men!

Leaving the Tuilleries gardens we turn down the Rue St. Roch.   Here is the church of St. Roch—the tombstone of the Revolution.   For it was here where Napoleon administered that whiff of grapeshot which blew the Revolution into space.   On October 5, 1795, the insurgent sections rose and marched against the Convention.   Section Lepelletier, with 40,000 fighting men behind it, storming down on the Tuilleries, as three years before St. Antoine had swooped down on the palace of the King.   But Napoleon was in command.   Napoleon, with some seven thousand men, *and artillery*—drew a steel girdle round the Tuilleries, and waited the attack, every gunner having his match burning.   He had not long to wait.

'' 'Fire!' says the bronze lips.   And roar and thunder, and roar and again roar continual, volcano like goes his great gun in the Cul de Sac Dauphin, against the Church of St. Roch; go his great guns on the Pont Royal; go all his great guns; blow to air some two hundred men, mainly about the Church of St. Roch.   The forty thousand yield on all sides; scour towards covert.   It was all finished by six.''

How vividly these famous localities call to mind those startling events in the history of this nation which caused

all the world to stand aghast in horror. It will take whole
centuries of peace and prosperity to wipe from the brow
of France such dark and devilish stains of blood.

We gladly turned away from such scenes and memories
and drove to what is considered the most noted and interesting industry of France—the Gobelin Tapestry Works.

These celebrated works, the only place in the world
where such tapestries are made, were founded in 1450 by
Jean Gobelin. It has acquired such a reputation throughout the world that the product of its looms are used only
for the decoration of State departments or as gifts to eminent embassadors. The walls of the building are adorned
by a number of magnificent specimens of the work representing some famous paintings.

The tapestries are exceedingly beautiful and the work is
very slow and tedious. About six inches square is considered a good day's work for a weaver, therefore many
years are required for the completion of some of the larger
designs. The Secretary noticed that the workmen were
engaged on some pieces which he had seen in their looms
over three years ago and yet the designs were not finished,
having several years of work yet ahead of them!

We were shown a number of pieces on which the price
was $10,000. The superintendent of the works permitted
us to go behind the looms so as to see the actual work of
weaving. The workman has a copy of the design beside
him and a basket of wools dyed in unchangeable colors,
each principal hue represented by twenty-four different
shades. One thread at a time is most carefully selected
and woven into place, then examined thoroughly to see if
it is exactly correct. It was hard for us to realize the
patience required for such work. Some of the larger pieces
represent the whole life of the workman given to its manufacture. As we noted this fact one of our party recalled
to our minds the following touching lines from Addison

Chester, which she impressively repeated as we looked upon the weavers:

THE TAPESTRY WEAVERS.

Let us take to our hearts a lesson,—
   No lesson can richer be,—
From the ways of the tapestry weavers,
   On the other side of the sea.
Above their heads the pattern hangs,
   They study it with care,
And while their fingers deftly work,
   Their eyes are fastened there.

They tell this curious thing besides,
   Of the patient, plodding weaver,
He works *on* the wrong side, evermore,
   But works *for* the right side, ever.
It is only when the weaving stops
   And the web is loosed and turned,
And he sees his real handiwork
   That his marvelous skill is learned.

At the sight of its delicate beauty,
   How it pays him for all it cost!
No rarer, daintier work than his,
   Was ever done by the frost.
Then the master bringeth him golden hire,
   And giveth him praises as well;
And how happy the heart of the weaver is
   No tongue but his own can tell.

The years of man are the looms of God,
   Let down from the place of the sun,
Wherein we are weaving always,
   Till the mystic web is done.
Weaving blindly, but weaving surely,
   Each for himself his fate;
We may not see how the right side looks.
   We can only weave and wait.

But, looking above the pattern,
   No weaver hath need to fear;
Only let him look clear into heaven—
   The Perfect Pattern is there.
If he keeps the face of the Saviour
   Forever and always in sight,
His toil shall be sweeter than honey;
   His weaving is sure to be right.

And when his task is ended,
  And the web is turned and shown,
He shall hear the voice of the master,
  It shall say to him ''Well done!''
And the white-winged angels of heaven,
  To bear him thence shall come down,
And God shall give him gold for his hire,
  Not coin, but a golden crown.

Returning to our carriages we drove into the commercial portion of the city and reined up in front of the Bourse or Stock Exchange. It was a lively day on the Exchange, and the great building was thronged with members thoroughly excited by their dizzy speculations.

Of course the party wanted to see the Frenchman engaged in his stock operations, so we alighted at the entrance to the galleries. Some three or four hundred members of the Exchange were crowding the long porch eagerly watching our movements. When our party appeared in the galleries we looked down upon a moving, yelling, shouting, excited mass of humanity which occupied the main floor of the Exchange to the number of about a thousand men. In a few moments they caught sight of the hundred North Carolinians watching them, and immediately their whole attention was turned to the galleries, while their significant gesticulations indicated that they were trying to learn who were their visitors.

Seeing this, the Secretary waved our American flag over the railing, and the effect was truly magical. Instantly every man waved his hat in the air, and the noisiest of enthusiasm prevailed everywhere. Stocks were forgotten for the time and a great burst of applause arose from that vast throng borne to us in a grand and continued wave of acclamation, ''Vive la Amerique!'' The scene was past description, and our guide informed us that such a thrilling event was never before witnessed in the French Stock Exchange, that its entire operations, involving millions of dollars, should be suspended while a welcome of intensest enthusiasm was being extended to the North Carolina teachers!

An officer of the Exchange came into the gallery and laughingly informed the Secretary that "The Bourse was charmed by its fair visitors and did not desire to attend to any more business while the handsome American party remained in the gallery."

We remained a few moments longer to enjoy our triumph and then retired. As we descended the stairway every member of the Bourse left the hall and gathered along our walk from the building, keeping up a vigorous shouting of "Vive la Amerique," until we were seated in our carriages and waved them a farewell with the glorious Stars and Stripes while the spectators slowly returned to their operations. North Carolina had again scored a victory, and honor and a recognition such as no other State had ever won.

It was dinner time and we were hungry, so we headed for our hotel.

Our route lay past the famous Morgue of Paris, and, at the request of some of the party, we stopped for a few moments for an inspection of this noted place. It is a small building, erected on the Isle de Cite immediately in the rear of Notre Dame. There are exposed here the bodies of all persons who die either from accident, suicide or suddenly, and the Morgue is scarcely ever empty.

When we visited the Morgue there were exposed on the marble slabs the bodies of three persons, two young women and an old man, all of whom had been taken from the river Seine that morning. There are about eight hundred bodies exposed annually in the Morgue, and a large majority of them are suicides. The lower class of French people seem to consider the Seine as a panacea for all troubles. Beside the bodies exposed are the clothes last worn, for the purpose of identification, and a new process of scientific refrigeration enables them to keep the bodies as long as three months.

NORTH CAROLINA TEACHERS' CUBAN TRIP.

All arrangements for our NORTH CAROLINA TEACHER'S charming winter trip to *Cuba* are now completed and the party is nearly made up in full.

The number of persons in the party is limited to *fifty* and it is a most congenial, select and cultured company of *teachers* and *their friends.* Young ladies need have no hesitation in joining the party as we have several experienced chaperons in the company.

The party will leave *Raleigh* for *Tampa, Florida,* via Atlantic Coast Line from Goldsboro, on Tuesday, *December 29, 1891.* Special sleeping cars will be engaged for the trip. The length of the tour is fifteen days inclusive.

At *9 o'clock, 30th,* we reach the Plant Line steamer at *Tampa* and step from our cars into our state-rooms. We will have a lovely sail through the *Florida Keys,* reaching *Key West* at *5 o'clock on 31st,* and will remain there about four hours, giving ample time to ride over that pleasant and interesting city.

On New Year's Day, just at sunrise, we will sail under the guns of the celebrated Morro Castle and enter the *Bay of Havana,* the most beautiful harbor in the world. From our steamer we will be transferred by the wagon-looking *Spanish boats* to the *Gran Hotel Mascotte,* most delightfully situated immediately on the Bay, which will be our headquarters while in Havana.

Cuba is a land of perpetual summer and you will need while there about such clothing as you usually wear in North Carolina during June and July. Carry just as little baggage as possible—a very small trunk or a medium size valise will be just the thing.

We will remain in Havana and vicinity until January 9th, each day visiting the famous places of interest in and about that wonderful "eleventh century city." Special examination will be made of the *Cathedral*, where repose the actual *remains of Columbus;* the noted *Cigar Factories,* the *Cemetery, Observatory, Morro* and *Cabana Castles,* the *Avenue of Palms,* the remarkable *Cuba Mission* in charge of Rev. Alberto Diaz, the *Cocoanut* and *Banana Groves,* the *Plaza de Toros* (Bull Fight), the *Theatres, Parks, Jesus del Monte,* the *Tacon Market, Matanzas,* the *Valley of the Yumuri,* riding through the most lovely valley in the world in the ancient volante, *Caves of Bella Mar, Sugar Plantations, Mountains,* etc.

The entire necessary expenses of the trip will be only *seventy-five dollars,* which is about one-half usual rates. Of course it will be well for you to carry a few dollars beyond this amount for purchases which you will want to make. Only the *Spanish language* is spoken throughout Cuba, but we will have competent *interpreters* with our party. Carry with you *United States money,* either gold, silver or paper. Our money is current at par, and exchanges can easily be made when you want "Spanish paper."

"Necessary Expenses" include round trip fares from Goldsboro to Havana, sleeping car berth, meals and stateroom on steamer, landing fee at Havana, and board at Hotel Mascotte while in Cuba.

The party will be *personally conducted* by the *editor of* THE NORTH CAROLINA TEACHER in the same satisfactory manner as were our previous "Teachers' Tours," to Washington City in 1887, New York and Niagara in 1888, and the memorable "Teachers' European Party" in 1889.

Each member of the Cuban party will make an *advance payment of ten dollars* to the editor of THE TEACHER and your *berth on the steamer* cannot be secured for you until this amount is paid. All other expenses are paid by *each person* while the tour is being made. The advance payment of ten dollars must be made *before December 10th* and

2

delay in forwarding the amount may cause the *loss of your place* with the party. If for any reason you cannot go and will give notice not later than *December 20th* the advance payment can be returned to you. This advance payment is put to your credit as part payment of your passage on the steamer.

The tour begins at *Goldsboro*, and all members of the party will assemble at that point on the morning of December 29, and our train leaves there at 3.15 o'clock P. M. Persons along the Richmond & Danville and Raleigh & Gaston railroads will take the early morning train for Goldsboro to make sure of connection with our train.

The tickets are good for thirty days thus enabling members of the party to remain longer in Cuba than our tour, or to stop over in Florida if desired. For those who remain longer in Havana we will secure an extension of our special low rates of board.

Each member of the party will need a Passport and this important document may be obtained of the Secretary of State, Washington, D. C., on payment of $1.00. Attend to this matter at once.

Persons desiring to join the party are requested to address, with references, the editor of THE NORTH CAROLINA TEACHER.

IF HE (the teacher) can turn your boys and girls into honest, earnest, scholarly, self-respecting, high-minded men and women, be he tall or short, young or old, graduate or no graduate, Baptist or Unitarian, Tammany Democrat or Prohibitionist, he is the man you want.—*C. W. Bardeen.*

A VERY BAD HABIT.

Some educators seem to delight in parading the short-comings of the teacher; and many outside of our ranks are wont to speak contemptuously of the district school. Believing that our rural school-teachers are, as a class, more than abreast with public sentiment, and knowing how hard a struggle many of them have had to reach their present standpoint, we have little sympathy with these carping critics.

The country teacher usually needs encouragement rather than ridicule; opportunities more than censure. Bring him into touch with his fellows, pay him living wages ten months in the year, hold up his hands, help him to feel that the little red school-house in which he teaches is, indeed, a pillar of state, the door to the kingdom of heaven on earth to many a child; in every way magnify his office, and he will put himself in the way of growing in order that he may become great enough to fill it.—*School Education.*

THE OLD NORTH STATE.

The *Philadephia Times* in speaking of the Southern Exposition at Raleigh, and of the late material growth of the South, has, among others, the following pleasant words to say of North Carolina:

"North Carolina is one of the most promising of the Southern States. It offers less temptation to wild speculation than some others, but it has more substantial wealth to invite the immigrant and industrial classes of all kinds than any other of the Southern States. It has the most homogeneous population and one of the most genial climates of any prominent agricultural State. It has fertile lands, vast forests, immense mineral resources, superb water-power and accessible markets, and is to-day a better field for young farmers than any State or Territory in the far West."

THE NORTH CAROLINA TEACHER takes special pleasure in publishing such kind and truthful mention of our beloved "Old North State." The opinion of North Carolina, as expressed so gracefully by the editor of the *Times*, is in full accord with the doctrine that we have been proclaiming in THE TEACHER since the day of its birth, nine years ago, that North Carolina is the most pleasant, prosperous, progressive and worthily prominent of all the splendid galaxy of Southern States.

WISE AND OTHERWISE.

A list of definitions, written by an old Siamese teacher who was trying to master English, includes the following: Wig—hypocrite hair. Flattery—a good kind of curse word. Whisky—sin water. Gold—a very good thing. Blew—a wind verb. Kick—a foot verb. Bow—a salute verb. Hop—a frog verb. Liar—a bad adjective of boy. Modesty—a good adjective of girl. Vine—a string tree. Cunning—a good word of philosophy man. Daughter—a girl-son. Bullet—a son of a gun. Sponge—water foam. Angel—God's boy. Large—an adjective of preacher. Preach—a missionary verb. Comfort—word of mother to crying child. Adulterate—a bad adjective of lying man. Admonition—word of Bible.

BEAUTIFUL THOUGHTS ON BOTANY.

Here are a few live words from Dr. Horne, of Allentown, Pa., concerning the study of botany. They are good. He says:

"Now for botany! School is being called, at this season, in the great kingdom of nature! We have just had a good, long recess. Now let us up and to work. The botany class should be organized at once. If there cannot be regular, systematic study made of botany, the next best thing, or, perhaps the first best thing should be done, namely, to study the vegetable world in an informal manner as a great object lesson.

There is vastly more sense, and profit too, in teaching children the names, character and characteristics of plants than in the distasteful rigmarole, practiced sometimes, of holding up an object and asking a number of hackneyed questions about it in a stereotyped style.

What a freshness and beauty, and, withal, what an interest in the kingdom of plants! Take out your pupils, and commence with the first flower whose head is lifted out of the snow-bank. Familiarize the children with every one of the first flowers of spring. Pass none, neglect none. If you don't know the name of the early peeper out of the ground which is brought to you, hunt up your botany and be determined that you will know.

Don't miss the early crocus, the daffodil, the trailing arbutus, the various anemones, the violets; dig up the beautiful colored skunk cabbage, smell your fingers after you handled it; you will thus learn to know it by the sense of smell as well as of sight; climb the trees and bring in branches of the maple with their early flowers; ransack meadow, field and woods; there are intensely interesting object-lessons to be studied everywhere."

HOW SOME GIRLS STUDY.

BY BELLE M'DONALD.

Did you ever see two girls together to study of an evening? I have, and it generally goes like this:

"In 1673 Marquette discovered the Mississippi. In 1673 Marquette dis—— What did yon say, Ide? You had ever so much rather see the hair coiled than braided?—Yes, so had I. It's so much more stylish, and then it looks classical, too; but how do you like——Oh! dear, I can never learn this lesson!

"In 1863 Lafayette discovered the Wisconsin. In 1863 Lafayette discovered the—well! what's the matter with me, any how! In 1673 Marquette discovered the Mississippi. I don't care if he did. I suppose the Mississippi would have gotten along just as well if Marquette had never looked at it. Now, see here, Ide, is there anything about my books that would give you to understand that I know when Columbus founded Jamestown, and how George Washington won the battle of Shiloh? Of course there isn't. History's a horrid study, anyhow. No use, neither. Now, French is much nicer. I can introduce French phrases very often, and one must know I have studied the language. What is the lesson for to-morrow? Oh, yes; conjugation of *parler*. Let's see; how does it commence? *Je parle, tu parle il, par-il pa-il*—well, *il* then!

"Conjugations don't amount to anything. I know some phrases that are appropriate here and there, and in almost every locality; and how's anybody going to know but what I have the conjugations all by heart?

"Have I got my geometry? No, I'm just going to study it. Thirty-ninth, is it not?

"Let the triangle A B C, triangle A B—say, Ide, have you read about the Jersey Lily and Freddie? I think it is too utterly utter.

"Oh! theorem.

"Let the triangle A B C be right-angled at B. On the side B C erect, erect the square A I. On the side—did I tell you, Sister Carracciola gave me a new piece to-day, a sonata? It is really intense. The tones fairly stir my soul. I am never going to take anything but sonatas after this. I got another new piece, too. Its name is Etudes. Isn't it funny? I asked Tom this noon what it means, and he says it is Greek for nothing. It is quite apropos, for there is really nothing in it—the same thing over and over.

"Where was I? Oh! yes; side A C the square A E. Draw the line—come on, let's go at our astronomy. It's on 'Are the planets inhabited?' Now, Ide, I think they are, and I have thought about it a great deal. I banged my hair last night. I wanted a Langtry bang just too bad for any use, but pa raved, and I had to give in. Yes, I think they are inhabited. I should like to visit some of them, but you would not catch me living in Venus. Eight seasons! Just think how often we would have to have new outfits to keep up with the styles.

"What! you are not going? I am so sorry, but I suppose you are tired. I am. It always makes me most sick to study a whole evening like this. I think sister ought to give us a picture."

And they go to school next morning and tell the other girls how awfully hard they had studied.

———

DID YOU attend the meeting of your Teachers' Council last month? If not, why not?

THE CHARM EXISTS.

Some ungallant man has said there is no special charm in talking with a woman simply on account of her sex.

This is wrong. There is an especial charm for the right kind of man in conversing with a woman for no other earthly reason than that she is a woman. Simply on account of her sex she calls forth a deference of manner, a different train of thought, a different line of conversation, a more delicate play of wit and humor, than men generally observe in talking to persons of their own sex.

And all this is only natural. Men are often argumentative and didactic in talking to men, but these two mental attributes should be laid aside when talking to women. They do not like to be preached at or "teached at," and they do like to share in the conversation; they like to have their opinions asked and listened to.—*Selected*.

ORGANIZE.

The teachers of any county of any State in this Union, who are not organized into a County association, are depriving themselves of an incalculable power for their own professional good. The meetings of the association should be monthly, and should be managed by the teachers themselves.

Numbers are a great consideration, but they are not essential. Where two or three leading, active teachers are gathered together, there will be profit, mutual improvement and increased professional power in their midst, and that to bless.

Do not depend on outside, foreign, "distinguished" talent for a meeting. This may be called in at times to give added power and interest, but while an association that is not self-sustaining is feeble, it is better than none.

The officers needed are a President, Vice-President, Secretary, Treasurer and Executive Committee.

The Executive Committee should be composed of the President, Secretary and three other members of the association. These three members may be changed every month, to adapt the committee to the neighborhood in which the association meets, if it meets at different places in the county, which is best until the association is permanently and prosperously established when it will be found best to meet at the county seat.

The programme of the next meeting should be prepared and published at *this* meeting and no one should be put on it whose consent to serve has not been obtained.

Full accounts of these meetings should always appear in the county papers. The Secretary must faithfully see to this. In these reports the efforts of home talent, and especially of the younger teachers, should always be praised, and the interest and profit heartily magnified.

The public should always be cordially invited to these meetings, but their presence is not essential. The more successful and prosperous the organization, the less will it depend on the public, and the more it will be a *teachers'* meeting.

The President should exert himself, spend money, write postals, talk and push the work.

Teachers who will not invest two or three dollars, if necessary, in traveling and other expenses to attend these meetings, should not expect people to invest much in them.

Organize, friends, organize, and have good times.—*Normal Exponent.*

[There are now about sixty live, working and interesting Teachers' Councils in North Carolina. They are doing a vast amount of good and furnish much enjoyment and mutual improvement to their members. It is a fact worthy of special note that those counties which have an energetic Teachers' Council at work stand first in educational activity and progress, and are of very great assistance in furthering the efforts of the County Superintendents.—EDITOR.]

A FEW WORDS ABOUT HISTORY.

The method of teaching Geography has undergone a revolution and the same changes are now being applied to the teaching of History.

In our boyhood days our study of Geography began with the hemispheres and the continents and it was only the children who remained at school long enough to complete the whole course that ever learned anything of their own country and state. The present and true method of teaching Geography begins with the school room and a careful study of directions, then through the town, the county, the state, the country and then the study of foreign geography becomes more practical and intelligible to a child.

History should be taught in the same manner. The study of general history as a beginning is entirely too distant and vague and the average pupil thus taught does not remember enough of history to pay for the time wasted in trying to study it. Even history of the United States is much too broad for a beginning.

Why not commence with the history of our own State, NORTH CAROLINA; with events which occurred in places we are familiar with and among people we know, and with causes that were prominent in the formation of our own individual surroundings and the establishment of our country?

The importance of the battle of Alamance in 1773, the Mecklenburg Declaration of 1775, and the Halifax Resolutions of 1776 have been underrated in the making of this American republic. The "Boston Tea Party," Plymouth Rock, Fanuel Hall and the battle of Lexington are constantly magnified and taught to our children; but the *first* resistance to the Stamp Act at Wilmington, the *first* independent government of North Carolina, the *first* bloodshed of the Revolution at Alamance, and the *first* North Carolina martyr to Southern Independence at Bethel, the splendid bravery of North Carolina soldiers in the wars of our country, the proud record of the state also in peace, are uncertain facts even to the people of North Carolina.

How this colony planted the first English settlement in America; how the high spirit of honor guided our people in all the early colonial days and has actuated all their transactions ever since; how the resistance of our pioneers to English tyranny influenced all the other thirteen colonies; how the action of this state in 1778 secured those important amendments to the original Constitution which have ever since formed the surest basis of American liberty; how North Carolina soldiers, though comparatively few in number, exhausted the army of Cornwallis, thus largely influencing his surrender at Yorktown; how North Carolina gave the first martyr to the cause of Southern Independence; how her soldiers saved many a hard-fought battle to the southern arms; the noble conduct of our people during the dark days of reconstruction oppression; how all these things were done ought to be taught with patriotic pride to the children of every school in North Carolina.

THE NORTH CAROLINA COLLEGE ASSOCIATION.

One of the most distinguished gatherings of educators the State has ever had was in the rooms of the Commissioner of Agriculture at Raleigh on Friday evening, October 16, during "Educational Week" of the Southern Exposition. The call was issued by a committee of the Teachers' Assembly, consisting of its president, Prof. Hugh Morson, and Prof. W. A. Withers, of the North Carolina College of Agriculture and Mechanic Arts.

All the leading educational institutions of the state were represented in person while many letters of regret were read from those who were absent. Among those present were: Pres. Geo. T. Winston, from the University; Pres. Taylor and Profs. Lanneau, Poteat, Brewer and Sledd from Wake Forest College; Profs. English, Welsh and Bandy from Trinity College; Prof. Currell from Davidson College; Pres. Holladay and Profs. Hill, Massey, Chamberlain, Kinealy, Withers and Emery from the Agricultural and Mechanical College; Pres. Abernathy from Rutherford College; Prof. Dinwiddie from Peace Institute; Prof. Bagley from Louisburg Female College; Pres. Brewer from Chowan Baptist Female Institute; Pres. Hugh Morson (Raleigh Male Academy), Secretary E. G. Harrell of the Teachers' Assembly, Superintendent of Public Instruction Finger, ex-Superintendent Scarborough, Prof. F. P. Hobgood, Prof. E. McK. Goodwin and Mr. B. S. Skinner.

Expressions of regret at their absence, but promising cordial co-operation in the cause, were sent by Pres. Shearer and Prof. Smith of Davidson College; Profs. Hume and Venable of the University; Pres. Crowell and Profs. Weeks, Armstrong and Steadman of Trinity College; Pres. Long of Elon College; Profs. Mills and Carlisle of Wake Forest College and Prof. Ellis of Fair View College.

Prof. Morson, of the Teachers' Assembly, called the meeting to order, and after explaining the object of the meeting, and how the movement originated at Morehead City in a suggestion by Pres. Taylor during the session of the Teachers' Assembly last June, he called Pres. Winston of the University to the chair.   Prof. W. A. Withers was asked to act as temporary Secretary.

Pres. Taylor of Wake Forest College was called on and in a few well chosen words showed how much good could be done to the cause of higher education by union, and not only to higher education, but to secondary education as well, for each had a mutual beneficial effect on the other.   He stated that if the Association were to die here without ever being born he would feel fully repaid, as he had met more of the professors of the state than he had ever known before.   He stated that his own case was probably representative of many others.

Prof. Withers spoke of the success of the College Association of the Middle States and Maryland, and the good accomplished by it, and thought "we can find a good model in it for our work."

On motion of Prof. English a Committee on Permanent Organization was appointed, with Pres. Taylor as chairman.   The Constitution as recommended by the committee was adopted.   The Association was organized with the representatives present from the colleges and the University as members.

Major S. M. Finger, State Superintendent of Public Instruction, was called upon, and stated how, as "President of the People's University of North Carolina," he felt a deep interest in the work of this Association and in all forms of education.   He spoke of the present unusual prosperity of the University and colleges, and attributed it to the prosperity of the public schools.   He "would be glad for this Association to help the public schools, if possible, and in doing so it would help itself. More money is needed, this State having less than any State in the South for the public schools. It is practically impossible to get more at present for the the tax for schools cannot be increased without making the amount for State and county purposes too small, so long as the Constitution remains unchanged. The public schools should be able to turn out boys ready for college, and for this more money is needed."

President Winston called attention to the fact that in Massachusetts the majority of students entering the Freshman class at Harvard College came from the city free high schools. This, too, is an institution which has as high requirements for admission as any in America. If it is a necessity for Massachusetts, it is also a necessity for North Carolina.

Professor Hugh Morson, President of the Teachers' Assembly, congratulated the Association on the step taken, and wished for it success.

On motion of Professor Lanneau, a committee consisting of Professor Hill as chairman, Professor Brewer, President Abernathy and Professor Bandy was appointed to nominate officers. The following were elected: President, Dr. George T. Winston, of the University; First Vice-President, Professor Charles E. Taylor, of Wake Forest; Second Vice-President, Professor N. C. English, of Trinity; Third Vice-President, Professor W. S. Currell, of Davidson; Secretary, Professor W. A. Withers, of Agricultural and Mechanical College, Raleigh.

After a discussion, which was participated in by Professor Hill, President Winston, President Abernathy, Professor Massey and Professor English, it was decided to have the next annual meeting in Greensboro about next Easter. It was also decided to request the Teachers' Assembly to set apart a day during its session as "College Day."

A vote of thanks was tendered to the Commissioner of Agriculture for the use of his rooms.

The Constitution provides that the object of the Association shall be "to consider the qualifications of candidates for admission to the colleges, and the methods of admission, the character of the preparatory schools, the courses of study to be passed in the colleges, including their number above; the relative number of required and elective studies in the various classes; the kind and character of degrees conferred, the organization, government, etc.; the relations of the colleges to the State and county, and any and all questions affecting the welfare of the colleges or calculated to secure their proper advancement.

The active membership consists of the Professors in the University and colleges of the State, while the associate members are the assistants in these institutions. Retired college Professors in this State and active or retired college Professors in any other State may be elected honorary members.

The decisions by the Association of questions not pertaining to its own government shall be always considered advisory and not mandatory, each institution preserving its own individuality and liberty of action upon all subjects considered.

The work has certainly begun under the most favorable auspices, and it is a grand step in the right direction.

Upon motion, Major Finger, State Superintendent of Public Instruction; Hon. John C. Scarborough, Ex-State Superintendent of Public Instruction; Dr. H. B. Battle, State Chemist; Col. Eugene G. Harrell, Secretary of the North Carolina Teachers' Assembly, and Mr. B. S. Skinner, superintendent of the Model Farm of the Agricultural and Mechanical College, were invited to meet with the College Association at Greensboro in 1892.

AN APOLOGY DEMANDED, AND CHEERFULLY MADE.

. We have received the following letter from a friend in. Virginia:

Editor North Carolina Teacher:

DEAR SIR: In the November number of THE TEACHER you state that Mr. Sheppe, editor of the Durham *Educator*, is a native of Virginia. This is a mistake. It is true that he did live in Virginia for a while, but he is from *Ohio!* Please make correction and necessary apology to *Virginia.*   Yours truly,

C. F. K.

LYNCHBURG, VA., October 29, 1891.

We were led into this error by Mr. Sheppe's own statement that he was a Virginian — an "F. F. V." We now gladly make the correction and most sincerely apologise to the grand Old Dominion for such a libel, though unintentional, upon her good name.

THE TEACHER will have nothing more to say upon this subject at present, as we are too busy to waste our time in resenting the slander and abuse which an Ohio sojourner may see fit to heap upon North Carolina and her teachers. They have never received any better treatment from such men and they do not expect anything different, nor do they mind it in the least.

NORTH CAROLINA is now attracting more attention than all the other Southern States. The noble character of our people, the fertility of our soil and the charm of our climate are beginning to be known and appreciated throughout this country. Much credit is due to our teachers for this happy condition.

JOHN W. STARNES,

PRESIDENT WESTERN NORTH CAROLINA TEACHERS' ASSOCIATION.

WESTERN NORTH CAROLINA TEACHERS' ASSOCIATION.

ORGANIZATION 1891.

JOHN W. STARNES, Asheville------ ------ ------ ----------President.
WALTER HURST, Barnardsville.------ ------ ------ -------- Secretary.
DAVID L. ELLIS, Fair View------ ------ ---- ---- ------ ------Treasurer.

This Association held a very pleasant and profitable meeting October 29–30, at Bryson City, in Swain County. The good people of the city vied with one another in their hospitality, and would not suffer the Association to be quartered at the hotels, but open doors and warm hearts made the teachers feel at home around their fire-sides *free of charge!* And not only did they do this,

3

but *en masse* they visited every sitting of the Association, and made their visitors feel their welcome.

Among the many good papers we noticed the following as being unusually full and interesting:

"Forming habits and developing character at school," by John W. Starnes. (By the way, Mr. Starnes was among the first to second the movement looking to the organization of the North Carolina Teachers' Assembly, and he has ever been its warm friend and supporter.)

"How should a teacher proceed to obtain a public school in North Carolina — to open, organize, conduct and close it?" by Superintendent C. B. Way, Buncombe County. This was the finest, most thoughtful paper we ever heard touching this very important topic.

"What are the prominent causes of failure in teaching?" Miss Florence Stephenson, Principal High School, Asheville. A most able and practical paper, full of inimitable wit and humor and solid blocks of common sense.

But the event of the Association was the address of Dr. G. T. Winston, President of the University of North Carolina, on "Education." The Doctor was never happier in speech nor of finer humor than in this address, which touched every heart in the crowded hall. The visit of Dr. Winston made every teacher better, for it would be impossible to associate with such an eminent scholar for two days and not be greatly benefited.

The Indian School, located in Swain County, under Government patronage, paid the Association a visit, and the bright faces of the "red-skins," rendered handsome by the impress of instruction, lent a peculiar charm to the gathering. The school has organized a full brass band; it can hardly be excelled in North Carolina for proficiency in volume and quality of music.

During the sessions a most cordial message of sympathy and encouragement reached the Association from the officers of the North Carolina Teachers' Assembly, and several letters of friends of the organization also came from various parts of the State.

Among the committees appointed was one on "Professional Standing," to which was referred the matter of a training-school for Western North Carolina teachers, presented and discussed by the editor of the *Western North Carolina Journal of Education*.

At the close of the Association all the vehicles of the city were at the disposal of the teachers, and they enjoyed a drive out into the beautiful country about Bryson City.

The next session of the Association will be held at Waynesville sometime in July, 1892.

There are signs of a grand onward march in the educational army in Western North Carolina, and we expect to see five hundred of the teachers of the thirteen counties west of the Ridge at the great Assembly gathering at Morehead City, N. C., June 21–July 2, 1892.   — D.

[For the North Carolina Teacher.]

FROM EASTERN NORTH CAROLINA.

——

I am not given to writing for journals and newspapers, but Mr. Sheppe, from Ohio (he is not a native of Virginia), says some things in the *Southern Educator*(?) which do not strike me as just the things to say.   Perhaps he expresses himself awkwardly and does not mean a reflection on the people of our Old North State.

In his *leading editorial* he virtually says that the people of North Carolina do not want better school-houses, better schools, better teachers. *The Educator* quotes THE TEACHER in referring to him as follows: "Tries to belittle

North Carolina and all her enterprises," and then calls on
THE TEACHER for "the proof or stand convicted of self-
confessed malicious falsehood."

The proof is in October number, 1891, of *The Educator*,
page 1. "Teach the people," says *The Educator*. "It is
folly to attempt to supply a demand that does not exist,"
says *The Southern*(?) *Educator*. "For if the people wanted
longer terms they would have them," says Mr. Sheppe,
of Ohio. "If they wanted better teachers they would
get them," says the October number of *The Educator*.
"If they wanted better school-houses it would be so ordered," says Mr. Sheppe. "The truth is, where school
facilities are bad (*poor*), the demand for better education
does not exist," says this editor from the Buckeye State.
Stand up and receive your sentence, Mr. *Educator*, for you
are *self*-convicted. We quote from your leading editorial
and prove that you not only "belittle" the people of North
Carolina, but reflect upon her teachers.

On page 350 of *The Educator* you refer to "the self-
constituted defender." In North Carolina you will find a
very large number of people "constituted" in the same
way. *The Educator* intended sarcasm, yet he could not
possibly have paid Colonel Harrell a higher compliment,
for the true Southerner knows how and when to defend
his people from "belittling" attacks and unjust reflections.
So mote it be!

If our poverty, and division of funds from taxable property owned by the whites goes to educate the "brother in
black," and which largely prevents longer school terms,
it *does not prove that we do not want more education*. It
is, however, very unkind for *The Educator* to misrepresent
us, and to send these misrepresentations throughout the
Northern States or elsewhere.

"Wake up public sentiment," says this "belittling"
editor. He reminds us of a man riding in a car back-

wards, for he does not see anything until his attention is called to it or he has passed it. Is not "public sentiment" on a boom in North Carolina? The Normals at University of North Carolina and Trinity; the Normals for five years in the Congressional districts; the County Institute work by Messrs. McIver and Alderman, aided by Messrs. Moses, Joyner, Blair, Hughes, Claxton, Noble, and others — all able workers in the cause — under the wise administration of the State Superintendent, Major S. M. Finger, aided still further by the press of the State, the teachers, and especially that able and "self-constituted defender," THE NORTH CAROLINA TEACHER, and our Teachers' Assembly — have made education *boom* in North Carolina more lively and earnestly than in any other State. Better repeat the call, with a little variation, and make it loud — "WAKE UP, MR. SHEPPE!!!"

The Educator (page 350), it seems, would have us forget *our* Pettigrew, the scholar and soldier. Now the names of Pettigrew, Pickett, and a host of others, should be as household words to *our* children. To have these names in our copy-books, readers and histories is not sectionalism; it is the preservation of our history — of the names and noble deeds of our ancestors — and it is both right and proper that it should be so.

In a very recent number of THE TEACHER appeared a just criticism on "Montgomery's History of the United States." Perhaps *The Educator* would have us use in our schools "Anderson's New Grammar-school United States History." On page 300: "Seven States were united in a confederacy, of which Jefferson Davis was the President, and Montgomery, Alabama, the capital." On page 327: "And though the news of the surrender of Johnston and of the capture of Davis reached them," etc. This is every word that is said of Mr. Davis; does not mention that he was from Mississippi, neither does it state that he was Secretary of War during the administration of President Pierce, was in the Mexican and other wars, was in the United States Senate, and held other important and honored positions.

On page 326 of this same so-called history, fine print (foot-note), we find as follows: "On this occasion Grant exhibited the greatest magnanimity. He declined to receive Lee's sword, and in his capitulation paroled him and his confederates.—Alexander W. Stevens, Vice-President of the Confederacy." Now here are two, if not three, wilful and inexcusable falsehoods: (1) Grant did not have the privilege to receive Lee's sword, for it was not tendered to him; (2) we do not believe the Vice-President and historian made use of any such statement; (3) the name of the Vice-President of the Confederacy was "Alexander *H.* Stephens." Nowhere else in Anderson's book does the name of Mr. Stephens appear. There is not a picture of a Southern man, who was in the Confederate service in any capacity, in this book. Bull Run (Manassas), page 304, the name of the General in command of the Southern soldiers does not appear. This book is advertised as "New, both in subject-matter and illustrations," and to this we most heartily agree, as there is but little of the truth between the covers of the book concerning the struggle for Southern Independence.

The Educator's quotation from THE TEACHER, "North Carolina for North Carolinians," is properly understood by us, for Mr. Sheppe doubtless would have Ohio furnish the teaching force for "tar, pitch and turpentine" boys and girls, as some Northern geographers delight to call them.

This sentiment, "North Carolina for North Carolinians," as ridiculed by *The Educator*, pervades every section of country. If not expressly stated, it is so plainly implied that "reading between the lines" in very many Northern books is an easy matter. We take it that you, Colonel Harrell, simply meant that sectionalism should be kept out of our schools, and that such books only as are national in their make-up should be used. To this all will agree, hence we can understand and do fully appreciate the warning you give against the use of school histories (so-called) which wilfully and knowingly and grossly misrepresent us. Preference should be given to home people, and we know of no reason why we should go from home to get teachers. If our University, male and female colleges, to say nothing of our most excellent and thorough city and private schools, cannot furnish our teachers, then we are, indeed, in a bad fix. But who will dare, question these things? At the same time, we have built no wall to keep out good men and women from other States, and we welcome all, including Mr. Sheppe, who will come, to come in earnest, to be one of us, and to help us on to further prosperity. As *The Educator* says, "Get in the swim!"

Now, Mr. Editor, this communication is written with kind motives, with the hope that Mr. Sheppe will, in future, so frame his language as to not reflect upon North Carolina and her people. We like Mr. Sheppe; we wish him abundant success, and we attribute his lack of appropriate language to express himself to his youth. As he grows older he may improve. We want him to remain in North Carolina; to "put a little tar on his heels" to help him to stick and to have the "sticking qualities" of our native Tar-heels.   *   *   *

CHOWAN COUNTY, N. C., November 4, 1891.

I WOULD have my children able at each moment from morning to evening to read on my face and to divine upon my lips that my heart is devoted to them; that their happiness and their joys are my happiness and my joys.—*Pestalozzi.*

THE EDUCATIONAL EXHIBIT AT THE SOUTH-
ERN EXPOSITION.

North Carolina has again placed herself proudly at the head of the column of States by the fine exhibit of her schools and their work at the Southern Exposition.

In nothing is the importance and progressiveness of a State estimated more than by the efficiency of its educational institutions. Superior school advantages first attract people to a State or city even before its material wealth is fully realized. In this test of merit, as in many others, North Carolina is specially and peculiarly successful.

First in magnitude, importance and interest in the educational exhibit is that made by our honored University. The display occupies about six hundred square feet, and includes a fine collection of specimens and models from the Scientific and Biological departments; the Chemical and Geological and Botanical laboratories; the Natural History Museum, and the Libraries. A number of elegant life-size oil paintings of prominent members of the Alumni adorn the walls, among which are the faces of Hon. JAMES K. POLK, President of the United States; Hon. WILLIAM A. GRAHAM, Vice-President of the United States; General WILLIAM R. DAVIE, General BRYAN GRIMES, General J. JOHNSTON PETTIGREW, Judge WILLIAM GASTON, Judge ARCHIBALD D. MURPHEY, and Rev. FRANCIS L. HAWKS, LL. D.

The arrangement of the exhibit was personally planned and superintended by Dr. George T. Winston, President of the University, and Mr. Hunter Harris, instructor in the Chemical and Geological departments.

Next to the University is the "North Carolina Teachers' Assembly Exhibit," which we have elsewhere noticed in full. The familiar faces of Presidents Fray, Lewis, Alderman, Winston, Smith, McIver and Morson, and of many well-known teachers in the various groups interest the visitor, while the North Carolina flag extends a patriotic welcome.

Next we have the splendid display of mechanical and industrial drawing and modeling from that department of the Charlotte Public Schools. Many of these specimens, which is the handiwork of children, would do credit to older and more experienced hands, and the entire exhibit is fully creditable to the splendid system of public schools of that greatly esteemed North Carolina city. A great many people carefully inspected the designs, drawings and models with special interest.

The Seminary for Girls at Lexington (Professor W. J. Scroggs, principal) is well represented by a number of excellent paintings and drawings from its Art Department. The high grade of work shown places this school among the best in our State, and is an earnest of the efficiency and thoroughness of its teaching.

Louisburg Seminary for girls also makes a highly creditable exhibit from its Art Department. Professor S. D. Bagley is principal of the school, and the Art Department is represented by a number of excellent paintings. North Carolina is proud of all such schools.

The "Miller Manual Labor School," of Crozet, Virginia, has a very large and fine exhibit of work from the various departments of that most excellent institution. Professor L. H. Vawter, a member of the Executive Committee of the Southern Educational Association, is President of the Miller School, and a more zealous, energetic and efficient worker in this special branch of our educational system can scarcely be found in the United States. The exhibit consists of drawings and models from the engineering department, mouldings and castings from the foundry, and a large number of specimens of work from the carpenter and blacksmith shops.

The Virginia Military Institute, the most celebrated military school in the South, has a good exhibit of mechanical drawings representing the excellent work of the senior classes of that institution.

The graded school at Reidsville, under the direction of Mr. E. L. Hughes, the Superintendent, makes a very creditable display of "free-hand drawing" by the pupils in the school, ranging from ten to twelve years of age. The little folks have done well in their work, and they show evidence of very careful training. Drawing is a most important subject and should be taught thoroughly and carefully in every school. The work exhibited by Mr. Hughes has been frequently examined and much complimented by educational visitors to the Exposition.

ANALYZING A WORD.

A teacher gave out words for analysis. "Banknote" was one of them, and the teacher's astonishment may be imagined when one young lady brought the following unique analysis: "Bank-note is a compound, primitive word, composed of 'bank' and 'note.' 'Bank' is a simple word, meaning the side of a stream; 'note,' to set down. 'Bank-note,' to set down by the side of a stream."

THE MAN who is poorest in grammar will usually prove loudest in his denunciation of it. He turns to language lessons to let himself down easily.—*School Moderator.*

North Carolina Teachers' Assembly.

ORGANIZATION FOR 1891–'92.

OFFICERS:

HUGH MORSON (Raleigh Male Academy), President, . . Raleigh.
EUGENE G. HARRELL (Editor TEACHER), Sec. and Treas., . Raleigh.

VICE-PRESIDENTS:

1. J. J. Blair (Supt. Graded Schools), ... Winston.
2. J. E. Kelly (Model Male School), ... Charlotte.
3. Miss Catherine Fulghum (Graded School), . . Goldsboro.
4. W. J. Ferrell (Wakefield Academy), . . . Wakefield.
5. Miss Lizzie Lindsay (Graded School), . . . Greensboro.
6. P. M. Pearsall (County Superintendent), . . Trenton.
7. Miss Lina McDonald (Graded School), . . . Winston.
8. T. J. Drewry (Horner Military School), . . . Oxford
9. Mrs. S. Montgomery Funk (Chowan Bap. Fem. Inst.), Murfreesboro.

EXECUTIVE COMMITTEE:

Hugh Morson, *ex officio*, President, ... Raleigh.
Eugene G. Harrell, *ex officio*, Secretary, . . . Raleigh.
Eben Alexander (University of North Carolina), . . Chapel Hill.
W. L. Poteat (Wake Forest College), ... Wake Forest.
James Dinwiddie (President Peace Institute), . . . Raleigh.
Charles D. McIver (Pres't Normal and Industrial School
    for Women), ... Greensboro.
J. Y. Joyner (Superintendent Graded School), . . Goldsboro.
A. C. Davis (Superintendent Military School), . . Winston.
E. E. Britton (Principal High School), ... Roxboro.

NINTH ANNUAL SESSION—JUNE 21 TO JULY 2, 1892.

F YOU want to know how to interest your school on the subject of drawing, be sure to attend the course of lessons given by the inimitable artist FRANK BEARD at the Assembly next June. Mr. Beard has no equal in America as a "chalk artist," and his work with the teachers at the Assembly next summer will be of the greatest practical value to them. The entire course of lessons and the evening entertainments will be free to all members of the Assembly.

THE SECRETARY OF THE ASSEMBLY will be glad to exchange "Proceedings" with every other State Teachers' association in the United States.

MRS. IDALIA G. MYERS, President of the Normal School at Washington City, has accepted an invitation to attend the next session of the Teachers' Assembly Mrs. Myers is one of the most efficient and progressive instructors in the art of teaching to be found in this country, and she will give our teachers the benefit of her large experience, study and observation in the work of the school-room.

ONE OF THE most interesting and valuable discussions at the next session of the Assembly will be upon the subject, "School Advertising." An entire day will be given to this practical topic, and many of the prominent teachers of the State who have made their schools successful by advertising will give their views to the Assembly for the benefit of the younger members of the profession.

THE "North Carolina Teachers' Assembly Exhibit" at the Southern Exposition attracted a great deal of attention. Strangers from a distance were specially interested in it, as it set forth the fact that North Carolina was far in the lead of all other States of the Union in the magnitude, pleasures and benefits of our great State organization of teachers. The exhibit included life-size portraits of each of the seven Presidents of the Assembly and of Hon. S. M. Finger, the State Superintendent of Public Instruction; also a number of photographs of the teachers on their various Assembly tours to Washington City, Niagara, Canada, Mount Vernon, and Europe. The North Carolina coat-of-arms was displayed with the group of pictures and the State flag proudly waved over all. A large printed tablet in the centre of the exhibit gave a short history of the Teachers' Assembly and its grand work during the eight years of its existence, and the results of its work were briefly summarized as follows:

1. Brought together thousands of teachers and friends of education in pleasant social intercourse.

2. Carried the teachers over North Carolina from the mountains to the sea.

3. Visited most of the prominent cities of the North and made a tour of Great Britain and other European countries.

4. Secured pleasant and remunerative positions for over five hundred of its members.

5. Erected a handsome and commodious Teachers' Assembly building at Morehead City, costing seven thousand dollars, for its annual sessions.

6. Brought to its meetings many of the most prominent educators and literary men and women of this country for special lectures.

7. Created a general educational revival in North Carolina, resulting in a large increase of the public school fund.

8. Secured the establishment of State Teachers' Institutes in every county of the State, and the institution of the State Normal and Training School for Young Women.

9. Fostered a sentiment of greater appreciation of our teachers and increased the attendance upon the schools.

10. Organized the Southern Educational Association, which represents over eighty thousand teachers in the South.

———

EVERY PUPIL should be required to memorize each day a lesson from some standard spelling-book. Nothing less than this daily exercise will make correct spellers, and you cannot afford to let your pupils go through life as a "bad spell."

IN THE SCHOOL-ROOM.

A PIECE OF ADVICE.

BY F. G. B.

HILDREN, I'm going to
give you all
A piece of good advice.
Remember now each word
I say —
I cannot give it twice.
You've doubtless heard it
many a time,
As told in prose and told in
rhyme.

Each morning early be at
school,
There study well, obey each rule;
Be sure your hands and face are clean,
Your hair well brushed when there you're seen.
At home take care to close each door,
And don't throw things upon the floor.
Follow these rules, and though you're small,
You'll find yourselves beloved by all.
                —*New York School Journal.*

"God asks, not 'To what sect did he belong?'
But 'Did he do the right, or love the wrong?'"
                —*Persian Poet.*

"AFTER GRADUATION—WHAT?"

Questions are asked in *Kate Field's Washington* as to whether the young ladies who read essays at their graduation on "The Archaic Heroine," "Lockyer's Meteoric Hypothesis," "Mediæval Universities," "The American Referendum," and other erudite themes, know anything about the subjects that "good wives" should be familiar with. "What do they know of domestic economy? Have they studied the properties of foods? Can they discourse on the relation of candy to loss of appetite? Can they do one thing well enough to earn their salt?"

Here is the opportunity for some of these girl graduates who have been through a course in "domestic economy" to take a simpler theme now and answer these pointed questions. The domestic department in education has existed long enough to have its defenders.

PREPARATION FOR READING.

To prepare for conducting your reading classes, try some such plan of study as this:

1. Make out a list of new or difficult words requiring class drill.

2. Decide what line of questioning will bring out the meaning of each sentence, paragraph, or entire lesson.

3. Decide what anecdote you may tell. '

4. Decide what stories the children may be led to tell in connection with the lesson.

5. Form a definite idea of the benefit which individual pupils and the class as a whole should receive from the lesson.—*Exchange.*

LIGHTING UP A CLOUDY DAY.

If anything unkind you hear
About some one you know, my dear,
Do not, I pray you, it repeat
When you that some one chance to meet;
For such news has a leaden way
Of clouding o'er a sunny day.

But if you something pleasant hear
About some one you know, my dear,
Make haste — to make great haste 'twere well,
To her or him the same to tell;
For such news has a golden way
Of lighting up a cloudy day.
                    —*Housekeeper's Weekly.*

TOWNS — A SUGGESTION.

Locate each large town in your State on an outline map, drawn on paper or the board, and tell of each one—

On what railroad is it located?

On what river or coast?

Tell its business.

How large is it compared with New York City? Chicago?

What large towns would you pass through in going from Raleigh to New York?

Name some city or village in which you are interested.

Describe (1) its location; (2) arrangement of streets; (3) principal public buildings; (4) one private building; (5) employment of its inhabitants.

Make an imaginary visit to-day to Raleigh; take one thousand dollars with you; tell what you see and what you buy.—*Exchange.*

[For the North Carolina Teacher.]
AUTUMN WHISPERS.

BY MITTIE MAY E., FAIR VIEW COLLEGE, NORTH CAROLINA.

Now the earth is wrapped in splendor,
Clothed in garments gold and crimson;
Nature's summer garb of emerald
Has been changed by Autumn's fingers.
Touched as by a magic paint-brush,
Bright and gay with flames of scarlet.
Now we hear the merry husker
Singing as the sheaves he garners,
Singing as the brown leaves rustle,
Reaping rich reward for labor.
Hearts with one accord are praising,
Thanking God for all His blessings
Showered upon His loving children,
Like the gentle rain of spring-time.
Skies of blue are bending o'er us,
While we sing to God our chorus.
God of all the earth and Heaven,
Prince of Peace to sinners given,
Hear Thy humble servants sing
Praises to our Lord and King!
Great has been Thy loving-kindness
Unto Thy unworthy children;
Help us all to love Thee more,
Do Thy will and serve Thee better,
And, when life on earth is ended,
And the Harvest Day has come,
May we be among the garnered —
Gathered to the Home above!

FOR THE DULL DAYS.

There comes many a day in every term of school when it seems that the children are less attentive than usual; in fact, the teacher feels that she is lacking in inspiration and enthusiasm. For just such days Professor Beer has prepared his "Talks with Pupils." The teachers who use it freely find that it "bridges over" these trying days and renews interest in the work when listlessness appears to take possession of the school, and,. to some extent, even the teacher. Try the "Beers Talks" for your dull days.

THE SPELLING MATCH.

FOR RECITATION.

They'd all sat down but Bess and me,
    I surely thought I'd win.
To lose on such an easy word,
     It was a shame and sin!
We spelled the longest in the book —
    The hardest ones — right through;
"Xylography," and "pachyderm,"
    And "gneiss," and "phthisic," too.

I spelled "immalleability,"
    "Pneumonia" — it was fun!
"Phlebotomy," and "zoöphyte,"
    Each long and curious one.
Then teacher gave a right queer smile
    When Bess spelled "aquarelle,"
And backward, quick, she turned the leaves,
    And then she gave out "spell."

I'm sure I never stopped to think
    About that "double 1,"
It seemed like such an easy word —
    But one can never tell.
"S-p-e-l," I spelled it —
    And how they all did laugh!
And teacher said, "I think, my dear,
    Too easy 't was, by half."

Now Bessie was not proud or mean;
    She said: "No wonder, Jane;
For were we thinking of big words,
    You'd spell it right again."
I'm glad that it was Bess that won,
    And not those others.   Well,
If I did miss one little word,
    I showed that I could spell!
                  —*St. Nicholas.*

BOYS.

Every now and then you hear some young man, with a cigarette between his teeth, bewailing the fact that he can't get to the front because the old men are in the way. They should know that there are plently of old men who are anxious enough to get out of the way of the young men if the young men will only get in the way of taking their places.

The trouble is that such a proportion of men have to live until they are old before they know how, or before they are willing to knuckle down.   Be earnest, active and diligent in business, and you'll find no one will hold you back.

EDITORIAL.

"Carolina, Carolina, Heaven's blessings attend her,
While we live we will cherish, protect and defend her;
Though the scorner may sneer at and witlings defame
her,
Our hearts swell with gladness whenever we name
her."

EDUCATIONAL WEEK AT THE EXPOSITION.

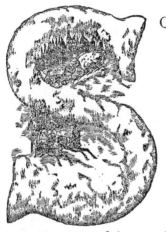 OUTHERN teachers have been interested in the Southern Inter-states Exposition, which was a grand . thing, bringing together thousands of our people to see the splendid resources of the various sections of our State and of the South. October 12 to 17 was set apart as "Educational week," at the request of the Teachers' Assembly, and it was a most successful occasion. There were present a large number of our most prominent educators, representing most of the leading schools of the State. Many of the teachers brought most of their larger pupils with them, and it was truly a pleasure to see these young people have so much enjoyment in their visit. It was a happy week. The weather was delightful, and both the elements and the people seemed to combine their powers to make school week the brightest, best and happiest time of the whole Exposition. Teachers met teachers and pleasant acquaintances

were formed which will be cherished through life. The occasion was almost equal to one of our Morehead City Teachers' Assemblies if social enjoyment and professional social intercourse is to be, for several years, the key-note of the educational prosperity of North Carolina. The exhibits of educational work by many prominent institutions throughout the country, which, through the energetic and efficient labors of Capt. C. B. Denson, chairman of the committee appointed by the Southern Educational Association, was so large and excellent, gave the teachers both pleasure and instruction.

SEND FOR our splendid "Premium List" of THE NORTH CAROLINA TEACHER. We think it will interest you.

THE CREATOR has given a great many more people the power to talk than He has the discretion as to what to say.

NORTH CAROLINA is to be developed, educationally, by her teachers. What are you doing towards this development?

WE ARE INDEBTED to the *School Bulletin*, of Syracuse, New York, for the cut which we use as a frontispiece in this number of THE TEACHER.

IF YOU KNOW of a teacher in this State who is not now a reader of THE NORTH CAROLINA TEACHER will you kindly send the name to us on a postal card?

DON'T LET the Christmas Holidays pass without having some kind of entertainment at your school. This will give enjoyment to your pupils and please your patrons.

THE *Southern Educator* of Durham and its Ohio editor must now do their own advertising, as we have "had our say" for the present, and now have other matters of more importance to talk with our readers about.

Do you know that North Carolina has the reputation of doing more "practical work" and less "foolishness" in her public schools than any other State in the South? This is a very desirable record and we are proud of it.

Are the city public schools amenable to the general School Law of the State—if so, how far? is asked by some of our correspondents. We refer the question to our State Superintendent of Public Instruction, Major S. M. Finger.

Only one North Carolina teacher attended the National Educational Association at Toronto, so far as we have been able to learn. There were present from the State some eight or ten other persons, comprising merchants, clerks, bankers and lawyers, all on a vacation sight-seeing tour.

The colored people of North Carolina have a very creditable history of their race for the use of schools, and they have adopted the name "Negro." The Teacher will therefore conform to their expressed desire and will also in future designate them as Negroes. It is the true name of their race and makes them a "nation," the same as any other distinct class of people.

Let the school supported by public taxation do its own work and do it well—thoroughly instruct a child in the regular public school course—and the people will be fully satisfied. This is all that the public school system is expected to accomplish, and it is all that it can, successfully, do. Do your duty well and attempt nothing else is all that is, or should be, required of every public servant.

Hon. J. G. Harris, State Superintendent of Public Instruction of Alabama and one of the Vice-Presidents of the Southern Educational Association, visited Raleigh on "Alabama Day" of the Southern Exposition — November 28 — and addressed the people in the main building on the subject of "The South's Wonderful Development." We partially claim Mr. Harris as a North Carolinian, as both of his parents were natives of Wake County.

THE TEACHER has enjoyed an unparalleled rush of renewals and new subscriptions during the past month. We have sent as premiums twelve sets "Six Great Books," forty-two sets "Ten Greatest Novels," twenty-seven sets "Dickens," five sets "Waverly," nine copies "Beers' Talks," fourteen "Black Beauty," and have also received thirty-one subscriptions without premiums, making one hundred and forty new subscriptions for the month. We thank you, friends!

THE VISIT of Hon. W. T. Harris, of Washington City, the United States Commissioner of Education, to the Exposition at Raleigh during Educational week was a proud and notable event. Since our teachers met Dr. Harris so pleasantly during his visit to the Teachers' Assembly at Morehead City last June, he has been a great favorite with the people of North Carolina. We hope to give our readers his strong address in full in an early number of THE TEACHER and commend it to their careful consideration.

EVERY SCHOOL AND COLLEGE in North Carolina, whether public or private, should have displayed prominently the "North Carolina State Flag." The flag can be easily and cheaply made and we will gladly send the design to any teacher on application. The highest order of patriotism is State pride, and we want every child of North Carolina trained to love and honor "The Old North State" as truly and sincerely as we do, and to cultivate and cherish an unwavering faith in North Carolina and a sacred pride in being a North Carolinian.

THE MOST appropriate of all gifts for any occasion is a good and beautiful book. It is always in excellent taste and it is a constant reminder of the donor, as it is also a con-

tinual well-spring of joy to the recipient. Messrs. Alfred
Williams & Company can supply anything you may want
in this line as a gift for the holiday season. For school
prizes, gifts to teachers, to pupils, to friends or relations,
for every style and novelty in the popular Christmas or New
Year Card, send to Messrs Alfred Williams & Company,
and your order will be filled by return mail.

DR. KEMP P. BATTLE, of the University, has done a
good work for North Carolina in the preparation of his
most excellent and instructive address on "The Life of
Jethro Sumner." Dr. Battle has done more to perpetuate
the memory of North Carolina than any other man in this
State, and his latest work is conceded to be his best. General Jethro Sumner was one of the most prominent men
in the history of our State, always "standing by" North
Carolina with a firm and patriotic devotion, and Dr. Battle
has done our State a great service in perpetuating the
memory of one of her most distinguished sons.

OF ALL the forty-four States of the Union the only one
which has "State Songs" is North Carolina. Our "Ho!
for Carolina" and "The Old North State" are cheered with
enthusiasm whenever sung, and they inspire a proud spirit of
patriotism throughout our State. Every true North Carolinian is in tenderest and heartiest accord with the patriotic
sentiment, "Carolina! Carolina! Heaven's blessings attend
her" and "Oh, there is no land on earth like this fair land
of ours." This spirit of devotion should be taught early
and continually to all the children in our schools until they
realize as we do the fact that North Carolina is truly the
greatest, grandest and bravest of all the States of America.

YOU CAN greatly increase the efficiency of your school
and arouse the interest of your patrons if you will introduce
a "drill feature." The manual of arms is a most admirable and beneficial exercise, and will be as much enjoyed

by the girls as by the boys. You can procure from Alfred Williams & Co., of Raleigh, an outfit of wooden guns, same size and style of the regulation army rifle, for fifty cents each, and a copy of the drill tactics for fifty cents. There is no sight more beautiful or interesting than a "company" of girls marching or executing the manual of arms. The exercise is as healthy as it is enjoyable, and for public entertainments or exhibitions nothing else takes near so well.

MANY of our educational exchanges are republishing Professor Greenwood's excellent article, "To Ten Thousand in a Year," which appeared originally in the *New York School Journal.* We notice, however, that some of the journals have stricken from the article the most valuable part, consisting of Professor Greenwood's strong and just denunciation of all the "shoe-peg, splint and tooth-pick nonsense" as so-called aids in teaching figures. The article appeared in full in THE NORTH CAROLINA TEACHER last month, and it was enjoyed by our readers. The shoe-pegs and tooth-picks must go — yes, they *are* going — out of all leading North Carolina schools, because such nonsense cannot continue in the face of public sentiment and educational experience.

COMBINED with the literary, musical and artistic education of the girls in the higher institutions there should be as much practical instruction as possible. For a long time a large company of young girls, under the charge of a lady of mature age, has appeared each morning at a meat market of New York, and while the lady orders the tradespeople to deliver certain quantities of the viands at her address, the girls stand about listening. The lady explains the different kinds of meat to the girls, and defines for them various ways of cutting. It is a class from a fashionable boarding-school obtaining instruction in the business of marketing and house-keeping. This kind of education should be given to every girl in the leading boarding-schools of North Carolina.

THE STORY of our "North Carolina Teachers Abroad" is now nearing completion and will be issued in handsome book form. The volume will comprise some four hundred pages, and will be illustrated by many engravings specially made for us, and thus the most important tour ever undertaken by the teachers of any State will be preserved in permanent form. Only a small number of copies of, the book will be published, and as a souvenir of the tour it will be invaluable to every member of the North Carolina party and their friends. The book will be beautifully bound in cloth and copies may be obtained for $1.50. Orders may be sent to the editor of THE TEACHER, and they will be filled as soon as the book comes from press. More than half of the entire edition is already sold.

SOMEBODY has started a publication in Richmond, Va., entitle "The New South." The misnomer should be promptly repudiated by all Southern people. Simply because the South is now the most prosperous portion of the American Union does not change our name to "The New South." All such efforts to "foreignize" our glorious South "makes us tired." No true Southern man can be guilty of a greater insult to our Sunny South than to try to change the name of our beloved country into "The New South." All these attempts to re-christen our beloved home comes from "The New North." Our country is *The South*, and nothing but the South. Persons who are not content to live in our country under the original and true name "The South" have full permission to go elsewhere or remain at home.

THERE have never before been such prosperous times with our schools as at the present. All the private schools are crowded with pupils, many of them being compelled to enlarge their buildings or seating capacity in consequence of so great an increase of patronage. This is specially gratifying, as the private school is to do the higher and finishing education of our children. The public schools are expected to give the masses a practical English education, but we look to the private institutions for the higher and complete education of our children. The private school has a place in our educational system which has never been, and cannot be, filled by the public schools. There is not the slightest conflict except when the public school tries to do what it should not, and cannot, do— assume the place of the Academy and prepare a pupil for college. It is far better for the public school to do its duty well than to attempt something greater and fail.

OUR TEACHERS have certainly done their part faithfully by the Exposition. A large number of them have individually visited the Exposition, while many more have acted upon the suggestion made by THE TEACHER and brought their schools with them. Our teachers have made the Exposition a great "Object Lesson" for their schools, and the pleasure and profit derived from the lesson have been of invaluable benefit to the pupils. There has scarcely been a pleasant day since the Exposition was fairly open that did not find from one to four of our enterprising and progressive schools from various sections of the State in charge of their teachers inspecting and enjoying the big exhibit of the State's resources, in a body. Some of the schools remained in the city from two to four days, and it has given us great pleasure to see the young people have such a good time. If all other people of our State were as true to North Carolina and her interests as are her teachers, what a grand forward movement would we see!

THE LARGE majority of the so-called "criticisms" of the North Carolina teachers and their grand Assembly by the pompous Mr. Sheppe, editor of the Durham *Educator*, is conceived in jealousy and born in his excessive vanity and conceit. His disease is therefore chronic and his present case is hopeless. His "adopted" native State, Virginia, could not tolerate his arrogance and pomposity, but North Carolina will try to be more lenient with this immigrating educational missionary and "organizer." North Carolina is as noted for her forbearance as for her other noble qualities, and this divine virtue will be exercised in Mr. Sheppe's behalf. Dr. Oliver Wendell Holmes has said a multitude of good things, but none better than this: "The human race is divided into two classes — those who go ahead and do something, and those who sit still and inquire, 'Why wasn't it done the other way?'" We commend this choice bit of human philosophy to the careful study of the editor of *The Southern Educator*, and will now leave him to his meditations.

WE EXTEND a most cordial welcome to *The Western North Carolina Journal of Education*, a new fraternal monthly co-worker for North Carolina and North Carolina's schools, admirably edited by our friends Mr. D. L. Ellis, President of Fairview College, and Mr. Walter Hurst, Principal of Mountain Dale Seminary, of Barnardsville. The publication is helpful to a teacher and patriotic in sentiment — the two principal elements desired in a journal for North Carolina teachers — and we wish it abundant success. The price is only fifty cents a year, and for $1.25 it will be sent with THE TEACHER for a year, including our premium for single subscriptions. We suggest to Messrs. Ellis and Hurst that they strike out the word "Western" in the name of their Journal, as North Carolina is but one State. There is no "Western North Carolina," "Eastern North Carolina" or "Central North Carolina" — we know of only *North Carolina*. North Carolina does not become a new State when it crosses the Blue Ridge or touches the seaboard, and it should not have a new name.

THE AWARD for the best account of "The Battle of Alamance and its Causes" has been given to T. W. Costen, Jr., of Guilford College, and the complete set of Dickens's works has been forwarded to him by express. We will publish the story as written by T. W. Costen, Jr., in next issue of THE TEACHER, and we think you will enjoy reading it. The committee of award was Capt. C. B. Denson of Raleigh Male Academy, Miss Edith Royster of Centennial Graded School, and Mrs. Lizzie Battle of St. Mary's School. The papers were all good, and specially meritorious were those written by JOHN GOLDSMITH BRAGAW, of Washington; MATTIE H. CARRAWAY, of Halifax; JOSEPH PHILLIPS and PERCY RAWLINS, of Battleboro; CORNELIA DEATON, of Mooresville; SAMUEL LONG, of Guilford College; JOHN A. MARTIN, WILLIAM MARTIN, J. L. MARTIN and JENNIE THOMPSON GAINEY, of Sherwood; E. L. ALEXANDER, of Hedrick; ANNIE BELLE SLADE, of Lennox Castle. We wish that we could send a set of Dickens to each of these boys and girls, for their work richly deserves it. Some of these young people are but eleven or twelve years old, and their story of the Battle of Alamance would do credit to maturer years.

THE NORTH CAROLINA TEACHER is the official organ of the Teachers' Assembly, and whenever any envious thrust is made at the Assembly, or at any other educational organization in North Carolina, by any person, native or foreigner, THE TEACHER will always be heard from very promptly and in unmistakable terms. It is the mission, as it is the pleasure of THE TEACHER to uphold without question the Executive Committee in any and all plans they may devise for the Teachers' Assembly, and for the pleasure, recreation and improvement of its members and friends. Besides, the Secretary and Treasurer has doubt- less proven his love for the Assembly by his work during the past eight years, having given a very large part of his time and labor for it, always refusing even the slightest remuneration for his services, while spending considerable sums of money in its interests. His reports have been promptly and regularly submitted at the proper times to the proper committees appointed by the Constitution to receive and audit them, and the reports have shown that there has not been a time within the past four years when the Secretary and Treasurer was not paying from three to eight hundred dollars months in advance for the Assembly, to be used in its building purposes and for expenses of the various committees. The reports have all been officially and regularly audited and duly signed by the committees and are filed for reference. The Secretary and Treasurer, the editor of THE NORTH CAROLINA TEACHER, has also paid the annual fee of $2 each year, although the Consti- tution did not require it of him.

ABOUT OUR TEACHERS AND SCHOOLS.

MISS LILLIAN COLLINS has a school at Newsom's, Va.

MISS A. C. HOOKER is teaching at Manteo, Dare County.

MISS BLANCHE WHITE is teaching at Nestoria, Dare County.

MR. JOHN A. MATTHEWS is teaching at Pamlico, Pamlico County.

MRS. GEORGE D. DRAKE is teaching at Castalia, Franklin County.

MISS BESSIE C. BECHAN is teaching at Troy, Montgomery County.

MISS IDA T. FROST has a school at Poplar Branch, Currituck County.

MISS LIZZIE JONES is in charge of a good school at Mill Creek, Per- son County.

MISS MAMIE WEBB, who is teaching at Wilson, visited the Exposition November 13.

MISS NELLIE CARPENTER (Trinity College, '92) is teaching at Tatum's, S. C.

MR. W. M. GILMORE is teaching in the High School at Tempting, Moore County.

MR. C. L. HAYWOOD (Wake Forest College), is principal of the school at Bryson City.

MISS W. T. DRAKE is in charge of the school at Willow Green in Greene County.

MISS SALLIE SHAW, of Pender County, has taken a school at St. Paul's, Robeson County.

MISS LILLIE LEA, of Anson County, has taken charge of a private school at Rome, Ga.

MR. SELL BRINSON (Wake Forest College), is teaching in the Graded School at New Bern.

MISS MAMIE L. CARVER has accepted a position in the Peabody High School, Lake City, Fla.

MR. J. C. LINNEY (Trinity College), is principal of the High School at Richlands, Onslow County.

GREENSBORO has been chosen as the location for the Agricultural and Mechanical College for Negroes.

MR. J. C. MASKE has been elected Adjunct Professor of Ancient Languages in Wake Forest College.

MR. WAYLAND MITCHELL (Wake Forest College), is principal of the High School at Aulander, Bertie County.

MISS ANNIE E. SPAIN, one of Pitt County's teachers, has taken a school at Whitaker's, Edgecombe County.

MISS OLLIE MOYE, of Wilson, has taken a position as teacher in Mr. C. H. James' school, at Grifton, Pitt County.

MR. ALLEN JONES, JR., and Mr. W. M. Gilmore, A. B., are principals of the High School at Pocket, Moore County.

MR. Z. D. McWHORTER is principal of the Institute at Greenville, with one hundred and ninety pupils enrolled.

MR. JOHN BENSON has a fine school a Juniper Bay near Lake Comfort, Hyde County, assisted by Miss Williams.

MISS CARRIE CARPENTER (Trinity College, '92) is principal of the Methodist Seminary for girls at Durham, N. C.

MR. B. W. GLASGOW (Davidson College), has accepted a position as teacher in the graded school at Coleman, Texas.

PROFESSOR W. J. SCROGGS, principal of the School for Girls at Lexington, spent some days at the Exposition in October.

MR. MOTT MOREHEAD (University North Carolina) is teaching French and Mathematics in the High School at Leaksville.

MR. W. O. HOWARD (Wake Forest College), is Professor of Latin and Mathematics in Jefferson Davis College, Mississippi.

MR. J. L. KESLER (Wake Forest College), formerly assistant in Raleigh Male Academy, has a fine school at Beaver Creek.

MR. H. A. FOUSHEE (Wake Forest College), is Professor of Mathematics in Chowan Baptist Seminary for Girls at Murfreesboro.

WAKE FOREST COLLEGE has an enrollment of two hundred and thirty students, the largest in the history of that splendid institution.

MR. E. C. WINGFIELD, of Virginia, is making a fine reputation in North Carolina as superintendent of the graded school at Shelby.

The College News is a lively young publication in the interest of Wake Forest College, edited by Mr. B. H. Matthews and Mr. B. W..Spillman.

MR. S. E. WARREN, principal of the Collegiate Institute at Wilson, visited the Exposition with a large party of his pupils on November 13th.

MR. JOHN A. GRAHAM, principal of the High School at Ridgeway, visited the Exposition on October 15th with a good number of his pupils.

MR. G. T. ADAMS, principal of the Academy at New Bern, visited the Exposition on November 29th with twenty-five young ladies of his school.

LOUISBURG COLLEGE for girls with its president, Professor L. W. Bagley, spent November 13th at the Exposition. The girls had a good time.

MR. B. K. MASON (Wake Forest College), is in charge of Cokesbury High School at Chalk Level, Harnett County. Over fifty pupils are enrolled.

THE High School at Menola, Hertford County, has an enrollment of forty-five pupils, and the number is increasing. Mr. J. P. Leitner is principal.

MR. BANKS WITHERS (Davidson College), is principal of the Thyrataria High School at Mill Bridge, Rowan County. The school is flourishing.

MISS ANNIE PATTERSON (Peace Institute), who has an interesting private school at Mangum, spent October 29th and 30th at the Exposition.

MISS ANNIE HUGHES, of Tarboro, attended the Exposition October 15th, accompanied by about twenty attractive young ladies of her excellent school.

REV. W. E. ORMAND, principal of the High School at Burlington, spent Thursday, November 29th at the Exposition accompanied by sixty of his pupils.

ON NOVEMBER 29th Captain John Duckett, principal of the High School at Hamilton, showed twenty young ladies of his school through the Exposition.

MR. A. P. WHISTENHUNT, of Catawba County, is principal of the Academy at Granite Falls. The school has bright prospects for a very satisfactory term.

MR. HUGH MILLER (University North Carolina), of Goldsboro, has accepted the Chair of Chemistry in the Agricultural and Mechanical College at Raleigh.

LIVINGSTONE COLLEGE at Salisbury is greatly prospering. It is a first class institution for the Negroes, and publishes a very creditable monthly entitled *The Living-Stone*.

MISSES JESSIE O. JONES, Daisy Newsome and Grace Brown, three of Hertford County's excellent young teachers, visited the Exposition on October 28th, 29th and 30th.

MR. B. T. H. HODGE, of Pocahontas, Va., has established an excellent school at Summerfield, Harnett County. It is an Academy of high grade and has a fine patronage.

ST. AUGUSTINE SCHOOL for colored boys and girls, at Raleigh, has an enrollment of seventy-eight pupils, the largest in its history. Rev. R. B. Sutton, D. D., is President.

MR. E. L. HUGHES, superintendent of the public school at Reidsville, accepted the same position in the schools of Greenville, S. C. We hoped he would decide to remain in North Carolina.

BINGHAM SCHOOL, now located at Asheville, began its fall term with seventy-five students, and there are new arrivals almost daily. We hope the enrollment may reach 300 during this term.

MR. LEON CASH is doing a fine work as County Superintendent of Davie County. He is inspiring his teachers with his own progressive spirit and consequently his schools are flourishing.

THIRTY lovely young ladies, pupils of the High School at Wakefield, Wake County, spent October 23rd at the Exposition, "chaperoned" by Mr. W. J. Ferrell, one of the principals of the school.

MR. E. W. SIKES has been elected Director of Physical Culture in Wake Forest College. He spent the summer in the gymnasium of Harvard College, preparing for the duties of his position.

WHAT a handsome publication is *The Trinity Archive* is in its new form. It is, besides, exceedingly well and ably edited, and is one of the very best college journals published in the United States.

6

THERE is to be hazing "no more forever" at the University or any North Carolina College. Davidson College gave her Freshman a royal welcome and reception at the opening of the present term.

WAKE FOREST ACADEMY is in charge of Misses Fort and Simmons, and a more excellent school of its class cannot be found in the South. The principals are teachers of rare ability and their school is "full to overflowing."

MISS CLAUDIA E. WAFF, of Gates County, is teaching at Cochran, Ga. Georgia seems to be very fond of North Carolina teachers, as they have captured a number of our best ones, for which they have our congratulations.

REV. J. A. BEAM is principal of the Institute at Bethel Hill, Person County. His assistants are Mrs. J. A. Beam and Miss Lula Ballentine. The school is in a most prosperous condition and has as many boarding pupils as can be accommodated.

CAPTAIN W. B. KENDRICK, the veteran school-book agent, has been quite an invalid for some time, but we are glad to see him getting well and again at active work. He is a native Georgian and a clever representative of a worthy State.

RALEIGH was proud to welcome the faculty of Trinity College with some two hundred of the students on "Trinity College Day," November 4th, at the Exposition. The unanimous opinion of Raleigh is that Trinity has "a splendid lot of boys."

KINSEY SCHOOL, at LaGrange, Professor Joseph Kinsey, principal, sent eighty-one of its fair young "School Girls" as its representatives to the Exposition on November 12th. The girls presented a handsome appearance in their neat gray uniform dresses.

A DELIGHTFUL Soiree Musicale and Reception was given by Professor Baumann's music class at Peace Institute on the evening of October 30th. The sweet music and charming company of the host of beautiful young ladies was enjoyed by hundreds of visitors.

MISS CORINNE HARRISON, of New Bern, has accepted a position in the Hemenway School at Norfolk, Va., specially being in charge of the Physical Culture Department. Miss Harrison is a fine teacher, and we congratulate our Norfolk friends on securing her services.

THE Academic Institute at Carthage, Moore County, has an excellent faculty, consisting of Misses E. A. Cole (Guilford College), and W. E. Evans (Hampden-Sidney), principals; with Miss Mary C. Bagwell, Miss Mary B. McIver, and Mr. W. P. Cameron, Jr., assisting. The school is prospering.

MR. J. E. KINSLAND has for several years been principal of the High School at Clyde, Haywood County. Under his judicious management the school has steadily prospered and increased its usefulness, and is now enjoying as wide a range of patronage as any other school in Western North Carolina.

Rev. J. M. Rhodes and wife, of Littleton Female Seminary, with twenty-five sweet young ladies of the institution visited the Exposition on November 18. It was a very cold day but the girls enjoyed their trip in spite of the weather. We are glad to know that this fine school is greatly prospering.

Davidson College was represented at the Inter-collegiate Southern Convention, held in Charleston, S. C., to organize a "Jefferson Davis Monument Association." We hope that every North Carolina college will join this Association, and thus honor the South's most distinguished and beloved statesman.

On "Masonic Day," November 18, the Oxford Orphan Asylum was represented at the Exposition by Dr. William S. Black, the Superintendent, several teachers, and about one hundred and twenty pupils. The pupils gave an excellent concert in the Exposition building, which was greatly enjoyed by a large audience.

The *University Magazine* (Chapel Hill) is doing a splendid work in encouraging its students and Alumni in the special original study of the History of North Carolina. And its work is meeting most gratifying success, as is shown in a number of most excellent historical articles which have recently appeared in its pages.

Mr. Charles Hall Davis is principal of the "University School" at Wilson. The institution is enjoying a marked prosperity, about sixty pupils being enrolled at the opening. Mr. Davis has introduced quite an innovation in school custom by changing the weekly holiday from Saturday to Monday, and the change seems to be preferred by both pupils and patrons.

"Wake Forest day" at the Exposition brought President Charles E. Taylor and almost the entire faculty and some two hundred students and many friends to the city on October 16th. The boys came through the city in grand style, making the air ring with their "college yell." They conducted themselves in an admirable manner throughout their visit and made many friends for the institution.

One of the brightest days at the Exposition was "Greensboro day," October 23d, specially made so by the presence of one hundred and fifty lovely young ladies of Greensboro Female College, accompanied by the President, Dr. B. F. Dixon. The "City of Flowers" was honored in its charming representatives. There are enrolled at Greensboro Female College 200 students, 160 of whom are boarders. This is the largest enrollment in the history of the institution. The school enjoys a splendid reputation at home and abroad for its very fine educational advantages.

THE schools for the Negro race in North Carolina are likewise enjoying an unusual prosperity, which is very gratifytng. Shaw University and Estey Seminary at Raleigh, Dr. H. M. Tupper, President, have an enrollment of about three hundred pupils. The Medical Department of this excellent institution is well patronized, and it has a faculty unsurpassed by any Medical College in the country.

NOVEMBER 5th was another big educational day at the Exposition. On that day there were present Horner School with about one hundred handsome soldier boys in charge of Colonel T. J. Drewry; Oxford Seminary for Girls, about eighty young ladies accompanied by Rev. Penick and several members of the faculty; Granville Institute, twenty young ladies with Miss Bettie Clarke, their principal; Oxford Home School, Mr. Faucette, the principal, with fifteen pupils, and one hundred and fifty pupils of Goldsboro Graded School in charge of Mr. J. Y. Joyner, the superintendent.

ELON COLLEGE is destined to be one of the most prominent educational institutions in the South. It is a co-educational school of high grade, and its graduates quickly secure good positions in schools as teachers or in business life. The institution is greatly prospering and well it deserves it. The *Elon College Monthly* for October is an excellent number, and specially fine is the article "Womanly Women," by Miss Irene Johnson, one of its editors. On November 5th Dr. Long, president of the College, accompanied eighty of his pupils to Raleigh for a day's visit to the Exposition.

DURING the Teachers' Institute at Ashboro October 28th to November 4th, there was a spirited public discussion between Mr. Marmaduke Robbins, of Ashboro, and Professor Charles D. McIver, the Institute conductor, as to the relative merits of the old and new systems of education. These public discussions are very beneficial, as they not only interest the people in the cause of education, but they rid our schools of useless "old fogyism," while they protect us from much of the objectionable machinery and humbuggery of the "new education." We hope these matters will be publicly discussed at every Institute.

"UNIVERSITY DAY" at the Exposition was October 15, and the Occasion was honored by the presence of Dr. George T. Winston, President of the University, accompanied by two hundred of the students. They filled the electric cars at the railroad station, rode up Fayetteville Street giving the "University yell" in thunder tones. At the Exposition grounds they formed columns of twos and marched through the buildings and halted before the University exhibit where they gave three rousing cheers for "The University," "President Winston," "North Carolina," "The Exposition," "The colleges for boys," "The schools for girls," "The city of Raleigh." Dr. Winston, upon call, spoke a few words of enthusiasm and the boys then had a "field day."

CUPID AMONG OUR TEACHERS.

'Tis said that "figures never lie,"
That one and one are always TWO;
But Cupid proves, with work so sly,
Some wondrous things that figures do.
And when he claims a teacher's hand
All rules of figures then are done,
Though TWO before the preacher stand
This one and one are ALWAYS ONE.

MISS EMMA WYNNE (Greensboro Female College), principal of the Sutherland Seminary, was married on October 5th, at her home in Warren County, to DR. W. P. HORTON, of Watauga County. The bride and groom are spending the winter in Baltimore.

MISS LINDA LEE RUMPLE, an accomplished teacher of music at Salisbury, was married on October 27th to REV. C. G. VARDELL, pastor of the Presbyterian church at New Bern. Rev. Jethro Rumple, D. D., father of the bride, officiated at the ceremony.

MISS LULA A. SPEED, a member of the Teachers' Assembly, who has been teaching at Lake Landing for several terms, was married on Tuesday, October 27th, to MR. STUART J. BECKWITH, of Hyde County. The ceremony occurred at Sunny Side, her home in Franklin County, and she will in future reside at Lake Landing.

PROFESSOR CHARLES E. BREWER, of Wake Forest College, married MISS LOVE BELL, of Shawboro, a member of the Teachers' Assembly, on October 28th. After spending several days most delightfully at Chowan Baptist Female Institute at Murfreesboro, the guests of Professor J. B. Brewer, the bridal couple returned to their home at Wake Forest.

MISS HANNAH SHINE ALLEN, of New Bern, a teacher in the academy at that city, and a charter member of the North Carolina Teachers' Assembly, was married on November the 4th to MR. CHARLES LUTHER IVES, of New Bern.

MR. THOMAS J. SIMMONS, of Wake Forest, Superintendent of the Graded Schools at Dawson, Georgia, married MISS LESSIE MUSE SOUTHGATE, principal of the Music School at Durham, on Wednesday, November 11. The ceremony was performed in Trinity Church at Durham.

MR. J. H. SMITH, one of Wake County's teachers, married MISS AMMA V. DUNN, of Neuse, on November 12th.

MISS LAURA BAILEY, a teacher in the Deaf and Dumb and Blind Institution at Raleigh, was married to MR. JOHN M. WYATT, of Raleigh, on November 12th. Rev. W. B. Wingate, of Greensboro, officiated.

IN MEMORIAM.

"Death hath made no breach
In love and sympathy, in hope and trust.
No outward sign or sound our ears can reach,
But there's an inward, spiritual speech
That greets us still, though mortal tongues be dust.
It bids us do the work that they laid down—
Take up the song where they broke off the strain;
So, journeying till we reach the heavenly town,
Where are laid up our treasure and our crown,
And our lost, loved ones will be found again."

ONE OF GOD'S SAINTS ON EARTH has gone to his eternal reward. Rev. Dr. BRANTLEY YORK passed away in great peace at Forest City, N. C., on the 7th of October, aged eighty-eight years. Sixty-four years ago he married Miss Fannie Sherwood, and fifty-four years ago he married Miss Mary W. Lineberry, who survives him, aged seventy-four. He was the author of an English Grammar; formerly known as "The Blind Man's Grammar." He was a man of talents, was a teacher for sixty years or more, and was blind for full forty years. In addition to this affliction, some ten years ago he was thrown from a buggy and suffered from a broken rib or otherwise. A most useful, benignant, gracious life has closed, and the man of God is now in the "saint's everlasting rest." He was a Methodist minister.

Dr. YORK was a remarkable man. He was twenty-four years old before he could read, and at thirty he was stricken with blindness. Notwithstanding early disadvantages and subsequent infirmity, he accomplished a work in life which will cause his memory to be honored as long as any who knew him shall live. He was the founder of Trinity College, of the college at Olin, and York Collegiate Institute, Alexander County; spent his life in teaching and preaching.

AT RECESS.

The books and slates now put away,
And let us laugh a little while;
For those who work there should be play,
The leisure moments to beguile.

KATIE (aged five years, who doesn't like to say "please")—"Papa, pass the bread." Papa—"If—what, my dear?" Katie—"If you can reach it."

"WHO'S WHISTLING in the school-room?" asked the teacher. "Me," said Johnny Jones; "didn't you know I could whistle!" And then the band played and the fun commenced.

NORTH CAROLINA STATE FLAG.

She thinks her thoughts in
    Greek,
While with a Chinese wash

The whole array of science
And problems mathematica
Whene'er she talks her he
    wise.;
But, to conceal their ignora

Not only is her learning far
But she in college tennis w
And in the college races on
Was always crowned the vic

A dainty pair of glasses on
Adds to her look of culture
But when discussing subjects

NORTH CAROLINA STATE FLAG.

(ENGRAVED EXPRESSLY FOR THE NORTH CAROLINA TEACHER.)

THE NORTH CAROLINA TEACHER.

VOL. IX.   RALEIGH, JANUARY, 1892.   NO. 5.

EUGENE G. HARRELL,   •   ▪   ▪   ▪   Editor.

A WONDER.

BY H. C. DODGE.

She is a college graduate.   Packed in her little head
Are all the living languages and many that are dead;
She thinks her thoughts in Latin and she whistles in high
    Greek,
While with a Chinese washee-man she easily can speak.

The whole array of sciences are at her finger tips,
And problems mathematical just bubble from her lips;
Whene'er she talks her hearers try their hardest to look
    wise;
But, to conceal their ignorance, they venture no replies.

Not only is her learning far ahead of any dream,
But she in college tennis was the captain of a team;
And in the college races on the lake and on the land,
Was always crowned the victor, to the music of the band.

A dainty pair of glasses on her dainty little nose
Adds to her look of culture and her statue-like repose;
But when discussing subjects with a Boston maiden's might
Her eyes flash through her glasses like a locomotive's light.

Oh, she is just a daisy.   Though the drawback of her sex
Keeps her from being President, her mind it doesn't vex,
For there are higher stations she is able to attain
By having so much knowledge in her active little brain.

And now the wonder cometh; this sweet college girl, who
    might'
Reform the very universe which men have ruined quite,
Stays at home to help her mother in the kitchen where
    she makes
The most delicious puddings, pies and home-made bread
    and cakes.

A man who thinks a woman's higher education tends
To make her hate domestic work, on which his bliss
    depends,
Should taste this maiden's cooking, for the more that
    women know
The more of sweet home happiness they're able to bestow.

SIGNS OF SPRING.

If you read these learned maxims and take note of each
small thing, you may come to be a prophet and foretell the
gladsome spring. When trees begin to blossom and the
violets to bloom; when the bull-frogs in the meadow warble
boom-ah-boom-ah-boom; when ducks are flying northward
and bright butterflies are out, and robins go housekeeping
in the broken waterspout; when grasshoppers are hopping,
and black bats come out at night, and venture in your bedroom attracted by the light; when birds fly down the chimney, and hens walk in the door, and beetles hold conventions in the center of the floor; when the mud is o'er your
shoetops as you cross the new-plowed land—you may count
on it as certain that sweet spring is near at hand.—*Harper's
Young People.*

North Carolina Teachers Abroad:

A SUMMER JAUNT

IN

England, Scotland, Ireland and France.

CHAPTER XXV.

FAMOUS ST. CLOUD.

ARRANGING THE TRIP—A LOVELY DRIVE—THE BOIS DE BOULOGNE—
A TOWER BUILT IN TEN DAYS—RUINS OF ST. CLOUD—ROADSIDE
BEGGARS—THE GRAND TRIANON AT VERSAILLES.

"TO-MORROW is our last day of sight-seeing in Paris," said the Secretary to the party while at the dinner-table on August 3d, "and we leave for London on Monday morning soon after breakfast."

"But we haven't seen Versailles yet," responded several of the girls, and we must visit that most beautiful palace in Europe, you know."

"Yes, I am anxious for you all to see the lovely and historic St. Cloud and Versailles," answered the Secretary, "but we haven't another day to spare unless you will consent to make a night journey to London on Monday. This will give us another day in Paris, and we will leave here at 8 o'clock Monday evening and thus we can have to-morrow at Versailles."

"We are willing to do that," said the girls. "We can certainly stand a night trip across the Channel in order that we may go to Versailles."

"All right," answered the Secretary, "that will be the plan then for to-morrow. But you girls must retire earlier this evening for you will have a rough trip on the Channel Monday night. We'll take a day, however, for resting in

London. Be ready at 9 o'clock to-morrow morning for a visit to St. Cloud, Versailles, and the porcelain works at Sevres."

"*Applez-moi a sept heures!*" said one of our prettiest girls, who did not neglect any opportunity to air her newly acquired language.

"*Je veux appellez vous de bon heure,*" in reply ventured the hall porter, who happened to be passing just then.

At 9 o'clock next morning our handsome excursion carriages were ready at the door of the hotel. In view of the longer drive than usual, an extra number of horses had been harnessed, and there were five beautiful iron-gray horses to each carriage.

"All aboard!" shouted Mr. Gallop, our clever guide with the "Cleveland white plug hat," and we were quick to obey the order.

The drivers cracked their whips and the impatient and spirited animals darted away at a full run with the heavy carriages and their thirty passengers. The air resounded with the deafening noise made by the great wheels of the vehicles and the clattering hoofs of the fiery horses over the cobble-stone pavement of the narrow Rue Matignon.

Our route through Paris was up the Champs Elysees to the Arc de Triomphe then turning to the left in the lovely Avenue du Bois de Boulogne which led to the Bois. This celebrated place covers nearly twenty-three hundred acres of land, and it is known throughout the world as one of the most beautiful parks on the globe. It is a favorite resort with the French people; it is equally so with the English, and more so with the impulsive American.

We entered the Bois de Boulogne at the popular hour— about 10 o'clock in the morning—for there were thousands of pretty and gay women and handsome men enjoying a delightful promenade, while the drives were crowded with rich turnouts and horse-back riders.

As the American flag was flown by the Secretary from our front carriage it won many a recognition and pleasant smile. Every American who caught a glimpse of the beloved, and honored star-spangled banner invariably took off his hat and waved it as enthusiastically as a Frenchman does at the sight of Meissonnier.

The Bois was originally a great forest and was kept filled with game. It was partly destroyed in 1814 by the allied forces, but Louis XVIII undertook the work of restoring its beauty, and under his direction new trees were planted. A little later Charles X kept game again in the forest, but during the Revolution, in July, the game, as likewise many Frenchmen, totally disappeared never to return. The completeness and beauty of the park now is the combined work of Louis XVIII and Charles X, assisted by over $400,000 in appropriations by the city.

Within the park are two very fine artificial lakes, and they are thronged with water-fowl which are on most friendly and intimate terms with the public. The lakes, in accordance with the Frenchman's fondness for big names, are called *Lac Inferieur* and *Lac Superieur*. The significance of the names are, however, reversed, and "Lake Superior" is not more than one-third as large or pretty as "Lake Inferior." In the larger lake is a picturesque island, upon which is an exceedingly Frenchy restaurant. It is reached by a bridge or ferry, and by either route the fare is "*dix centimes*" (two cents).

The Route de St. Cloud took us through the Bois de Boulogne into "the country" towards the little historic village of St. Cloud. We were all familiar with this place from our geographical and historical studies, but when the Frenchman spoke of it as "Son Clu" we hardly recognized it as Saint Cloud of our school-days. We were still more mystified when the Versailles of our childhood and our American tongues became "Varecæ" when given to us in the language of the Napoleons.

It was a question for frequent discussion among the teachers, while in Paris, whether or not in their future work the patrons of the schools and the public generally would tolerate the true French pronunciation of the French proper names by their pupils. Shall these foreign words be presented to the children of North Carolina in English dress or in the costume of their native country? We have not been informed that the query was satisfactorily and unanimously answered.

"Ladies and gentlemen," said our guide as we approached a neat suburban residence surrounded by a grove of thick trees—and we were all attention—"a few years ago a French nobleman made a wager that he could build a tower within ten days. The bet was taken up and he hired his workmen and set to work on the task, and it was actually completed within the time. There it is just to your right, its top rising above that grove of trees." We all looked and saw the trees and the tower in the midst of them, and exclaimed, "How wonderful!"

A lovely ride of about four miles, partly along the picturesque bank of the Seine river, then diverging slightly among those elegant suburban chateaux which delight the traveler's eye, again turning toward the river, brings us across the famous bridge and immediately our horses were reigned up in the historic village of St. Cloud. The stop was just in front of a restaurant and a cool fountain. As the horses were watered we indulged in a light luncheon of grapes and other fruit.

A short five-minutes walk up a little slope of a hill brought us to the Palace of St. Cloud—or rather its ruins.

This beautiful palace in the days of its full glory was one of the most attractive places in the environs of Paris.

It was built by Louis XIV in 1658, who afterwards presented it to his brother the Duc d'Orleans. The lovely Marie Antoinette was so charmed by the place that it was purchased for her in 1782 by Louis XVI. The Palace was built upon a hill which is cut away just in front of the building some twenty feet down into a level space which forms an exquisite garden. At the top of the flight of steps which leads to the garden our party stood for a few moments to enjoy the charming scene before them. In the distance the city of Paris is spread before us as some great panorama of beauty, in the midst of which rises the immense Eiffel Tower, like some sudden spectre, startling us with its nearness and its marvelousness. Then looking higher into the heavens we see the huge captive balloon, some thousand feet nearer the sky than the tower, swaying in the wind and seeming eager to break from its captivity and soar with its human voyagers into fatal freedom beyond the clouds.

The magnificent gilded dome above the tomb of Napoleon is flashing the rays of the noonday sunlight towards us as from a glittering mountain of gold. Surely nowhere else in Europe, nor in any other country, is there spread a landscape of such exceeding grandeur and loveliness as that upon which we now look!

The Palace of St. Cloud was a favorite resort with the Emperor Napoleon I, and he said it was because from this elevation he could see the whole of Paris like a map lying before him. In 1815 Blucher established his headquarters at St. Cloud, and on the third of July the second capitulation of Paris was signed in the chateau. The famous proclamations by Charles X, abolishing the freedom of the press and establishing a most unpopular election law, were signed here on July 25, 1830, which resulted in the revolution of July. Napoleon III was also very proud of St. Cloud and spent his summers there, and Queen Victoria was entertained here on the occasion of her visit to Paris in 1855.

The park and garden of St. Cloud and the Trocadero adjoining are noted for their rare beauty, and they are ornamented with many artistic fountains and numerous statues and vases, some of which are genuine antique and exceedingly valuable. The fountains play occasionally during the summer and they always attract great crowds of people.

This elegant Palace, of which now only the outer walls remain, forming a hollow square opening towards the Seine, was destroyed by the French in 1870, while throwing shells from Fort Valerian into the wood to dislodge the German army.

Of course the French people assert that the Germans burned the Palace while they occupied the town, therefore history is likely to have a continual conflict of opinion as to which nation belongs the credit for the present ruins of the St. Cloud Palace.

Our carriages were sent to the rear of the town to meet us at the northern entrance to the park while we strolled leisurely through these most charming grounds so as to enjoy all the fairy-like pleasure of the place. At the steps of one of the park terraces we found an amateur French photographer, and the party were soon posed upon the steps for a picture of the group, which we intended to present to our Teachers' Assembly.

Again taking our carriages we continue the drive to Versailles. The route is through the magnificent forest of Ville d'Array, in which are buried the Prussian officers who were slain during the siege of Paris. The road through the forest is quite hilly and at each ascent where the horses came to a walk the party was beset by beggars of various ages and degrees of ingenuity. They ran by the side of the carriages as they moved slowly up the hill, and while they collected a few centimes they accompanied their petitions by a most horribly squeaky accordeon, which tried to render the Marseillaise, but about half the notes were cut short by its consumptive bellows.

The most successful of the roadside beggars presented their claims in rather a novel manner. There was the same short-winded accordeon, the same dirty, half-clothed child-performer on the instrument. There was a girl about thirteen years old, rather good looking, dressed in full-rigged ballet costume, though wearing long pantalettes ruffled at the bottom and fastened around her ankles. She was mounted on stilts which were strapped to her legs, lifting her about four feet from the ground, and on these stilts she danced with considerable skill to the music of the accordeon. She kept good time, never lost a step or her balance, and the movements were executed with remarkable skill. Of course when the girl came alongside our carriages with the plate held out in her hands she received a liberal contribution.

About half a mile from Versailles we came to the Grand Trianon, a lovely villa, built by Louis XIV for Madame de Maintenon. The building is all on the ground, there being but one story; it is semi-circular in form and contains a number of most beautiful and richly furnished apartments. In the principal rooms but one color prevails in furnishing, and in some rooms the color is blue, in others light green, but the most attractive one is the golden room of Napoleon I. In the Grand Vestibule the celebrated trial of Marshal Bazaine was conducted in 1873. There are several magnificent paintings to be seen and some very fine and valuable specimens of Japanese and Sevres porcelain add to the adornments of the rooms, particularly the "Victoria Room."

A short distance from the Grand Trianon is the *Musee des Voitures*, an exceedingly interesting place. This building contains a fine collection of state carriages and harness

from the time the Empire was founded to the baptism of
the Prince Imperial in 1856. The imposing vehicles present an imposing scene of glitter and gold, and a visitor
from such a plain, practical country as America is almost
dazzled with the gorgeousness of these royal equipages.
The bridal carriage of Napoleon I and the coronation
carriage of Charles X were specially magnificent. They
were made entirely in gilt, nothing but the tires of the
wheels appearing different from gold. The coronation
coach is said to have cost over $200,000!

Through a long, straight and wide avenue of incon-
ceivable beauty we proceeded to Versailles.

CHAPTER XXVI.

CHARMING VERSAILLES.

TRYING TO ORDER LUNCH—THE FAMOUS PALACE—GLORIES DEPARTED
YET LINGERING—THE HOME OF EMPERORS—A PRESENTATION—
"CAROLINA, CAROLINA, HEAVEN'S BLESSINGS ATTEND HER"—HIS-
TORIC APARTMENTS—A WALTZ IN THE GRAND GALLERY.

We reached Versailles about noon, and it was planned
that we would have a lunch before visiting the palace.
Accordingly we repaired to a *caffé*, and as neither the proprietor nor a single servant about the premises knew a
single word of English, some of the party found it quite
interesting in trying to get their orders filled.

"*Garcon!*" said one of the girls to a waiter, "*apportez-
moi*, if you please *du boeuf roti*—roast—*caffé* and milk—*du
lait—du pain—*"

"*Excuse moi*," interrupted the man, "*je ne puis parle
pas Anglaise*," and he gave his shoulders a shrug and a lift
to his eyebrows such as is seen nowhere but in Paris.

"Ah! Miss Mattie," said Prosessor Winston after we
had all laughed heartily at the struggle of the young lady

with the language, "you must give him a very different kind of French before you will get the roast beef, coffee, bread and milk."

"But I know the French *is* correct, Professor," returned Miss Mattie, "because it is just as I learned it at school."

"And it may do very well for the school room," said our guide, "but the average Frenchman must hear his language pronounced very differently before he can understand it. Conversational French cannot be learned except from a French teacher, or by a residence in France."

As we were taking lunch we were besieged by numbers of vendors of French caps, flowers, music, fruit, "the only complete Guide-book to the Palace," pictures, souvenir albums, etc. These street merchants comprise children from four years of age to the grandfather of sixty, and their persistency was both interesting and amusing.

Having concluded our lunch, we followed our guide to the famous palace, which has figured so prominently in the sad history of France since 1671. The central portion is the original chateau of Louis XIII, who was so much pleased with the spot during a rest on the hill while hunting that he determined to erect the chateau as a hunting-lodge. To Louis XIV the palace owes its beauty and magnificence as a royal residence, and he constructed it according to designs by Mansart, the most celebrated architect who ever lived.

The amount of material used in the building and the vast number of workmen and horses that were engaged in the work seems almost beyond belief. It is said that there were at one time working upon the terraces and park over 36,000 men and 6,000 horses. The palace and its furniture cost over $200,000,000, and Louis XIV bankrupted the Empire twice by his extravagance in this building. At the time of his death, in 1750, he became ashamed of his reckless waste of the treasure, and that the cost of his extravagance should never be known he commanded that all papers, records and bills connected with the erection of the palace should be brought to his bedside and burned.

Louis XV was born here and also died here. The unfortunate Louis XVI resided here until 1780, when he was taken to Paris and imprisoned. Shortly thereafter the palace was visited by an infuriated mob, which included many thousand women, and as they thronged the court-yard the Empress appeared at an upper window, and by her appeals quieted the clamor and the mob returned to Paris. Since that time the palace has remained uninhabited.

In 1795 the building was used as a great manufactory of arms, and in 1815 it was pillaged and greatly injured by the Prussians. It was temporarily occupied by Louis XVIII, Charles X and Louis Phillippe, and from September, 1870, to March, 1871, during the Franco-Prussian war, it was the headquarters of the King of Prussia. A large portion of it was then used as a military hospital. King William of Prussia, on the 18th January, 1871, was here proclaimed Emperor of Germany. The negotiations between Prince Bismarck and Jules Favre on January 23, 24, 26, 28, which decided the capitulation of Paris were here held, and on March 12, 1871, the seat of the French Republic under the presidency of M. Thiers was located here after the German troops had departed. From this place the plans for crushing the French Commune were directed by Marshal MacMahon.

In the centre of the court is a splendid bronze equestrian statue of Louis XIV, and the pavilion near bears an interesting inscription, which indicates the vanity of the Emperor in these words, "*A toutes les glories de la France*," which the guide interpreted for his American company as "To all the glories of France." As our party gathered about the statue to examine it, Professor Winston stepped upon the pedestal, raised his hand to command attention and said:

"Ladies and gentlemen: In behalf of this most pleasant party I desire to express our appreciation to Major Eugene G. Harrell, who so wisely planned our trip and has so safely and satisfactorily conducted the party through all these thousands of miles of travel and sight-seeing. His unceasing care and attention have brought us to our journey's end without accident, loss or trouble, and as a slight token of our appreciation of his services we present to him this diamond scarf-pin, which we beg that he will accept."

"And, ladies and gentlemen," said Col. W. J. Martin, of Davidson College, "that is not enough. I move that this party do give to Major Harrell a formal vote of our hearty thanks for the unprecedented success of the trip, and for his uniform patience, kindness, courtesy and good nature at all times, which have promoted in such large degree the pleasures of our tour."

The vote was cordially and unanimously given; and the Secretary, as best he could, expressed his appreciation of the exceedingly kind sentiments of good will so heartily and pleasantly uttered, and his thanks for the beautiful and valuable souvenir of the friendship of the party which had been presented. In return he felt compelled to say that a a very large part of the credit for the success, pleasure and satisfaction of the tour was due to each member of our memorable party, who had exhibited likewise such good nature, congeniality, patience, consideration and thoughtfulness on all occasions.

The whole party then sang "Carolina, Carolina, Heaven's blessings attend her," with such spirit and enthusiasm, and the beautiful Stars and Stripes were worn so patriotically as astonished our guide, the natives of Versailles, the guards of the palace and perhaps even the colossal statue of Louis XIV, which was then being so highly honored.

Again following our guide we crossed the threshold of this splendid palace, the glories of which have thrilled all the world with admiration, though it is sad to reflect while we enjoy these famous works of beauty and art that they were provided at the cost of bankrupted and prostrated France!

As we enter the *Historic Musee* the effect of the grandeur is almost overpowering, and we can find expression for nothing more than "Isn't it grand! superb! magnificent!" The foundation of this museum alone cost over $3,000,000! There is nothing else on earth to rival the collection of historical paintings which are to be seen in this interminable number of apartments in the palace. To walk through the rooms hastily without stopping to examine a single painting would require over two hours' time, there being something more than five miles of pictures to be seen. We were not surprised to know that under Louis XIV the inhabitants of the Castle numbered over ten thousand, comprising princes, lords, flatterers, high and low officers and servants of the king, queen, dauphins, dauphinesses, princes and princesses, and valets of all sorts and ranks for the royal family.

To describe everything that is beautiful and bewildering in this famous palace would require a year of hard work and comprise several volumes. The massive ceilings, exquisitely lovely in their paintings and their wedge-wise gilded stones, the great marble, mosaics, sculptured and gilded wainscots, door tops, chase and gilded copperworks, ancient furniture, pictures, statuary, busts, tapestry and drapery, and the greatest profusion of the finest and most costly specimens of decorative art of the seventh and eighteenth centuries, combine in a scene of magnificence and grandeur that the recollection of it as we now write seems but some day-dream of loveliness which we once enjoyed— we scarcely know where.

Under the leadership of our excellent guide (who, by the way, is an Englishman, and he delights to tell of the departed glories of France while occasionally sandwiching a word or two about the present glories of England) we visit in the most satisfactory manner each of the noted rooms of the palace, while the leading points of interest are clearly explained to us. We are impressed with the great number of historical paintings which are intended to glorify the great Napoleon and Louis XIV. Specially beautiful are the apartments of Louis XV and Madame Adelaide, which required eight years in their preparation. Madame Adelaide performed on the violoncello, and all the fresco decorations in her room represent musical instruments. Everything in the apartment is sculptured and gilded in the finest manner. The Opera Hall, which occupied nearly twenty years in its construction, was used for great banquets under the reign of Louis XV; the apartments of the brilliant Marie Antoinette represent the combined taste of both Louis XIV and Louis XV, and they are indeed brilliant. The Hall of Hercules has one of the largest ceiling and single paintings in existence, being 150 feet, and in the picture there are one hundred and forty-two figures represented. The various halls are named for the special style and designs in paintings and sculpture which adorn them, and particularly noticeable and lovely are the Halls of Abundance, where it was the custom of Louis XIV to receive, three times a week, all the nobility who inhabited other portions of the castle; Hall of Venus, in which is the Ambassador's Staircase, a masterpiece of architecture and decorative art; Hall of Diana, where is to be seen a table of Louis XIV in Florentine mosaic, which is one of the rarest pieces of furniture to be found anywhere; Hall of Mars, for the concerts and balls; Hall of Mercury, occupied by Louis XIV in 1701 as a bedroom. Before the bed there is a chased silver railing which cost over $200,000. Hall of Apollo, in which is a magnificent silver throne nearly seven feet high, most expensively upholstered in crimson velvet.

Leaving the Hall of Apollo, we entered the Great Gallery, or Glass Gallery, which exceeded anything in beauty which we had heretofore seen. This Great Gallery is two hundred and forty feet long, thirty wide, and forty feet high. There are seventeen large windows, between which are seventeen arcades wholly of magnificent mirrors, which multiply objects innumerably.

From the windows is an exceedingly lovely view of the park, the gardens and their picturesque sheets of water, in which are located the wonderful fountains which have excited the admiration of the world. Immediately in front of us are the Fountain of Apollo and the Basin of Neptune, two of the grandest of the water-figures. In their construction the imagination of heathen mythology, combined with French art, have begotten exquisite designs which fascinate the beholder with their massiveness, extravagance, and loveliness. There is such tasty grouping of nymphs, dolphins, gods, goddesses and chariots, that if we were suddenly and unexpectedly to look upon such a scene we would be prone to believe that we stood upon the borderland of that country in which lived the all-powerful genii of the Arabian Knights.

In this room Queen Victoria led the dance in a celebrated feast of Louis XIV, and as soon as we were informed of this by the guide of course a number of our ladies and gentlemen participated in a waltz on the same floor in memory of the Queen and Louis XIV. Among the couples were seen our affable Professor Winston and the Governor's daughter, Miss Fowle. The French say that this beautiful hall was desecrated and disgraced by the Germans on January 16, 1871, when they here proclaimed the King of Prussia Emperor of Germany.

We next entered the Bed Chamber of Louis XIV, containing the bed upon which he died September 1, 1715. From the balcony of this room the chamberlain announced to the people the death of the King by exclaiming, "*Le Roi est mort!*" and then he broke his wand of office. He then took a new one and exclaimed, "*Vive le Roi!*" and the government began to exist under its new king. From the balcony of the window in this room Louis XVI and Marie Antoinette appeased the howling and infuriated mob of Parisians and promised that they would make their residence in Paris. In the private apartments of Marie Antoinette are some very rare and fine specimens of cabinets of the Louis XVI era. Near these apartments is the Queen's Room, which has been occupied by Queen Marie Therese, wife of Louis XIV; the Dauphiness of Bavaria, wife of the Grand Dauphin, son of Louis XIV; the Duchess of Burgundy; the Infanta of Spain, betrothed to Louis XV; and Queen Marie Antoinette for nearly twenty years. The guide added to our interest by informing us that nineteen princes and princesses were born in that room !

HOW TO TEACH COMPOSITION.

1. Add to the children's conversational vocabulary all the new words in the reading lesson.

2. Develop the power of oral expression in your pupils by a few well prepared questions on the lesson.

3. Let children describe pictures in books, each write a sentence about it on slate; then on blackboard. Let teacher correct what pupils cannot. Then all write sentences correctly.

2

4. Let the teacher write questions on the board about the lesson; the children write the answers at their seats on slates, and bring them to recitation.

5. Occasionally read a short story and require the children to reproduce it in their own language.

6. Allow impromptu composition to take the place of reading every Friday afternoon.

7. By judicious management letter-writing may come in at the close of the second school year.

8. Whenever the pupil can tell a story pretty well, require him to write out the same.

9. Correct one fault at a time.

10. In all your methods in all studies, develop the power of *correct* expression.

11. There should be much pen, pencil and crayon-work in our schools.

12. Commend the best your pupils can do.

13. Business forms should also be taught.

14. All exercises should be carefully criticised, and one criticism to each pupil is better than many general ones.

15. Methods that lead to composition writing are: (*a*) Sentence making; (*b*) filling blanks in sentence making; (*c*) capitalization; (*d*) punctuation.

16. Results of oral instruction should be expressed in composition.—*The Fountain.*

BRIGHT GIRLS.

Speaking generally, it is statistically shown that the average school-girl is brighter than the average school-boy. And since this is so it is but fair to conclude that a woman who has had the same social advantages as the man with whom she is conversing is actually superior to him in cleverness and tact. She may not have had equal educational advantages, but perhaps she had those which, in rounding up character, are quite as good as his, though different, for while the young man is in college studying books the young woman is learning life at first hand.

GIRLS WHO MAKE POOR WIVES.

It is "the worshipped daughter," who has been taught that her whims and wishes are supreme in a household, who makes marriage a failure all her life. She has had her way in things great and small; and when she desired dresses, pleasures or journeys which were beyond the family purse, she carried the day with tears or sulks, or by posing as a martyr. The parents sacrificed and suffered for her sake, hoping finally to see her well married.

The average man is blind to the faults of a pretty girl. He thinks her little pettish ways are mere girlish moods; but when she becomes his wife and reveals her selfish and cruel nature, he is grieved and hurt to think that Fate has been so unkind to him.

SLEEP FOR SCHOOL-CHILDREN.

We all know how much greater is the need of sleep for children than for grown persons, and how necessary for their good it is to be able fully to satisfy this need; but how great it is generally at any particular age of the child is very hard to define exactly.

The amount varies under different climatic conditions. In Sweden we consider a sleep of eleven or twelve hours necessary for the younger school-children, and of at least eight or nine for the older ones. Yet the investigations have shown that this requirement lacks much of being met in all the classes through the whole school.

Boys in the higher classes get little more than seven hours in bed; and as that is the average, it is easy to perceive that many of them must content themselves with still less sleep. It is also evident from investigations that the sleeping time is diminished with the increase of the working hours, from class to class, so that the pupils of the same age enjoy less, according as they are higher in their classes.

It thus appears constantly that in schools of relatively longer hours of work the sleeping time of the pupils is correspondingly shorter. In short, the prolongation of the working hours takes place at the cost of the time for sleep.— *Exchange.*

EDUCATE THE YOUNG MEN.

A writer in the *New York Sun* asks: "Does it pay to educate young men?" It pays to give all young men a common school education, provided Religion be joined as a fourth to the three R's, though it may not be possible to acquire it at school.

But whether it pays to give a college education to young men depends. It would be a woeful waste of money, time, and nerve tension, if all the young farmers, and mechanics and clerks of the country were made to take a four years' college course—four valuable years lost to the farm, shop, and store.

On the other hand it pays to send young men to college who will utilize that education in after-life by contributing to the cause of popular knowledge and by doing something for the benefit of others.

When improvements are made in the country a careful survey of the land is made, that its facilities may be utilized to the best advantage. When it is proposed to educate a boy, make a careful survey of him and find out whether he has facilities for acquiring and utilizing a college education, before sending him for a prize which he would not value. A painter assayed to become an artist and stopped at a sign-post. A farmer took his boy out of college where he was idling, learning nothing, because he did not "propose to spend a thousand dollars on a five-dollar boy." Both incidents are suggestive, and may serve a purpose in helping answer the interrogative, "Will it pay to educate the young man?"—*Christian at Work.*

TROUBLE WITH THE GRAMMARIANS.

A writer in *The Christian World* sends up this little rocket to shed light upon the confusion existing in the minds of many very well educated people in regard to the use of the two words "sit" and "set"—a confusion similar to that which seems to attend upon the choice of saying "will" or "shall":

"A man, or woman either, can set a hen, although they cannot sit her; neither can they set on her, although the old hen might sit on them by the hour if they would allow. A man cannot set on the wash-bench, but he could set the basin on it, and neither the basin nor the grammarians would object. He could sit on the dog's tail if the dog were willing, or he might set his foot on it. But if he should set on the aforesaid tail, or sit his foot there, the grammarians, as well as the dog, would howl. And yet, strange as it may seem, the man might set the tail aside and then sit down, and neither be assailed by the dog nor the grammarians.''

THE GIRL WHO TEACHES.

Sound health is a prime necessity for any worker in the world, no matter what the line of work may be, but it becomes of the greatest importance if the work is to be carried on in the school-room, writes Caroline B. Le Row in the September *Ladies' Home Journal.* There not only the physical, but the nervous and mental forces are taxed to their utmost.

The young graduate has hitherto gone to school to sit comfortably at her desk; to stand occasionally for recitations; to use her voice but little; to have constant variety in her work; to enjoy her recess with perfect freedom and in congenial companionship.

As a teacher she goes to school to stand upon her feet all day long; to use her voice incessantly, perhaps, too, in a large room filled with the tumult of the street; to keep noisy, and, very likely, rebellious and disobedient children not only quiet, but interested, and to spend the recess in care of them in the halls and the yard.

Besides this she is to stimulate their brains, and a certain amount of time—usually prescribed by a board of education, the members of which know little of the capacity and possibilities of the youthful mind—is allotted her, in which she must, somehow or other, succeed in teaching them a certain number of facts—no allowance being made for the slowness, stupidity or disorder which increases the friction of the work and delays the doing.

No matter how complete the education, or how enthusiastic the spirit, the power for physical endurance is absolutely necessary.

THE WELL-BRED WOMAN.

One hears and reads more about the hoyden than the well-bred woman, but some one has recently taken occasion to say the following words for the latter: This sweetly austere and gently repellant lady does not wear paint on her lips or lampblack on her eyebrows. She does not make up a gaudy toilet for the street, there are no diamonds in her ears, no feathers in her bonnet, no stick pins in her jacket nor jewel pins in her hair.

Her umbrella is not silver trimmed, neither is her purse. She doesn't stare you out of countenance; her remarks are not cutting, and her voice is never audible to a third person. She is a gracious creature; her influence is divine, her acquaintance a boon and her friendship a blessing. Best of all her name is legion.—*Exchange.*

DRESS OF TEACHERS.

"Which of these young ladies would I select for the ideal teacher?" asked an observer of herself as she watched the bright-faced students of a normal school strolling arm in arm through one of the corridors of the building. "Not this one," looking at a pretty girl whose disordered, even untidy, dress betrayed a very unpromising carelessness. "Nor this," as her eyes fell on an intelligent looking young woman, severely neat in dress, but, alas! laced into a long, tapering bodice that made one wonder on what anatomical principal she could possibly have been constructed.

"If I were selecting an assistant for a school of my own would I really reject an intelligent, energetic, and capable-seeming candidate because her ideas of dress did not agree with my own?" Not quite that, but, other things being equal, I should certainly prefer a teacher whose dress was neat, well chosen, and hygienic, to one who was untidy or dressed in violation of well-known laws of health.

For one thing, no woman in a tight dress, collar, or shoes can possibly have thorough command of her mind or her temper; the whole intellectual and emotional tone is lowered, just as the physical powers are limited. The energy used merely in resisting the disadvantages of a hampered dress might accomplish much if set free and properly employed.

Then, too, I should be somewhat unwilling to trust the practical judgment of a teacher who was so *un*practical as to wear a dress that must be more or less injurious to her. However high her intellectual aims and ideas, I should fear there was something lacking in her conception of well-rounded development for her pupils.—*N. Y. School Journal.*

THE BEST USE OF TIME.

A boy who is good for anything does not want a long vacation that he may do nothing, or in order to rest.

Most boys are not tired, even at the end of the school year. What they do want is activity, and that means education of another sort from what school-life ordinarily gives.

The summer vacation is too long for any one, teacher or scholar, who does not use a good part of it for education. There is a growing appreciation of this fact among educators and among parents.

Summer schools and summer camps have grown rapidly in number and consequence of late. The study of Nature interests more people every year. The development of amateur photography means a great advance in outdoor facilities for education. Everybody travels nowadays, and there is no better way to learn.—*Exchange.*

THE UGLY GIRL.

It is a strange fact that " the ugly girl " is rather a favorite than otherwise, although "a thing of beauty is a joy forever." When we look at her we lament the shape of her nose, we sigh over the cast in her eye, we deplore the dullness of her complexion, we can find nothing to praise; but perhaps she smiles, or she has a bewitching manner. She knows the spell which puts everyone at his ease; she owns the charm which makes others pleased with themselves; and then we are wont to say that there is no such person as the ugly girl. But to those who do not know her, who do not come under the magnetism of her presence, she remains the ugly girl to the end of the chapter, and when she marries and carries off the best match of the season, perhaps, prettier women are at their wits' end to know what attractions she possesses superior to their own.

What is it that redeems the ugly face and makes it shine with comeliness, so that we sometimes would not exchange it, with all its misshapen features, for the beauty of Aphrodite? The plain face which is alive with intelligence, which beams with an expression of refinement and good nature, which culture and high-mindedness animate, becomes sometimes finer and more effective than mere prettiness, mere pink and white loveliness, mere shapeliness and symmetry of feature.

A pretty face has been known to pall upon one, but who has sounded the depth of attraction which resides in a mobile countenance where the features may be found to swear at each other, so to speak? But the ugly girl must choose her colors and fashions wisely. She must not be ultra and conspicuous; she must know how to bring out whatever charms exist in her face or figure, if she would overcome the defects; if her nose is large, the hair on the top of her head will be most becoming; if her face is heavy, a turban hat that covers the forehead will add to its disfigurement; if her ears are large and ill-shapen, she should not wear ear-rings. She should first of all recognize her defects.

The ugly girl has some advantages over her pretty sister; she does not fade so early, or at least her fading is not so palpable, and she is usually a better-looking matron than a girl.—*Selected.*

THE SESSION of the Teachers' Assembly at Morehead City this summer will be a grand educational jubilee in North Carolina. Everything that the teachers have asked of the Legislature has been granted, and all the schools of the State are in a prosperous condition. Such a satisfactory state of affairs will be duly celebrated when thousands of our teachers gather at Morehead City in June.

IN THE SCHOOL-ROOM.

AS YOU GO THROUGH LIFE.

Don't look for the flaws as you go through life;
    And even when you find them,
It is wise and kind to be somewhat blind
    And look for the virtue behind them,
For the cloudiest night has a hint of light,
    Somewhere in its shadows hiding;
It is better by far to hunt for a star
    Than the spots on the sun abiding.

The current of life runs every way
    To the bosom of God's great ocean;
Don't set your force 'gainst the river's course
    And think to alter its motion.
Don't waste a curse on the universe—
    Remember it lived before you;
Don't butt at the storm with your puny form,
    But bend and let it go o'er you.

The world will never adjust itself
    To suit your whims to the letter;
Some things must go wrong your whole life long,
    And the sooner you know it the better.
It is folly to fight the Infinite,
    And go under at last in the wrestle;
The wise man shapes into God's plan
    As the water shapes into a vessel.
                —Ella Wheeler Wilcox.

LAUGHING.

A hearty laugh, which is ever in order, stirs up the physical man from the center to the circumference, and tends to improve the whole physical and spiritual being. It promotes animal health and spirits, and is to the man what the tides are to the ocean; it stirs up the sluggish depths, prevents stagnation, and keeps the whole system fresh and wholesome. It is what the Gulf Stream is to the ocean—a vivifying and warming element. The convulsion produced by hearty laughter penetrates to the minutest blood vessel, and causes the blood to flow with a freshened impulse.

Laughter shuts the mouth of malice and opens the brow of kindness. Whether it discovers the gums of infancy or age, the grinders of folly or pearls of beauty, whether it racks the sides or deforms the countenance of vulgarity, or deep-lines the visage, or moistens the eye of refinement—in all its phases, and on all faces, comforting, relaxing, overwhelming, convulsing, throwing the human form into happy shaking and quaking, a laugh is a glorious thing.— *Exchange.*

THE RAINY DAY.

Now comes the days of trial to the district school-teacher. The bad weather, the cold and the wet will compel the pupils to remain indoors at recesses and noonings. The room will lack ventilation, pupils will feel the effects of it, and it will take tact, patience, wisdom, pluck to make all go along smoothly now. Secure, if possible, some good reading—some choice story—reading it during half of the nooning.

Geography games, history recitations, spelling matches, puzzles, conundrums, dissected maps, sliced pictures, etc., will prove helpful. At any rate, have order in the house at all times. No loud talking, uproarious laughter, scuffling, running or the like, should be tolerated for a moment at any time in the school-room. Sing, march, visit, study, read—but at all times have it understood that the teacher governs uninterruptedly and on all parts of the school premises from morning till night of every school-day.— *South Western Journal of Education.*

HOW TO CURE ROUND SHOULDERS.

A stooping figure and a halting gait, accompanied by the unavoidable weakness of lungs incidental to a narrow chest, may be entirely cured by the very simple and easily performed exercise of raising one's self upon the toes leisurely in a perpendicular position several times daily.

To take this exercise properly one must be in a perfectly upright position, with the heels together and the toes at an angle of forty-five degrees; then drop the arms lifelessly by the sides, inflating and raising the chest to its full capacity muscularly, the chin well drawn in, and the crown of the head feeling as if attached to a string suspended from the ceiling above. Slowly rise on the balls of both feet to the greatest possible height, thereby exercising all the muscles of the legs and body, then come again into standing position without swaying the body backward out of the perfect line. Repeat this same exercise, first on one foot and then on the other.

It is wonderful what a straightening-out power this exercise has upon round shoulders and crooked backs, and one will be surprised to note how soon the lungs begin to show the effect of such expansive development.—*Exchange.*

DISCRIMINATION IN WORDS.

Pretty refers to external beauty on a small scale.

Grace of manner is a natural gift; elegance implies cultivation.

Well-bred is referable to general conduct rather than individual actions.

Beautiful is the strongest word of its class, implying softness and delicacy in addition to everything that is in similar words.

Courtesy·has reference to others, politeness, to ourselves. The former is a duty or privilege to others; the latter is behavior assumed from proper self-respect.

Benevolent refers to the character of the agent acting; beneficent, to the act performed.

Charitable is restricted to alms-giving, except when used in reference to judgment of others.

Lovely is used only where there is something more than external beauty, when there is a combination of personal beauty and pleasing manner. .Faultless features do not make a lady lovely who is disagreeable in disposition.

ABOUT MEN.

He who knows not, and knows not he knows not, is a fool; shun him.

He who knows not, and knows he knows not, is simple; teach him.

He who knows, and knows not he knows, is asleep; wake him.

He who knows, and knows he knows, is wise; follow him.

BEFORE YOU ARE FIFTEEN.

The other day one of my girls opened a letter from a girl friend and read: "While I was away this summer I learned something to be ashamed of: all other girls had some accomplishment, and I had not one. So I came home and cried about it, and thought myself all over, and found I couldn't sing, or play (well), or paint, or—anything. Then I cried again, and what do you think? Mamma suggested the kitchen. Awful thought! But I am doing it. Come and eat my bread and cake and ' pisen things. ' "

Now, girls, before you are fifteen, do you not wish to learn (and do) the pretty accomplishments of home?

Here are fifteen rules: (You do not believe there can be so many?)

1. Shut the door, and shut it softly.
2. Keep your own room in tasteful order.
3. Have an hour for rising, and rise.
4. Learn to make bread as well as cake.
5. Never let a button stay off twenty-four hours.
6. Always know where your things are.
7. Never let a day pass without doing something to make somebody comfortable.
8. Never come to breakfast without a collar.
9. Never go about with your shoes unbuttoned.
10. Speak clearly enough for everybody to understand.
11. Never fidget, or hum, to disturb somebody.
12. Never help yourself at the table before you pass the plate.
13. Be patient with the little ones, as you wish your mother to be with you.
14. Never keep anybody waiting.
15. Never fuss, or fret, or fidget.

How many can you add ?   Look at your own faults and
see.   I might add fifteen more, but I would rather you
would think of them yourself.   The girl who wrote this
letter is one of the most attractive girls I know, because
she is so sweet at home.

Oh ! I wish I had put in: Never contradict or be pert,
and think you know best.

You think it is too bad to give you so much to do at
home, when home is the stupidest place in the world, and
you like the other girls' homes better than your own? And
it is so much easier and pleasanter to do these things in
the other girls' homes.

When I was a little girl I liked a great deal better to
dust, or sweep, or take care of the baby next door, and it
never made me tired.

And you say I haven't made a rule about fancy-work or
plain sewing.   That is for you to do.   Or charity work,
and you love to do that.

Have you heard the story of the Princess Maud of Wales
and her new way of doing "charity work"?

Her mother gives her an allowance, a part of which she
spends in charity, but she has so many calls upon her
sympathy that the allowance cannot meet them all; but as
she cannot have anything more from her mother, she must
make it herself.   There's nothing, girls, like finding things
out for yourself.   That is the blessing of the "short allowance."

There is a great flock of pea-fowl at Sandringham, and
Princess Maud gathers the feathers that are continually
dropping and weaves them into fine screens and fans to be
sold at charity fairs.

Because they are made by a princess people are eager
to buy them; but they would not buy them if they were
not well made, and something that lasted.—*Home Journal.*

Southern Educational Association.

ORGANIZATION 1891-1892.

SOLOMON PALMER, PRESIDENT, East Lake, Florida.
EUGENE G. HARRELL, SECRETARY AND TREASURER, Raleigh, N. C.
W. T. WATSON, ASSISTANT SECRETARY, Memphis, Tennessee.

THIRD ANNUAL SESSION, ATLANTA, GA., JULY, 1892.

VICE-PRESIDENTS:

1. E. B. PRETTYMAN, Maryland.
2. JOHN E. MASSEY, Virginia.
3. B. S. MORGAN, West Virginia.
4. S. M. FINGER, North Carolina.
5. W. D. MAYFIELD, S. Carolina.
6. S. B. BRADWELL, Georgia.
7. A. J. RUSSELL, Florida.
8. J. G. HARRIS, Alabama.
9. J. R. PRESTON, Mississippi.
10. W. H. JACK, Louisiana.
11. J. M. CARLISLE, Texas.
12. J. H. SHINN, Arkansas.
13. W. R. GARRETT, Tennessee.
14. ED. PORTER THOMPSON, Ky.
15. W. E. COLEMAN, Missouri.

EXECUTIVE COMMITTEE:

Solomon Palmer, *ex officio* Chairman, East Lake, Alabama.
E. G. Harrell, *ex officio* Secretary, Raleigh, North Carolina.
1. J. H. Phillips, Superintendent City Schools, Birmingham, Ala.
2. W. H. Sutton, Superintendent of Schools, Jackson, Mississippi.
3. Thomas D. Boyd, President State Normal, Natchitoches, La.
4. O. H. Cooper, Superintendent City Schools, Galveston, Texas.
5. J. W. Conger, President Ouachita College, Arkadelphia, Arkansas.
6. J. M. Stewart, Agricultural and Mechanical College, Lake City, Fla.
7. J. M. Greenwood, Superintendent Schools, Kansas City, Missouri.
8. R. N. Roark, State Normal College, Lexington, Kentucky.
9. Frank M. Smith, University of Tennessee, Knoxville, Tennessee.
10. Euler B. Smith, President State Association, LaGrange, Georgia.
11. Edward S. Joynes, University of South Carolina, Columbia, S. C.
12. Hugh Morson, President Teachers' Assembly, Raleigh, N. C.
13. C. E. Vawter, Superintendent Miller Industrial School, Crozet, Va.
14. W. R. White, Superintendent of Schools, Morganton, W. Va.
15. Daniel Gilman, Johns Hopkins University, Baltimore, Maryland.

THE "PAPERS" of the session at Chattanooga are about all in hand and the proceedings are in press. We regret the delay, but you know that young organizations must move a little slowly at first, and as the Southern Educational Association has not yet accumulated a large fund for current expenses, it was necessary for us to secure a certain amount of advertising patronage before sending copy of proceedings to the printer.

THE INTEREST of teachers throughout the South in their Southern Educational Association is daily growing. The universal sentiment, as gathered from letters to the Secretary, is for the next session to he held in Atlanta, July 4 to 7, 1892. We have been promised one-fare rate by the railroads, and the people of Atlanta will do their best to make the meeting a most enjoyable one. Of course the question of time and place of meeting is to be officially chosen by the Executive Committee. There is every indication that the attendance at next session will reach the thousands. The committee will meet February 5.

WILL THE brethren of the Southern educational press please urge that on the programme of each State Teachers' Association in the South, there be set apart a day specially devoted to the consideration of the objects and interests of the Southern Educational Association. There are over eighty thousand white teachers in the South, and we want to see the time when at least fifteen thousand of them will attend the meetings of their Southern Educational Association. The North Carolina Teachers' Assembly has already placed on its next programme the discussion, "What the South Expects from the Southern Educational Association." At the close of the Assembly session the North Carolina teachers will have an excursion to Atlanta, and we hope to have the State represented by several hundred teachers in the meeting of the Southern Educational Association.

North Carolina Teachers' Assembly.

ORGANIZATION FOR 1891–'92.

OFFICERS:

HUGH MORSON (Raleigh Male Academy), President, . . Raleigh.
EUGENE G. HARRELL (Editor TEACHER), Sec. and Treas., . Raleigh.

VICE-PRESIDENTS:

1. J. J. Blair (Supt. Graded Schools), ... Winston.
2. J. E. Kelly (Model Male School), ... Charlotte.
3. Miss Catherine Fulghum (Graded School), . . Goldsboro.
4. W. J. Ferrell (Wakefield Academy), . . . Wakefield.
5. Miss Lizzie Lindsay (Graded School), . . . Greensboro.
6. P. M. Pearsall (County Superintendent), . . Trenton.
7. Miss Lina McDonald (Graded School), . . . Winston.
8. T. J. Drewry (Horner Military School), . . . Oxford
9. Mrs. S. Montgomery Funk (Chowan Bap. Fem. Inst.), Murfreesboro.

EXECUTIVE COMMITTEE:

Hugh Morson, *ex officio*, President, ... Raleigh.
Eugene G. Harrell, *ex officio*, Secretary, . . . Raleigh.
Eben Alexander (University of North Carolina), . . Chapel Hill.
W. L. Poteat (Wake Forest College), ... Wake Forest.
James Dinwiddie (President Peace Institute), . . . Raleigh.
Charles D. McIver (Pres't Normal and Industrial School
for Women), ... Greensboro.
J. Y. Joyner (Superintendent Graded School), . . Goldsboro.
A. C. Davis (Superintendent Military School), . . Winston.
E. E. Britton (Principal High School), ... Roxboro.

NINTH ANNUAL SESSION, MOREHEAD CITY, JUNE 21 TO JULY 2, 1892.

ASSEMBLY NOTES.

MISS BESSIE WORTHINGTON, of Rocky Mount, teacher of music in the Seminary for Girls, at Charlottesville, Virginia, will have charge of the musical part of the Assembly programme during the session this Summer.

THE ATLANTIC HOTEL COMPANY will have entire management of the hotel this summer, and they promise the very best of accommodations for the teachers and their friends during the session of the Assembly. Several changes will be made in the Atlantic Hotel, and all are in the interest of the guests.

THE "WESTERN NORTH CAROLINA TEACHERS' ASSOCIATION" promises to send about five hundred teachers from beyond the Blue Ridge to the Teachers' Assembly this summer. The western delegation will have a most cordial reception and welcome at Morehead City.

AT THE close of the session of the Teachers' Assembly on July 2d there will be an excursion to Atlanta to attend the meeting of the Southern Educational Association which convenes on July 4th. The railroad ticket will be only one fare for the round trip, and we hope that several hundred North Carolina teachers will join the excursion to this great meeting of the teachers of the South. The excursion train will leave from Morehead City, and persons desiring to secure this special rate must be at Morehead City with the party.

THE EXECUTIVE COMMITTEE OF 1890–'91, to whom was given the power to designate the place for the next annual session of the Assembly, have decided in favor of Morehead City. Cordial invitations were in hand from the University at Chapel Hill, the Woman's Christian Temperance Union at Waynesville, the Atlantic Hotel Company at Morehead City, and the Hotel Company at Hot Springs. Asheville would not submit in writing the proposition made at Morehead City last Summer, although we made repeated efforts to get the invitation properly before the committee. The votes by the committee were received in writing.

THERE IS no place, after all, that can afford such genuine enjoyment and needed recreation to a tired teacher as a visit to the Atlantic Ocean. The pleasures of surf-bathing, the delights of sailing over the waters, the excitement of trolling, the recuperation of the salty southwestern sea-breeze, and the many physical benefits received at the seaside cannot be equaled by any other place on earth. A two-weeks' sojourn at the seaside during the session of the Teachers' Assembly will do more towards restoring exhausted nature than anything else within our knowledge. It was for this special reason that the Teachers' Assembly established its permanent home at Morehead City on the shores of the fascinating Atlantic, Nature's great sanitarium for tired humanity.

THE NEW EXECUTIVE COMMITTEE of the Assembly met in Raleigh on December 28th. President Morson presided and nearly every member of the Committee was present. A large amount of work was done on the programme for the session next June, and every effort will be put forth to make this the best of all the sessions of the Assembly. There are to be some new and interesting features in the programme, of which due announcement will be made. The annual report of the Secretary and Treasurer was submitted with the report of the Auditing Committee, and both were approved and filed as usual. There seems to be universal approval among the teachers of the decision of the committee to continue to meet at Morehead City, where we have every convenience for the Assembly work.

THE SPECIAL COMMITTEE appointed by the Executive Committee to audit the books and accounts of the Secretary and Treasurer for the fiscal year 1890–91, comprised Capt. C. B. Denson and Prof. E. McK. Goodwin, of Raleigh. The work was performed on December 17th, and the following report was submitted by the Committee:

ANNUAL REPORT OF SECRETARY AND TREASURER.

EUGENE G. HARRELL, *Secretary and Treasurer,*
In account with North Carolina Teachers' Assembly.

1891.   DR.

Jan. 1. To balance from 1890	$ 238 92
" Amount from H. Morson, Treasurer	49 40
" " " Talmage's lecture	435 30
" " " dues, 1891	1,051 00

CR.

Jan. 1. By amount paid note and interest (building)	$ 720 58
" " " expenses of Executive Com.	27 60
July 1. " " " Dr. T. De Witt Talmage	500 00
" " " sundry freight bills	17 05
" " " special lecturers	18 75
" " " repairs on building	26 25
" " " postage on printed matter	28 40
" " " postage on letters	16 00
" " " A. Williams & Co. for st'nery	22 20
" " " for medals and engraving	44 00
" " " Mott Hester, janitor 1 month	20 00
" " " Edwards & Broughton for printing	46 75
" " " E. M. Uzzell for printing	31 50
" " " E. A. Alderman, Training School Committee	30 00
" " " Chas. D. McIver, Training School Committee	30 00
" " " for telegrams	2 18
" " " printing proceedings, ½ cost	87 50
Aug. 15. " " " on teachers' building	792 00
" " " sundry bills—hauling, packing, &c	16 76

$1,774 62 $2,477 52

Balance due Secretary _____$ 702 90

The undersigned Committee have examined the books and accounts of the Secretary and Treasurer, and find them correct.

C. B. DENSON,
E. McK. GOODWIN.

RALEIGH, N. C., Dec. 18, 1891.

TEACHERS will be glad to learn that Mr. T. F. Donnelly, author of that excellent little book, "Barnes' Primary History of the United States," has kindly consented to attend the Assembly this Summer and give a little talk upon the subject "How to Make the Study of History of Most Value and Interest to Pupils." Mr. Donnelly speaks as well as he writes, and he will delight his fine audience of teachers at Morehead City.

THE TEACHERS' CUBAN PARTY.

The editor of THE NORTH CAROLINA TEACHER has gotten up and personally conducted within the past few years six special parties of tourists in our country and abroad, comprising in the aggregate over seven hundred people. Each trip has been exceedingly pleasant and entirely satisfactory in every way; and in all the tours, embracing over twenty-five thousand miles of travel by almost every conceivable mode of conveyance, there has never been an accident, a loss, or a single case of serious illness. For such rare good fortune, surely we have reason to be profoundly thankful.

Of all the tours that we have conducted, there has never been a more charming and congenial party, more satisfaction and enjoyment, or a more signal success than in our fifteen days' visit to Cuba and Florida. Every mile of the trip was comfortable and delightful, and each day brought a new round of surprise and pleasure.

On December 29th, our party, consisting of fifty persons, the limited number, set out upon this memorable tour to the Queen of the Antilles. The company was divided into two sections at the start to accommodate members in different portions of the State. Each section began the trip at Goldsboro, one on the Atlantic Coast Line via Wilmington, Charleston and Savannah, and the other on the Richmond and Danville Railroad via Raleigh, Charlotte, Atlanta and Macon. The two sections were united at Jacksonville and remained together during the remainder of the tour.

Our journey was rested by a stop over of three hours at Atlanta and Jacksonville. At both of these cities we were met by a number of friends, who extended to us many attentions and courtesies. We are under special obligations to Col. W. A. Turk and Mr. Hopkins, of Charlotte; Mr. Hawkins, Mr. Lucas and Mr. Rafftery, of Jacksonville; Mr. Woodlief, of Sandford, Florida, and Mr. Taylor, of Atlanta, all prominent railroad officials, for many kindnesses and courtesies which added greatly to the comforts and enjoyments of our trip. And to all the conductors on the railroads along our route are extended cordial thanks for their very kind attention and valuable assistance.

At Port Tampa, Florida, we embarked on the excellent steamer *Mascotte*, commanded by the genial Captain Hanlon, and the sail among the Florida Keys was most placid and enjoyable. We reached Key West at 5 o'clock P. M., on January 1st, and while the steamer was receiving and discharging cargo we had several hours to ride over that interesting city. At night we had the opportunity of attending a Spanish ball in Key West, where for the first time we saw the famous *danza*.

On Saturday, the 2d of January, just at sunrise, we sailed under the guns of the celebrated Morro Castle and entered the lovely Bay of Havana. As soon as the steamer was safely anchored in the bay a tug-boat came alongside, which had been previously chartered for our party, and in a few moments we were comfortably located in our rooms at the Grand Hotel Mascotte, which had been selected as our home while in Havana. Among the friends who were on the tug to meet us were Mrs. M. Trigo, Misses Blanca Trigo and Fidelia Gonzales, and Rev. Alberto Diaz the most prominent Protestant minister in Cuba. As we left the steamer we gave three rousing cheers for Captain Hanlon and his associate officers on the *Mascotte.*

We can truly say that the city of Havana was "turned over to our party," for every public building and many of the elegant private residences were freely opened to us as had never been done before. Wherever we went—in the stores, on the streets, in the omnibuses, or railroad cars, every attention and consideration was shown to the "North Carolina Party." On the morning after our arrival the newspapers of Havana announced the event and published the names of the party, and thus we were known wherever we went.

The week was spent most pleasantly in visiting Cabana Fortress, Morro Castle, the Governor General's Winter Palace, all the Cathedrals, the Tomb of Columbus, the Parks, the Catholic and Baptist Cemeteries, Cigar Factories, Sugar Plantations, Matanzas, Carmela, Jesus Del Monte, Guanabacoa, and all the country surrounding Havana. The manners and customs of the people were carefully studied, and we do not think that any people ever got such a clear insight into Cuban life as did our party.

We are under great obligations to Lieutenant Muller, Commander of Cabana Fortress, and to his excellent wife, for many enjoyable courtesies which they extended to us during our visit to that celebrated prison. They kindly accompanied us throughout our visit and opened to us many doors which have been inaccessible to all other people. Mrs. Muller is a New York lady, and it was delightful to hear her speak the American language so fluently.

The Grand Hotel Mascotte is pleasantly situated on the Bay of Havana. It is free from dust and noise, while the rooms, service and fare were entirely satisfactory to us. The charming daughters of Mr. Carbonell, proprietor of the hotel, Misses Josephine and Sebastiano, were particularly attractive to our party, and they received many cordial invitations to visit our American homes. Miss Josephine has learned to speak American, as she says, *"muy pocito,"* (very little), but it was a talisman to the hearts of our people.

The weather in Havana was indeed delightful. While North Carolina and other portions of the United States were trudging through deep snows and shivering in cold rains and icy winds, we were basking in the warm sunshine of a summer day, wearing summer clothing, bathing in the open air, and enjoying all the fruits and vegetables of the summer season! As we wiped the perspiration from our faces and vigorously manipulated the fan it was hard to realize that we were living in January instead of July. Fortunately for our greater comfort in sight-seeing the weather during our stay in Cuba, even at 85°, was much cooler than is usual in a tropical winter, in fact the Cubans said that it was "cold," and they shrugged their shoulders very significantly while telling us that it was the "coldest weather that had been known in Cuba within thirteen years!"

There are so many things to be said about our happy mid-winter trip to Cuba that we must defer them until another number of THE TEACHER.

MEMBERS OF THE CUBAN PARTY.

COL. EUGENE G. HARRELL ---------------------------Raleigh, N. C.
JOHN N. HARRELL.-------- ------ ----- ----------- --Raleigh, N. C.
REV. BENNETT SMEDES, D. D.---------- --------- Raleigh, N. C.
JUDGE JOHN GRAY BYNUM --- ----- ----- --------Morganton, N. C.
CAPT. T. R. ROBERTSON ----------------- --------Charlotte, N. C.
MR. T. B. SEIGLE ------- -------- ----- --------Charlotte, N. C.
MR. HAL B. SMITH --------- ------ ----- --------Charlotte, N. C.

CAPT. E. C. HOLT ----------------------------------Burlington, N. C.
MR. J. H. ERWIN----------------------------------Burlington, N. C.
DR. J. A. WILLIAMSON------------------------------Graham, N. C.
MR. J. S. RAMSEY ---------------------------------Statesville, N. C.
MR. A. M. FRY-------------------------------------Bryson City, N. C.
MR. H. A. LONDON, JR-----------------------------Pittsboro, N. C.
MR. I. A. FONVILLE--------------------------------Goldsboro, N. C.
MR. L. D. GIDDENS---------------------------------Goldsboro, N. C.
MR. H. A. CASSIN----------------------------------Atlanta, Ga.
MR. BURRUS CORPREW-------------------------------Norfolk, Va.
MR. R. H. RICKS-----------------------------------Rocky Mount, N. C.
MISS MATTIE FULLER--------------------------------Raleigh, N. C.
MISS MATTIE HIGGS---------------------------------Raleigh, N. C.
MISS TRULETTA KRETH-------------------------------Raleigh, N. C.
MISS JANIE WARD-----------------------------------Raleigh, N. C.
MISS LAURA CARTER---------------------------------Raleigh, N. C.
MISS K. CARTER------------------------------------Raleigh, N. C.
MISS KATIE MCMACKIN-------------------------------Raleigh, N. C.
MISS JEANNIE WILLIAMS-----------------------------Fayetteville, N. C.
MISS MARY L. TAYLOR-------------------------------Fayetteville, N. C.
MISS ETTIE BROWN----------------------------------Fayetteville, N. C.
MISS ROSA LILLY CUMMING---------------------------Wilmington, N. C.
MISS NELLIE MORRISON------------------------------Athens, Ga.
MISS BESSIE WORTHINGTON---------------------------Rocky Mount, N. C.
MISS FANNIE BURWELL-------------------------------Charlotte, N. C.
MISS JOSEPHINE EPPES------------------------------City Point, Va.
MISS ELFRIDA EPPES--------------------------------City Point, Va.
MISS E. FOWLER------------------------------------Tampa, Fla.
MISS ALICE S. HARVEY------------------------------Snow Hill, N. C.
MISS MARTHA WILLIAMS------------------------------Wilmington, N. C.
MRS. J. B. NEATHERY-------------------------------Raleigh, N. C.
MRS. JULIUS LEWIS---------------------------------Raleigh, N. C.
MRS. LAVINIA BALL---------------------------------Raleigh, N. C.
MRS. PRESTON CUMMING------------------------------Wilmington, N. C.
MRS. T. R. ROBERTSON------------------------------Charlotte, N. C.
MRS. B. W. CRANE----------------------------------Baltimore, Md.
MRS. J. G. BYNUM----------------------------------Morganton, N. C.
MRS. BESSIE LEAK----------------------------------Burlington, N. C.
MRS. E. A. CORPREW--------------------------------Norfolk, Va.
MRS. FANNIE COX BELL------------------------------Richmond, Va.
MRS. MARTHA JUSTICE-------------------------------Waycross, Ga.
MRS. H. A. CASSIN---------------------------------Atlanta, Ga.
MRS. M. HOLMAN------------------------------------Tampa, Fla.

EDITORIAL.

"Carolina! Carolina! Heaven's blessings attend her,
While we live we will cherish, protect and defend her;
Though the scorner may sneer at and witlings defame her,
Our hearts swell with gladness whenever we name her."

LET YOUR TEACHERS' ASSOCIATION LIVE.

Don't make the programme of your State or county
teachers' association too long. Don't try to discuss too
many subjects at a sitting. Don't allow any written
papers to be over twenty-five minutes long, and don't permit extempore speeches to go beyond fifteen minutes.
Don't try to tell all you know about a subject—that might
require a day or two—but give the main points concisely,
and this can be done in twenty minutes. Don't try to give
an audience more mental food than can be properly diges-
ted and thus spoil an intellectual feast. The speaker at an
educational meeting whose written paper is only twenty
minutes, or whose extempore remarks are not over ten
minutes, will always have the average audience of teachers
"thoroughly with him"; but the forty to fifty-minute
speaker, and the thirty-minute debater—well, we feel sorry
for them, as also for their audiences. Many fine educational meetings are killed at the beginning of their sessions by long-winded papers. "Short and to the point"
is the demand of the times, and no person who cannot
adapt himself to this desire should ever accept an invitation to speak to an audience of teachers. It is sad, indeed,
when we have to write as an epitaph upon the grave of
a defunct teachers' association this significant record,
"Talked to Death," and yet nine-tenths of the once pros-

perous and enjoyable associations which have departed this life were talked into eternity. If your teachers' association is destined to cease its existence, let it enjoy a natural death—don't let it be murdered by long-winded papers upon dry-as-dust subjects. No public speaker should be vain enough as to suppose that he can hold the attention of an audience for an hour or more in discussing a subject which he has perhaps studied for a life-time. If it is an important topic he will accomplish more good in a ten-minute than by a forty-minute paper, however carefully prepared. Most educational speakers are enthusiasts in their special lines of work—audiences are not so and cannot be made so in an hour. Don't try it. It is harder to keep the attention of an audience of teachers than of any other class of hearers—why it is we do not know, but it is true, nevertheless.

WE HAVE all had a pleasant holiday, now let us get back to hard work in earnest, for much is to be done this year, and there should be no idle moments.

THE TEACHERS' ASSEMBLY has been the principal agency in supplying over four hundred of our teachers with good schools, and this grand work will continue.

THIS NUMBER of THE TEACHER is not fully up to our standard, in consequence of the absence of the editor until late in the month with his Teacher's Party in Cuba.

INDEED, we thank our readers for so many compliments paid to the Christmas number of THE TEACHER. It affords us great pleasure to know that we have been able to give pleasure to others.

ARE YOU going to try to make this the best educational year that North Carolina has ever seen? The teachers have the power to do this, and it is only necessary that every teacher shall do the very best work that he can.

WE ARE under obligations to a large number of our County Superintendents of Public Instruction for many favors which we constantly receive at their hands. If at any time we can be of service to them, they may command us.

IF YOU need supplementary reading for your advanced classes, use "Black Beauty." It will intensely interest your pupils and inspire a lesson of humanity towards animal nature which will prove valuable throughout life.

WE WELCOME to the ranks of educational journalism in North Carolina *The Mountain School Journal.* It is published at Highlands, N. C., and Mr. T. G. Harbison, Principal of Highlands Normal School, is editor. It is a neat and helpful journal, and is issued monthly for twenty-five cents a year. We wish you success, brother Harbison.

THE TEACHER has been truly flooded with new subscriptions and renewals during the past month. One of the favorite premiums desired seems to have been "Black Beauty," and we are glad of it, for this wonderful book is in the interest of animals, and surely kindness to these dumb creatures and servants of mankind is one of the most divine attributes of human nature.

SOME MEETINGS we want especially to keep in mind for the year and begin to make arrangements to attend: The ninth session of the North Carolina Teachers' Assembly, Morehead City, June 21 to July 2; the third annual session of The Southern Educational Association, Atlanta, Ga., July 4–7. These two great meetings are of peculiar value and importance to North Carolina teachers, and progressive teachers cannot afford to be absent.

WE HAVE been working for several years upon a grand "Teachers' Tour to California and the Yellowstone Park." The trip is to occupy about six weeks, allowing eight days for the World's Fair in Chicago. We propose to make the trip across the continent with the party in a special train of Pullman palace cars provided with buffet and baggage car. The party will be a select one and positively limited to one hundred persons. When arrangements are complete the itinerary of the tour will be announced.

THE CROWNING literary glory of the United States and of this age is the new "Webster's International Dictionary." The publishers have recently spent $300,000 upon revision of the great book, and the work represents the best literary work of over a hundred of the most eminent scholars of this century. No North Carolina school is s) limited in funds that it can afford to be without this absolutely essential aid in teaching constantly in the schoolroom. The new "Webster" is truly "a thing of beauty and a joy forever."

THE TEACHERS of North Carolina who are best and most favorably known to the brotherhood are those who are every year pleasantly and socially met in the meetings of the Teachers' Assembly at Morehead City. The teacher who habitually stays away from those great annual reunions is almost entirely forgotten by the profession when "the honor-roll is called." A teacher must associate freely with the brotherhood and with the people if he does not want his influence to go out like a snuffed candle. It is impossible to "stay to yourself" and at the same time "reach the people."

MANY TEACHERS have taken our advice concerning the State flag, and now this beautiful emblem of North Carolina patriotism is proudly displayed in their school-rooms. We have received so many applications for the design that we had Mr. T. C. Harris, of Raleigh, to engrave the design of our State flag expressly for THE TEACHER, and we now present it to you beautifully printed in its appropriate colors. The flag is easy to make, and it should be prominently displayed in every school-room in North Carolina, and thus teach your boys and girls the important lesson of patriotism and State pride. The first duty of a North Carolina teacher should be to teach her pupils to cordially love and believe in North Carolina.

THE TEACHER proposes, in future, when speaking of our language, to call it "American." Our country now comprises near sixty-five million people and the sun never sets on our territory; therefore we think that America is important enough in the world to have a language of our own, and it is "American." The people of England speak "English," a language very much like ours, but it is not quite "American." We live under the great American flag and speak the American language. Of course our people understand "English," although in many respects the American tongue is very different. It is generally conceded by scholars that in a few years the American and English languages will be universally spoken throughout the civilized world.

WE THINK you will enjoy our prize essay on "The Battle of Alamance" by T. W. Costen, Jr., which will be published in THE TEACHER. The paper is clearly and thoughtfully written, and does great credit to the little boy who wrote it. In addition to the papers mentioned in December number of THE TEACHER, we have also received excellent ones from J. O. Matthews, Owensville; Della Collins, Currie; and Ethel A. Wicker, Wicker. We thank our little friends sincerely for their most creditable work in North Carolina history, and we feel quite sure that all these young people have been benefited by their literary efforts. The children enjoy the study of North Carolina history, and it is making of them men and women of whom the State will be very proud in a few years.

THE COTTON CROP is short and the price is very low, and the cry of "hard times" is abroad in the land. The "cry" is, however, much more with the people than is the fact. But even though we are experiencing a temporary period of "hard times," do not let this keep your children from school. There is now more reason than ever why they should be acquiring an education, and it is of more pleasure and value to them in hard times than when money is plentiful. Our public schools are good, and the private schools and colleges of North Carolina are equal to any in this country, and you cannot afford to keep your children away from school. It is worth any sacrifice on your part to have them in school. The education which you can now give your children will be of far more practical value to them than any sum of money which you may hope to give to them in the future. Your son or daughter with an education has a great advantage in life, whether it is to be spent on the farm, in the store or in the professions, and the education can be made to provide a living when all other things fail. We give you the counsel of experience and close observation in urging you to *keep your children in school.*

EVERY MAIL brings new subscriptions or renewals to THE TEACHER. While this is indeed gratifying, yet we derive much more pleasure and satisfaction from such expressions, gathered from letters, as these: "Consider me a life-membe of THE TEACHERS' Subscription List." "THE TEACHER is 'North Carolina to the backbone,' and this delights the heart of every North Carolinian!" "Your firm and true loyalty to the State is refreshing in this age of 'foreignizing.'" "THE NORTH CAROLINA TEACHER has done more to build up the educational interests of our State and purify our methods of public education than any and all other influences in the State." "THE TEACHER, in its honest reflections of public sentiment, has banished from our public schools much of the nonsense of educational cranks and fanatics, and for this special reason 'may it live long and prosper.'" "I like THE TEACHER because it is an educational journal with an opinion of its own, and its original views are, in the main, correct. It 'toadies' to nothing and to nobody, and I admire its independence." "THE TEACHER has built up a strong sentiment of State pride in North Carolina, and for that great service alone it should receive the blessing of generations." "I like your views on the 'New South;' they are original and patriotic and true." These are a few actual clippings from the many kind and complimentary letters on the editor's desk.

ABOUT OUR TEACHERS AND SCHOOLS.

MR. W. M. BOONE is teaching in Franklin county.

MR. J. A. WHITEHEAD is teaching in Perquimans county.

MR. WALTER HOLLAND has a good school in Iredell county.

MISS NANNIE PARKS has an excellent school in Randolph county.

MR, E. F. EARLY has a flourishing school in Marion county, S. C.

MISS LILLIE NICHOLSON has taken charge of a school in Pitt county.

MISS BETTIE H. WELLS has an interesting school in Nash county.

MISS MITTIE CRAWFORD has taken a school in Montgomery county.

MR. WILLIAM H. GRADY has a school full of pupils in Duplin county.

MISS JULIA ALSTON has an interesting private school in Granville county.

MISS JENNIE WILLIS is teaching an excellent school in Pamlico county.

MISS MAUD CHEARS writes that she has a fine school in Rockingham county.

MISS JULIA E. LOCKHART is in charge of a good school in Anson county.

MISS BESSIE EAGLE has a good school in Iredell county, not far from Statesville.

MISS MOLLIE D. ANDERSON is principal of River Hill Academy, in Iredell county.

MISS CORINNE BARNES is teaching in the family of O. W. Sutton, in Wayne county.

MISS NANNIE SHEARIN is in charge of one of the best public schools in Warren county.

REV. T. O. FULLER, A. B., is principal of the Graded School for negroes at Franklinton.

MR. P. P. PEARCE is principal of Brown Mountain School, with thirty-six pupils enrolled.

MISS MARY E. BROWN is in charge of the school at Adams' School-House, in Onslow county.

MR. WALTER FEIMSTER, with Mr. Burke, is conducting a prosperous high school in Iredell county.

MISS MAMIE WILSON is principal of Bethel Academy, and about thirty-five pupils are enrolled.

MISS ETHEL WICKER, of Cumberland county, has a fine school of forty scholars in Harnett county.

MRS. J. L. BUTT, *nee* Miss Maggie Smith, is teaching in Beaufort county. Her school is a success.

MR. G. I. SMITH has been elected principal of the flourishing Piney Grove High School in Sampson county.

MRS. FANNIE COX BELL, a member of our Cuban party, has accepted again a position as primary teacher in the Winston Graded Schools.

MISSES AGNES GRADY AND MAY ABBOTT, two of Lenoir county's excellent teachers, are each in charge of flourishing public scools.

THE Durham people regret very much to give up Mr. L. B. Edwards, who leaves them to take a position as teacher in the Public Schools of Asheville.

MR. Y. D. MOORE is principal of Willow School, in Henderson county. Mr. T. A. Drake is his assistant. The school is prospering, and it prepares boys for college.

MISS BETTIE HOLLAND is in charge of Olive Public School, with a very large attendance, and she writes that her patrons seem to be quite enthusiastic on the subject of education.

MISS KATHLEEN ELMORE (Oxford Female Seminary) is principal of Union Academy, Sampson county. The school is a new one, but it is flourishing greatly in such skillful hands.

THE Executive Committee of the Western North Carolina Teachers' Association will meet in Asheville on Saturday, February 27th, to select time and place for next session of the Association.

PROFESSOR R. L. HAMBERLIN, Instructor of Elocution in Richmond College, has been secured by the University of North Carolina to give a six-weeks' course in elocution there, beginning this month.

MISS FANNIE DANIEL, one of the progressive teachers of Pitt county in renewing her subscription, writes, "I enjoy reading THE TEACHER ever so much, and cannot do without it." Thank you, Miss Fannie.

THE Graded Schools at Statesville are flourishing greatly under the excellent management of the superintendent, Mr. D. Matt Thompson. Eight teachers are employed and near four hundred pupils are enrolled.

PROFESSOR F. P. HOBGOOD has entirely recovered his health and again assumes the presidency of the Seminary for Girls at Oxford. He is one of the most prominent educators of our State and we are delighted to have him again in the work.

MR. ROBERT E. WARE informs us that his school in Cleveland county is in fine condition, forty-five pupils enrolled. He adds: "I am well pleased with THE TEACHER and derive much benefit from it. I read every number with the greatest interest." Thanks.

REV. DR. THOMAS HUME, of the State University, has been invited to deliver a lecture before the American Institute of Christian Philosophy, in New-York, July 12. The invitation is by Dr. Charles F. Deems, Archdeacon MacKay Smith of the Episcopal church, and others.

MT. OLIVE, in Wayne county, is blessed with four excellent schools and all the teachers are name Smith and are not related to one another; Mr. J. E. Smith, of the Academy; Mr. E. S. Smith, of the Public School; and Misses Clara Smith and Lou Smith have private schools.

MR. ERNEST P. MANGUM left a great many friends in Asheville when he accepted the position of Superintendent of the Graded Schools at Concord. We congratulate the people at Concord on their good fortune in securing the services of Mr. Mangum as manager of their schools.

THE TEACHERS of Moore have a fine Teachers' Council, Mr. D. R. McIver is President, and Mr. E. A. Cole is Secretary. At the meetings of the Council the teachers very properly (as at the Teachers' Assembly) combine instruction and entertainment, consequently the meetings are greatly enjoyed.

MR. WASHINGTON DUKE, of Durham, has already paid to Trinity College $85,000, and he proposes to contribute $35,000 more, provided the Methodists will raise an additional $50,000 to equip the new main building of the college. This is the largest gift to education by a Southern man within thirty years. Hurrah, for North Carolina!

THE GROWTH of Fairview Academy, W. T. Whitsett, A. M., superintendent, Gibsonville, has been so rapid during the past few months that it has become necessary to erect a new building to accommodate the increasing number of students. The building now in course of erection will contain music-rooms, society halls, a chapel 50 x 60, etc. This will place Fairview Academy in the very front rank of North Carolina preparatory schools.

CUPID AMONG OUR TEACHERS.

'Tis said that "figures never lie,"
That one and one are always TWO,
But Cupid proves, with work so sly,
Some wondrous things that figures do.
And when he claims a teacher's hand
All rules of figures then are done,
Though TWO before the preacher stand
This one and one are ALWAYS ONE.

MR. ROBERT L. MADISON, principal of Cullowhee High School in Swain County, married MISS ELLA V. RICHARDS, his teacher of Art, on November 25th, 1891, Rev. W. S. Barrows, officiating.

MISS ANNIE L. FLEMING, teaching at Middleburg, was married to MR. CLYDE HARRIS, of Louisburg, on December 2d, 1891.

MISS MAMIE J. KIMBALL, of Middleburg, a teacher and a member of the Teachers' Assembly, was married on December 16th to MR. ROBERT L. BENNETT, of Littleton. The ceremony was performed by Rev. N. B. Cobb, D. D., of Raleigh.

MISS CLAUDIA E. PRINCE, a member of the Teachers' Assembly and one of the best teachers of Harnett County, was married on December 23d, at Chalk Level, to MR. JOHN K. SESSOMS, of Georgia. After the wedding festivities the bride and groom left for Pearce, Georgia, their place of residence.

COL. T. J. DREWRY, junior principal of the famous "Horner School," at Oxford, married MISS LUCIE N. MORECOCK on December 23d, at Norfolk, Va. Rev. W. E. Evans, D. D., pastor of Granby Street Methodist Church, performed the marriage ceremony.

On January 6th, 1892, at New Hope Church in Caswell County, MR. J. M. LONG married MISS WINNIE J. TAYLOR, Rev. J. H. Shore officiating. They were both members of the Teachers' Assembly at Morehead. They took a Southern tour to Florida.

MR. T. C. BUCHANAN, principal of a flourishing academy in Caldwell County, married MISS ANNIE GREENE, of Mitchell County, one of his students, on Sunday, January 17th, 1892. The bride and groom had known each other but ten days.

MISS MARY E. BALL, a teacher, of Greensboro, was married to Mr. EDWIN L. MILLER on January 27th, 1892. Their home will in future be Seneca, Kansas.

IN MEMORIAM.

' Death hath made no breach
In love and sympathy, in hope and trust.
No outward sign or sound our ears can reach,
But there's an inward, spiritual speech
That greets us still, though mortal tongues be dust.
It bids us do the work that·they laid down—
Take up the song where they broke off the strain ;
So, journeying till we reach the heavenly town,
Where are laid up our treasure and our crown,
And our lost, loved ones will be found again.''

MR. W. C. PULLEN of Nash County, one of our most faithful teachers, died suddenly at Ringwood on Saturday, December 5th. He had just taken charge of the school at Ringwood, Halifax County, and had been teaching there but two months.

MISS MAMIE L. CARVER, of Fayetteville, died at Lake City, Florida, January 21st, 1892. She had been teaching in Peabody High School in Lake City since October last, and died of nervous prostration. A correspondent writes : "She had a sweet disposition, a noble character, and had made many friends here."

MISS MAMIE L. SHERWOOD, daughter of Mike S. and Maria L. Sherwood, died in Greensboro, November 23d, at 4 o'clock A. M., after a brief illness.

· Miss Mamie was much beloved and respected by all who knew her, and she will be sadly missed by a large circle of friends and many children in the graded schools where she ·has so acceptably held the position of teacher for many years. The warmest and tenderest sympathy of the community goes out to the stricken mother and brothers and sisters. The funeral took place at West Market Street Church, conducted by Rev. Solomon Pool, D. D.

A precious one from us has gone,
    A voice we loved is stilled ;
A place is vacant in our home
    Which never can be filled.

God in His wisdom has recalled ·
    The boon his love had given ;
And though the body moulders here
    The soul is safe in Heaven.

                                        SISTER.

AT RECESS.

The books and slates now put away,
And let us laugh a little while;
For those who work there should be play,
The leisure moments to beguile.

"Johnny, said the pretty teacher "what is a kiss?" "I can't exactly put it in words," returned the boy, "but if you really wanter know, I can show yer."

HARD ON MILTON.—Teacher—"Try to remember this: Milton, the poet, was blind. Do you think you can remember it?" "Yes ma'am." "Now, what was Milton's great misfortune?" "He was a poet."

A FRENCH LITERARY MAN writes to an American literary friend that he is learning English without a teacher, from a text-book and dictionary, and adds, "In small time I can learn so many English as I think I will come at the America and to go on the scaffold to lecture."

HIS WAS THE GREATEST ACCOMPLISHMENT.—"Yes, my wife is learning Delsarte, my daughter is learning elocution, and my boy is learning the mandolin. Oh, we shall soon be the most accomplished family in town." "We? What are you learning, pray?" "To endure."

RATHER A BLUNT ANSWER.—A teacher was impressing upon the scholars of the primary school the importance of perspiration. Having, as she thought, fully explained the matter, she asked, "Now, Johnnie, if the pores of the skin got filled up, what would happen?" Johnnie thought a moment, then answered briskly, "We'd bust."

A SCHOOL INSPECTOR asked the class the question, "What is a statesman?" After a little hesitation one of the boys stood up and answered, "One who makes speeches." "Not bad," said the inspector, smiling encouragingly, "but not quite right. For instance I make speeches, but am not a statesman." Another moment's hesitation and then the boy said, "One who makes good speeches."

A NEW SCHOLAR.

ANNIE LEONE HUGHES, daughter of Mr. E. L. Hughes, superintendent of Reidsville graded school, was born on November 29th, 1891. The charming little lady was introduced to our Cuban party while on the train the 29th of December.

THE NORTH CAROLINA TEACHER.

VOL. IX.　　RALEIGH, FEBRUARY, 1892.　　No. 6.

EUGENE G. HARRELL, ＝ ＝ ＝ ＝ ·Editor.

THE OLD–TIME PEDAGOGUE.

They call 'em all perfessers now, these chaps 'at teaches
　　school,
'Cause they deal out eddication by a more refinin' rule.
But tho' the intellectual parts with sciences they clog,
Th'aint nary one is ekal to the ol'-time pedagogue.

Jerusha! If he had a case of tutorin' to do,
He'd make the other feller do a little tootin, too.
And ef the mental engine sorter settled in a cog,
With ile of birch he'd start 'er, would the ol'-time peda-
　　gogue.

His train o' knolledge hadn't no currickerlums, or sich,
He engined 'er an' fired 'er an' tended to the switch.
An' jus' as easy as a beaver toppled from a log
He'd land yer at yer station, would the ol'-time pedagogue.

But now-a-days they say a college course is just the cheese,
An' what's a college course but atherletics, ef yer please?
An' that we got—onless my brain is side-tracked in a fog—
In allerpathic doses from the ol'-time pedagogue.
　　　　　　　　　　　　　　　—*Public School Journal.*

DISPLAY THE North Carolina State Flag in your school-
room and thus teach your pupils patriotism.

North Carolina Teachers Abroad:

A SUMMER JAUNT

IN

England, Scotland, Ireland and France.

CHAPTER XXVII.

FRENCH HISTORY AND FRENCH ART.

The Gallery of Battles at Versailles—An English
Guide and George Washington's Picture—The
Porcelain Works at Sevres—Seeing the work—
Some Valuable Porcelain—Plassidy, the Founder
of Ceramic Art—"The Best Day in Paris."

WE ARE still wandering as if entranced among the
thousands of bewildering fascinations of the matchless Palace of Versailles. Nothing else on the globe equals
the grandeur of this famous palace. We do not know that
we will ever again see these incomparable beauties, therefore we are making the best possible use of our time while
here.

The great hall of the palace at Versailles is the *Galerie
des Batailles*, which has the surprising dimensions of three
hundred and ninety feet in length and forty-two feet in
width. Seventy rooms of the palace were destroyed to
create this immense gallery of the battles. It contains thirty-
three superb battle-scenes in the history of France, and
busts of eighty prominent generals who have fallen in
battle.

As we passed on down the gallery, our English guide
seemed to be specially desirous to explain the paintings
which were on the left side of the hall while he kept his
back to the right. We didn't at first understand this.

"Here, ladies and gentlemen," he said, "is a very fine painting by Scheffer, representing the battle of Tolbiac; and this handsome piece is the work of Schurtz, and shows Count Endes defending Paris against the Normans; and here is—"

We had been listening on the left while looking on the right, and just here, about the centre of the hall, we suddenly discovered why it was that the Englishman was not so much interested in explaining the pictures on the right side of the gallery.

An immense painting by Couder was at this point suspended on the wall, entitled "The Siege of Yorktown, conducted by Generals Rochambeau and Washington."

As the title would indicate, of course the French artist had made his General Rochambeau the most prominent figure in the scene, and as both Rochambeau and *Washington* were too prominent for our Englishman, he preferred to pass the picture by. But this snubbing of our Washington did not accord with the intense patriotism of our American party, and we wanted to know all about the picture.

"Hey, there! old friend Gallop," said the Secretary, "tell us about this picture over here." The whole crowd turned towards Washington and waited for the guide to answer.

The Englishman, however, was equal to the occasion.

He scratched his head, looked towards the ceiling and said, "Oh, that is—is—is a—; yes, that is a scene in the—in America before the British captured the United States!" He laughed heartily, in which we heartily joined and waved our American flag while he ran off down the hall.

If the British haven't captured all the United States this summer, they certainly have captured by their cleverness a large portion of our population which is now sojourning on the British side of the Atlantic.

As we feast our eyes on these marvelous evidences of the departed glories of France, we cannot shake off a slight feeling of sadness which comes over us.

Our reflection wanders far back into the past centuries, and, in imagination, we see marching about the gorgeous apartments of this vast palace the thousands of gay, giddy devotees of fashion and folly, and among that great and changing throng of people we behold the reckless and dissolute Louis XIII; the extravagant, vain, immoral and haughty Louis XIV; the modest, virtuous and retiring Queen Marie Theresa; the beautiful and dashing Queen Marie Antoinette, descendant of the Cæsars, and once the brightest jewel in the Court of France; the gentle and lovely Dauphiness Adelaide; the charming, fascinating, graceful and bewitching Creole Empress Josephine, who, while all the courtiers of Europe revolved around her, displayed such noble traits of character and exhibited such unaffected kindness that she won all hearts, the lowly and the exalted alike; the dignified, aimable and cultured Marie Louise; the proud and ambitious Corsican "Little Corporal" Napoleon, and the noble Italian and Christian Queen Marie Amelie.

And in the coming and going of these royal spectres of the past, we read the eventful and bloody history of France.

We did not give any special time to examining the fountains about the park and gardens, as the water was not flowing at that time. There was to be a grand illumination of those wonderful masterpieces on Sunday night in honor of the Shah of Persia, and our visit to them was therefore deferred to that time so that we might see them in their grandeur and complete beauty.

Our interest in the strangely fascinating pictorial palace being so intense we did not note the rapid passage of the time until we suddenly discovered that it was late in the afternoon, and as we intended to visit the celebrated porcelain factory at Sevres, about six miles distant, we saw that only by very fast driving could we reach Sevres before five o'clock, at which time the manufactory was closed.

Therefore we hastened to our carriages, the drivers cracked their whips and the heavy vehicles soon sped away, and we left that enchanted palace and "all the glories of France" to the admiration of other tourists who will visit it during the coming centuries and marvel at its splendor, just as we have done to-day.

Our drive to Sevres was through a lovely portion of suburban France, every mile of which is full of historical interest.

Pausing but a moment at the little towns of Viroflay and Chaville we hasten on and reach Sevres at 5.20 o'clock, after the porcelain works had been closed for twenty minutes.

But we were determined to see the factory if possible, and Americans are not easily turned aside from their intentions, so a few gratuities properly applied by our guide soon opened the factory and a workman showed us the process by which that most beautiful and expensive porcelain is produced.

The workman placed a lump of clay about the size of a cocoanut on the revolving rod, and it seemed that it was simply a touch of his fingers here and there which shaped it alternately into the most graceful vases, urns, bowls, pitchers, &c. Then by a slight touch of a sharp instrument he formed an exquisitely beautiful cup which he handed to one of our ladies. When she took it into her hand it crumbled into dust.

Many of the party brought away pieces of the lump of clay which the workman had manipulated for us. The process of firing and ornamenting the vessels was explained to us in French while our guide interpreted.

In the exhibition rooms and the *Musee Ceramique* we examined some wonderful specimens of porcelain representing the art in the various ages. We thought of buying some genuine article of Sevres manufacture as a souvenir, but on learning that the cups and vases which we wanted were priced from fifteen to forty dollars, we changed our minds as to souvenirs and decided that the articles could not be carried to America without risk of being broken!

There are some porcelain vessels on exhibition in the museum worth $20,000.

This celebrated porcelain factory is the result of the discoveries in ceramic art made by Plassidy, whose history of the struggle in his researches and investigations is sad and touching.

Plassidy was sure that the art had by no means reached perfection, and he believed that a certain degree of temperature and time for firing the porcelain would produce a more beautiful effect than anything before attained in the manufacture of the ware. In his experiments he had exhausted his own funds, and he resolved to make one more effort to develop the perfection in porcelain which he desired.

He therefore prepared another furnace and borrowed all the money that his friends would lend him to keep up the fires. These funds were also soon exhausted and he could borrow no more. The ware was not sufficiently fired and the furnace was cooling for the need of more fuel! What should the poor man do? Not another franc could he beg or borrow, and the fires *must* be kept up or else he would again fail.

In his extremity he hesitated no longer, but cut up his furniture, his bedstead, chairs and tables, and with them he kept the furnace heated until he had attained success and produced the first of that marvelously beautiful porcelain that is now made at Sevres, and which is the wonder and admiration of connoisseurs in ceramic art throughout the world, and which has never been equaled or even successfully imitated anywhere else on the globe.

Indeed, it is not strange that in the court at the main entrance to this noted manufactory there should stand in eternal brass a splendid statue of PLASSIDY, the author and founder of ceramic art.

Our drive back to Paris in the afternoon was highly enjoyable, it being the most pleasant part of the day, and just at the time when all Paris was out for a drive.

Along the smooth pavement of the suburban streets our horses dashed at a rapid gait, then through the lovely avenue Victor Hugo, to the Arc de Triomphe and down the grand Champs de Elysees, where thousands of handsome vehicles of every description were dashing along with fair occupants of every nationality.

Our beautiful American Stars and Stripes gracefully flying from the first carriage attracted great attention and excited the constant admiration of the people along that crowded thoroughfare. A waving of hat and a face full of smiles frequently seen in cabs as we met them, indicated that some delighted American traveler had seen his national flag, and that sight always brings a joyful and patriotic recognition in any land where a citizen of the United States may be found.

Reaching our hotel about seven o'clock we found dinner awaiting us, and a hungry crowd of North Carolinians were soon doing full justice to it without taking time to ask about the ingredients of the various French dishes on the bill of fare. Frequently, however, during the meal, the diners found time to say, "This has been our biggest and best day in Paris."

THE EDUCATIONAL EXPOSITION at the Teachers' Assembly this summer will indeed be a big thing. Twenty-three prominent schools have already applied for space for exhibits.

A TALK WITH GIRL GRADUATES.

BY KATE FIELD, EDITOR OF "WASHINGTON."

Kate Field has said a great many wise things, but nothing more sensible than the following counsel to girl graduates. Our teachers most pleasantly remember Miss Field in her visit to the Assembly in 1889.

"Some people make us feel pleasant in reading the nice, pretty things they write, others encourage us with their strong hopeful style, while some really give one the blues. Now here comes the "woman editor," strong, terse and strikingly original at all times, and none the less so in this talk with the girl graduates, and if she makes no one feel, she surely will make her readers, as they follow her through the following pointed paragraphs, do a little thinking. Miss Field says:

"Dear graduates, I don't know what it is to be a graduate myself. I never went to school after I was fifteen, and I never learned anything at school after I was twelve. Not being a graduate, the world having been my university, you girls can probably teach me ologies and osophies I never heard of, yet I am asked to give you advice!

I want to ask you a few questions.

Do you really know anything thoroughly well? Are you mistress of your own language? Can you speak it purely and musically, or do you torture sensitive ears by talking through your noses with slovenly enunciation.

Do you sign your name so they who run may read, or does it require an expert to decipher it? I ask feelingly. I've been an editor just one year and a half, during which time I have gone more or less mad over more atrocious chirography than I dreamed possible in a nation of alleged universal education. The number of women who can't or won't write their names clearly is shameful. That so few women charm by refinement of speech tells a sad story of illiterate homes and culpable teachers.

Can you write an intelligent letter, spelled and punctuated properly throughout,—such a production as you would not be ashamed to have picked up in the street or read aloud in a court-room? If not, you may know something of ancient history and decline Latin verbs, but you are an awful failure in English.

Can you keep accounts? No? Then all your geometry won't avail you in facing a hard and practical world.

Have you a practical knowledge of physiology and hygiene? Did you ever study your own wonderful mechanism and the laws by which it is governed? Have you been taught to stand in awe of your own stomach? Have you learned what foods you can digest and what you cannot?

Do you realize that a sound mind is only possible in a sound body? Do you wear such clothing as gives perfect freedom to the vital organs? If not, your teachers have neglected to impress upon you the most important of all knowledge, the knowledge of yourself.

Can you earn your own living? If not, dear graduates, it seems to me that your lives so far have been thrown away, and the sooner you begin again the better.

There are exceptional men and women who are a law unto themselves to whom schools and universities are more or less a nuisance. These people, having rare talents, are to be given their heads and let alone. Sooner or later they work out their own salvation in their own way, and the world is the gainer. The general average of human beings stand upon a commonplace plane, and if they don't do commonplace duties well they fail to fulfil their destiny.

Taking it for granted, therefore, that many of you graduates do not feel called upon to startle the world with the corruscations of genius, that you are going home to be a comfort to fond parents, let me ask whether you are good housekeepers. Can you cook? If not, in the name of common sense, of the man you propose to marry, of the friends who may visit you, of an innocent posterity, don't rest until you have learned the business of almost every woman's life, which is to keep house well and economically. The woman who can't turn her servants out of doors and do their work better than the best of them, has no right to marry unless she has money enough in her own right to employ a skilled housekeeper to carry out her orders.

Dear graduates, cooking is the alphabet of your happiness. I do not hesitate to affirm that this republic, great as her necessities are in many directions, needs cooks more than all else. The salvation of the national stomach depends upon them. We are a nation of dyspeptics, and Americans are dyspeptics because they eat the wrong foods, badly cooked, which they drown in ice-water. They are dyspeptics because our women don't know the rudiments of their business, and resign their kitchen into the hands of incompetent servants, of whom they are afraid, and whose impudence they frequently endure through sheer helplessness. Be cooks first, and anything you please afterwards. On you posterity waits.''

THE FRIENDLESS GIRL.

I don't mean by this the girl who is alone in the world, but I mean the girl who thinks she cannot make friends, and who has become morbid and unhappy about it.

In the first place, friends are not blocked out like caramels; you may have no end of acquaintances—pleasant ones—but friends come with years. The two weeks' acquaintance is not the one with whom it is wise to be confidential, nor should you count upon her eternal fidelity.

My dear girl, in this busy world so many people have so much to do that they cannot form many close friendships, and they choose the people they prefer. If you are absolutely friendless, in the sense that I mean, the fault must lie a little with you. Probably you are a wee bit selfish, and selfishness and friendship, like oil and water, do not mingle well. You claim that you love everybody. Now love is too precious a thing to give to every one.

Suppose I tell you a little story: There were once two beautiful fox-terriers; when a stranger came to the house where they lived one of them rushed to meet the visitor, lavished caresses upon her, and quickly coiled itself in a most comfortable position on her lap. The other dog stood quietly by; if it were asked for a paw, it gave it, but always retreated and sat down beside its master.

Somebody said one day, speaking of the first: "How different this dog is from the other; it is so much more affectionate!" "Oh, no," said their master, "you are very much mistaken; the dog who is so affectionate with you, gives its affection to every stranger it meets; the other one waits until it knows you well and then from that time on it is your friend, and is ready to greet you and show signs of its friendship.

"When I was ill, the dog that you call the affectionate one preferred to stay with strangers; the other one rested at the foot of my bed and refused to stir. When my sister sat there crying because of some trouble that had come to her, the dog that loved everybody went into another room, but the other dog went up to her, licked the tear-stained hands, looked up into her face with his soft brown eyes as if he were trying to say, 'I'm your friend, don't worry.'"

This points a little bit of moral, and it means that while you can have plenty of pleasant acquaintances you will find that a *few* friends are best worth having; and that—I must repeat it—if you are friendless, there must be a fault in you that is the cause.—*Exchange.*

THE "SCHOOLMA'AM."

In view of the fact that there will be a great many North Carolina teachers in Chicago visiting the World's Fair, the following article from *The Interior* (Chicago) is somewhat prophetic:

"The schoolma'am is in Chicago, thousands upon thousands of duplicates of her. The cool, level eye, the exact propriety of speech, the neat but plain apparel, the quickness and directness of ocular observation, the self-confidence which comes of self-support.

The schoolmarm! She is conjugations and equations preserved in sugar. She is dignity and propriety after the similitude of ripe peaches and whipped cream. In these days everybody cannot marry a schoolmarm, but the time was when everybody who was anybody did, because all the nice girls took their turn at it.

The thousands, more or less, of schoolmarms in Chicago now are just a little more professional in their airs than they were thirty or forty years ago, because teaching is more of a profession. The schoolmarm now is usually a graduate of the "Normal" and a sort of "Normal" atmosphere prevades her presence. She talks Normalese.

But a fellow is coming along to each one of them who will break through all that. She will wash the ink off her fingers, she will lay aside the grammar and the algebra and the chalk. She will heave a happy little sigh as she glances around at the empty little desks, and as her eye follows the receding, homeward-bound throng of children.

Then she will turn a tender face toward the new path of life—with one to lead the way—and her schoolmarm days—happy days—will be over forever.

God bless the schoolmarms now and forever! They are just the pink, the perfection, the carved capitals of womankind. You cannot say anything so nice of them that any old fellow who was married from thirty to forty years ago will fail to say: ' Amen—that's so, brother!'

That is because he married one himself.''

THE MAP MAKERS ARE WRONG.

"The publishers of school maps," says a teacher in the St. Louis *Globe-Democrat*, " are responsible for more errors than any other class of people on the planet.

"They use sometimes half a dozen different scales of size in a single book, and it is impossible for children to get a correct idea of the relative sizes of different countries because of the lack of uniformity in the scale.

"In an atlas for school use all the maps should be on the same scale, otherwise most incorrect ideas will be formed.

"I recently asked a bright schoolboy, who had just finished the study of geography and laid it by because he knew all about it, how large he supposed Arabia was. He reflected a moment, and then, with some confidence, replied that Arabia was about the size of Massachusetts. I suggested the possibility of his being mistaken, when he got his atlas and showed me that Arabia and Massachusetts were nearly the same size, that is, on the map.

"He opened his eyes when I explained to him the mysteries of the scale, and that instead of being a mere speck Arabia was as long as from St. Paul to New Orleans, as wide as from St. Louis to New York, and contained more than one-third as many square miles as the United States. He had been misled by the maps, as his teacher probably had also, and thousands of other people besides.

"A uniform scale would prevent many false ideas, and if a national series of text-books is ever adopted the atlases should have that feature prominent."

[For the North Carolina Teacher.]

EDUCATION AND LEARNING COMBINED.

BY E. H. ATWOOD, LINCOLN PARK, N. J.

With both education and learning, we, as teachers have to do. But the two are often confounded, for while education may include learning, the latter often excludes the former. To a large extent this has been the case in our common country schools, but is not confined to them alone. In many of our higher schools, and even in our colleges, have true educational principles been lacking.

Learning has indeed been the leading feature, and to this end pupils have been crammed and scholars studied until it seems as if their very heads would burst with knowledge. Education is the concrete, combining knowledge and practice, giving occupation to both body and mind, while learning is too often purely abstract.

Education that is thorough tends toward making the "perfect" man. Learning is apt to make a man disproportionate, very much like the caricatures so often seen in our illustrated papers of great men with "large" heads and "slim" support.

Man is so constituted that unconsciously he yields to educational forces. These forces being either good or bad, how careful he ought to be.

One need not learn unless he choose, but he cannot escape education. Not that learning is to be despised, or treated at all lightly, for education, to be thorough, *must* include this, and as we gain far more from books than by experience, great care should be taken lest they become too great a prop and we too indifferent.

In the first stage of a child's life many educational forces appear. He seldom learns to read until nearly six, but oh! if his parents are faithful what a number of disciplinary lessons he has had, and *by experience* how many! Thus when he is placed under our charge he has been *educated* up to a certain point, but is not *learned* from books.

And how carefully ought we to see that as he enters the vast field of learning his *education* still continues.

How many times does the high school or college graduate, thinking his diploma will certainly give success in the branch of business which he has so thoroughly studied, find to his sorrow that learning is *not* education.

His schoolmate left school at fifteen, entered a store as clerk and now is a successful merchant. Why? Because he became educated to the business. He has had the actual practice. This is not an isolated case. Thousands of our young men have learned by bitter experience that theory and practice are quite different.

What shall we say, then? That in order to succeed one must not study books, not become learned? No, not by any means. Books are of untold value and *must not* be neglected. They may become great helps toward education.

The truth is just here, *we fail to join the two;* they should go hand in hand. The first young man had the actual practice while studying to be a merchant, the abilities of both being equal, would have far outstripped his school-mate. He would have had a higher standing socially and a wider field of usefulness.

And right here the question may be asked, why cannot the business principles learned at school be applied when we enter life's work? They *must* be applied and could, *if we only knew how.* Here lies the difficulty. Is not too much dependence put upon books? Do we not feel too secure, and become too indolent to investigate and practice?

An easy chair by a cosy fireside has its attractions, and we had much rather stay in it than venture out in storm or darkness.

American people are fond of ease—their children none the less so. Have not books become to them an easy chair, where they spend many moments in the pleasure of taking *in* new ideas—moments of pure receptiveness—rest?

Our educational leaders of to-day are working up to this, and as a natural result are following closely Pestalozzi's plans and Frœbel's methods. We are entering a *new* era, and to it all honor and great success. An era when diplomas held by graduates will mean something more than learning merely—they will mean a *knowing how.*

How proud, then, we ought to feel, that we are of that vast army of workers who try to educate and instruct, so that their pupils shall be not ornamental only, but useful and practical as well—men and women who have the *why* and *how* combined, whose education is both extended and thorough.

NORTH CAROLINA TEACHERS are moving in the matter of a State Educational Exhibit at Morehead City in June, and at Chicago in 1893, and success is assured.

[For The North Carolina Tacher.]

THE BATTLE OF ALAMANCE AND ITS CAUSES.

PRIZE ESSAY, BY T. W. COSTEN, JR., NEW GARDEN, N. C.

One of the most memorable battles that was ever fought upon North Carolina's soil was the battle of Alamance, for it was there that our forefathers first shouldered their arms and marched to the defense of their country. Oppressed as they were by England's tyrannical sovereigns and ruled by despotic governors, their free, brave and liberty-loving spirit was aroused, and they could no longer stand the oppressive laws of the tyrants.

From the year 1729, when North Carolina became subject to England, to the year 1765 the colonists lived at peace with the "Mother Country." Although the colonists did not think at any time that England had the right to make them pay tax, for "taxation without representation" they considered unjust, still no strife, war or contention of any importance prevailed among the people. And it was not until the English Parliament passed a law called the "Stamp Act" that a rebellious spirit arose in the colonists, and they declared that no such law should prevail in the colony.

Tryon, the Governor of North Carolina, who was a very deceitful man, had succeeded by his polite and winning ways in gaining many friends in the colony, but he could not show them the advantage of a "Stamp Act," for the people knew that it was not for their good but rather to help fill England's coffers with gold.

So when the Governor, on the 6th of January, 1776, issued a proclamation announcing that stamps had arrived. from England and were ready for use, the people became so aroused and excited, not only in North Carolina, but in all America, that England had to repeal the law.

2

About this time many emigrants came from the Old Country to America and settled in the central and western parts of North Carolina. Farming being the chief occupation of the people at this time, these people had to resort to it, and as they had settled in the part of the country which was adapted to the raising of grain, they turned their attention to the raising of wheat, which they considered as their moneyed product.

After harvest they had to carry their wheat to market, which was at Cross Creek, now Fayetteville, North Carolina. Most of these farmers lived a great distance from this place, and we can say that they labored under many disadvantages, for wheat was exceedingly low, and they hardly realized enough from it to buy salt for family use.

At this time they were oppressed by heavy taxes, each man being assessed twelve dollars poll tax and seventy-five cents per hundred acres of land. These taxes were increased by dishonest sheriffs until the people were unable to pay them. The officers were growing rich by draining the money out of the poor farmers' pockets.

Colonel Edmund Fanning, Register of Deeds in Orange county, had become rich, and was the "leader in this oppression." Herman Husbands, a Quaker preacher, was a native of this same county. He saw and realized the hardships that these people were undergoing, so he besought them to bind themselves together in a "Mutual Protection Association" against their oppressors, which they did, and their order was known as the Regulators. This order was only organized for protection, not to create any disturbance; but the Governor and his followers thought different, therefore they did what they could to disorganize them.

Many troubles arose. Among the first was the taking of a horse that belonged to one of the Regulators who went to Hillsboro to see the Sheriff, but the horse was taken back by force. That night Husbands was arrested but gave bail and was released until Superior Court. When he was going out of Hillsboro he met several hundred of his men coming to his rescue. Governor Tryon thinking there would be a rebellion, raised an army of eleven hundred men in Mecklenburg and Rowan counties and marched back to Hillsboro.

Court was in session, Husbands was released, but other Regulators were heavily fined, while Colonel Fanning was fined only one penny in each of five cases where he had been accused of extortion in office.

By the Governor raising an army of men and the Court's favoring the English officers more than they did the Regulators the people were aroused more and more, and things continued to grow from bad to worse until Husbands was dismissed from the "House of Assembly" and put in prison for talking about Judge Maurice Moore. He was released, and his being released caused him to stop several hundred men who had started to release him, and who would have probably done much damage. In 1771 Governor Tryon went into the eastern counties and raised an army of eleven hundred men and marched them to Orange county to put down what he called the "rebellion of the Regulators."

On the 16th of May, 1771, Governor Tryon, with his eleven hundred men met a company of Regulators numbering two thousand men at Alamance. Governor Tryon fired the first shot and ordered his men to fire. A battle then ensued in which good fighting was done until the amunition of the Regulators gave out and they had to retire from the field, driven back but not conquered. Many valiant heroes lay dead upon this field of carnage; fell fighting for their rights, resisting British oppression, and their names are cherished in our memories as being the first to take up arms in defense of their homes.

But all that North Carolina gained from the battle was that many of these despotic officers left the province.

SAVE THE BOYS.

Why do the boys drift away from the upper grades of school?

One writer says it is because the teachers are mostly women, and the boys of the "hobbledehoy" age need masculine government and masculine leadership. But the drift out of the school is as great in the high school where there is usually at least one male teacher.

Another says it is because the boys are anxious to be earning something, or their parents are anxious for them. but in these days girls can earn money as well as boys, and girls cling to school longer than boys on an average. Still there is doubless something in this argument, especially for what may be called the middle class of families, whose boys are not ashamed to hire out to work at anything, but whose girls are inclined to play lady and only engage in certain selected occupations. In this class the girls largely aspire to be teachers, to attain which distinction a considerable degree of education is required, which accounts for many girls staying in school.

But in every village or city many boys may be seen on the streets who are not at work and who are not in school. These truants are not only a loss to the school, but they are a loss to the community as well. Boys and girls who are at work may be losing one form of education, but they are gaining another education of moral and intellectual value.

Boys, and girls, also, if there are any such, who are not at work and not in school, but on the streets, are also gaining an education, such as it is. They are being educated in idleness, in love of evil comradeship, in vices of various kinds, and are on the road that may lead to crime. Most professional criminals are recruited from this class. Most tramps were first truants on the street. Most of the gangs of rowdies in the cities are filled up from time to time by the boys who ought to have been at school or at work.

These statements show that the danger of truancy is not measured by mere numbers, and the value of a good school in diminishing truancy is not limited to the amount of arithmetic and geography which can be drilled into reluctant brains.

Boys who are kept busy at school or at some gainful occupation are saved from the great temptations of idleness.

The value of farm life is that there is always work to be done, and that the temptations of street life are absent. Cities are the nurseries of crime.

To thoroughly deal with this problem two things are needed—truant-officers and ungraded departments. Truant-officers are needed to bring in the boys; ungraded departments are needed to take care of them after they are brought in. The truants, and also other boys who are out of grade for good or bad reasons, should be placed where they can study something new and valuable to them, and not be obliged to drop back below where they belong, because they are not ready for the next higher grade.

With these two aids many a truant boy can be saved, at little cost to the community, who might otherwise be a burden and a terror, as a rowdy, a tramp, a criminal and finally as a pauper.

Save the boys.—*Wisconsin Journal of Education.*

THE PUBLIC GRADED SCHOOLS in North Carolina do not make sufficient effort in behalf of the boys and girls in the suburbs of the cities. These children most need the school and yet they are allowed to stay away and grow up in crime.

IN THE SCHOOL-ROOM.

SUGGESTIVE.

To the lovers of epigramatic, straight-forward advice, the following exhortations, among a hundred similar ones in the same circular, will be appreciated. They are given by a county superintendent to his teachers:

Teach the outline map of North Carolina to the school. If they say the preceding teacher taught it, do not let this make any difference with *your* teaching it again.

If there is a globe in the school-room use it. If you do not know how to use it, *learn* how.

Read each issue of your educational journal. If you do not take a journal *you should*.

Do not think you can teach successfully and also run to parties two or three nights each week. Just as sure as you do this you will be the subject of the talk of the neighborhood.—*Adapted.*

EXERCISES IN LETTER–WRITING.

Write a business letter on one of the following themes:
1. Order a book.
2. Order a newspaper.
3. Apply for a situation.
4. Decline an offer of a situation.
5. Ask for a recommendation.

FASTIDIOUS SPEECH.

How many people are there who pronounce any proportion of their words correctly, not merely by reason of clipping and mouthing, but by ignorance of good usage.

We find them everywhere, and they lay the accent on the first instead of the second syllable of "acclimate" for example; they pronounce the second syllable of "acoustics" *coo* instead of *cow;* they do not put the accent on the last syllable of "adept," as they should do; they leave the *u* sound out of "buoy"; they pronounce "duke" with the sound of *oo* instead of with the simple long *u;* emphasize the first instead of the second syllable of "enervate," and sound the *t* in "often."

They are astonished to know that "precedence" has the accent on the second syllable, and "placard" on the last; that "quay" is called *key;* that "sough" is *suf;* that the *z* instead of the *s* sound is to be given in "sacrifice," and the reverse in "rise" that "subtile" and "subtle" are two different words; that the last syllable of "tortoise" is pronounced *tis* instead of *tus;* that it should be "used" and not *ust;* and that it is not the "zoo" but the *zoological* gardens where one goes to see the chim*pan*zee, and not the chimpan*zee.*

It is quite time, we think, when we hear one of these talkers, for some of the fancy work and fancy studies of the day to be dropped and a little hard work on the dictionary put in their place.—*Exchange.*

DID you ever try to interest your pupils in a school saving bank? Such an institution can be very easily managed, and nothing can be better for teaching business ideas and principles.

PROPER NAMES IN GEOGRAPHY AND HISTORY.

Some one, somewhere, has said:. "In teaching geography or history, write on the blackboard every proper name when used for the first time. · Let every pupil copy it on slate or note-book. Let one or two spell it orally. Reserve two or three minutes at each recitation for a review in spelling proper names. Let the pupils sometimes spell orally; and sometimes write from dictation the names selected by the teacher.

"Frequently give, as an exercise, a list of proper names to be brought in class neatly written, and properly spelled. If you do not use some such device, even though you may have a class finely informed on the subject-matter, you will be mortified whenever they are put to a test on the spelling of the names of persons or places."

This same method may be carried out in other branches, in teaching the spelling of common names, especially in physiology and arithmetic.—*Iowa Normal Monthly.*

THE SIGN OF EQUALITY.

Mathematical readers will be interested in the following quotation from Robert Recorde, who introduced the sign of equality into algebra.

Recorde was the first English author who wrote on the subject of algebra. In his treatise called "Whetstone of Witte," published about 1557, he says:

"To avoid the tedious repetition of these words, is equelle to, I will sette, as I doe often in worke use, a paire of parallel lines of one lengthe, thus: =, because no 2 thynges can be more equalle."

SHE COULD AND SHE COULDN'T.

FOR RECITATION.

She could sing and she could play,
She could dance from night till day,
She could while the hours away,
    So 'tis said;
She could skate and she could paint,
She could play the patron saint,
But she couldn't and she wouldn't
    Make a bed.

She could walk eight miles a day
And play tennis charmingly,
Flirting in a saucy way,
    Little scamp!
She could drive and play base-ball,
She could make a stylish call,
But she couldn't and she wouldn't
    Clean a lamp.

She could swim and she could row,
She could always have a beau,
And I'm sure that we all know
    She was shy.
She could laugh and she could prance
She could play a game of chance,
But she couldn't and she wouldn't
    Make a pie.

She could etch and write a book,
She could vanquish with a look,
She could win by hook or crook,
    I confess;

She could scold and she could flout,
She could cry and she could pout,
But she couldn't and she wouldn't
    Make a dress.

She could talk of church affairs,
But knew naught of household cares;
But I'm sure that none compares
    With sweet Nan;
Even if she couldn't bake
Bread and pies and angel cake,
She entrapped and she captured
    A rich man!   —*Bar Harbor Bazoo.*

A PRACTICAL SPELLING LESSON.

Lay aside for a day the spelling-book, and try an exercise like the following:

Let the pupils take their slates and write their own names in full.

Write the teacher's surname.

Write the name of the county in which they live, the State, their post-office address.

Tell where Scotchmen came from.

Tell how old a boy is who was born in 1879.

Write the names of four winter amusements; of four summer amusements.

Write how many days in this month.

Write what we plant to get potatoes.

Write a definition of a druggist.

Write the names of six pieces of furniture.

Write the names of six kinds of tools.

Write the names of the seven days.

Write the name of the year, month and day of the month.

Write a verse of poetry and a verse of Scripture from memory.—*American Journal of Education.*

LITTLE FOLKS AT PLAY.

Children who drill
Seldom are ill,
For sinking, tiptoeing, and right and left going,
And shouting and clapping, and measured out tapping,
Strengthen their limbs,
Drive away whims,
Make faces shine brightly, make spines grow uprightly;
So, I suppose,
Illness all goes.

Children who learn
Bodies to turn,
And bodies to bend low, and noddles to send low,
And elbows to fetch out, and fingers to stretch out,
Seldom look pale,
Delicate, frail,
And seldom are sulky, and seldom too bulky,
And seldom are spiteful but always delightful.
So, then, we will
Beg leave to drill.

—*Exchange.*

USE YOUR GIFT of speech to give comfort, joy, cheer, and hope to all about you. Use it to encourage the disheartened, to warn those who are treading in paths of danger, to inspire the indolent with holy motives, to kindle the fires of heavenly aspiration on cold heart-altars.

North Carolina Teachers' Assembly.

ORGANIZATION FOR 1891-'92.

OFFICERS:

HUGH MORSON (Raleigh Male Academy), President, . . Raleigh.
EUGENE G. HARRELL (Editor TEACHER), Sec. and Treas., . Raleigh.

VICE-PRESIDENTS:

1. J. J. Blair (Supt. Graded Schools), ... Winston.
2. J. E. Kelly (Model Male School), ... Charlotte.
3. Miss Catherine Fulghum (Graded School), . . Goldsboro.
4. W. J. Ferrell (Wakefield Academy), . . . Wakefield.
5. Miss Lizzie Lindsay (Graded School), . . . Greensboro.
6. P. M. Pearsall (County Superintendent), . . Trenton.
7. Miss Lina McDonald (Graded School), . . . Winston.
8. T. J. Drewry (Horner Military School), . . . Oxford
9. Mrs. S. Montgomery Funk (Chowan Bap. Fem. Inst.), Murfreesboro.

EXECUTIVE COMMITTEE:

Hugh Morson, *ex officio*, President, ... Raleigh.
Eugene G. Harrell, *ex officio*, Secretary, . . . Raleigh.
Eben Alexander (University of North Carolina), . . Chapel Hill.
W. L. Poteat (Wake Forest College), ... Wake Forest.
James Dinwiddie (President Peace Institute), . . . Raleigh.
Charles D. McIver (Pres't Normal and Industrial School
    for Women), ... Greensboro.
J. Y. Joyner (Superintendent Graded School), . . Goldsboro.
A. C. Davis (Superintendent Military School), . . Winston.
E. E. Britton (Principal High School), ... Roxboro.

NINTH ANNUAL SESSION, MOREHEAD CITY, JUNE 21 TO JULY 2, 1892.

ASSEMBLY NOTES.

YOU will find the Atlantic Hotel and the Teachers'
Building wearing a handsome new dress of paint when you
go to the Assembly this summer. There are also a number of other pleasant surprises in contemplation.

Two things which every teacher in the South owes to the profession—attend first the State meeting of your co-workers, and then the meeting of your Southern Educational Association. These two great gatherings will give inspiration for a year of very pleasant and successful work.

THE Woman's Christian Temperance Union will have charge of the programme on Friday, June 24th. We expect addresses from Mrs. Lucy Hunt, of Massachusetts, Mrs. M. M. Snell, of Mississippi, and a number of other prominent members of the Union, upon "The Method and Manner of Temperance Teaching in the Public Schools," and kindred subjects. Mrs. S. E. Craven, of Concord, is arranging this programme, and she will give the Assembly a most instructive and interesting day.

MR. JOHN O. PLANK, of Chicago, has been engaged by the Atlantic Hotel Company to manage the hotel this season. He is one of the most expert hotelists in this country, having had much experience in the management of some of the most popular summer hotels in America. He knows the wants of guests and he knows how to supply them in the most satisfactory manner. The Teachers' Assembly and the summer visitors to charming Morehead City are to be congratulated on being the guests of Mr. Plank.

THE TEACHERS' ASSEMBLY EDUCATIONAL EXPOSITION this summer is going to be a big thing. The leading schools have already asked for space for their exhibit, and the displays will fill the Teachers' Building. Among the schools which have already secured space for exhibits are the University, St. Mary's School, Peace Institute, Agricultural and Mechanical College, Institution for the Deaf and Dumb and Blind, Granville Institute, Thomasville Orphanage, Graded Schools at Raleigh, Wilmington, Charlotte, Goldsboro, Lexington Seminary, Mt. Olive High School, and the four colleges for boys.

DR. EDWARD S. JOYNES, of the University of South Carolina, has kindly consented to attend the Assembly this summer and address the teachers. This distinguished Southern educator will find a great many of his strong friends at Morehead City, who have been long using his excellent text-books of modern languages. Dr. Joynes is a most able and fascinating speaker, and at the meeting of the Southern Educational Association on Lookout Mountain last summer hundreds of southern teachers were charmed by his able and eloquent address. We extend to him in advance a most cordial welcome to Morehead City.

ARE YOU preparing your educational exhibit for the meeting at Morehead City? We know of eight or ten new scholars that a certain school secured on account of the fine exhibit made by that school in the Assembly's Educational Exposition at Morehead City in 1890 and 1891. We know of a graded school superintendent who was elected to a better and more remunerative position specially by reason of the exhibit of work at Morehead City which had been done by his pupils. No graded school or private boarding-school, no college nor the University can afford to be without representation in the Assembly's Educational Exposition this summer.

COLONEL JULIAN S. CARR, one of the most successful business men of the South, has accepted an invitation to address the Teachers' Assembly this summer upon the timely and important topic, "What Business Men Expect of the Public Schools." Every superintendent and teacher of public schools ought to be present and hear this suggestive question discussed. It is proposed to inquire into and to show whether or not the schools supported by public taxation are doing the work which has been assigned to them by our Constitution and the School Law. Several public school officers will take part in the discussion of this interesting question.

THE "Inter-Collegiate Oratorical contest" for the Teachers' Assembly gold medal will be one of the new and most interesting features of the Assembly programme this summer. There will be but one speaker admitted to the contest from each society of our four principal colleges for males; the oration is to be original and the length of the speech is limited to fifteen minutes. All the colleges will be represented by their best speakers in this contest and there will be hundreds of friends of each institution present on the occasion. College societies who propose to enter the contest are requested to notify the sceretary as early as possible, so that the programme may be properly arranged.

IT IS PROPOSED to make the work of the Teachers' Bureau of the Assembly much more effective this year than ever before. Every teacher who desires a better position for next year, should address the chairman of the Bureau, Mr. David L. Ellis, Fair View, N. C., for "Information blank." Many applications have been filed already. Schools in need of teachers could not do better than to secure their teachers through the Assembly Bureau, because the chairman has had seven years experience in this special work, and thus he knows the qualifications of a large number of our best teachers better than anyone else No charge is made for any work done by the Assembly Bureau for our teachers, the only requirement being that they be *bona fide* members of the Assembly, and hold its certificate of membership for 1892, whether they can attend the Assembly or not. The Bureau filled forty positions last year, and over 1,000 communications passed through the hands of the manager. This is but one of the many practical benefits which members of the teachers' Assembly derive from the great organization.

THE Assembly programme this year will be more of a "popular" character than ever before. It is intended to

make all the work of special interest to " the people," and
we would be glad to see present several thousand persons
who are not teachers. The Teachers' Assembly intends
to keep away, as far as possible, from the "normal school
idea," and it strives to be what it set out to be— "a people's educational meeting under the direction of the teachers." Our great summer educational gatherings at Morehead City will, of course, be under the entire management
of teachers, but the objects of the meetings, as set forth in
our constitution, will be closely followed in arraging the
programme—"health, rest, recreation, and mutual improvement. The Teachers' Assembly is for the people,
and we want the people to attend it and enjoy it, and then
all the educational interests of North Carolina will be promoted to a most satisfactory degree. The teachers and
" the people " are to control the the destiny of North Carolina, and the object of the Teachers' Assembly is to bring
together annually all the people of North Carolina in a
good social and enthusiastic meeting to consult together
for the best interests of our State. If there should ever
exist a demand for a strictly professional and exclusive
meeting of teachers, perhaps somebody will undertake to
organize it.

WE HAVE about completed arrangements to have an
evening's entertainment by the "University Glee Club,"
of Chapel Hill. This is one of the very best college·
musical organizations in this country, and their songs have
received enthusiastic praise from their audiences. Their
presence at the Teachers' Assembly will add very much
to the enjoyments of the session. The Glee Club will
be assisted in their entertainment by several members
of the Assembly, comprising the finest musical talent in the
State.

THE RAILROADS have, at the special request of the Executive Committee, made a new arrangement for Assembly tickets this year. The rate will be the same as heretofore, about one-and-a-quarter cents a mile each way, and the membership coupon for two dollars will be attached to each ticket to be paid with the fare. When you get to Morehead City, present the ticket to the Secretary and Treasurer, and he will take off the coupon and give you a "certificate of membership" which alone will secure for you the rate of one dollar per day at the Atlantic Hotel. All female members of the Assembly will have one dollar refunded to them by the Secretary and Treasurer on presentation of their ticket and coupon as the fee for women is only one dollar per year. This is an excellent arrangement, and saves you all the trouble of sending fees to the Secretary for your certificate. You simply buy the railroad Assembly ticket and come along. Persons who live on the lines of railroad which do not have on sale the coupon tickets can pay the membership fee when they arrive at Morehead City and secure the certificate of membership.

THE "QUEEN OF THE WEST INDIES."

NUMBER II.

Cuba comprises about forty-four thousand square miles of area, about four-fifths as large as North Carolina, but we do not believe that so much to interest and delight a traveler can be found anywhere else on the globe within the same area.

All other foreign countries, in their liberal contact with other nations, have necessarily kept up somewhat with the

3

manners and customs of the age, but the visitor to Cuba feels that he has been transported by some sudden and mysterious power into a land of the eleventh century. The antiquity around him, even of the things that are new, gives him unceasing cause for amazement and delight.

He finds that many Cuban ways are very different from the ways of all other people of the world, and he is surprised to notice that some of their habits are just the opposite of ours. Specially noticeable of these differences are the customs in Cuba to eat breakfast at noon and dinner at sunset; bring a person to you by motioning with your hand for him to go away; to have preaching in the church at 8.30 A. M., and Sunday-school at 11 o'clock; to put keyholes upside down on the doors; to applaud in the theatre by a prolonged hiss; to hold a person as guilty in the courts until he can prove himself innocent; to impose a fine of $12.50 on a housekeeper for cleaning up and repairing a premises and nothing for letting the house be dirty; to pay the priests promptly, but never attend the church services; to sell postage-stamps everywhere except at the post-office; to be unable to obtain revenue stamps from government officers (they must be bought of brokers on the streets); for servants to expect no fees and tips from a traveler; to live on the lower floor of a house and do the cooking upstairs; to have men for washerwomen, chambermaids and nurses instead of women; to look for plows, rakes and other hardware in a "chocolate shop"; and to see only men attend a burial at the cemetery while all women remain at home. But it is astonishing how quickly we become accustomed to these things and "fall in with the ways of the people."

On Sunday, while in Havana, we attended, at 9 o'clock A. M., high mass in the handsome Merced Cathedral. This building ranks as one of the most elegant religious edifices on the ear.h. All its appointments are truly magnificent, and at the close of the service we had the privilege and pleasure of examining all the interesting features of the building under the conduct of a most charming Spanish lady whom we met at the services. The lady was educated in Mobile, Alabama, and spoke American very well.

From the Merced church we went to the Cathedral of Havana, which was also celebrating high mass for the New Year Sunday. The service there was conducted in person by the Bishop of Havana in gorgeous robes of royal purple, assisted by twenty priests clad in richest of vestments. At the conclusion of the service the Bishop and all the officiating priests marched down the north aisle to the door, and large numbers of devout Catholics knelt before the Bishop and reverently kissed his hand.

Cuba people are not noted for their church-going proclivities. At this special high-mass service in the great Cathedral there were present just sixty-two persons besides the twenty officiating priests. Even of that small attendance thirty persons were from our party. It is often the case that a priest conducts a service when he is the only human being in the church except the sexton.

This cathedral enjoys the proud distinction of being the true resting-place of the great discoverer, CHRISTOPHER COLUMBUS. We listened to the history of the interment, walked close to his tomb and placed our hands tenderly upon his marble bust and believed that we were standing near the actual remains of the discoverer of our country. Other claims and statements have been made, but we are yet unshaken in our faith that the remains of Columbus truly rest in the Havana Cathedral.

In the evening most of our party attended services at the famous Baptist Cuba Mission, conducted by Rev. Alberto Diaz. This is the most remarkable and successful foreign mission work done by any denomination of Christians in any part of the world. The building, purchased by the Southern Baptist Convention of the United States for the church, was the famous "Theatre Jane" (pronounced Har-ny), situated in the centre of Havana. The mission was established about nine years ago, and there are now fifteen regular Cuban ministers, and over 18,000 members of the church, and accessions made at almost every meeting.

Dr. Diaz seated our entire party with him on the platform, and at the conclusion of the service he stated that all his members desired to clasp hands with the American party, therefore we stood in a line in front of the pulpit while the congregation passed by us, a cordial handshake and a pleasant word being received from each person. During the service, Miss Bessie Worthington, of Rocky Mount, one of our party, sang a charming solo, and at the conclusion of the service our party gathered around the organ and sang a number of inspiring "Gospel Hymns."

There were stopping at our hotel, the Mascotte, several leading members of the grand Spanish Opera Company, then playing in Havana. A very strong mutual attachment soon existed between our party and those ladies and gentlemen with wonderfully trained voices, and they made the parlor ring with sweet melody in the early evenings for our enjoyment.

There was no conversation between the parties except through an interpreter, because neither knew a word of the language of the other, but every lady seemed to be very happy with one another just the same. One of the ladies of the Opera Company, Miss Amalia Paoli, made a desperate effort to learn at least a few American words, and she was rewarded by sufficient success to say, when putting her arm lovingly around some charming girl of our party, "Me loves you," and the act amused us very much.

On our last morning in Havana, just before going on board our steamer all the party gathered in the parlor, being joined by all our kind Spanish friends, and for an hour we sang with intensest enthusiasm all our favorite Southern airs, " Old Folks at Home," " Dixie," " Old North State," " Ho, for Carolina," " Bonnie Blue Flag," " The Mocking Bird," and others. Our audience was highly entertained by our melody of patriotism, and many of them went on board our tug-boat, and accompanied us to the steamer, where, under the flutter of the Stars and Stripes, the *adios* were spoken.

It is a matter of great gratification to the American to realize that the beautiful emblem of his beloved country is honored in every land wherever displayed.

The steamer was soon loosed from her moorings and we regretfully turned our eyes toward the beautiful Cuban capital, while the vessel slowly steamed out of the placid bay and ominously began to yield to the motion of the " white caps " of the Gulf of Mexico, and the unmistakable warnings of sea-sickness prevailed upon us to postpone writing the conclusion of this tour until a more convenient season.

THE ASSEMBLY PROGRAMME.

Teachers are requested to send to the Secretary at once any suggestions they may have to make as to subjects which they desire to have placed on the programme for discussion, and all suggestions will be submitted to the Committee. By this means it is intended to present the best and most practical work that has ever been done by the Assembly.

Southern Educational Association.

ORGANIZATION 1891-1892.

SOLOMON PALMER, PRESIDENT, East Lake, Florida.
EUGENE G. HARRELL, SECRETARY AND TREASURER, Raleigh, N. C.
W. T. WATSON, ASSISTANT SECRETARY, Memphis, Tennessee.

THIRD ANNUAL SESSION, ATLANTA, GA., JULY 6-8, 1892.

VICE-PRESIDENTS:

1. E. B. PRETTYMAN, Maryland.
2. JOHN E. MASSEY, Virginia.
3. B. S. MORGAN, West Virginia.
4. S. M. FINGER, North Carolina.
5. W. D. MAYFIELD, S. Carolina.
6. S. D. BRADWELL, Georgia.
7. A. J. RUSSELL, Florida.
8. J. G. HARRIS, Alabama.
9. J. R. PRESTON, Mississippi.
10. W. H. JACK, Louisiana.
11. J. M. CARLISLE, Texas.
12. J. H. SHINN, Arkansas.
13. W. R. GARRETT, Tennessee.
14. ED. PORTER THOMPSON, Ky.
15. W. E. COLEMAN, Missouri.

EXECUTIVE COMMITTEE:

Solomon Palmer, *ex officio* Chairman, East Lake, Alabama.
E. G. Harrell, *ex officio* Secretary, Raleigh, North Carolina.
1. J. H. Phillips, Superintendent City Schools, Birmingham, Ala.
2. Dabney Lipscomb, Middleton, Mississippi.
3. Thomas D. Boyd, President State Normal, Natchitoches, La.
4. O. H. Cooper, Superintendent City Schools, Galveston, Texas.
5. J. W. Conger, President Ouachita College, Arkadelphia, Arkansas.
6. J. M. Stewart, Agricultural and Mechanical College, Lake City, Fla.
7. J. M. Greenwood, Superintendent Schools, Kansas City, Missouri.
8. R. N. Roark, State Normal College, Lexington, Kentucky.
9. Frank M. Smith, University of Tennessee, Knoxville, Tennessee.
10. Euler B. Smith, President State Association, LaGrange, Georgia.
11. Edward S. Joynes, University of South Carolina, Columbia, S. C.
12. Hugh Morson, President Teachers' Assembly, Raleigh, N. C.
13. C. E. Vawter, Superintendent Miller Industrial School, Crozet, Va.
14. W. R. White, Superintendent of Schools, Morganton, W. Va.
15. Daniel Gilman, Johns Hopkins University, Baltimore, Maryland.

THE EXECUTIVE OFFICERS of the Southern Educational Association are preparing a full circular of information concerning the approaching session in Atlanta. This circular will be mailed to several thousand prominent teachers throughout the South and to all educational journals. Persons receiving copies are requested to give the information the widest possible circulation in their sections.

THE DAILY sesssions will be held in Georgia's matchless Capitol building, where there is ample accommodation for the general meetings, and for the sessions of the various departments. There are six separate departments in connection with the Association work including "Superintendence," "Higher Education," "Secondary Education," "Southern Literature," "Pedagogy" and "Kindergarten and Primary Education." The railroads throughout the South have been asked to make a rate of *one fare for the round trip* with membership coupon of two dollars attached to each ticket. No doubt the request will be granted, and the liberal rate will bring together thousands of the South's best teachers in consultation at Atlanta.

THE PROGRAMME for the meeting of the Southern Educational Association at Atlanta in July will comprise interesting and important papers from the most eminent of the South's teachers. Among the important subjects to be discussed, are: "Thorough Training of Girls;" "What the people expect of the Public Schools;" "Industrial Training of Young Women;" "How can the People be Interested more in Popular Education;" "Pure English for Americans;" "Physical Culture in the Public Schools;" "The Teacher's Code of Ethics;" "The First Year's Work of the Teacher;" "Legal Relation of Teacher, Pupil and Patron;" "A Southern Literature for the South," and a number of other topics, equally as important and interesting, will make one of the best programmes ever seen at an educational meeting in this country.

THE EXECUTIVE COMMITTEE of the Southern Educational Association met in the parlor of the Kimball House in Atlanta on the 5th of February. President Solomon Palmer was in the chair, Secretaries E. G. Harrell and W. T. Watson reported the proceedings, and there was present a full representation of the fifteen Southern States. We do not think that a more enthusiastic and working meeting has ever been held by an Executive Committee of any organization. Governor Northen, School Commissioner Bradwell and City Superintendent Slaton met with the Committee; and there were also present with the Committee several prominent members of the Association, including Hon. J. H. Shinn, ex-President, and Superintendent of Public Instruction for Arkansas; Hon. J. R. Preston, Vice-President, Superintendent of Public Instruction for Mississippi; Hon. W. R. Garrett, ex-President National Educational Association, Superintendent of Public Instruction for Tennessee; Prof. Wharton S. Jones, of Memphis; Prof. C. J. Ramsey, Clinton, La.; Prof. F. M. Roof, Birmingham, Ala.; Prof. Frank Goodman, Nashville, Tenn.; Prof. Euler B. Smith, President Georgia State Teachers' Association. The claims of Birmingham, Montgomery and Atlanta were considered as a place for holding the next session of the Association, and the vote was unanimously given to Atlanta. The time selected for the meeting is July 6–8, 1892. Governor Northen pledged the heartiest support of all Georgia to the Association, and State Commissioner Bradwell promised an attendance of one thousand Georgia teachers. In addition to the regular programme, several pleasant excursions have been planned to interesting points in Georgia, including a visit to Indian Springs, and to Cumberland Island on the Atlantic Coast.

EDITORIAL.

"Then let all who love us, love the land that we live in,
(As happy a region as on this side of Heaven);
Where plenty and freedom, love and peace smile before us,—
Raise aloud, raise together, the heart-thrilling chorus,
Hurrah! hurrah! The Old North State forever!
Hurrah! hurrah! the good Old North State!

OUR SCHOOLS AT THE WORLD'S FAIR.

North Carolina must have a grand educational exhibit at the World's Fair in 1893. No State in the South has made more progress in educational matters within the past few years than North Carolina, and no State can make a better exhibit than ours.

To have a creditable display, much work is to be done both by teachers and pupils, but we hope that our teachers and pupils are so inspired with patriotism and State pride that the work will be joyfully undertaken and promptly performed. Every leading private and public school in the State should be able to make a good exhibit, and if there are any that can exhibit nothing, then such schools should be reorganized, for their work does not reach the standard of public duty and expectation. The State Board of Agriculture offers to pay all transportation both ways on articles sent for educational exhibition at Chicago, and will provide ample space for each exhibitor. We would suggest that you send for exhibit paintings, drawings, mechanical models, essays, specimens of penmanship, map drawings, and mouldings, botanical and mineral specimens collected and arranged by pupils. Also, if possible, send a drawing or painting, nicely framed, of your school building and surroundings, and inscribed underneath the picture a brief synopsis of the work done by your institution, its scope and names of the Faculty. Hon. S. M. Finger, State Superintendent of Public Instruction, has been selected by the North Carolina World's Fair Committee to superintend the educational exhibit from this State, and he will be glad to furnish teachers at any time whatever information may be desired in this matter. It will be nearly eighteen months before the articles are wanted for the World's Fair, and we begin this work so long in advance so that none of our prominent schools will fail to make an exhibit for the lack of due notice.

WE DESIRE to receive copies of the annual reports of all School Superintendents in this country, also copies of the proceedings of each State Teachers' Association in the South. For these things we will gladly make any return of courtesy that may be in our power.

NORTH CAROLINA boys and girls are studying North Carolina history. There has never before been seen in the State such an active interest taken in our history. In almost every school there is a class in either Spencer's or Moore's history of North Carolina, and in many schools both books are used.

FIFTY COPIES of "Black Beauty" were sent to new subscribers as premiums during the past thirty days. Every teacher, every child and every citizen of North Carolina ought to read this fascinating book upon the humane treatment of animals. "Black Beauty" is the autobiography of a beautiful black horse, and the noble animal tells his own story charmingly. We send a copy of this famous book to every new subscriber or renewal of subscription to THE TEACHER.

WE HAVE just secured a new edition of Dickens' complete works, fifteen large volumes, with large clear type, paper-bound, which we will send by mail, post-paid, with THE TEACHER for a year for only $2.50. This is the biggest and cheapest offer in standard books within our knowledge. We will also mail a set of the books to any person who will send us four new subscribers to THE TEACHER.

TO EVERY music teacher in North Carolina, sending us one dollar for a year's subscription to THE TEACHER, we will give twelve pieces of vocal and instrumental music of our own selection. The music is regular size and style, and the published retail prices of the pieces are from twenty-five cents to one dollar each. In ordering, state whether you want the pieces instrumental, vocal, or assorted.

THE DEMAND for copies of THE TEACHER containing the design of the North Carolina State flag has been unprecedented, and it quickly exhausted the extra edition of THE TEACHER. We have, however, a few copies of the State flag design, and will gladly supply any teacher desiring them so long as the supply holds out. We believe that during this school year over a thousand teachers in North Carolina will proudly display our State flag in their school-rooms. "So mote it be," and may the number be ten thousand instead of one thousand.

NORTH CAROLINA schools are enjoying a very prosperous spring term. While there is not quite so much building and improving of school property as usual, yet all the schools are full of pupils and the teachers are doing excellent work. The public schools have opened well since the holidays, and most of our counties will have nearly a four month's term, some of them longer. If our government should ever succeed in having a fair, honest and accurate census taken, North Carolina will, in many things, stand at the head of the list of Southern States.

WE WILL gladly furnish any public or private school in North Carolina with a first-class teacher, in any department, upon short notice, and without any charges or fees whatever. This is one of the special missions of THE TEACHER, and we have already supplied several hundred school vacancies with teachers. Sometimes we have on file more applications for positions than we have schools, and at others we have more schools than teachers, but we generally succeed in satisfying all applications in due time.

THE MOST thoroughly abused educational method in this age is the so-called "kindergarten." It is nominally "picture teaching," "object teaching" or "play teaching," but generally it is dealing with children as if they were idiots—entirely devoid of all thinking faculties. The mother who really desires not to have the mind of her children dwarfed into imbecility should be careful to keep them away from most of the present "kindergarten schools." The "object teaching" craze which places tiny dolls, tooth-picks, splints, beans and other nonsense before a child for the purpose of teaching numbers and for "developing the mind" will effectually destroy the thinking powers of your child, and the "sand table" for "teaching geography" will make an intellectual nothing of your boy or girl. The whole country is denouncing the "kindergarten fraud" and the "tooth-pick-splint-and-bean" nonsense in emphatic and unmistakable terms. Doubtless the kindergarten was originally a good thing, and there is yet some good in the method, but since the idea has fallen into the hands of fanatics it has lost most of its usefulness. In a Northern Sunday-school, where the kindergarten method is employed in teaching the scriptures, a teacher recently had the children singing "ding, dong, dell," to represent death in the crucifixion, while she made a number of marks on the black-board with red chalk to illustrate the shedding of blood! Poor children.

ABOUT OUR TEACHERS AND SCHOOLS.

Mr. L. A. Garner is teaching in Carteret County.

Mr. W. H. Grady has a good school in Duplin County.

Miss Mary Arrington has a good school at Whitaker.

Mr. A. L. Johnson has a good school in Yadkin County.

Miss Lena Allen (Peace Institute) has a fine music school at Durham.

Miss Julia Lane has charge of a good public school in Craven County.

Mr. J. B. Mills has a public school of forty pupils in Carteret County.

Mr. J. B. Parsons is principal of Catherine Lake Academy in Onslow County.

Messrs. H. O. Piner and M. L. Scott have charge of the public school at Morehead City.

Professor F. A. Fetter has an enrollment of one hundred pupils in Kernersville High School.

Mr. P. C. Duncan has, in Mitchell County, one of the most prosperous public schools in North Carolina.

Miss Marietta Sutton has an interesting private school at the residence of Mr. Uzzle, near Kinston.

Mr. J. W. Phillips has the public school at Marshallburg in Carteret County, with forty-five pupils enrolled.

Davidson College has in attendance one hundred and fifty-four students, the largest enrollment in its history.

Professor Baumann's music class at Peace Institute, Raleigh, entertained their friends in a charming *soirée* on February 13th.

Rev. J. A. Campbell has one of the most successful schools in Harnett County. One hundred and ten pupils are now enrolled.

Rev. J. B. Game is Principal of Ashboro Academy for Boys and Girls. Students are prepared for the University or any of our colleges.

Rev. B. W. Spilman (Wake Forest College) has charge of the public school at Smyrna. He has organized a military company among his students.

Several new Teachers' Councils have been organized in the State since the new year, and they are doing good work. Is your county organized?

Miss Willie Brown Graves, one of the most honored graduates in music of Peace Institute, has been engaged as assistant teacher of music for the spring term.

THE TEACHERS of Buncombe County will hold their next quarterly meeting at Asheville, February 27, 1892. An attractive programme has been made out for the occasion.

MR. D. MATT THOMPSON is succeeding admirably as superintendent of Statesville Graded Schools. Over five hundred pupils are enrolled and steps are being taken towards erecting a $10,000 building.

GREENSBORO COLLEGE FOR GIRLS has renewed the publication of its charming journal *The College Message*, and the January number contains a good portrait of the President, Dr. B. F. Dixon, with a sketch of his life.

TRINITY COLLEGE has an enrollment of two hundred students for the spring term, which will be the last term at the old location. The new buildings at Durham will be completed this fall, and Dr. Crowell expects to open the term with three hundred boys.

MISS LILLIE LEA has returned from Rome, Georgia, and takes charge of Leasburg Academy. The school opened on the 15th inst. with twenty-five pupils, with prospects of ten more to enter in a few days. We welcome Miss Lea home to the Old North State.

OUR UNIVERSITY has two hundred and forty-one students, the largest enrollment since 1861. Dr. Winston, the energetic and enthusiastic President, is succeeding in most effectually "reaching the people" and awakening an increased interest in collegiate education.

PROFESSOR THOMAS M. HUFHAM is President of Mars Hill College, Madison County. One hundred and ninety-three students are enrolled, the largest enrollment of any educational institution in Western North Carolina. The College has one large brick building, and another nearly completed, also a good library of four hundred volumes.

MISS SUDIE GAY, a very talented and successful student of the Wilson Collegiate Institute, went to Stanhope, Monday, at the urgent request of the Principals of the Stanhope Male and Female Academy, to take charge of the departments of Music and French in that school for a week or two, the teacher s of those departments being absent on account of sickness.

THE SCHOOLS of Raleigh are greatly increasing in popularity and prosperity. People throughout the State and the whole South realize the many valuable advantages which a boy or girl has who is educated at the Capital, and thus it is that every room at Peace Institute is full of girls, St. Mary's School is overrun with pupils, and Morson and Denson's Academy has an enrollment which beats all past record. Each of these schools has a larger patronage than ever before in its history. Besides, the schools of Raleigh have been remarkably free from cases of serious illness among the pupils during the general epidemic of "grippe" and pneumonia which has prevailed in other communities.

THERE SEEMS to be a martial spirit in the air. Mr. W. R. Skinner of New Berne, proposes, at an early day, to open a military school at Clinton, in Duplin County. This will make eight schools in North Carolina where the boys wear uniform.

THE THREE LITERARY SOCIETIES of Fair View College, aggregating about sixty members, hold joint public exercises March 4th, 1892. These Societies have shown much interest in their work. The ladies' Society, "The Philozelian," arranges the musical programme for all the public exercises of the College and for the young men's Societies, the "Agatheridon" and the "Erosophia."

THE EXECUTIVE COMMITTEE of the Western North Carolina Teachers' Association will hold a meeting in the city of Asheville, February 26th, for the purpose of deciding upon time and place for the next annual session of the Association. The place will doubtless be Waynesville, N. C., and the time about June 14–18, so as to give delegates to that meeting ample time to reach Morehead City in time for the North Carolina Teachers' Assembly, June 21st.

MR. ANDREW J. CONNER, the efficient County Superintendent of Northampton County, as another evidence of his enterprise, has begun the publication of a county educational journal. It is well edited in the special interests of the schools and the Northampton Teachers' Council. Both the journal and its progressive and energetic manager, friend Conner, have our very best wishes. Nearly every teacher in Northampton County will attend the Teachers' Assembly at Morehead City this summer.

THE NORMAL DEPARTMENT of Fair View College has now fifteen teachers pursuing the special course arranged for the Buncombe County public school teachers. This course embraces the required studies of the State list, and a two month's study of current and general pedagogical literature, with experimental class-work in the classes of the school. At the close of the work, those who pass the required examination will receive the diploma of this department, entitling candidates to the degree of Licentiate of Instruction.

FRIENDS ELLIS AND HURST have gotten up an extra good number of their journal for January. It contains full proceedings of the session of the Western North Carolina Teachers' Association with several portraits of prominent members. We are glad to see that they have adopted the advice of THE TEACHER, and that they do not try to form another State in North Carolina west of the Blue Ridge named "Western North Carolina," hence the name of their journal will in future be the *North Carolina Journal of Education*.

CUPID AMONG OUR TEACHERS.

'Tis said that " figures never lie,"
 That one and one are always TWO;
But Cupid proves, with work so sly,
 Some wondrous things that figures do.
And when he claims a teacher's hand
 All rules of figures then are done,
Though TWO before the preacher stand
 This one and one are ALWAYS ONE.

REV. J. B. GAME, Principal of Cedar Grove Academy, married Miss IRENE HUGHES of Roxboro on Monday February 15th.

MISS ANNA WILLIAMSON, a teacher in the Winston Graded School, was married on December the 29th to LIEUTENANT WALTER LEAK of Winston.

MR. E. P. MENDENHALL. Principal of the High School at Swepson-ville, married Miss MATTIE DAVIS of Yadkin College, his music teacher, on Sunday, February 7, 1892.

MISS MARY F. McDONALD, a teacher in Fair View College, Buncombe County, was married in the chapel of Fair View College on Thursday, February 4th, to Mr. J. W. JONES.

MISS ELLA S. PARKER, daughter of the late Captain W. C. Parker of Raleigh, who has been, for several years, in charge of a school near Wilton, N. C., was married on January 20th, to DR. T. B. LAWRENCE of Granville County.

A NEW SCHOLAR.

RICHARD HENRY LEWIS, son of Mr. Elisha B. Lewis, of Asheville Graded School, was born at Kinston on Wednesday, February 10, 1892.

IN MEMORIAM.

—

' Death hath made no breach
In love and sympathy, in hope and trust.
No outward sign or sound our ears can reach,
But there's an inward, spiritual speech
That greets us still, though mortal tongues be dust.
It bids us do the work that they laid down—
Take up the song where they broke off the strain ;
So, journeying till we reach the heavenly town,
Where are laid up our treasure and our crown,
And our lost loved ones will be found again.''

—

MR. DAVID E. TAYLOE, the faithful and efficient County Superintendent of Public Instruction of Bertie County, died at his home in Windsor on Sunday, January 24, 1892.

MISS FANNIE S. MYRICK, formerly a teacher of music in Wesleyan Female College at Murfreesboro, and also at Littleton Female College, died at Murfreesboro February 6, 1892.

MISS MINNIE BEARD, of Kernersville, died in South Carolina on February 15th. She was a graduate of Salem Female Academy and had been teaching music in South Carolina. She was greatly beloved by a large circle of friends.

AT RECESS.

—

The books and slates now put away,
And let us laugh a little while ;
For those who work there should be play,
The leisure moments to beguile.

—

"*Capital* punishment," so the boy said when the schoolmistress seated him with the girls.

TEACHER—"What is an 'April fool,' Robby ?" Robby—"The man who takes off his winter clothing on the first warm day."

4

A MERE CHANCE.—Professor—"To what circumstance is Columbus indebted for his fame?" Johnnie—"To the circumstance that America had not yet been discovered."

TEACHER IN ELEMENTARY GERMAN—"Now, Miss Mildred, you may decline a kiss." Miss Mildred (slowly)—"Excuse me, but I don't think a kiss can be declined. I never could decline one."

AN OBSERVANT PHILOSOPHER.—"Why should we not cry over spilled milk?" asked the teacher. "Because," replied the favorite scholar, we can recover about half of it by going to the nearest hydrant."

"I had to be away from school yesterday," said Tommy. "You must bring an excuse," said the teacher. "Who from?" "Your father." "He ain't no good at making excuses; ma catches him every time."

A LIMITED EDUCATION.—"Little Waldo Beaconhill was in a predicament to-day. A lady gave him a 'Robinson Crusoe,' in words of one syllable, and he couldn't read it. Poor child! He cried for twenty minutes." "That's queer, Waldo can read." "Yes, but only in words of eight syllables."

A POOR SCHOOL.—Jenks—"You are sending your boy to Prof. Teachim's classical school, are you not?" Winks—"Not now. I took him out. He was growing up a perfect ignoramus." "He was?" "Yes. Why, after three years at that school he didn't know any more about the United States than an editor of a London paper."

"NOW, BOYS," said the Boston public school teacher, just beginning a talk on "patriotism." "what is the meaning of the letters G. A. R. which we see so many men wearing on the lapel of the coat?" "Great American Robbers," said the smart boy on the back seat, and patriotism vanished from the school-room for that time.

HOW TO KEEP BOYS ON THE FARM.—"He told his son to *milk the cows, feed the horses, slop the pigs, hunt the eggs, feed the calves, catch the colt and put him in the stable, cut plenty of wood, split kindling, stir the milk, put fresh water in the creamery after supper, and be sure to study his lessons before he went to bed.* Then he hurried off to the club to take a leading part in the question, "*How to keep boys on the farm.*"

VISITOR (addressing a public school in New York)—"In the year 1825, my dear young friends, several boys walked from Salem to Boston and back, a distance of thirty miles, to hear Daniel Webster speak. If there were no railroads nor means of transportation to-day, would the boys of the present generation undertake such a journey, do you think?" Small boy (after a long silence)—"No, sir." Visitor—"Ah! and why?" Small boy—"Because Mr. Webster is dead."

THE NORTH CAROLINA TEACHER.

VOL. IX.   RALEIGH, MARCH, 1892.   NO. 7.

EUGENE G. HARRELL,   =   -   =   =   Editor.

PASSING THE PRIMARY SCHOOL.

Each morning, as we slowly pass
    The city's streets along,
We hear the voices of the class
    Ring out the Nation's song.
The lassies' treble piping clear,
    The laddies' deep bass growl,
And from the boy who has no ear
    A weird, discordant howl.

With swelling hearts we hear them sing
    "My country, 'tis of thee!"
From childish throats the anthems ring
    "Sweet land of liberty!"
Their little hearts aglow with pride,
    Each with exultant tongue
Proclaims: "From every mountain side
    Let Freedom's song be sung!"

Let him who'd criticise the time,
    Or scout the harmony,
Betake him to some other clime,
    No patriot is he.
From scenes like these our grandeur springs,
    And we shall e'er be strong,
While o'er the land the school-house rings
    Each day with Freedom's song.
                  —*Boston Courier.*

North Carolina Teachers Abroad:

A SUMMER JAUNT

IN

ENGLAND, SCOTLAND, IRELAND AND FRANCE.

CHAPTER XXVII.

"SUNDAY" IN PARIS.

THE FAITHFUL HISTORIAN—FRENCH SUNDAY IS SIMPLY A DAY IN
THE ALMANAC—WHEN IN PARIS DO AS THE PARISIANS DO—MASS
AT THE MADELAINE—"TO THE EXPOSITION"—A GRAND FUNERAL
AT THE PANTHEON—MILITARY PARADES—THE HIPPODROME—SEE-
ING THE FOUNTAINS PLAY AT VERSAILLES.

SEVERAL highly esteemed members of our party
endeavored by persuasion, threats and bribery to
prevent the Secretary from writing this chapter, setting forth the manner in which a distinguished party of
teachers from good old conservative North Carolina spent
a "Sunday" in the gay French Capital. But, as we have
before announced in this volume, as historian of this memorable tour it is our bounden duty to chronicle events as
they actually occurred, and so here goes for the facts in
this case.

Sunday, so-called, is a very different day in Paris from
what it is in North Carolina, in Scotland, or in London.
We have tried faithfully to observe Sunday, when there is
any Sunday, in whatever country we chanced to be.

There is no Sunday in Paris in the usual sense of the
word. It does not even appear in the French Almanac.
They have a day in their calendar, *Dimanche*, which about
corresponds to the same time in the week or month as the
American Sunday, but it is totally unknown in Paris as a

day of religious observance. It is simply placed at regular intervals in each month as a holiday, or *fête* day; or, as the American would express it, "a day for painting the town red." If the French calendar was built in strict accordance with French custom, the week would comprise Monday, Tuesday, Wednesday, Thursday, Friday, Saturday and Big Day, which last day is simply a day for leaving off regular work, changing your clothes and having a big time.

It is well known to our readers that during the reign of the "Goddess of Reason" in Paris, the people, in order to abolish forever even the suspicion that Sunday was a day for religious observance, decreed that the day should be stricken from the calendar and that the "day of rest" should occur every tenth day instead of the seventh. The plan succeeded, and although the government has since then restored "Sunday" to the seventh place in the calendar of the week, the ancient religious idea in the day has never been permitted to return to it.

All real travelers have faithfully heeded the very sensible injunction, "When you are in Rome you must do as Rome does," and our party also acknowledged this wise philosophy, and "accepted the situation."

We decided that we would try to *begin* the day in accordance with our American custom, however different might be the continuation and ending thereof, so we promptly attended "High Mass" at 9 o'clock in the Church de Madelaine. As we entered the building we found a great many people standing, while there were a large number of unoccupied chairs in the auditorium. We did not understand what this meant as we marched into the room and seated ourselves, but we were soon enlightened on the subject by the prompt appearance of an officer of the church in a brilliant red uniform trimmed with gold, who proceeded to collect from each one of us twenty cents for the use of the chairs. We paid the money more for the " big of the

thing" than for any other reason, and then watched the
priests, choir-boys, attendants and supernumeraries perform
the mysterious and wholly unintelligible ceremony of High
Mass.   This service is conducted in Latin, mainly for the
reason that the French people cannot understand it; and,
with the exception that a few devout persons seemed to
offer prayer at certain intervals, the entire audience appears
to be wholly indifferent to the proceedings.· There is a
continual buzz of conversation and the rustle of feet, to
which the priests pay no attention, interrupted only by the
uniformed officers in their search for the francs and other
revenue of The Church.   The Sunday service in a French
church is only a prescribed ceremony, without the slightest
suspicion of real worship of a Divine Being embodied in
the formula.

It may be said, however, to the credit of our party, that
many of our girls hunted up the celebrated McAll Mission
in Paris, to which they gave their encouragement and
presence on this memorable Sunday in Paris.   This Mission is under the auspices of the Presbyterians, and it is
doing a most wonderful and satisfactory work in Paris.

Leaving the Church of the Madelaine it was asked,
"Where shall we go now?"

"To the Exposition," replied the Secretary, "as that
seems to be the least objectionable place, according to American ideas, for spending a Sunday afternoon."

Therefore we repaired to the Exposition.   The buildings are all open on Sunday, the machinery is at work,
and all the amusements and entertainments of the "Big
Show" are open for the enjoyment and recreation of visitors.   We enjoyed the music, and watched the vast crowd
of people until four o'clock, witnessing interesting sights
and scenes and incidents peculiarly French, but which we
do not propose to record in this book, knowing that North
Carolina is expected to maintain that same conscientious
dignity and good name abroad as it possesses at home.

After a refreshing lunch at Spier & Pond's famous restaurant in the main building of the Exposition we wended our way to the Pantheon, where was to occur a most memorable service. It was the funeral ceremony on the occasion of removing the bodies of Lazare Carnot, the organizer of victory; of Marceau, the military hero of the first Republic; of La Tour d'Auvergne, the immortal Grenadier; and of Baudin, slain on the barricades in defence of his country's laws, from Rouen to the Pantheon amid a display of civic and military splendor almost unprecedented.

President Carnot and wife, as chief mourners, were present on the occasion with all the officers of the French Government, and the ceremony was the most imposing witnessed in Paris since the memorable obsequies of Victor Hugo. Thirty organized deputations were also present, and such an array of brilliant uniforms is rarely seen anywhere. Several speeches were made by distinguished men of France, after which the military garrison of Paris marched past the President in salute. This beautiful display continued for over an hour, receiving enthusiastic applause from a hundred thousand spectators. The remains of the famous dead were then placed with great ceremony in the crypts of the Pantheon, the four caskets resting in the same tomb. The bodies of these famous Frenchmen had been resting in various cities of France for fifty years or more.

The real gayety of Sunday in Paris begins after the noon lunch. The entire population is out-doors, and every human creature seems possessed of but one single idea—enjoyment. This enjoyment they are determined to have in some way, even if it is to be found only in looking at the various parades which specially occur on Sunday afternoon.

The great attraction is the military display. The measured tread of the soldiers, the bright-red uniforms, the glittering brass buttons, the waving of silk banners and the sprightly music of the brass bands have a peculiar charm for the French people—especially for the women, and thousands and thousands of them always turn out to see the soldiers parade.

The French army is not, however, a very imposing object. The soldiers are all small men, seemingly about half-grown boys—nine out of ten faces in ranks being entirely beardless. Some of their military organizations bordered closely on the ludicrous, and the average company of French soldiers consists of about thirty boyish men, an immense banner and a brass band of some forty pieces, the idea seeming to be that it is more important to have a large band than a large company.

Every company has a name and a motto, and some of the inscriptions on their banners are "immense." We saw a company comprising twenty-four boys in their "teens" and a brass band of sixteen pieces, carrying a banner on which glittered in gold the thrilling words, "The Hope of France." From other ranks equally small, bright banners sported in the breeze heralding to the world that there were now passing "The Paris Guard," "The Invincibles," "The Nation's Glory," "The Spirit of Napoleon," "The Defenders of Liberty," and "The Protectors of Our Country."

After faithfully "taking in" all the parades we decided that we would also "take in" the great Hippodrome, or circus, as it is better known to us at home.

Sunday in Paris is the biggest day of all with the theatres and all other places of amusement. The people then have nothing to do and they want to be amused—they *will* be amused. Managers fully realize this fact, and they present their very best performances and charge more for admission on Sunday than on any other day of the week.

The Hippodrome is situated near the Exposition grounds, and soon after dinner a number of our party were seate within that spacious enclosure, seeming wholly oblivious as to the day and all other surroundings. It really seems that a traveler is wholly relieved of all restraints of law or custom.

Upon taking our seats a little girl handed us a programme of the performance, and placed a low stool under our feet. We found this stool exceedingly comfortable, and while enjoying it the girl was continually saying to us something that sounded very much like "poor boy," whereupon "the General" declared that the girl could not possibly be a poor boy, and therefore he would pay no attention to her demands as a "poor boy." However, one of our party unfortunately translated the words into "*pour boire*," and this information cost each of us about a franc for the notorious "poor boy" which is found throughout all European countries. We enjoyed the Hippodrome very much, there being many interesting features which we had never seen in an American circus.

The Sunday newspaper told us that "the fountains and park of Versailles will be illuminated to-night in honor of the Shah of Persia." The grand fête was also to celebrate the centenary of the French Revolution with special commemoration of the historical sitting of August 4, 1789.

To illuminate these famous fountains costs about $13,000, and this is done but once each year, except on very rare occasions. The illumination of the fountains at Versailles is such a noted occurrence that this magnificent celebration draws thousands of people from all parts of Europe. A large number of our party had an early supper and repaired to Versailles to witness this rare and brilliant spectacle.

. If it is possible to produce "Fairy-land" on earth, French ingenuity has surely accomplished this at Versailles when the fountains are illuminated. It is a sight of such magnificence and splendor that it can be seen nowhere else on earth, and which when once witnessed can never be forgotten. It is estimated that half a million of people saw the display on that Sunday evening, August 4, 1889. Everywhere in the park and for considerable distance away there was a vast jam of that immense crowd of people.

At 8 o'clock P. M. the magnificent Neptune Basin was illuminated, while the vicinity was lighted up by sixty-four glass porches and fifty thousand colored lamps arranged gracefully in rows. At 9 o'clock there was a gorgeous pyrotechnical display in connection with the fountains. All the jets were colored, and some curious and startling effects were produced by "water-fires" in the basin.

Half an hour afterwards, while we gazed in wonder at the beautiful scene, the shrubbery throughout the immense park suddenly became one bewildering blaze of light, continuing to the great triumphal arch at the end of the glittering amphitheatre, which formed the chief scene of a *fête* which was declared to be altogether unique in France. It is impossible even to attempt to describe the glories of that scene, and as we looked upon it, charmed and fascinated, it was difficult to realize that such brilliancy and beauty could be produced on earth.

We were informed by an official who was assisting in managing the grand display that the illuminations and playing of the fountains during those two hours cost over $16,000. But the people patronized the great show with the same liberality as it was conducted, and they paid over $100,000 for seeing the gorgeous display. There is nothing "small" about France, except the size of her people.

When the guards of the palace turned out the first light within the fountains, there was a grand and simultaneous every-man-for-himself kind of a stampede to catch the trains for Paris. With our usual good luck, we succeeded in getting (or rather being borne along in the jam) aboard the first train. This train carried at least five thousand people to Paris on that trip, although it was made up to hold only about one thousand.

We were packed so tight in that little French train that we almost forgot it was Sunday, and could breathe only every once in a while; but we reached our hotel, however, in comparative safety a short time before breakfast, and the Secretary spent the remainder of the night in dreaming that he was being used as a fender between two great ocean steamers that were lying alongside each other, while the waves of the sea gave the vessels just enough motion to flatten him out like a pancake with each swell of the water.

ABOUT SCHOOL PRINCIPALS.

BY J. M. GREENWOOD, KANSAS CITY, MISSOURI.

1. Will his manner attract or repel teachers, pupils and parents?

2. Is his voice pleasing, or harsh and grating?

3. Is he pedantic and pretentious, or manly and dignified?

4. Is he fidgety and nervous, or quiet and equable?

5. Is his eye restless and foxy, or calm and penetrating?

6. Is his face deceitful, or pleasant and honest?

7. Is his walk hesitating and unsteady, or direct and firm?

8. Is his judgment wavering and fitful, or judicial and impartial?

9. Is his judgment narrow and selfish, or broad and liberal?

10. Is his scholarship weak and restricted, or comprehensive and accurate?

11. Is his health tottering, or is it vigorous and strong?

12. Is his moral nature weak and vacillating, or is it noble and elevated?

13. Has he stagnated, or is he still elastic and buoyant?

WOMEN OF THE SOUTH.

———

Anyone who has met the Southern woman in the North knows she is an example to Northern women in her conduct of business matters, writes Helen Watterson, in the *Pittsburg Dispatch*. There are in New York probably as cosmopolitan a set of working women to-day as can be found in any quarter of the globe drawing breath and salaries. You will find a Western woman often working for less than she is worth. Sometimes it is because she really doesn't know what she's worth, and sometimes because she doesn't care what she's worth.

Not so with the Eastern girl. To settle a business matter with her is quite another thing. She seems to regard the money part of it as an incident, an after-thought. She insists on treating it with a fine contempt, and speaks of it as "compensation," until a man feels that he has been guilty of an indelicacy in mentioning it. And it isn't affectation so much as a kind of inbred nonsense that business life hasn't taken out of her yet.

But the Southern woman, bless you! there isn't a bit of nonsense about her. She's the furthest seeing, the shrewdest, the best match of man in business matters of any woman you can find. With the offer of her services comes the statement of the sum of money she expects for it. While the employer haws and hedges—as he is sure to do—she hums "Dixie" and looks out of the window. She knows he will take her terms, and she means to give him full return for what she gets. Then when all this is arranged she insists on having a good stout contract made. Then she goes to work with a calm heart.

It is by no means to be inferred from this that the Southern woman is a grasping creature. Not in the least. She's generous to a fault in the use of her money. The strangest part of it all is that this unusual business instinct should be found imbedded in such sentiment as you find in the Southern woman. The Western woman isn't sentimental at all; the Eastern woman is only contemplative and reflective; the Southern woman, with all her experience and shrewdness in money matters, hasn't lost a bit of the deliciously romantic charm that characterized her "before the war." She works royally, but never for an instant relinquishes her belief that no woman ought to work. She still looks up to a man as a god-like and superior creature, and never accepts the fact that a woman should ride in anything but her own carriage, go out after dark without an escort, or open the door for herself.

And it's a good belief. It isn't comfortable for her always, because she finds things so at variance with it, but it's good for men to feel that somebody still insists upon and expects from them all things that are gentle and unselfish.

WAR PRICES IN DIXIE.

Here is a list of prices taken from the bill of the Oriental Restaurant, at Richmond, under date of January 17, 1864:

Soup, per plate	$1 50
Turkey, per plate	3 50
Chicken, per plate	3 50
Rockfish, per plate	5 00
Roast beef, per plate	3 00
Beef-steak, per dish	3 50
Ham and eggs	3 50
Boiled eggs (2)	2 00
Fried oysters	5 00
Raw oysters (6)	2 00
Cabbage	1 00
Potatoes	1 00
Pure coffee, per cup	2 00
Pure tea, per cup	2 00
Fresh milk	2 00
Bread and butter	1 50

WINES, PER BOTTLE.

Champagne	$50 00
Maderia	50 00
Port	25 00
Claret	20 00
Sherry	35 00

LIQUORS, PER DRINK.

French brandy	$3 00
Rye whisky	2 00
Apple brandy	2 00

MALT LIQUORS, PER BOTTLE.

Porter	$12 00
Ale	12 00
Ale, half-bottle	6 00

CIGARS.

Fine Havana	$2 00

HALF A DOLLAR FOR ALL.

That's what it will cost to get into the World's Fair grounds.

People who may have been expecting to work off any counterfeit coins when they go to the World's Fair in 1893 are doomed to disappointment. It will cost everyone a genuine half dollar to get inside the gates.

The men who will take in the cash and hand the tickets out through the apertures of their little booths will be selected with especial regard to their ability to pounce upon a counterfeit, not only by its weight or its feeling, but by the looks of it a yard off. And it will cost everybody a half a dollar. There isn't going to be any half-price for children.

Once inside the gates, however, there will be no occasion for the visitor to be diving into his pockets every few minutes for additional coins with which to secure admittance to some particular exhibit or show that wasn't included in the original price of admission. No circus-tent-side-show business will be tolerated. If the fat woman, the man with the monster performing snakes, or the howling dervishes manage to get their tents within the enclosure they will have to perform for nothing.

The management does not propose to have the visitors "held up." Only one exception will be made to this rule. The natives from India, Egypt, Russia and Corea may possibly be permitted to give entertainments peculiar to their own countries in some one room of their own houses, but at the same time all the remaining portions of the structure will have to be kept open in order that the ordinary visitor who may not care about taking in the show can wander about at will and study the people and their customs without extra charge.

DEFENDS THE PUBLIC SCHOOLS.

Rev. H. M. Simmons, of Minnesota, recently preached a sermon in reply to Benjamin Reece's argument in the *Popular Science Monthly* against the value of schools to prevent crime, and Herbert Spencer's similar conclusions in *Social Statics* forty years ago. He said :

"There was plenty of truth in those conclusions. Geography will not keep a man from murder, or grammar from stealing, or logarithms make him love his fellow-men, and even the ability to read will not necessarily help his morals, especially if it be concentrated upon the *Police Gazette.* The mental training, too, obtained from schools may all be used for bad purposes, and, seeing how many college graduates get into prison and how many more deserve to, we conclude that it often is so used. And millions of men who could not read have still had more virtues than even a theological seminary can give.

"But the general influence of learning is not the less against crime. Reading at least prevents the idleness which sends so many into saloons and sins innumerable, and, bad as much of it is, far more has a humanizing and broadening influence. Mental discipline also is a moral discipline, and studying Greek or even memorizing the capes and creeks of Asia is at the same time giving the man a power of self-control which will help him to withstand temptation. Nor can anyone see how many of our criminals are unable to read, without concluding that illiteracy is not merely an attendant but a cause of crime, and that mere learning does help to prevent it. And when we add to mental training the manual and moral, which are advancing in schools everywhere, this true education must certainly check crime.

"Nor are the statistics so much against this conclusion, as the unreliability of census reports leaves us room to doubt whether crime has increased so fast in this country as is commonly declared. Whatever increase there is may be accounted for by many causes, such as the growing concentration in cities, the great social changes, the discontent of the poor and eagerness of all to get rich, the intemperance and immigration. And if the old methods of education cannot counteract these dangers, the true methods can and do. Few schools have tried true education until recently. Most have sought to educate only the head, and that in the poor way of stuffing with geographical data and historical dates and theological dogmas. But the education which seeks to train head and hand and heart together, for better life and social relations, has shown itself able not merely to prevent crime, but even to cure criminals.

"The typical criminal, with abnormal body and brain, with vicious instincts and ungovernable temper, without will power or conscience, and characterized by 'utter untruthfulness,' is about as hopeless a case as can be imagined. Yet the Elmira Reformatory takes such, and by the curriculum of strict diet, baths, massage, dumb-bells, steady work, learning a trade, close study, training of habits, incentives and gains, makes new men of them and reforms 80 per cent.

"The somewhat similar system adopted throughout England and Ireland has had a most telling effect in diminishing crime there. When so many criminals can be cured, there is no doubt but a true education can do the easier work of keeping men from becoming criminals.

"We need a better prison system in this country in place of the present no system. Now prisoners of all sorts are sometimes herded together in idleness, sometimes treated with cruelty and sometimes with laxity, and the last census report tells of a murderer who, under the Southern system of leasing out prisoners to private parties to be taken care of, was leased out to his own wife, and was spending his term of punishment at home in full happiness.

"We need to go behind the prisons and work for the diminution of poverty, and avarice, and intemperance, and the causes of crime. And we need more of that true education which strengthens men to meet temptation and avoid crime; not merely a mental, but a moral education; not the religious education which teaches men to be saved by the deeds of somebody else, but to save themselves by their own deeds, and save each other by honesty and kindness. But such an education will be religious in the highest sense.

"The Talmud tells how in a time of drouth and prayers for rain no prayer availed except that of one girl who was a 'teacher of children;' and the teaching of children, if rightly done, is a prayer which will be answered with results richer than rain."

"SHORT-CUTS" ARE DISAPPEARING.

It is refreshing to find so little said lately with regard to short-cuts, improved methods, etc. There could be no objection to any of these were there not so many of them delusive. We want always the best methods, but these are not always short methods or "improved methods."

Teachers will do well always to seek and use the best, but the success of any method usually lies more in the teacher and his application of the method than in the method itself.

There are few who, if they strive diligently and properly, may not make good teachers, and these few are the only ones who should be weeded out as speedily as possible.

Let a young man strive earnestly for success in the work of teaching, and in most cases he will find it within his grasp, whatever the method he pursues to reach it.—*Educational News.*

AN OPEN LETTER.

Editor North Carolina Teacher.

DEAR SIR—Will you please inform me when the State Normal and Industrial School for Young Women will open for the admission of students, and what is to be the character of the instruction therein offered to girls? My daughter is anxious to earn a living for herself, but does not know how to do a single practical thing sufficiently well to apply for a position. I hope to have your early reply.

Yours truly,   MRS. A. M. T.

Wilson, N. C., February 25, 1892.

As we have lately received several inquiries about the school, we will try to give a general reply to this open letter.

The "Normal and Industrial School for Young Women" is a State institution, organized in response to the persistent appeals of the Teachers' Assembly. It is the outcome of the very first effort in the history of North Carolina looking to the assistance of girls in acquiring a practical education. The State has been helping the boys for a hundred years in securing an education, but never has a single cent been appropriated for the girls until this Normal and Industrial School was asked for by the Teachers' Assembly.

The building has been located at Greensboro, and it is rapidly nearing completion, and it is expected that the school will be regularly opened for students about September, 1892.

The course of instruction will be, as the name indicates, normal and industrial, and such as is contemplated in the act of Assembly which establishes the institution. The girl will be educated in such a way as will prepare her to teach school, or will best enable her to make a living or fit her for the duties of practical life. It will be entirely different from any school for girls now existing in the State, in the fact that industrial training will form a principal feature of the instruction. In addition to the ordinary curriculum of a normal school, which is preparation for teaching, the girls will be instructed in short-hand, telegraphy, typewriting, dressmaking, housekeeping, sewing, cooking, marketing, bookkeeping, mechanical drawing and other thoroughly practical subjects which belong to industrial education. The school will be for girls just what the Agricultural and Mechanical College at Raleigh is for boys.

There are in this age many new occupations of usefulness opening up for girls, and there is a growing necessity for them to earn their own living and independence, and North Carolina never did a wiser thing than when it established this school which shall prepare our girls to fill these various positions of usefulness.

At the Normal and Industrial School there will be no charge for any tuition, and only a nominal expense, "not over $8 a month," for board. All books and material for study and work will also be without cost to pupils. We think that the Board of Trustees of the institution intend to make it of the greatest possible practical benefit to North Carolina girls.

[For the North Carolina Teacher.]

SOME MISFIT NAMES OF PLACES.

BY T. C. HARRIS, RALEIGH, N. C.

If a stranger from another State were to look over a map of North Carolina he would find some perplexing cases, where the names of certain towns seem to be a misfit as regards the names of their respective counties. This may sometimes account for mail-matter going wrong or

2

failing to reach the person addressed within a reasonable time.

For example, he would expect to find both Asheville and Ashboro in Ashe County, but instead of that arrangement he finds the former in Buncombe and the latter in Randolph County. He would naturally look for Greensboro and Greenville in Greene County, instead of Guilford and Pitt, while he would see Pittsboro not in Pitt County at all, but in Chatham. Beaufort ought to be in Beaufort County, instead of Carteret, while Washington, in Beaufort County, should be in Washington County. Mooresville, in Iredell County, should be in Moore County, and Jonesboro, in Moore County, would seem best suited to Jones County. Haywood, in Chatham, ought to be in Haywood County, while the capital of that county would just suit Wayne.

Why was not Jackson put in the county of that name instead of Northampton, and Franklin, as well as Franklinton, in Franklin County? Then there is Macon, in Warren County instead of Macon, and Hertford in Perquimans instead of Hertford County. Yanceyville, in Caswell County, he could see as well in Yancey County, and Rockingham he would put in Rockingham County, instead of Richmond.

Columbus is in Polk County, and Polkton is in Anson County, while Columbus County has not even Columbia. Davidson College is not in Davidson County, nor is Yadkin College in Yadkin County. Neither Alexanders nor Alexandriana is in Alexander County. Graham would seem best in Graham County, and Lenoir just suits Lenoir County. Vanceboro might have been put in Vance County, instead of Craven, Gaston in Gaston County, and Madison in Madison County, instead of Rockingham.

There may be other cases of apparent misfit, but these are enough. So when you direct a letter be sure to "put the county on."

DO YOU SPEAK "AMERICAN" OR "ENGLISH?"

Some of our friends have disagreed with THE TEACHER as to whether or not we speak the American or English languages. 'Tis true that there are numbers of slang expressions in the American tongue and many bad and incorrect words, but they are distinctively American just the same, and the fact that they exist does not form any part of the question as to the right of America to have a language of its own. There are even more slang speeches and objectionable words in the English language and with them we have nothing to do or say ; but as to whether or not you speak "American" or "English" examine the following list of a very few differences between the two languages :

AMERICAN.	ENGLISH.
Telegram.	Wire.
Ticket office.	Booking office.
Buying a ticket.	Booking.
Railroad.	Railway.
Railroad track.	Permanent way.
Rails.	Metals.
Depot.	Station.
Switch.	Points.
Street car.	Tram car.
Freight train.	Goods train.
Cars.	Carriages.
Conductor.	Guard.
Engineer.	Driver.
Fireman.	Stoker.
Locomotive.	Engine.
Baggage.	Luggage.
All aboard.	Seats, please.
Matches.	Lights.
Beer.	Ale.
Switching cars.	Drilling cars.
Trains meeting.	Trains crossing.
Freight cars.	Goods van.
Parquet.	Pit.
Englishman.	Hinglishman.
Store.	Shop.

There are hundreds of other things which are expressed by entirely different words. In money we have the sovereign, which is also a "quid," and in Yorkshire sometimes called a "thick 'un." A shilling is a "bob"; a sixpence, a "tanner"; a ten-shilling gold piece is "half a quid and a "thin 'un"; while a crown or five-shilling piece is a "plunk" or "big 'un." The half-crown is known as "two-and-six," sometimes "two and a tanner."

It is likewise the habit of the most intelligent English people to drop the "h" in words where it should be used and to put it where it does not belong. The Englishism "The 'orn hof the 'unter his 'eard hon the 'ills," is familiar to every schoolboy, and it is a fair representation of the difference between the English and the American languages.

There are several hundred words in general use which the Englisman will spell differently from the American and we give a few common words with the English orthography: publick, almanack, ardour, armour, bevelled, boddice, cancelled, cheque, scimetar, counsellor, defence, despatch, drought, gaiety, gypsey, jeweller, labour, marvelling, modeller, parlour, pædo-baptism, plough, rumour, sceptre, sideways, sceptic, stye, tumour, vapour, villany, waggon, wilful, woeful, worshipper, yolk.

The two languages are, as we admit, very much alike, and perhaps the many differences would not be much noticed unless attention was called to them, but they exist just the same, and as no American uses the Englishisms in literature or in speech it cannot be claimed that we speak the English language, therefore it must be admitted that America has a language of its own and that it is *American*.

We concede that some of the words and expressions we have mentioned are used only by English cockneys, but it is well known that most of these expressions and words are universally employed by all the most educated people of England, and this evidence is sufficient to make them a part of the "English" language and not of the "American."

IN THE SCHOOL-ROOM.

IT MAKES A DIFFERENCE.

, FOR RECITATION.

A boy will stand and hold a kite
From early morn till late at night,
   And never tire at all.
But, oh! it gives him bitter pain
To stand and hold his mother's skein
   The while she winds the ball.

A man will walk a score of miles
Upon the hardest kind of tiles
   About a billiard table.
But, oh! it nearly takes his life
To do an errand for his wife
   Between the house and stable.

A girl will gladly sit and play
With half a dozen dolls all day,
   And call it jolly fun.
But, oh! it makes her sick and sour
To 'tend the baby half an hour,
   Although it's only one.

A woman will—but never mind!
My wife is standing close behind,
   And reading o'er my shoulder.
Some other time, perhaps, I may
Take up the theme of woman's way,
   When I am feeling bolder.
            —*Detroit Free Press.*

HOW TO PRONOUNCE "BENEATH" AND "NEPHEW."

There is an effort among some public school men in this country to compel our children to pronounce "beneath," *beneethe*, and "nephew," *nevue*. Do not permit your child to be taught such an absurdity, for there is not the slightest standard authority for such pronunciation unless we consider English cockneys as authority, and such "authority" should not be for even one moment tolerated among educated people in America.

Such pronunciations as "beneethe" and "nevue" are simply some of the ridiculous results of affectation and too much "New Education." Even the better class of people in England, where such orthœpic monstrosities are said to have been born, always pronounce these words as "beneeth" and "nefue," just as all the most distinguished scholars in America pronounce them.

We are glad to know that this imported caricature in pronunciation has never obtained a footing in North Carolina schools—our teachers are wisely content to speak the pure American language without any cockney embellishments or variations. America may have its Bowery and street hoodlum slang which sometimes finds its way even into polite society, but such words and expressions are no part of the American language, any more than the dialect in use among the bog-trotters of Ireland is a part of the English language.

THE "North Carolina Practical Spelling Book" is now in press and will be ready for the school-room in about sixty days. We believe that the teachers of the State will be pleased with the book.

A COMPOSITION.

———

[The following composition was written by little Lena D. Cherry, of Miss Gertrude Bagby's school at Vandemere. A year ago the little girl could not read or write, and this is her first effort at writing a composition.—EDITOR.]

WHAT I LIKE ON A COLD DAY.

I like a cold day when I have a good fire to sit by. I like to put on my warm cloak and gloves and go out doors and run on the frozen ground and play in the snow.

I don't like to go to school on cold days. I had rather stay at home by the fire and play with my dolls.

I like ice in the winter time but better in the summer when the weather is warm.

It is now a rainy and cold day and I like to sit by the fire and eat nuts, apples, candy and oranges.

———

PRONOUN FOR ARTICLE.

———

An incident occurred recently which illustrates the absurdity of the very common habit of using the personal pronoun where the article should be used.

At a Teachers' Institute a young pedagogue was at the blackboard demonstrating a mathematical problem, and at a certain stage of the process a reduction from feet to inches was necessary. Turning to his audience with a flourish of the crayon, he says: "I will now reduce my feet!" All eyes were immediately fixed upon those members, and the laughter that convulsed the audience somewhat disturbed the proposed reduction!

ABOUT BABIES.

Who does not love the merry little creatures, with their bright eyes, sweet voices, innocent ways, and vociferous squalls, particularly while cutting teeth? We involuntarily shrink from the man who does not love children, until we have some of our own, and try to undress the baby some night when the mother is absent.

Dear little children! How much they add to the beauty and loveliness of the earth, and how much walking it takes to quiet one, when there is no soothing syrup handy. What dear little sleep-destroyers they are! Fresh from the hand of the Creator—with spirits unclouded by sorrow, unstained by sin—how it can occupy simultaneously both sides of the largest sized bed.

Like the birds and flowers, they help to make up the poetry of existence, and it can also make an old bachelor in the adjoining room use language which if uttered on the street would get him into the penitentiary for two years.

They are so fragile that there mingles with our love tender anxiety that shadows and subdues our warmer emotions, and yet that same baby if taken to a theater can stay awake and bawl until the last act.—*Exchange.*

WHAT A BUSHEL OF CORN WILL DO.

From a bushel of corn, a distiller gets four gallons of whiskey, which retails at $16. The government gets $3.60, the farmer who raised the corn gets forty cents, the railroad gets $1, the manufacturer gets $4, the retailer gets $7, the consumer gets six months, and the special policeman gets a fee if he runs him in.

ADVICE TO GIRLS.

Don't be silly about the men.

Don't fail to take a man at his word when he says he is poor.

Don't be rude to a man in order to show your independence.

Don't let a man impose upon you, simply because he is a man.

Don't think because a man likes you that he wants to marry you.

Don't believe everything a man tells you, either about himself or yourself.

Don't be familiar with men, and don't permit familiarities from them.

Don't conclude that a man is a gentleman simply because he has the appearance of one.

Don't think that a man is not in love with you because he has not proposed to you.

Don't think because a man is a graceful and interesting talker that he is everything else desirable.—*Exchange.*

ABOUT THE WORLD'S RULERS.

According to an eminent German statistician the world has had 2,550 Kings or Emperors who have reigned over seventy-four peoples. Of these 300 were overthrown, sixty-four were forced to abdicate, twenty-eight committed suicide, twenty-three became mad or imbecile, 100 were killed in battle, 223 were captured by the enemy, twenty-five were tortured to death, 134 were assassinated and 108 were executed.

THE DERIVATION OF "AMERICA."

[As the people of our country are now interested in the great World's Fair, commemorating the discovery of this continent, it is well to be informed as to the derivation of the name given to America.—EDITOR.]

In a paper read before the Society of "Americanistas," in Paris, on October 15, 1890, entitled "A Philological Study of the Origin of the Name America," Bishop Carrillo, of Yucatan, a well known author on American linguistic matters, maintained that when Cortez landed on the coast of Yucatan, and on what is now known as the Mosquito Coast, the whole country was possessed by the Aztecs, and was known by them as Am-eli-ka, which in the Aztec tongue meant "The Windy Country, or the Country of High Winds."

This name of "Am-eli-ka" was easily corrupted in pronunciation into "America" by the old Spaniards. The Italian geographer, Alberic Vespucci, prefixed it in place of the name by which he had been christened, and became known as Americus (Amerigo) Vespucius, in the same manner as the distinguished English geographer Gordon had prefixed "Chinese" to his name, and became known to the world as Chinese Gordon.

DERIVATION OF SEVERAL WORDS.

"Canter" is an abbreviated form of Canterbury gallop, so called because pilgrims to Canterbury rode at the pace of a moderate gallop. A "grocer," so says the dictionary, was originally one who sold by the gross. A "grenade" derives its name from its shape, which resembles a pomegranate. A "biscuit" means "twice baked," because, according to military practice, the bread or biscuits of the Romans were twice prepared in the ovens.

Did you ever notice the leaves of the "dandelion?" They are said to resemble, in form and size, the tooth of the lion, and so the French call it the *dent de lion* and we "the dandelion."

The Pope was formerly called "the pape," which means the same as "papa," or father. "Vinegar" came from two Latin words, "*vin*" and "*acer*," meaning "vine" and "sour."

These are only a few of the many curious and interesting things we found in an afternoon's search in the old dictionary.

When you are at a loss for something to do follow our example, and you will be surprised at the many bits of information you can pick up in a little time.

TO SCHOOL-GIRLS.

You would think it a pleasant magic if you could flush your flowers into a brighter bloom by a kind look upon them; nay, more, if you had the power, not only to cheer, but to guard them—if you could bid the black blight to turn away, and the knotted caterpillar spare—if you could bid the dew fall upon them in the drought, and say to the south wind in frost, "Come, thou South, and breathe upon my garden, that the spices of it may flow out!"

This you would think a great thing; and all of this (and how much more than this!) you can do, for fairer flowers than these—flowers that would bless you for having blessed them, and will love you for having loved them—flowers that have eyes like yours, and thoughts like yours, and lives like yours; which, once saved, you save forever. Is this only a little power?—*Ruskin.*

[By Request.]
PRACTICAL WORK IN NUMBERS.

GAUGING CASKS.

Measure diagonally, *in inches*, from the centre of the bung to the chime : cube and divide by 370 and the answer will be in gallons.

Should the bung not be in the centre, measure both ways to chime, add the measurements, take half their sum, then cube and divide by 370 to get gallons. If a remainder, multiply by four and divide by 370, etc. This rule has been found correct by actual measurement.

HOW LONG IS THE ROPE?

In yards, what is the length of a rope tied to the neck of a horse, which would allow him to feed over an acre of land? Solution :—The area to graze is an acre, 4,840 square yards ; as the area of a circle is obtained by squaring its diameter and multiplying by $\frac{11}{14}$, so dividing the area by $\frac{11}{14}$ and taking the square root of the quotient will give the diameter. The rope is fastened, say, to a stick in the center of the circle, and, therefore, being half the distance only, we divide by two.

Three men bought a grindstone 32 inches in diameter, A paying 70 cents, B 50 cents, C 40 cents. They agree that A shall grind off his share first, then B and then C. How much will each grind off?

Solution :—The semi-diameter of the grindstone is 16 inches, which squared=256. A paid $\frac{7}{16}$ of the money, then $\frac{7}{16}$ of 256=112, which taken from 256, will leave B and C's portion, or the semi-diameter for them. 256—112=144, and $\sqrt{144}$=12, the semi-diameter for B and C. 16—12=4 inches, A's portion. B paid $\frac{5}{16}$ of the money, then $\frac{5}{16}$ of 256=80, which taken from 144—B and C's portion, will leave C's 144—80=64 and $\sqrt{64}$=8 inches C's portion, and 12—8=4=B's portion.

Southern Educational Association.

ORGANIZATION 1891-1892.

SOLOMON PALMER, President, East Lake, Florida.
EUGENE G. HARRELL, Secretary and Treasurer, Raleigh, N. C.
W. T. WATSON, Assistant Secretary, Memphis, Tennessee.

THIRD ANNUAL SESSION, ATLANTA, GA., JULY 6-8, 1892.

VICE-PRESIDENTS:

1. E. B. Prettyman, Maryland.
2. John E. Massey, Virginia.
3. B. S. Morgan, West Virginia.
4. S. M. Finger, North Carolina.
5. W. D. Mayfield, S. Carolina.
6. S. D. Bradwell, Georgia.
7. A. J. Russell, Florida.
8. J. G. Harris, Alabama.
9. J. R. Preston, Mississippi.
10. W. H. Jack, Louisiana.
11. J. M. Carlisle, Texas.
12. J. H. Shinn, Arkansas.
13. W. R. Garrett, Tennessee.
14. Ed. Porter Thompson, Ky.

15. W. E. Coleman, Missouri.

EXECUTIVE COMMITTEE:

Solomon Palmer, *ex officio* Chairman, East Lake, Alabama.
E. G. Harrell, *ex officio* Secretary, Raleigh, North Carolina.

1. J. H. Phillips, Superintendent City Schools, Birmingham, Ala.
2. Dabney Lipscomb, Agr. and Mech. College, Middleton, Miss.
3. Thomas D. Boyd, President State Normal, Natchitoches, La.
4. O. H. Cooper, Superintendent City Schools, Galveston, Texas.
5. J. W. Conger, President Ouachita College, Arkadelphia, Arkansas.
6. J. M. Stewart, Agricultural and Mechanical College, Lake City, Fla.
7. J. M. Greenwood, Superintendent Schools, Kansas City, Missouri.
8. R. N. Roark, State Normal College, Lexington, Kentucky.
9. Frank M. Smith, University of Tennessee, Knoxville, Tennessee.
10. Euler B. Smith, President State Association, LaGrange, Georgia.
11. Edward S. Joynes, University of South Carolina, Columbia, S. C.
12. Hugh Morson, President Teachers' Assembly, Raleigh, N. C.
13. C. E. Vawter, Superintendent Miller Industrial School, Crozet, Va.
14. W. R. White, Superintendent of Schools, Morganton, W. Va.
15. Daniel Gilman, Johns Hopkins University, Baltimore, Maryland.

THE SOUTHERN PASSENGER ASSOCIATION has granted the rate of *one fare for round trip* to the meeting of the Southern Educational Association in Atlanta, July 6–9, and a coupon for $2.00 membership fee will be attached to each ticket.

THE SOUTHERN EDUCATIONAL ASSOCIATION has a great many friends in the North. The Secretary has just visited the Northern cities, and he was much pleased to find there a large number of well-wishers for the continued prosperity of the Association. Everybody realizes the important influence which it is to exert upon the educational work and interest of the South.

THE PROCEEDINGS of the Session of 1891 on Lookout Mountain have been printed in neat and attractive style, and the volume is now being mailed as rapidly as possible. A careful reading of the journal will convince you that no abler educational papers have ever been submitted to any educational organization on this continent. The South may justly feel proud of this volume, which speaks in thunder-tones the profound scholarship of our Southern teachers.

"CIRCULAR OF INFORMATION NO. 1," which has just been issued and circulated by the executive officers of The Southern Educational Association, has created a grand wave of enthusiasm among the teachers of the South in the interests of their Association The Secretary is almost flooded with letters from every portion of the South giving warmest assurances of the very heartiest coöperation in all the work and plans of the Association. The South is aroused as never before on the great educational question. The educational press in the South is also united in its efforts for the success of the Association—all of the journals publish liberal extracts from the official circular.

North Carolina Teachers' Assembly.

ORGANIZATION FOR 1892.

OFFICERS:

HUGH MORSON (Raleigh Male Academy), President, . . Raleigh.
EUGENE G. HARRELL (Editor TEACHER), Sec. and Treas., . Raleigh.

VICE-PRESIDENTS:

1. J. J. Blair (Supt. Graded Schools), ... Winston.
2. J. E. Kelly (Model Male School), ... Charlotte.
3. Miss Catherine Fulghum (Graded School), . . Goldsboro.
4. W. J. Ferrell (Wakefield Academy), . . . Wakefield.
5. Miss Lizzie Lindsay (Graded School), . . . Greensboro.
6. P. M. Pearsall (County Superintendent), . . Trenton.
7. Miss Lina McDonald (Graded School), . . . Winston.
8. T. J. Drewry (Horner Military School), . . . Oxford
9. Mrs. S. Montgomery Funk (Chowan Bap. Fem. Inst.), Murfreesboro.

EXECUTIVE COMMITTEE:

Hugh Morson, *ex officio*, President, ... Raleigh.
Eugene G. Harrell, *ex officio*, Secretary, . . . Raleigh.
Eben Alexander (University of North Carolina), . . Chapel Hill.
W. L. Poteat (Wake Forest College), , . . . Wake Forest.
James Dinwiddie (President Peace Institute), . . . Raleigh.
Charles D. McIver (Pres't Normal and Industrial School
    for Women), ... Greensboro.
J. Y. Joyner (Superintendent Graded School), . . Goldsboro.
A. C. Davis (Superintendent Military School), . . Winston.
E. E. Britton (Principal High School), ... Roxboro.

NINTH ANNUAL SESSION, MOREHEAD CITY, JUNE 21 TO JULY 4, 1892.

ASSEMBLY NOTES.

REV. THOMAS DIXON, JR., North Carolina's famous pulpit orator, will deliver a lecture to the Assembly on July 2, and will preach in the Assembly Hall on Sunday morning, July 3.

THE SECRETARY is now sending out the first official circular for 1892, giving information in regard to the coming session of the Assembly. County Superintendents will supply any person with the circular who may desire it; and when you have read it please send it to some friend.

REMEMBER that under the new arrangements as to Assembly tickets, you pay the membership fee when you buy the ticket and are saved the trouble of sending it to the Secretary as was done heretofore. The Secretary has already returned some fees which had been recently sent to him. There will be, however, a few branch roads in the State that will not have the "membership coupon" attached to the ticket, and from those points it will be necessary to send the annual dues to the Secretary as heretofore, for which the certificate will be returned.

THE "MUSIC CONTEST" for the Assembly Medal this summer will be confined exclusively to instrumental music. The same rules will be observed as last year, except that each member of the committee will be instructed to judge upon some particular point without regard to any other feature of the playing. Any girl who has been a pupil in any North Carolina school within the past two years may enter the contest. The Secretary already has in hand the names of several young ladies who intend to enter the contest, and all others who desire to take part are requested to give notice as early as possible. These music contests will be of great value to those who take part in them, and the Assembly has no difficulty in securing a good position as music teacher for every young lady who enters the contest, as the entry is in itself evidence of special musical talent, skill and cultivation.

THE TEACHERS IN CUBA AND FLORIDA.

NUMBER III—(CONCLUDED)

As our steamer sailed down the charming Bay of Havana, under the frowning guns of Cabana Fortress and Morro Castle, and out into the broad Gulf of Mexico with her prow pointed homeward, we began to fully realize what a delightful visit we had enjoyed to Cuba, the lovely Queen of the Antilles.

Our party was a most select and congenial company, and during the ten days that we had spent constantly and so pleasantly together it had become truly a large and sympathetic family. This fact added very greatly to the pleasures of our jaunt and gave to us such enjoyment as is never. seen in promiscuous parties of tourists. We enjoyed our joys with one another, we groaned in our sea-sickness with one another, we laughed at our entertainments with one another and we talked about our pleasant experiences with one another, each one feeling a special friendly interest in the other. This is the peculiar charm and privilege of all the North Carolina Teachers' parties of tourists, and with no other travellers within our knowledge are these most necessary conditions of enjoyment and comfort to be found.

The sail to Key West was "a little rough," as our excellent stewardess expressed it, but our party had become such good sailors that there was very little sea-sickness, and all were present at each meal and fully ready to go ashore at Key West and again "take in the town." ·

What a bright, beautiful, calm and peaceful Sunday dawned upon us next morning! The Gulf was as smooth as a mirror, the air was as balmy as spring, the sky was as clear as crystal, and even the gulls that flitted lazily around

The Mascotte seemed to be trying to tell us that it was the holy day. Not a sick person in all the party. Everybody was on deck enjoying each others company and the inspiration of the warm Southern sunshine.

At 11 o'clock we all assembled in the Social Hall to engage in a very pleasant devotional service, conducted by our beloved chaplain, Rev. Bennett Smedes, D. D., of Raleigh. In all the prayers, responses and hymns there seemed to prevail a spirit of peculiar inspiration, thankfulness and earnestness, prompted by the realization that our tour had been wholly without accident, sickness, trouble, or loss of any kind.

After the services an informal meeting was called by the editor of THE TEACHER, to which all the party assembled, when he told them that during the short week which we had so pleasantly spent in Havana the wife of our esteemed Captain Hanlon had met a terrible death in a railway accident at Tampa, and that the faithful engineer had been killed in a most painful manner while serving the electric dynamo on our steamer. The tenderest sympathies of our company were feelingly expressed for these afflicted families, and Judge John Gray Bynum added very touching and appropriate remarks. A committee was appointed, comprising Judge J. G. Bynum, Rev. B. Smedes, D. D., Captain T. R. Robertson, Mr. L. D. Giddens and Mr. A. M. Fry, to prepare suitable resolutions of respect and sympathy, and they were promptly forwarded to Captain Hanlon.

"Uncle Sam" was very kind to his returning children upon their arrival at Port Tampa, and the ordeal of the Custom House was relieved of all its expected horrors by the exceedingly prompt, efficient and courteous management of the government officials at that point. Our baggage was quickly examined "with neatness and dispatch," and we were soon "on our way rejoicing."

While the baggage was being examined the editor made satisfactory arrangements for the party to spend the night at the magnificent Tampa Bay Hotel, which is situated at Tampa, about nine miles from our landing port. This hotel is truly one of the most magnificent in the world, and it is so lovely and grand in all its appointments that it is impossible to even attempt to describe its beauties. It was our good fortune to arrive upon the "opening night" for the season; in fact, it was our honor and privilege to open this famous hotel for the season of 1892, and truly we did ample justice to that elegant "opening dinner."

According to the itinerary of our tour we were due at home on the next day after leaving Tampa Bay Hotel, but as each member of the party yet had a small amount of unexpended funds, it was decided that we would enjoy the rare sights of Florida for a few days, the famous land of alligators, orange groves and fine hotels.

We set out from Tampa for a trip down Indian River, but unfortunately we were a day ahead of the little tri-weekly boat. But we did not suffer much by the mishap, for we spent the day at Enterprise, one of the most charm-ing winter resorts in Florida. The little village is on Lake Monroe, just opposite Sanford. It has a large, new and comfortable hotel, fine fishing and gunning, but best of all for us the hotel has a magnificent large grove of heavily-laden orange trees, all the privileges of which are entirely free to its guests.

"Orange-grove privileges" were never more appreciated or fully enjoyed than they were by our party, and we feel entirely safe in saying that our fifty people within twenty-four hours pulled from the trees and ate at least five thou-sand of those delicious oranges. It was impossible to find a girl who was not either sucking an orange or just pulling another from the tree, and many brought away branches of the trees bearing the luscious fruit.

While at Enterprise the party divided into two sections—
one making a trip on the lovely Indian River, while the
other section went to St. Augustine, where we were soon
comfortably quartered in the elegant Alcazar Hotel, which
is an annex of the celebrated Ponce de Leon Hotel. "The
Ponce" was not to open for guests until several days after
our departure from St. Augustine, hence the manager
was deprived of the pleasure of our company as guests.
We compromised the disappointment, however, by going
through the gorgeous structure on a tour of inspection.
Some idea of the matchless grandeur of the building and
furniture may be formed from the knowledge of the fact
that the hall clock cost thirty thousand dollars, and several
centre-tables in the parlor cost over twelve thousand dollars
each !

The winter guests are trying to pay for these expensive
equipments by crowding the hotel to overflowing at a rate
of board from ten to fifty dollars per day. But the season
is very short, and even with this large patronage and high
prices the Ponce de Leon expends over one hundred thousand dollars every year in excess of its receipts.

St. Augustine is a charming tropical city, and the air
was almost as warm and balmy as in Cuba. Several of our
party, including Misses Fannie Burwell, Nellie Morrison,
Mattie Fuller, Capt. T. R. Robertson and the editor of
THE TEACHER, enjoyed a most delightful bath for an hour
in the swimming-pool of the Alcazar Hotel in the open air
on the morning of January 14th, and the water and air
were as warm as we have it at Morehead City in July !

There are a great many interesting historical places and
things among the Spanish remains at St. Augustine. We
took a carriage drive over the city and visited every place
of importance, including a trip through the dungeons of
the "Old Fort" where prisoners were put to death some
three hundred years ago, and where Geronimo and his cut-

throat band of Indians should likewise have perished while they were temporarily confined in the Fort a few years ago.

Just after the party had boarded the train at St. Augustine *en route* for home, the company was called to "attention" by Captain Robertson. Then, in a neat little speech, spoken with his usual eloquence and grace, he presented to the editor of THE TEACHER, in behalf of the memorable North Carolina Cuban party of 1892, a fine silk umbrella, with handle of ivory and silver, appropriately engraved, costing $25, as a reminder of the pleasure which each member of the party had derived from the tour, and of their gratification at the perfection of all the arrangements of the trip. The editor returned thanks as best he could for this most pleasant surprise,—and he would not part with this proud souvenir of the trip for five hundred dollars.

On our homeward journey we again enjoyed many acts of kindness extended to us by the railroad officials, for which those gentlemen have our sincerest thanks. At Jacksonville, even during our short stop of one hour, we received special favors from Mr. W. H. Lucas, agent of the Richmond and Danville Railroad; Colonel Davidson, of the South Florida Railroad, and other officials, which added very greatly to our comfort and to the accommodation of delayed members of the party. Upon arriving in Atlanta, by the favor of Mr. James L. Taylor, General Passenger Agent of the Richmond and Danville Road, our tickets were made available for transportation on the "vestibule train," thus enabling us to reach our homes several hours earlier than by the regular trains. Such timely courtesies as these enter largely into the pleasant memories of a tour, and they were fully appreciated by our party.

We reached our homes on January 15th, without accident, loss or sickness, or trouble of any kind, perfectly delighted with our holiday trip to the West Indies, and already making a good beginning in forming a large party for the same trip next winter.

Among the many pleasant recollections of the trip, we had the satisfaction of knowing that the "necessary expenses" of the tour had come within the appropriation of $75, and this is a very important matter with travellers. This amount was divided as follows: Ticket to Port Tampa and return, $26.40; to Havana and return, $28; board in Havana, $16; landing fees, $2; passports, 30 cents; visit to Morro Castle, $1; meals *en route*, $1.30; total, $75. Sleeping-car berths are always considered as *extras* in all parties of tourists, they being not a necessary part of the transportation but luxuries which are entirely optional with each traveller. The three days which we spent in Florida was also an extra expense, as this part of the trip was planned after we had left Havana on the homeward journey.

THE GREATEST SUCCESS.

The North Carolina Teachers' Assembly is considered by the educators of other States also to be the most successful and enterprising State organization of teachers in this country. The Secretary receives many letters from other States asking for copies of our constitution, with information as to our plan of work, and why it is that our meetings are the largest in the United States and have such gratifying effect upon the school legislation of North Carolina. One of the secrets of the unparalleled success of our Assembly is the fact that *the teachers and "the people"* come together in the meetings, thus bringing them into unity of effort in behalf of the schools of the State. The plan upon which the Teachers' Assembly is organized is original and is entirely different from that of any other educational organization in the Union, and it has proven to be the best plan for best results.

EDITORIAL.

UNJUST DEDUCTIONS FROM TEACHERS' SALARIES.

The poorest paid public servant in this great and rich country of ours is the teacher in the city free schools. The Superintendents, without a single exception within our knowledge, all receive large salaries *for the year*, while the teacher is employed by the term of five to nine months, is paid by the month just sufficient to keep fed and clothed with moderate comfort, and yet for every legal or special holiday of one or more days a pro rata reduction is taken from the teacher's meagre salary! This is absolutely wrong! No deductions from the Superintendent's salary is made for holidays or for several months of summer vacation, nor should there be any deduction; no merchant deducts from his clerk's wages for every day of holiday or recreation; no reputable farmer deducts from the wages of his laborer for every rainy day (and the farm hand who receives $10 or $12 a month and board *for the year* is better paid than the average teacher in the free schools); no church deducts from the pastor's salary when he has a vacation; neither should there be a deduction from the teacher's salary for occasional holidays. The average teacher earns every dollar received from the public school fund, and also fully earns the few legal holidays which occur during the school term, without being forced to pay for them from a salary so meagre that it will hardly support life during the year. The teachers are not responsible for the occurrence of legal holidays, nor should they be compelled by school boards to suffer by reason of them. Teachers prefer to do their regular work rather than be forced to take a rest and pay for it. The teachers are not employed by the day or paid by the day, nor should deductions by the day be made against their insignificant salary. The taxpayers of North Carolina are not so unappreciative of the faithful work of the teachers in our free schools that they are not willing to *give* instead of *sell* them the legal holidays, and school committees need not think that they have the approval of the people of our State in making these picayunish deductions from the salaries of teachers whenever a day of rest is appointed by the State or nation.

A FEW YEARS AGO the craze in the Boston public schools was "teaching Geography"; now it is "Ling's Gymnastics." Every craze has its day in Boston.

AT THE OPENING exercises of your school in the mornings have all the children to rise at their places and salute the North Carolina State Flag draped over the platform, and sing one stanza of "The Old North State," "Ho, for Carolina," or "My Country, 'tis of Thee."

ONE OF THE strongest evidences that North Carolina is making rapid educational progress is the fact that our teachers are keeping abreast with the spirit of the times by reading a great many professional books, while nearly all the regular teachers in the State are subscribers for THE NORTH CAROLINA TEACHER. The teacher who is a liberal reader of professional books and journals cannot fail to attain success in the school-room.

NORTH CAROLINA has never had a more energetic and efficient Superintendent of Public Instruction than Hon. S. M. Finger, the present incumbent. There has been more real educational progress under his administration than at any other period in the history of public schools. His well directed efforts now being made in behalf of a good educational exhibit at Chicago by North Carolina schools are certain to be rewarded by success.

THE ANNUAL REPORT of the State Auditor gives the following interesting information as to taxes for public education: The total State taxes for schools is $712,489; number of white polls paying taxes, 153,486; Negro polls, 60,832; school taxes paid by whites on property, $283,953; school taxes paid by Negroes on property, $8,735; total assessed valuation of property in the State, $216,872,374. According to this report it will be seen that the Negroes pay less than four per cent. of the property tax for schools, and less than one-third of the poll-taxes. The Constitution provides that the whites and Negroes shall have equal school privileges and facilities.

THE FEBRUARY NUMBER of THE TEACHER was held for ten days in the Raleigh post-office, waiting for a ruling from the Department at Washington concerning a supplement. This country is in great need of a Postmaster General who will attend to the business of the office, and who will employ as assistants only persons who know or will learn something of the postal laws. The present Post-office Department at Washington has the rare faculty of rendering such absurd and outrageous rulings, wholly unsustained by the law, that it may be verily considered the joke of the nineteenth century. It is gratifying to see that the press of the country is exposing the iniquities, frauds and absurdities of Wanamaker, Hazen & Co., who have charge of the Post-office Department of the United States.

THE TEACHER has about succeeded in getting our people rid of that foreign stigma "The New South" so far as North Carolina is concerned.   The term is sometimes used here by some foreign capitalists who may have invested a few dollars in a mine or in "booming" town lots, but the native North Carolinian has repudiated the insult just as he has that other insult "The Rebellion," as applied by the same foreigners to the War for Southern Independence. May this rejection of a new and false name, "The New South," be hearty, unanimous and emphatic throughout all the South, that our children may continue to live in the glorious land in which their ancestors were born—THE SOUTH.   The term "New South" will soon be in such bad odor in North Carolina that a public speaker who uses it as a name for our country will be hissed by his audience. In fact, we have been informed that a certain teacher in North Carolina was recently hissed by his class when he attempted to name our country "The New South"; the inherent love of our boys and girls for their country could not be thus insulted without prompt resistance.   May such true patriotism ever control the people of THE SOUTH!

THE INTERESTING annual report of Dr. George T. Winston, President of the University, shows that of one hundred and twenty-six new students received this term the private high schools and academies of the State sent ninety-six, while the high school departments of the public graded schools sent only nineteen.   There are in North Carolina eleven city graded schools which have a high school department, and if only nineteen boys were prepared for the University by all of these public high schools, the question might properly be asked, "Does it pay to try to prepare boys for college at public expense in the graded schools?"   The facts in the case seem to justly warrant a most emphatic answer, No.   A careful examination of results of the high school work in the free schools shows that only about six per cent. of the number of children in the schools remain long enough to even reach the high grade, and of those who complete the course only about two per cent. ever go to college. Besides, the public high school cripples the fund which should pay reasonable salaries to teachers for thoroughly educating boys and girls in the English branches so that they may become good citizens and earn a living, and they destroy the private schools which have been, are now, and always will be, the principal feeders to the University and the colleges. We have no desire to disagree with any public or private educator in North Carolina, but we all must acknowledge that *facts* speak louder than theory or argument in this matter of high school education at public expense. Theories are pretty and sentimental, but facts are exceedingly stubborn things. Theories are as we would have things, while facts show what they are, and facts are not easily controverted by theories. Don't try to do it. The pages of THE TEACHER are open to full and free discussion of this interesting and important subject.

ABOUT OUR TEACHERS AND SCHOOLS.

MISS MARY P. PARKER is teaching in Bertie County.

MISS LIZZIE SHERROD is teaching at Conoho, Martin County.

MISS HATTIE DAIL has a fine school at Stella, in Carteret County.

MISS BETTIE CURRIE has a prosperous school in Rockingham County.

MISS GERTRUDE BAGBY, of Kinston, is teaching in Pamlico County.

MR. E. L. FOX is principal of Friendship Academy, Alamance County.

MR. F. A. FETTER has a good school of eighty-five pupils in Forsyth County.

MR. P. E. JOHNSON has a prosperous school at Rome, in Johnston County.

MISS CORA S. BORDEN has a flourishing public school in Pender County, with thirty-seven pupils.

MISS MEDDIE STEWART has forty-four pupils enrolled in the Maxton School, of which she is principal.

MR. D. T. OATES is principal of South River Baptist Institute, in Sampson County, and the school is prospering.

MISS SALLIE GARRETT is in charge of the Department of Music and Art in Friendship Academy in Alamance County.

MR. J. W. KENNEDY is principal and Miss Olive Lyda is assistant in the management of Pigeon River Academy, Haywood County.

MISS MINNIE L. SMITH, a member of the Teachers' Assembly, has a fine school of fifty-one pupils at Green Springs, South Carolina.

MISS LULA JONES has an enrollment of sixty-four pupils in Cary Academy, of which she is principal. Miss Ada Owen is assistant.

MISS ALICE FALLS is one of the enterprising teachers of Gaston County. She has a public school of thirty-eight scholars at Pisgah Church.

MR. HUGH A. PRIEST is preparing to take a school in Richmond County. As the first important step thereto he subscribes for THE TEACHER.

MR. T. J. SHAW has a fine school in Swain County with ninety-four pupils enrolled. He writes that he finds "a great deal of help in THE TEACHER."

MR. W. L. BREWER has a progressive and interesting school of sixty-four pupils in Alleghany County; and he writes that "THE TEACHER is a splendid magazine for teachers, and I cannot do without it." Thanks, friend Brewer.

THE YOUNG LADIES and teachers of Kinsey Seminary, LaGrange, visited the New Bern Fair in a body, on Februrary 22, and charmed the people of eastern Carolina. The institution had a very fine exhibit in the Art Department of the Fair.

MRS. W. H. SPEIGHT is in charge of Fremont Academy, which is conducted under the auspices of the New Bern District of the Methodist Episcopal Church. Her daughters, Misses Alma and Daisy, are assistants in the school. One hundred and fifty pupils are enrolled,

MR. J. A. STEWART is now teaching in Wake County, and he writes: "We are getting on nicely, with ninety-nine pupils enrolled. Next week our enrollment will go over one hundred. We have a very interesting class in North Carolina History. Glad to see THE TEACHER again."

THE DAVIDSON COLLEGE YOUNG MEN'S CHRISTIAN ASSOCIATION held a brilliant reception in their new hall February 1 to introduce the public to their parlor and reading-room, which have just been handsomely carpeted and furnished with elegant sets of furniture in cherry and antique oak. The carpet, stove and furniture of the reading-room, costing nearly one hundred dollars, were presented by Messrs. H. Baruch, Andrews, and Bros. Kaufman and Davis, of Charlotte, and the parlor completely furnished at an expense of $190 by Dr. and Mrs. J. B. Shearer, of Davidson College.

BUNCOMBE COUNTY is not to be outdone in her educational work. The Quarterly County Teachers' Association held its third session of the current year at Asheville the last Saturday in February, with about seventy-five teachers present. Interesting addresses were made by Superintendent Claxton, of the city schools; Professor Arnold, of Asheville Female College; President D. L. Ellis, of Fair View College; Miss Florence Stephenson, of Home Industrial School; Professor Walter Hurst, of Barnardsville, and others. County Superintendent Way is a live worker, and as President of the Association he serves very acceptably.

THE EXECUTIVE COMMITTEE of the Western North Carolina Teachers' Association met at Asheville, February 26th, to decide upon time and place of meeting for the Association. Several places were represented, but the decision of the committee was for Waynesville, N. C., and time selected was June 14th to 18th. A Programme Committee of four—Chairman Starnes, *ex officio;* Secretary Hurst, *ex officio;* Treasurer Ellis, *ex officio;* Dr. R. H. Lewis—and Miss Florence Stephenson, were named to arrange work for the Association. Great enthusiasm prevails among the teachers, and there is every prospect of a fine attendance in June. One attraction of the Association will be the presence of Rev. Thomas Dixon, who will make a special lecture before the Association.

AT RECESS.

The books and slates now put away,
And let us laugh a little while;
For those who work there should be play,
The leisure moments to beguile.

PUPIL (in class in punctuation, reading)—I saw Lily a charming girl. Teacher—Well, what would you do? Pupil—Make a dash after Lily. Teacher—Right.

"ROBERT, you may give the name of some wild flower," said the teacher in botany. Robert thought awhile and then said: "Well, I reckon Injun meal comes about as near being wild flour as anything I know of."

GUEST—So you are hard at work studying French? What is the object of that? Waiter—I've been offered a steady job at big pay over in Paris if I learn. Guest—Humph! There are plenty of French waiters in Paris. Waiter—Y-e-s, but you see they can't understand French as Americans speak it.

VISITOR—When I passed your daughter's door, coming down, she stood before the glass making horrible grimaces. I'm afraid she isn't well. Matron—Did she have a book in her hand? Visitor—Yes, I think she had. Matron—She is all right; that was the Delsartean method of looking pleasant.

A YOUNG MINISTER, unexpectedly called upon to address a Sunday-school, asked, to gain time, "Children, what shall I speak about?" A little girl on the front seat from the public school, who had herself committed to memory several declamations, held up her hand and in a shrill voice inquired, "What do you know?"

THE TEACHER had been giving a class of youngsters some ideas of adages and how to make them, and to test her training she put a few questions. "What is an idle brain?" was one. "The devil's work-shop," was the prompt response. Then there were several more till this one came: "Birds of a feather do what?" "Lay eggs," piped a small boy before anybody else had a chance to speak."

IN MEMORIAM.

"Death hath made no breach
In love and sympathy, in hope and trust
No outward sign or sound our ears can reach,
But there's an inward, spiritual speech
That greets us still, though mortal tongues be dust.
It bids us do the work that they laid down—
Take up the song where they broke off the strain ;
So, journeying till we reach the heavenly town,
Where are laid up our treasure and our crown,
And our lost loved ones will be found again.".

MISS NETTIE MARSHALL, a teacher in the Institution for the Deaf and Dumb at Raleigh, died, after a brief illness, on March 11, 1892, in the fortieth year of her age. She was a member of the Teachers' Assembly since its organization, and was acknowledged one of the best teachers in the South. She was a sister of Rev. M. M. Marshall, D. D., of Raleigh.

THE NORTH CAROLINA TEACHER.

VOL. IX.   RALEIGH, APRIL, 1892.   NO. 8.

EUGENE G. HARRELL,   =   =   =   =   Editor.

TO THE MODERN TEACHER.

You must get a "broad, gray line,"
   And be sure of the "free arm movement."
"Do, me, sol," of course "on time,"
   And the "sewing" needs improvement.

The "Ling System" is introduced,
   And "Sloyd Work" is cited,
"Compositions" oft produced,
   "Language Work" not slighted.

Of "Supplementary Reading," many lays,
   "Thought Problems" you must hoard.
"Around the World in Eighty Days,"
   And go on the "molding board."

"History" with "Old Colonial Times,"
   And "Boys of '76."
"Word Lessons," just so many times.
   "Monthly Reports" to fix.

"Test Papers" face you by the score.
   "General Lessons" every day.
More, and more, and more, and more.
   What, think you, should be the pay?
         —*American Teacher.*

CHAPTER XXVIII.

OUR FACES TURNED TOWARDS HOME.

OUR LAST DAY IN PARIS—EXTRA TOURS ARRANGED—A ROUGH NIGHT
ON THE CHANNEL—RESTING IN LONDON—THE GRAND MILITARY
REVIEW—THE FLYING AMERICAN TRAIN—ANCESTRAL HOME OF
WASHINGTON—THE LAND OF SHAKESPEARE—A RAILROAD WON-
DER—AGAIN IN GLASGOW.

 ELL, young ladies,"
said the Secretary next
morning as we assembled
in the dining-room, "our
charming tour is now
practically ended, and
we are about to turn
our faces again towards
home. Whatever else there is in Paris that you desire to
see must be seen to-day, as we leave at 5 o'clock on our
return to London. I advise you, however, to take as much
rest to-day as possible, for the weather indicates that we are
likely to have a rough night on the Channel."

"All right, Major," laughingly replied one of the girls,
"we don't mind the Channel, and we haven't time to rest,
so we will finish 'doing' this wonderful city to-day, and
be ready to leave at 5 o'clock."

And all spent the day as they were most inclined, some shopping, others revisiting the art galleries, but most of them simply strolling about the boulevards and public parks watching the ever-changing and interesting mass of humanity.

As several members of the party desired to remain longer in Europe, visiting Italy and the far south, Germany and Switzerland, much of the day was occupied in making up these sections and arranging tickets for the tours. There was very little trouble, however, in securing satisfactory rates and accommodations, for the valuable assistance of our tourist friends, Messrs. Gaze & Sons, soon planned just the very trips that were desired.

In the afternoon, when these small parties began to leave upon their tours, we felt the first pangs of separation and the sadness of the "good-byes" which were soon to be spoken to all these dear friends whom a month's pleasant journeying together had united almost as a great family of natural brothers and sisters.

The remainder of our party, sixty-four persons, left Paris at 5 o'clock P. M., August 5th, for Dieppe, with our faces turned towards home.

It matters not how pleasant may be a tour in a foreign land, nor how long or short may be the absence, when the trip is ended and the time for returning home is at hand there is as much joy in turning towards our home land as there was in setting out upon the journey. After many days of sojourn in a strange land and contact with those only who are strangers to us, how the heart yearns to be again with those whom we know and love.

It was a rough night on the Channel. The wind had been blowing a brisk gale all day, and it had worked up a very characteristic "choppy sea," which was sufficient to satisfy the most exacting of those who desired to see a "rough Channel."

There was a great crowd of visitors leaving Paris, and the little steamer was filled to its utmost capacity. Every part of the vessel was thronged with people merrily chatting and laughing over the memories of their experiences and pleasures of the gay French capital.

We were hungry, and there was a rush for supper, but the meal was scarcely finished before there was almost a simultaneous rush for the rail in order to get rid of it. The wind was shrieking maliciously, and the pleasant chatting had become vainly suppressed groaning.

There were many nationalities represented on board, and it was amusing to listen to the various comments upon the condition of things. The Englishman, between his paroxysms, called it "a nasty sea;" the Frenchman gritted his teeth and mumbled "*Parbleu!*" the German endeavored to ease his agony by frequently expressing his opinion, "Mein Gott, I will die!" while the American party almost unanimously agreed that when they again reached the land nothing should induce them to leave it, even to cross the ocean in order to get home. The Secretary feared that the whole party would remain in England, and in his moments of saneness, between the throes of sea-sick anguish, he had fully decided to remain with them.

We all succeeded, however, by some unaccountable means in living through that awful night, and entered the port of New Haven just about sunrise. So sudden was the change from the violent pitching of the sea to the placid water of the harbor that we did not have time to finish our sea-sickness before landing, although the malady had nearly finished us.

In our forlorn condition of body and mind, even the custom house had no terrors for us, and our struggle with the English tariff ceremonies became wholly a mechanical transaction in which we could scarcely appreciate the dignity of our position as parts of the machine. Our whole object in life at that time seemed to be simply to get into the railway cars and go to sleep, and that cherished object was attained at the earliest possible moment.

The railway guards thoughtfully woke us up when we entered Victoria Station in London. We were yet sea-sick, and were longing to reach our hotel. The Secretary had telegraphed our departure from Paris in order that the proprietor of the Manchester Hotel should have rooms ready for the party. Upon our arrival we found everything prepared for us, and within an hour every person was in bed and asleep, having previously given orders that we were not to be called until dinner, at 6 o'clock P. M.

The order was carefully obeyed, and for nine hours we slept the sleep of the weary. Some of the party did not put in an appearance until the breakfast hour next morning.

All of London was greatly excited in consequence of a magnificent review of the English troops by the Emperor of Germany at Aldershott the following day, the 7th of August. The ceremonies were to conclude by a thrilling sham battle, in which the infantry, cavalry and artillery should be engaged. Of course the general excitement likewise affected the North Carolina party, and therefore as soon after breakfast as possible we joined the vast throng of people and set out for Aldershott.

Our government continues in such a chronic state of peace that a large standing army is not at all necessary, and it is a rare thing to see an imposing military review in our country, but to witness such a magnificent and dashing array and movement of soldiers as it was our privilege to see at Aldershott on that day, is an event which occurs but once in a lifetime. The occasion was the grand review of the English army by William II, Emperor of Germany.

The weather was exceedingly pleasant (for England), and at an early hour thousands of people were moving towards the vast parade ground at Aldershott, about six miles distant from London. The main feature of the day was the brilliant sham battle by two armies of fifteen thousand soldiers each.

The Northern Army, commanded by General Sir D. C. Drury Lowe, was supposed to be defending the city of London from an invasion by a southern army under Major General Williams, which had landed on the south coast. The two armies included, besides the infantry, four thousand six hundred horses and ninety-three guns. The movements began about 8 o'clock, and as the various brigades took their positions among the hills and the plains the marching was a sight so beautiful that it will never be forgotten.

In the rear of the infantry were the cavalry and artillery, and a battery was posted far to the rear to defend in a flank movement.

While the opposing armies were manœuvering the distinguished reviewing officers took their position on a hill to the eastward of the battlefield. Many of our party were close enough to recognize the Emperor and various members of his escort.

The Emperor of Germany was specially accompanied by the Duke of Cambridge, who is at the head of the English Military Affairs, and standing near were Lord Wolseley, Sir Evelyn Wood, Sir Redvers Buller and General Hannon. On the left of the Emperor were Prince Albert Victor of Wales and Prince Henry of Prussia, and the royal occasion was also graced by the Princess of Wales and her two lovely daughters, Victoria and Maud.

The fight was commenced by the southern Army, and the opposing scouts were at once thrown out.

It was soon seen that General Williams had the advantage of position, and he made several flank movements which were simply superb. The battle was a hot one, the gallant charges of cavalry, the fierce blazing of the field batteries, and the brilliant stands of the infantry formed a martial panorama which thrilled every heart in that vast concourse of near two hundred thousand spectators.

Victory rested on the banners of the invading army, and after three hours of battle the defenders began a retreat, it having been outflanked and its centre broken. One of the most interesting features of the engagement was the construction within half an hour of a bridge by General Lowe's Engineer Corps to provide for his retreat across a small stream of water.

About 2 o'clock the smoke of battle had cleared away, and the two armies were soon in position for the grand review. This beautiful spectacle continued about two hours, and the splendid marching did not indicate any fatigue from the battle of the morning. Each body of troops, infantry, cavalry and artillery, marched past the reviewing ground with the precision of machinery, and the Emperor seemed to enjoy the sight as much as any member of our party who had never before seen anything so grand and imposing.

We reached our hotel just in time for the 6 o'clock dinner, thoroughly prepared to enjoy it, even though we were then full of martial enthusiasm and inspiration. It is a well known fact that tourists are always tired and always hungry, and of course our party came within the universal rule.

This being our last evening of sight-seeing in London, we wanted to make the best possible use of it. Therefore, as soon as the dinner was finished all the members of the party again set out for the various places of amusement and entertainment which abound in that great city. The immense stores, the gaily thronged parks and highways, the art exhibitions and the theatres were the principal objective points of visit, while the Secretary called upon the railroad officials to arrange coaches for our departure next day.

It had been our desire and intention to visit Stratford-upon-Avon, the historic home of the world's greatest dramatist, and our regret may be imagined when we learned that all visitors to Stratford were obliged to remain there over night, and that it was impossible to visit the place upon any other conditions. As we were then in London on August 7th, and our steamer sailed for New York from Glasgow at at 10 o'clock on the 9th, we were compelled to admit that our long desired visit to the home of Shakespeare seemed to be now exceedingly uncertain.

The Secretary, however, determined that the trip should not be so easily given up, and after half an hour's consultation with the President of the London and North Western Railroad he had secured for our North Carolina party, by the courtesy of that most considerate and accommodating railway company, a special train of first-class cars and one of the best engines on the road.

Our train was to leave London at 5 o'clock A. M., reach Stratford at 12:·30 P. M., remaining there two hours, then run through to Glasgow by 8 o'clock P. M., a total distance of five hundred and thirty miles! Thus we were enabled to go from London to Glasgow, visiting Shakespeare's Home *en route* within a day, and this had never been done by any other company of tourists.

The party having been notified of the arrangement, we were all ready promptly at 5 o'clock next morning when the railway omnibuses called at the Manchester Hotel for us and our baggage. We were quickly seated in our railway coaches, and the train dashed out of the Station with the speed of the hurricane, while the guards looked after us in amazement at the enterprise of "that American party."

Sixty, seventy and eighty miles an hour our train glided "over the metals," not making a single stop until we reached Blisworth, where we left the main line to take a branch road to Stratford, about fifty miles distant, while our special train ran up to Rugby Junction to await our return by a different route.

In a few moments after leaving Blisworth we reached Morton Pinkney, an insignificant station apparently, but possessing a wonderful interest for us, it being near the ancestral home of Washington, the grandfather of our GEORGE WASHINGTON, the first President of the United States.

About three miles to the left of the Station, sitting upon a slight hill is the little village of Sulgrave, and just outside the village, stands the ancient manor house erected by Laurence Washington in 1650, still bearing over the main entrance the family coat-of-arms, the Shield and Stars and Stripes with his crest, a raven, above it.

When the civil war began in England, the sons of Laurence Washington took the side of the King, and the second son, John, had the honor of knighthood conferred upon him in 1622 at Newmarket. When the tide of war turned and the Commonwealth governed England, this John Washington and his brother Laurence deemed it more prudent to emigrate, and, therefore, in 1657 they landed on the free shores of America and settled at Bridges' creek, in Virginia. A century later, in the war of the Revolution, George, the grandson of that Sir John, was a colonel serving under General Braddock, and he soon became General Washington in command of the American army, and afterwards was inaugurated the first President of the United States.

The coat-of-arms which his ancestors brought to Virginia with them from the old homestead at Sulgrave, became, with slight alterations, the famous "Stars and Stripes" of the first American Republic, and their crest, the raven, was changed into that renowned bird of liberty, the "Spread-eagle of the American Union." Of course we waved our American flag most vigorously and patriotically over this historic place of such peculiar interest to us.

We had but a very few moments for our thoughts to dwell upon the historic ancestry of the great Washington, for our train quickly pulled up at the station of Stratford, and then followed a rush for the little village.

What emotions crowd the breast as one beholds for the first time the house in which Shakespeare was born. One feels the presence of the divine power which from this humble spot gave humanity its greatest genius.

The house stands now as it was then. The exterior is strikingly familiar to all lovers of the poet. The solid framework of beams, girders and posts is painted black and shows through the plaster stucco which forms the outer covering in place of weatherboarding. It is a very old style, but still to be seen in many of the old English towns.

You can distinguish the house a good distance off. The black and gray striped appearance of the front and the peculiar gable-shaped windows mark it at once. Instinctively you stop and gaze upon it with rare and strange emotions, felt perhaps nowhere else upon earth. Reverence, pride, wonder, human sympathy are blended with a sense of weakness and of power that are called forth by contemplating the works of God in nature. When we stand for the first time in Henley street, opposite to the birth-place of Shakespeare, one feels somewhat as he does when he beholds for the first time the mountains, or the ocean, or Niagara.

The place belongs to the town of Stratford, and it is guarded with loving pride and reverence. An elderly lady (now dead) was in charge as we entered. She had been there over a quarter of a century, and her face was now a part of the place. She had seen there, and escorted around, nearly all the great men of the world of this generation. She kindly ushered us in, and our party spread over the house, looking at the various mementoes. Here was a case containing many specimens of Shakespeare's handwriting and his seal. The chirography was simply illegible. As Mark Twain has said of the handwriting of Christopher Columbus, "A six-year-old boy in the schools could do better."

A library in the building contains all books ever written about Shakespeare, and various editions of his works. There are many Shakespearean portraits and a very full set of engravings.

The most interesting spot in the house is the room where he was born, containing the furniture that belongs to the family. The room is large, but very plain. The plaster is very old and stained and cracked. It would fall down, but it is supported by iron strips. In this room cried and squalled and smiled and shook its tiny fist the infant Shakespeare. Little did his humble mother dream that she had given the world its greatest poet, philosopher and moralist. Everyone stood silent and speechless in this sacred place. The purest and deepest emotions were evoked in our hearts, and we felt almost as if we had received personal knowledge of Shakespeare. Several of the young ladies had cause to use their handkerchiefs, and the Professor was profoundly affected. We all registered our names along with those of Scott, Dickens, Irving, Queen Victoria, Bismark, the Czar of Russia and thousands of others who had stood in this spot and felt the same strange and elevating emotions.

About a mile from Stratford is Anne Hathaway's Cottage, a perfect specimen of the plainer farm cottage of Shakespeare's day. The roof is straw-thatched; the fireplace is very broad and there are seats *inside* the fireplace on either side of the logs of wood, where sat the person who attended to the roasting of the mutton or beef. There doubtless sat Shakespeare with the hot blood of youth firing his imagination and painting Miss Anne as a fairy. The buxom woman wound the boy about her fingers, and the greatest genius on earth was led captive by his passion and the physical charms of a plain country woman.

"The thoughts that you cannot tie with hoops of steel, a girl's hair lightly binds." Crowds of people go constantly to this cottage and pluck a flower or a blade of grass from the yard, or drink of the spring and sit upon the oak bench in the fireplace. How intensely does humanity long for the human. How unable are we to free ourselves from the power of personality. God himself recognized this weakness in mankind and sent down His revealed truth in the person of a human creature like ourselves.

What a story would be written could we know Shakespeare's full career! What a story of passion, of heartache, of developing power, of humanity. It would·be in one sense the life of man—a weak, puling baby; a wild, wayward boy; a hot-blooded youth, wedded to a woman several years older; a father, a runaway from home, a fortune-seeker in London, a menial, an actor, a playwright, a man of society, a friend of princes and lords, a mirror and glass of nature and humanity, a SHAKESPEARE. He returned to Stratford, built a magnificent residence called " New Place," and was the social magnate of his native place. The city has erected memorial buildings in his honor—a theatre, library and picture gallery. They are rich with priceless relics.

The Cathedral contains his tomb, and here lie all that is left of this immortal genius. He is buried under the floor back of the chancel railing. Over. the tomb is the following inscription, said to have been written by Shakespeare himself :

> " Good Friend for Jesus sake forbeare
> To Digg the Dust encloased heare
> Blest be Ye man Yt spares thes stones
> And Curst be He Yt moves my bones."

Attempts have been made to open the grave and move his bones, but his curse is still potent, and the reverence of the English people guards sacredly this spot. He needs no Westminster Abbey. Let the winding Avon enfold him in its embrace till all are called at the judgment day.

The Secretary, by much persuasion and bribery of the janitor of the church, was permitted to cover this famous inscription with printing ink and take an impression on paper as a rare and valuable souvenir of the visit of this famous party of North Carolinians to the grave of Shakespeare. The exact impression of this celebrated epitaph, printed direct from the grave-stone, is now framed and hung in the North Carolina Teachers' Assembly Building at Morehead City, the most valuable of all the decorations in that building.

Ours was truly "a flying trip" to Stratford, but we are sure that few persons have ever seen more of that interesting locality, however long may have been their visit.

At Rugby Junction we again boarded our own special train at 3 o'clock P. M. We were then three hundred miles from Glasgow, and were due there at 8 o'clock. The Secretary asked the engineer, a noble specimen of humanity, if he could make the trip within schedule time. "Oh, yes," he replied, smiling, "we have but one stop for coal and water, and we will make the run at fifty to eighty miles an hour, according to the grade of the road."

No "Flying Dutchman" or "Flying Scotchman" ever approached the velocity of that train. We overtook numbers of fast trains which were side-tracked for us to pass. We were compelled to close the windows, for the speed almost took away our breath. The road-bed was so level that there was but little rocking to the train, scarcely as much as there is with a train in America running at forty miles an hour.

We were moving so fast that we could hardly see the people who looked at our train in wonder from the doors and windows of their houses as we dashed past them. A shrill whistle of the engine told us when we were rushing through a town or city, and that was all we knew of them. Bridges, trestles, roads, forests, towns, rivers, mountains and lakes were approached and passed in the twinkling of an eye.

At 8 o'clock precisely our train stopped at the Central Station in Glasgow, and as we stepped from the cars a railway official informed us that "no such a run has ever before been made by a train in Great Britain."

We were soon comfortably roomed in the two large hotels, St. James and St. George, situated around St. George's Square in Glasgow. It was our last night to be spent in the "Old World," and the visions of our slumbers brought to us that night many pleasant scenes and incidents of the memorable tour, and there was regret that the journey was ending. But happy dreams of "Home, Sweet Home," also came to us as we slept, with sweet consolations of hope and affection, and our hearts longed "to greet you all once more."

[For The North Carolina Teacher.]

COUNTRY SCHOOLS AND CITY SCHOOLS.

BY MISS WILLIE T. HALL, CALDWELL INSTITUTE, N. C.

The country is, in some respects, a better place for a school than the city.

If we will only look for a few moments into the crowded city with its stifling atmosphere, thronged streets and unhealthy localities, and then out into the country at its quietude, its shady groves and forests, and its ever-pure and invigorating air, we will be fully convinced, without further argument, which place would be the better to send the youth of our land to be educated.

One of the first reasons for saying the country is better is health. Someone may say we are not speaking of health, it is education; but what would an education be worth to us if we had no health?

Go for a few moments into one of the hospitals of New York and there view suffering humanity for a short time, and I am confident that we would never again fail to be thoughtful of our health. We might have the wealth of Vanderbilt or the wisdom of Solomon, and without health it could be of but little pleasure or benefit to us.

The law of nature requires that we should have two thousand feet of fresh and pure air every hour, but we know that it would be almost impossible to obtain that quantity in a large city with its crowded houses, filthy streets and gutters.

So we must resort to the country with its broad acres of land which are standing uninhabited, with nothing to make the atmosphere foul and impure.

Second, the temptatious are more numerous and much greater in the city than they are in the country.

When we are passing through the streets of some city, what is it we see oftener than large bar-rooms with pool and billiard tables inviting the young men as they pass that way to come in and spend their money for strong drinks, and their afternoons in gambling, which is to-day a curse to thousands of young men of our country, who otherwise would be noble young men.

The ball-rooms, theatres and opera-houses are not much less numerous than the bar-rooms, inviting both sexes to come in and waste their time and means, thowing them away, doing themselves and others no service whatever. Who would wish to send boys and girls to such places as that to meet all those temptations, which so few would be able to resist? I dare say, none.

The older and wiser people would much prefer sending their children to the country, where they can spend their leisure hours in rambling through forests, admiring the beauties of nature and plucking the beautiful flowers with which God has clothed this great universe, that they may cheer and brighten the paths of His creatures as they wander to and fro over this earth. And I am sure no one would appreciate them more than a school-girl.

Here in the country we find no such temptations to tempt the young as we do in the cities.

Third, there are less attractions in the country. In the city there is always something to attract the attention of the student from his books.

Out in the country we find none such; but there they can have outdoor games for amusement and recreation when necessary.

Fourth, it is less expensive. I don't think I would be speaking falsely, if I were to say that we could attend school twenty months in the country for the same amount it would require for ten months in the city, and learn just as much at one place as the other. Is this, too, not a great advantage, especially to the poorer classes, as it enables them to obtain an education when they could never do so otherwise.

Numbers of boys and girls are now in school preparing themselves for usefulness in life, and if they were not in the country they could never do it.

We know by experience that the country is *decidedly* a better place for a school than a city. If it had not been, why would our forefathers have selected farms and places in the country to found the institutions of Trinity, Davidson, Wake Forest, the University and other colleges?

We cannot doubt but that it was for the best; if it had not been, they would never have been half so successful as they have. They were wise men. They knew what was best for the young people of our country.

Some may argue that children learn so much more by observation when they are in the city; but I think it just as necessary to learn something about that which God has created and placed here in this world as it is to learn so very much about human inventions, style and fashion, for there are plenty of children living in towns and cities who have never seen so small a thing as a duck or guinea.

Would they not be surprised if they were permitted to see the animals roaming through the open country?

Plant schools in the country; send the boys and girls where they will be free from so many temptations; send them where they will find health, peace and pleasure.

KEEP THIS IN MIND.

Don't find fault with the work of your predecessor. He may not have done so well as you, or as you expect to do, but you will add no strength to the character of your work by finding fault with his.

If your work is better, your pupils and the public will soon appreciate the fact and give you all due credit and possibly more than due praise; and how much more gratifying it will be to have it come because it is deserved!

It is, of course, possible to criticise your predecessor's work and show the blunders he made, but is it generous? Do you strengthen your own character by seeking for flaws in the character of others? If so, yours must be one that greatly needs strengthening. It is only the smallest that need to stand on the prostrate bodies of others, that they may make themselves visible to the world at large.—*Educational News.*

2

ADVICE TO YOUNG MEN.

Don't think that a cigarette smoker is likely to be employed as clerk or book-keeper by a careful business man.

Don't think that every girl who smiles at you is in love with you.

Don't take liberties with sisters of other young men that you would not be willing to see those men take with your sisters.

Don't make the meetings of the Young Men's Christian Association an excuse for going away from home every night.

Don't ask every girl you meet for her photograph or a lock of her hair. To comply with similar requests from other young men would be, the one very expensive and the other very inconvenient to her.

Don't try to make people believe that you " know it all, " simply because you have been to college, for sensible persons are not to be caught that way, and they well know that colleges cannot supply a deficient brain.

Don't be ashamed to be seen engaged in any honest work.

Don't spend even a single dollar in amusement or for entertainment if you are in debt to any person, because the dollar does not belong to you.

Don't think you will have the respect of persons who hear you speak flippantly of your father, your mother, or of any other lady.

Don't think that you can live with less work in any other State than in North Carolina. All the poor men who have tried to live without work starved to death just as they thought they had learned the art.

Don't loaf, don't chew tobacco, don't smoke, don't drink intoxicating liquors as a beverage, and don't be a religious crank.

WHY THE TEACHER SHOULD BE EARLY.

A teacher should be at the school-house early every day for the following, among many reasons adduced:

1. *To set an example.*—As the teacher, so will the pupil learn to be.

2. *To prevent damage.*—Children arriving at the school-room early get to playing in and about the room, and very frequently do unintentional damage.

3. *To see that all is right.*—There are many little things to be "put to rights" or arranged before school opens. Fires and ventilation must be looked after early in the day.

4. *To secure ventilation.*—The house, shut up from the time the school closed the day before, is unhealthy, and should be opened and fully aired in season to be warmed and closed at school time.

5. *To greet pupils.*—Children kindly and cordially greeted on arriving at the school-house are far less inclined to torment the teacher through the day.

6. *To administer discipline.*—A kind greeting and a kind word of discipline spoken to one who has been careless or misbehaved the day before, when he can thus be approached alone, is far more effectual than detention at night or punishment in the presence of the school.

7. *To help those needing assistance.*—During the school but little personal assistance can be given. If an industrious pupil thinks that he can be helped in some difficult point if at the school-house before school time, he will appreciate and avail himself of the opportunity.

8. *To win the love of the pupils.*—Kind greeting, kind words and kind assistance will win the love of the pupils, whether they are themselves the recipients or see it given to others.—*School Bulletin.*

A LETTER FROM CUBA.

[We think our readers will be interested in this letter from a little Cuban girl.   She is only thirteen years old, is a native of the island and has learned the American language by hard study.   The letter is well written and punctuated, and we think that it is also well expressed.   We hope that Pura may enter some excellent North Carolina school as a pupil.—EDITOR.]

HAVANA, CUBA, March 15th, 1892.

MR. EUGENE G. HARRELL, *Raleigh, N. C.*

DEAR SIR:—I have not forgotten my promise to write a letter for your TEACHER, but I have been so busy with my school work and our church attentions all this month, and besides I am so much afraid of writing in a foreign language, which I am learning now and know but little.   And also my father has been out in February last on trip to New York and back to Cuba, and I wished him to see my letter and correct it.   He arrived here in the last week of past month and he brought to me many nice things from that great city.

Our mission work is growing every day in number of members and in spirit.   I am sorry that you and the teachers' party did not visit us.   My father is the pastor and we hold meetings every Sunday at 12 o'clock and at 7:30 P. M.   Our church is called "Pilar Baptist Church," and is situated in the Pilar, a district of this city at three miles distant from Mr. Diaz's church.   We are 207 members and the Sunday-school has near 200 children and five children.   We have also a day mission school where boys and girls are taught reading, writing, Bible, grammar, arithmetic, geography, drawing, singing and others; it is a very interesting school, as every visitor says.   My father is the director and my mother is a teacher, as well as Miss Gutierrez and myself for the little ones learning to read. Mr. Ecay is another teacher for boys. This day school numbers 160 boys and girls. Why did you not visit it? It is a free school and my father has established it to form Christian people for the future, as he says.

I have received your nice paper, THE NORTH CAROLINA TEACHER. Many thanks for it. I have read the article on Cuba and I think they have exaggerated to you our customs: the time for meals is according with the house you are at; we at home here breakfast at 9 in the morning and dinner at 4 P. M., and in this way many of the things mentioned in that article.

Well, my friend, I know that you liked our island and I hope to see you again in it. Let me salute from this paper every one of the teachers of your party as well as every one of the girls of "Peace Institute," and every person who cares there for this Cuban work.

My father and mother send kind regards.

Truly your friend,

PURA J. COVA.

SOMETHING QUEER IN THE NUMBERS.

—

Mr. John W. Kirk, the white-haired veteran, who was with Morse when the first working telegraph line was stretched, and who stood beside the great inventor when the first message was transmitted from Annapolis Junction to Washington, has made, during his life, a great many interesting calculations in numbers. The two most remarkable numbers in the world are 3 and 7.

"The numeral 7," says Mr. Kirk, "the Arabians got from India, and all following have taken it from the Arabians. It is conspicuous in Biblical lore, being mentioned

over 300 times in the Scriptures, either alone or com-
pounded with other words. It seems a favorite numeral
with the divine mind, outside as well as inside the Bible,
as nature demonstrates in many ways, and all other numbers bow to it. There is also another divine favorite, the
number 3—the Trinity. This is brought out by a combination of figures that is somewhat remarkable. It is the six
figures 142,857.

"Multiply this by 2, the answer is 285,714.

"Multiply this by 3, the answer is 428,571.

"Multiply this by 4, the answer is 571,428.

"Multiply this by 5, the answer is 714,285.

"Multiply this by 6, the answer is 857,142.

"Each answer contains the same figures as the original
sum and no others, and that three of the figures of the sum
remain together in each answer, thus showing that figures
preserve the Trinity.

"Thus 285 appears in the first and second numbers,
571 in the second and third, 428 in the third and fourth
and 142 in the fourth and fifth.

"It is also interesting to note that, taking out of any
two of these sums the group of three common to both, the
other three, read in the usual order from left to right, will
also be in the same order in both sums.

"Take the first and second sums, for example. The
group 285 is common to both. Having read 285 out of
the second sum, read right along and bring in the first
figure of the thousands last. It will read 714. All the
others will read in the same way.

"Again, note that the two groups of threes in the first
sum are the same as the two groups of threes in the fourth,
reversed in order, and that the same thing is true of the
second and third. The last multiplication has its groups
of threes the same as those of the original number, reversed
again.

"Examine these results again, and you will see that in these calculations all the numerals have appeared save the 9. Now multiply the original sum by the mighty 7—the divine favorite of the Bible and of creation—and behold the answer! The last of the numerals, and that one only in groups of three—again the Trinity!

$$\begin{array}{r} 142,857 \\ 7 \\ \hline 999,999 \end{array}$$

"No other combination of numbers will produce the same results. Does not this show the imperial multipotent numeral 7 and its divinity?"—*New York Sun.*

A MUCH NEEDED SOCIETY.

It would seem that with the hundreds of various societies which are working to secure the attention and support of the people, surely there is no possible room or demand for any other society. And of all these organizations North Carolina has a full share.

There is great need, nevertheless, of another society. If we complied with a ridiculous custom of the times and should designate our proposed new society simply by its initials, they would be S. F. K. M. A. W. A. H. A. N. I. O. G. T. L. O. S. M., which, being translated into pure American, would be "Society for keeping men and women at home at night instead of going to lodge or society meetings."

It is customary, you know, to give a name to a society which is so long that nobody will ever take time to announce it, but use initials only, as "Y. M. C. A.," "W. C. T. U.," "N. E. A.," "S. P. K. C.," "S. P. C. A.," and so on, *ad disgustum.*

But the new society for which there is so great need would not be known by the eighteen initials as above, but would simply be called the " Home Society." Its principal objects would be to provide entertainment for young people at home, so as to prevent this promiscuous " running out at night "; to introduce socially our boys and girls to one another, so that they would find pleasure in one another's company in the evening gatherings at private houses where the brothers, sisters, and all members of the families could find entertainment.

THE TEACHER cannot look with much favor upon any society or organization, Christian or secular, which habitually draws our young men away from home and the family circle, and takes them "down the street" at night. This constant attendance upon night meetings is the prominent feature of weakness in the " Young Men's Christian Association." This Association has done and is doing a valuable work with homeless boys in large cities, but, in our judgment, there are few night meetings that can be of near so much benefit to a young man as an evening spent at home amid the refining influences of his own or some other pure and congenial family circle.

The "gymnasium," the "singing meeting," or the "committee meeting" at the Young Men's Christian Association rooms has sometimes been the cause of a boy going astray by getting him into the habit of being frequently away from home and on the street at night. This fact proves that while an object and work may be good the results may be very undesirable. All work should be viewed from every possible standpoint.

Let us, therefore, constitute ourselves and our boys and girls into a great brotherhood—the Stay-at-home-at-night Society, whose principles provide that after dark we will generally be found enjoying our own homes, or pleasantly visiting some other home equally as pleasant.

IN THE SCHOOL-ROOM.

WHAT CHEWING GUM DOES.

Chewing gum tends to distort the face. It produces a sort of vacant stare or hungry expression, such as may be seen on the face of a child that has to wait for the second table. The gum-chewing habit will in a short time remove the fine lines from the best molded face.

Have you ever noted the deformity in the face of a nail-biter? It is distinctly marked, and nearly the same in all cases. Defective sight, however, is probably the most prolific cause of distortion of the face. This defect is largely due to poor light in school-rooms and close application to study at night by gaslight.

A little attention to these matters may save your girl from growing up ugly.

THE WOMAN WHO LAUGHS.

For a good everyday household angel give us a woman who laughs. Her biscuit may not be always just right, and she may occasionally burn her bread and forget to replace dislocated buttons, but for solid comfort all day and every day she is a paragon. Home is not a battle-field, nor life one long, unending row.

The trick of always seeing the bright side, or, if the matter has no bright side, of shining up the dark one, is a very important faculty, one of the things no woman should be without.

We are not all born with the sunshine in our hearts, as the Irish prettily phrase it, but we can cultivate a cheerful sense of humor if we only try.—*Rural New Yorker.*

GOOD ENGLISH.

There is an old story of the advice of William Cullen Bryant once gave to a young man who offered him an article for *The Evening Post*, which is so good that it will bear frequent repeating:

"My young friend, I observe that you used several French expressions in your article. I think, if you will study the English language that you will find it capable of expressing all the ideas that you may have. Be simple, unaffected; be honest in your speaking and writing. Never use a long word when a short one will do. Call a spade not a well-know oblong instrument of manual industry; let a home be a home, not a residence; a place, not a locality, and so of the rest. When a short word will do, you always lose by using a long one."

IS IT SUCCESS OR FAILURE?

We would like to know what has been the observation of principals and superintendents as to the results of the teaching of the effects of stimulants and narcotics as affecting the habits of the boys, especially the tobacco habit.

Theoretically the law is all right, but when we see a boy who in the morning has been taught, scientifically, the evils resulting from the use of tobacco, stand upon the street corners and puff away vigorously at a cigarette, we confess to a doubt whether this department of physiology has any material influence over the boy's habits.

The tobacco habit is doing the boys more injury than liquor, and the habit seems to be on the increase in spite of the teachings against its use.—*Central School Journal.*

SENSIBLE HINTS ABOUT ADDITION.

When you are ready to teach addition, teach it as a subject in and of itself. Do not mix it up with multiplication and division. Teach one thing at a time and do it well. Addition is the foundation of work in numbers, and good teaching here helps all the other work. Make haste slowly; spend very little time in explaining that ten units of one order make one of the next higher. You can teach that principle to little children every day for a year and then they will not understand it, though they may repeat the words for you. When you are ready to begin carrying show the class how it is done, and let the explanation of the principle go to a future time. Make a sharp distinction between adding and counting. Counting is not addition and is the bane of addition work. The pupil who does not know instantly the sum of 6 and 8, does not add though he may be a perfect counter. Addition is knowing at once the sum of two numbers, and the sum is known because it has been well memorized. We do not reason sums, differences, products and quotients; we reason to determine whether we shall find a sum difference, product or quotient, and as soon as we have decided what to find the memory carries the work to the determined end.

Do not forget that the 45 combinations are the foundation of all addition work. They are made by adding one to each of the nine figures, two to each of the nine, three to each, and so on. Here are the 45 combinations. This first of 20 involves no carrying and are easily taught

1 1 1 2 1 2 3 2 1 6 5 4 7 6 5 4 8 7 6 5
1 2 3 2 4 3 3 4 5 1 2 3 1 2 3 4 1 2 3 4

Here are the 25 that involve carrying. Teach them well. They are the root of difficulties in addition. Call the pupil's attention to the fact that nine and seven always produce a 6, 7 and 5 a 2, 5 and 5 a 0, and so on through

the 25 combinations.   The reason for this will be apparent
when you come to add columns.

5 6 7 8 9 6 7 8 9 6 7 8 9 6 8 9 7 8 9 8 9 8 9 8 9
5 4 3 2 1 5 4 3 2 6 5 4 3 7 5 4 7 6 5 7 6 8 7 9 9

Seek accuracy first, then rapidity.   A well taught class
in its second year in school should give correctly these 45
sums in at least 45 seconds. . Be on your guard against
counting.   Teach only as fast as you can teach well.—
Central School Journal.

FOR THE ARITHMETIC CLASS.

I.

A cunning fox was bounding at a rapid pace,
When up jumped a rabbit, which he gave a chase;
Just sixty yards were there between
The fox and rabbit by us seen;
As the cunning fox jumped eleven feet,
The rabbit made eight in quick retreat.
Now, James, tell me how far the rabbit ran,
Before the cunning fox upon him sprang.

II.

Which will enclose the largest ground,
A fence made square, or one made round,
Two panels to each rod of land,
Ten rails to each we understand;
And every rail in each suppose
To just one acre of land enclose;
The next thing is to tell exact
How many acres in each tract?

[We will give a nice book of poems to the school-boy or
girl who first sends us correct solutions of these two problems. The problems must be solved without assistance
from any source.—EDITOR.]

BEFORE SCHOOL AND AFTER SCHOOL.

[This bright little recitation can be made very effective, with a little attention paid to a change of voice at each change of phrase. The title "Before School," should be pronounced distinctly, and followed at the end of the tenth line with "After School."]

"Quarter to nine! Boys and girls do you hear?"
"One more buckwheat, then—be quick, mother dear!
 Where is my luncheon box?" "Under the shelf,
 Just in the place you left it yourself!"
"I can't say my table!" "O, find me my cap!"
"One kiss for mama and sweet Sis in her lap."
"Be good, dear!" "I'll try."—"9 times 9's 81."
"Take your mittens!" "All right."—"Hurry up, Bill;
 let's run."
With a slam of the door, they are off, girls and boys,
And the mother draws breath in the lull of their noise.

* * * * * * * * *

"Don't wake up the baby! Come gently, my dear!"
"O, mother! I've torn my new dress, just look here!
 I'm sorry, I was only climbing the wall."
"O, mother, my map was the nicest of all!"
"And Nelly, in spelling went up to the head!"
"O, say! can I go on the hill with my sled?"
"I've got such a toothache." "The teacher is unfair!"
"Is dinner 'most ready? I'm just like a bear!"
Be patient, worn mother, they're growing up fast,
These nursery whirlwinds, not long do they last.
A still, lonely house would be far worse than the noise;
Rejoice and be glad in your brave girls and boys!
                                        —*Selected.*

A COMMENCEMENT DAY ODE.

No more "Gliding down life's river,"
  No more " Drifting out to sea,"
No more "Farewell, thee, kind teacher,"
  Willie has taken his degree.

No more "Sad the parting words we utter,"
  No more "Let us ever faithful be,"
No more "Tender memories fondly cherished,"
  Willie has taken his degree.

No more "Brave the world with firm endeavor,"
  No more "Strive to do the best we can,"
No more "Show the world that we are in it,"
  Willie now is quite a man.

—*Westfield Standard.*

BEAUTIFUL HANDS.

Beautiful hands are those that do
Work that is earnest, brave and true,
Moment by moment, the long day through.

THE NORTH CAROLINA PRACTICAL SPELLING BOOK is rapidly piling up its orders. It is likely that the entire first edition of ten thousand copies will be sold within sixty days after coming from press. The demand for the book will be very large and will extend into other States.

North Carolina Teachers' Assembly.

ORGANIZATION FOR 1892.

OFFICERS:

HUGH MORSON (Raleigh Male Academy), President, . . Raleigh.
EUGENE G. HARRELL (Editor TEACHER), Sec. and Treas., . Raleigh.

VICE–PRESIDENTS:

1. J. J. Blair (Supt. Graded Schools), ... Winston.
2. J. E. Kelly (Model Male School), ... Charlotte.
3. Miss Catherine Fulghum (Graded School), . . Goldsboro.
4. W. J. Ferrell (Wakefield Academy), . . . Wakefield.
5. Miss Lizzie Lindsay (Graded School), . . . Greensboro.
6. P. M. Pearsall (County Superintendent), . . Trenton.
7. Miss Lina McDonald (Graded School), . . . Winston.
8. T. J. Drewry (Horner Military School), . . . Oxford
9. Mrs. S. Montgomery Funk (Chowan Bap. Fem. Inst.), Murfreesboro.

EXECUTIVE COMMITTEE:

Hugh Morson, *ex officio*, President, ... Raleigh.
Eugene G. Harrell, *ex officio*, Secretary, . . . Raleigh.
Eben Alexander (University of North Carolina), . . Chapel Hill.
W. L. Poteat (Wake Forest College), ... Wake Forest.
James Dinwiddie (President Peace Institute), . . . Raleigh.
Charles D. McIver (Pres't Normal and Industrial School
    for Women), ... Greensboro.
J. Y. Joyner (Superintendent Graded School), . . Goldsboro.
A. C. Davis (Superintendent Military School), . . Winston.
E. E. Britton (Principal High School), ... Roxboro.

NINTH ANNUAL SESSION, MOREHEAD CITY, JUNE 21 TO JULY 4, 1892.

OFFICIAL CIRCULAR OF INFORMATION.

THE ASSEMBLY AND ITS WORK.

The work of the North Carolina Teachers' Assembly is annually growing in interest and value to the teachers of our State, and to its influence is largely due the general prosperity which is now being enjoyed by the schools throughout our borders.

Its delightful mid-summer meetings in the teachers' own "home by the sea," at Morehead City, bringing together many thousand teachers and their friends for most profitable educational work and in charming social intercourse, have given a new encouragement and inspiration to the teachers and induced a stronger support and appreciation of the teachers' work among those who patronize the schools. And the enjoyments and benefits which the teachers and friends of education in North Carolina are to derive from the Teachers' Assembly are yet but just beginning to be realized.

Besides the intellectual and social enjoyments of the Teachers' Assembly, the physical benefits which are derived from the trip cannot be overestimated. There is nothing which can so completely and effectually restore strength and energy to thoroughly exhausted nature as the rest and recreation of a sojourn at the seaside. The pure salt air, the plunge in the splendid surf, the excitement of fishing and sailing and the inspiration of the presence of the mighty ocean soon make us forget the fatigue of the school-room, and every hard-worked teacher finds the recuperation so greatly needed.

There is no place in the United States so valuable to the North Carolina teacher as the sessions of the Teachers' Assembly.

PRACTICAL AID TO TEACHERS.

During the past nine years in which the Assembly has been at work it has secured good, paying and pleasant school positions for nearly six hundred of its members. This represents a great deal of correspondence and careful work and no litle expense, but the Assembly has done all the work and paid all the expenses, and there has not been the cost of even a single cent to any teacher or school officer.

The practical benefits of this feature of the Assembly work are increasing each year, and the Teachers' Bureau of the Assembly enjoys such confidence among school principals and committees that its recommendation is generally all that is needed by a competent teacher towards securing a good position.

At each session of the Assembly there is present a large number of school officers for the purpose of selecting teachers and assistants for their schools.

It is intended to organize an Assembly Examining Board which shall meet each day during the session of the Assembly and carefully examine teachers desiring positions. This board will be composed of the most prominent and successful educators of our State, who well know by experience just what qualifications and attainments a competent teacher should possess, and to applicants, whose examination is satisfactory, an official ''Certificate of Proficiency in Teaching'' will be given, with the seal of the Teachers' Assembly affixed. This certificate will be of inestimable value to a teacher in this or any other State in the Union, and it will almost invariably procure a good school position for a teacher when a place is wanted.

THE PROGRAMME FOR 1892.

The Executive Committee has been hard at work to prepare a programme for the coming session which shall be of the greatest possible interest and benefit to the teachers who desire to make steady progress in their work.

To this end the very highest ability among the profession in North Carolina has been placed at the disposal of the committee for selection, and liberal use has been made of this array of talent, ability and experience.

3

The work of the session will be properly classified and assigned to special days for each department. Among the days so far appointed are, "Popular Education," "Classical," "Academical," "County Superintendence," "English Literature," "Modern Languages," "Temperance" and "General History." Each day is in the charge of a special committee, which will arrange an excellent programme of live and interesting subjects, with the very best of our popular speakers to present them.

In addition to this regular work, there will be two public entertainments and a special course of instruction to teachers by the inimitable "Frank Beard," who, as a popular and witty "Chalk Artist" and lecturer, has no equal in America. His instruction will have special reference to the use of the blackboard in the school and Sunday-school, by every teacher, in rapidly illustrating important lessons and information. Engagements have also been made with Rev. Thomas Dixon, Jr., who is perhaps the most popular and fascinating platform speaker in this country, and with the University Glee Club, whose unique entertainments never fail to charm an audience.

Every feature of the programme is entirely free to all persons who hold Certificates of Membership in the Teachers' Assembly.

The committee has also secured lectures from some of the most prominent educators in the country, and specially pleased will the teachers be to meet Dr. Edward S. Joynes, of the University of South Carolina; Hon. Frank M Smith, of the University of Tennessee; Hon. Josiah H. Shinn, State Superintendent of Arkansas; Mr. T. F. Donnelly, of New York, author of "Barnes' Primary History of the United States," Mrs. Idalia G. Myers, of Washington, D. C., Prof. H. J. Hamill, the celebrated authority on "Voice Culture and Natural Elocution," and other noted educators and literary men and women.

Among the entertainments will be a musical and literary evening by members of the Assembly and a concert by the Glee Club of the University of North Carolina, Every day will be a day of profit and enjoyment, and County Superintendents cannot too strongly urge their teachers to attend the Assembly this year. There will also be an Inter-Collegiate Oratorical Contest for the Assembly gold medal, and an Instrumental Music Contest by pupils from the female schools of the State.

RAILROAD RATES, BOARD AND MEMBERSHIP COUPONS.

The railroads throughout North Carolina have always shown a peculiar interest in the Teachers' Assembly, and have encouraged the work in every possible way. The rate at which tickets to the Assembly are sold is lower than that given to any other organization in the United States, being only about *one and a half cents a mile* each way.

Assembly tickets will be on sale this session to Morehead City from June 18th to 30th, good to return until July 15.

The annual fees from members of the Assembly are $2 for males and $1 for females, and at the earnest solicitation of our Executive Committee a coupon for $2 will be attached to each railroad ticket. This will save all trouble in sending to the Secretary for the Certificate of Membership. At Morehead City the ticket is to be presented to the Secretary, who will take up the coupon and issue a certificate, only upon which can the reduced rate of board at the Atlantic Hotel be secured. To each female member of the Assembly $1 will be returned by the Secretary when the ticket with coupon is presented to him, as the annual fee for women is only $1. The $2 coupon attached to railroad ticket pays the membership fee for 1892.

The rate of board at the Atlantic Hotel is $2.50 per day, but to those who hold the Teachers' Assembly Certificate the rate is *only $1 per day.* These rates and conditions will be strictly adhered to this session.

Mr. John O. Plank the well-known and most successful hotel man of Chicago, will have entire management of the Atlantic Hotel this summer, and he guarantees every possible accommodation and comfort to the Assembly during the coming session. Rooms may be reserved in advance by writing to Mr. Plank, and we feel safe in assuring teachers that their requests will be faithfully attended to. A number of improvements are in contemplation in and about the Atlantic Hotel which will add to the comforts and popularity of this famous summer resort.

THE EDUCATIONAL EXPOSITION.

This valuable department of the Assembly work, inaugurated three years ago, has been increasing in magnitude and importance. The interest has never been so great as at this time, nor have our schools been so well prepared to make a good exhibit. Nearly all the available space in the ten large rooms and the auditorium of our Teachers' Building has been engaged by schools for their exhibits.

Among the leading institutions reserving space are the University, Trinity, Davidson, Wake Forest, Agricultural and Mechanical, Elon and Guilford Colleges, Peace Institute, St. Mary's School, the female colleges at Greensboro, Oxford, Louisburg, Murfreesboro, Durham, the Institution for the Deaf and Dumb and the Blind, the High Schools at Roxboro, Mt. Olive, Leaksville, Liberty, New Bern, and the Graded Schools at Raleigh, Greensboro, Goldsboro, Tarboro, Winston, Durham, Wilmington and Charlotte.

A careful inspection of this Educational Exhibit will alone be worth to a progressive teacher many times the small expense of attendance upon the Assembly. There will also be exhibits by several Northern publishers and manufacturers of school furniture and other supplies.

It has been proven by careful observation that it pays a school to make an exhibit at the Assembly, and surely every public or private school has something creditable to send to the Exposition at Morehead City.

THE TEACHERS AND THEIR FRIENDS.

One of the main objects of the Teachers' Assembly is to bring together annually in pleasant social intercourse and consultation the teachers and all friends of education. The Assembly was organized for this particular purpose, and it is not intended or desired that it shall be an exclusive meeting of teachers.

The Constitution, therefore, wisely provides that all friends of education, patrons and possible patrons of schools, school committees and the public generally may attend the delightful sessions of the Assembly upon the same conditions and terms as regular teachers.

The Assembly cordially invites the people of North Carolina to meet with the teachers in their great educational gatherings, to confer with them as to the educational needs of our State, to take part in the discussions and to enjoy with the teachers all the pleasures of the seaside and all the exercises and entertainments of the Assembly programme.

It is a pleasure to note that a very large number of these friends, ladies and gentlemen, attend the Assembly each year, and it is hoped that the number may increase until many thousands of "the people" shall annually meet with the teachers in their most delightful Assembly. The programme provides instruction and entertainment for all, and there is ample time given to recreation and amusement.

THE TEACHERS' SUMMER HOME.

No place can begin to compare in value with the seaside as a restorer of tired physical nature in the early spring and summer. The exhilaration of the strong south-western sea-breeze soon brings renewed life to the body and roses to the cheeks.

The Assembly did its wisest act in locating its large, convenient and beautiful Teachers' Building and permanent home at Morehead City, where there is plenty of room, plenty of amusement and instruction, unequal facilities for the work, an immense hotel which can "entertain the Assembly in one house," and at much less expense than would be incurred at any other place in the State. Thousands of teachers have said that they can "have more instruction and enjoyment with less money at Morehead City during the session of the Assembly than at any other place on earth."

It is one of the principal objects of the Assembly to provide for its members the greatest amount of benefit and entertainment for the smallest possible expense. That the Assembly has succeeded in this effort may be realized in the fact that a teacher from the most remote portion of North Carolina can leave home on Monday, June 20th, for Morehead City, remain there during the entire session of the Assembly, paying railroad fare both ways and board at the Atlantic Hotel, all at a cost not to exceed $25. A week may be spent at the Assembly by a person coming from a point within three hundred miles of Morehead City at a total cost under $15, including railroad fare and board.

At this rate of travel and board surely every teacher can afford to attend the grand meeting of the Assembly this year.

PLEASURE TOURS.

The Teachers' Assembly has, under the exclusive management of the Secretary, made several exceedingly successful and enjoyable tours. They have included trips to the extreme western part of our State, Washington City,

New York, Niagara Falls, England, Scotland, Ireland and France, and to Cuba and Florida. In the aggregate these select parties have numbered seven hundred persons, and there has never been an accident or a serious case of sickness during the tours. At the close of the coming session of the Assembly a large party of teachers and their friends will leave Morehead City on the morning of July 4th for a trip to Atlanta, Georgia, to attend the session of the Southern Educational Association, which meets July 6–9. The fare will be very low, and tickets will be sold at Morehead City to Atlanta and return *from the point where your Assembly ticket ends.* By this plan there will be no loss on the Assembly ticket, and thus the party can start at the same time and on a special train from Morehead City.

No arrangements can be made for persons to join this party at the reduced rates who are not present at Morehead City on July 4th, the day of departure for Atlanta.

A visit to the South's most important city and to this grand gathering of the leaders in Southern education will be an event to be remembered with pleasure for a long while.

HUGH MORSON, *President.*

EUGENE G. HARRELL, *Secretary.*

Raleigh, N. C., April 1, 1892.

MISS GERTRUDE JENKINS, of Salem, has been engaged as stenographer and typist for the coming session of the Assembly. She is one of the most expert short-hand reporters in the South. It is intended that the published proceedings of this session shall be more complete than ever before.

EDITORIAL.

"Carolina! Carolina! Heaven's blessings attend her,
While we live we will cherish, protect and defend her;
Though the scorner may sneer at and witlings defame her,
Our hearts swell with gladness whenever we name her."

Our Students' Camera is a very popular premium which The Teacher offers. We have supplied the camera to several new subscribers during the past month, and all are greatly pleased with the little wonder.

The "Grube Method" of teaching arithmetic has been rightfully called, by experienced teachers, simply a most "ingenious device for killing time." In the hands of a teacher who is not very specially endowed with the rare trait of originality, this senseless and continual use of objects will prove to be a successful maker of ignoramuses of the unfortunate pupils.

The total enrollment at the meeting of the National Educational Association in Toronto in 1891 was 4,788. This is only about 1,500 more than enrolled at The North Carolina Teachers' Assembly. It is evidence that the teachers of the South do not attend the Northern association except simply as a summer excursion. It is confidently expected that the Southern Educational Association will, in a very short time, be a much larger body than the Northern.

Messrs. Alfred Williams & Co. have in press a "Text-book on the Constitution of North Carolina" for the use of schools and colleges. There are a complete set of carefully prepared "Questions on the Constitution," by

Hon. Kemp P. Battle, LL.D., Professor of History in our University, who is the highest authority upon North Carolina historical matters now living in our State. The little book comprises about sixty pages, is substantially bound and will be sold for twenty-five cents. It should be studied in every high school, academy and college in North Carolina, and by both girls and boys.

PLEASE REMEMBER, dear friends, that THE TEACHER is not a school-book or a text-book upon methods of teaching. It is an *educational journal*, striving to be only a medium of communication between teachers and the people. You need not look in THE TEACHER for "busy work," "school devices," etc., because such things do not come within the scope of our work, and they are all discussed in the various books on teaching. THE TEACHER has a much higher aim. We are working to make North Carolina schools the very best in this country, and North Carolina teachers the most appreciated of our people.

IT WAS OUR privilege and pleasure to spend a few moments with Mr. M. C. S. Noble, Superintendent of the Wilmington Graded Schools, in a visit to his Union School on the 7th inst. It is truly a model building and a model school. Over four hundred and fifty pupils are enrolled in that school, and they were all assembled in the large auditorium at the time of our visit, and by request they sang so charmingly and touchingly that old Southern song, "I'm gwine back to Dixie," that we are yet enjoying the inspiration of the music and the occasion. The school is collecting a good library, now having some five hundred choice volumes which are liberally read by the pupils.

TO A TEACHER one of the most valuable things we know of is a practical knowledge of stenography. It is within itself almost an unlimited capital for work. Besides the pleasure that comes from the ability to make verbatim reports of lectures, sermons, addresses and other important public exercises, a good short-hand writer is rarely without a good paying position. The art of stenography is not difficult to acquire if proper attention and application is given to it, and every teacher has plenty of spare time to give to the study, and the opportunities for practice are without limit. Two months of regular and systematic practice will give you a working knowledge of short-hand with which you would not part for any reasonable consideration.

PLEASE, FRIENDS, do not speak or write of The North Carolina Teachers' Assembly as the "N. C. T. A.," nor the Southern Educational Association as the "S. E. A." We know that you are so overwhelmed with work that you really haven't time to mention these great organizations except by their initial·letters, but we hope that you will spare just four seconds of your time in designating these associations by their proper names when you have occasion to speak of them. When we see organizations spoken of or written about as "N. C. T. A.," "S. E. A.," "N. E. A.," "Y. M. C. A.," "W. C. T. U.," "A. & M.," and so on, we must confess that it seems to us as if pure laziness had instigated this initial language. We recently noticed that a very important article in a prominent educational journal bore the senseless hieroglyphic heading "S. E. A." Our sympathies are with that overworked editor who did not have time, or energy, to write correctly the name of the subject of his excellent article.

IT GIVES US great pleasure to have such cordial words of endorsement of the plan of work upon which our Teachers' Assembly is based from such eminent and high authority as Prof. J. B. Merwin, editor of *The American Journal of Education*, St. Louis, Mo. He writes: " I want to commend most earnestly your idea of making the meeting at Morehead City a 'people's meeting.' We need to reach *the people*, and the teachers ought to be entirely relieved of anything like 'normal methods,' or any other methods at these great gatherings; they ought be only a means of re-creation for the teachers. The teachers have all that they can do, and I wonder that they do so much, with what they have to contend with. These great gatherings should be a means for *instructing the people in the work* the teachers do, and in the work of *educating the children.*'' We notice that several other State associations of teachers are following the example of the North Carolina Teachers' Assembly, and are discarding from their programmes all the "cut-and-dried" and "dry-as-dust" class of work. A normal school is one thing and a teachers' association is another.

· ABOUT OUR TEACHERS AND SCHOOLS.

MRS. J. C. FINCH is teaching at Edenton.

MISS LEE ARRINGTON has a school at Castalia.

MISS MATTIE H. FLYNN is teaching in Hertford County.

MISS BEULAH JAMES has a good school in Duplin County.

MISS VICKIE HARRIS is teaching at Grissom, Granville County.

MR. L. E. GIBSON has a progressive school in Richmond County.

MR. C. M. COPE is one of the successful teachers of Davie County.

MISS KATE BROWN is teacher of the Primary School in Kenansville.

MISS PATTIE B. COOPER teaches public school at Hilliardston, Nash County.

MRS. MARTHA BECK DRAKE has a primary school at her home near Castalia, Nash County.

MR. E. E. BLOUNT, of Haywood county, has taken charge of a school at Middleburgh, Kentucky.

SENATOR JOHN G. CARLISLE, of Kentucky, will deliver the Commencement Oration at the University June 1st.

THE NORMAL AND INDUSTRIAL COLLEGE FOR YOUNG WOMEN will begin its first term in September with a good enrollment of students.

MR. GREY KING and Miss Tempe Lou King have charge of the Male and Female Academy at Cedar Rock, Franklin County.

MR. R. W. MILLARD, a teacher of forty years experience, has been elected County Superintendent of Public Instruction of Duplin County.

MISS META CHESTNUT, of North Carolina, is Principal of Minco Academy in Indian Territory. She writes, "We are all *Southerners* here."

MR. F. L. McCOY (Trinity College) and Mr. R. N. Hadley (Thompson Business College) are in charge of the Literary and Commercial Institute at Rochélle, Georgia.

MISS EMILY G. GILLIAM, a North Carolinian now at Franklin, Va., will be pleased to have a situation as teacher in some school or private family for the fall term.

SENATOR MATT. RANSOM has accepted an invitation to address the Literary Societies of Wilson Collegiate Institute on June 1. The school is for girls, and it is enjoying a prosperous term.

MR. GEORGE F. CRUTCHFIELD has just completed the term of a good public school at Buckhorn in Orange County. Sixty-three pupils were enrolled, and he is now in charge of a private school at some other place.

MISS EMMA F. WEBB has a very interesting school at the little town of Union, in Hertford County. Twenty boys and girls are enrolled, and they are preparing an enjoyable entertainment for the close of the school.

MRS. T. V. FAUCETTE, of Milton, has charge of an excellent school at Oxford, and the school will be well represented in the Educational Exposition at Morehead City during the session of the Teachers' Assembly.

MRS. R. R. FLEMING, one of Pitt County's best teachers, recently married, writes: "I am no longer a teacher, but cannot do without my old friend, THE NORTH CAROLINA TEACHER, and I therefore enclose one dollar to renew my subscription."

THE ENTERPRISING NORMAL SCHOOL at Elizabethtown, Bladen County, entered upon its sixth term April 18th. Mr. S. M. Lloyd is Principal, and he is assisted by Messrs. S. P. Wright, W. H. Graham, J. M. Lloyd and E. A. Carroll. Two hundred and thirty-nine pupils have been enrolled.

THE EASTER music and services by the young ladies of St. Mary's School at Raleigh far surpassed in excellence and beauty any similar occasion in the past. The chapel was thronged by delighted visitors on Easter Sunday. On Tuesday following Dr. Smedes gave the girls an outing and a switchback ride in the Exposition grounds, and a great many friends shared with them the enjoyments of the day.

MR. ERNEST P. MANGUM is succeeding finely as Superintendent of the Graded Schools at Concord. He has the heartiest support of the community, and he is promised that the school shall soon have new and larger buildings—which they are greatly in need of.

PROF. J. H. KINEALLY, of the Agricultural and Mechanical College, will deliver an address to the Chamber of Commerce and Industry of Raleigh and the citizens generally on Tuesday evening, April 26, on "The Duties of a Citizen."

THE LATEST REPORT shows that North Carolina had only thirteen representatives in the National Educational Association at Toronto last year, and five of the number were teachers. Let us have at least five hundred representatives in the meeting of our Southern Educational Association at Atlanta in July.

MISS LILLA B. REESE is teaching at Sigma. In renewing her subscription to THE TEACHER she writes: "I have received the 'Waverly Novels.' Am wonderfully pleased with them. Anyone might own them, they are so cheap. THE TEACHER is better than usual. Every number gets better. It is a great help to me."

A SITUATION AS TEACHER is wanted by Miss Carrie W. Coghill, who is a graduate of Western Maryland College. Teaches the English branches, Latin, French and German, Music on Piano or Organ, Calisthenics, Club-swinging, etc. She prefers to teach music, elocution and calisthenics. Address her at Rocky Mount, N. C.

REV. N. M. SHAW, for several years principal of the school in Kenansville, and for three years County Superintendent of Public Instructions, Duplin County, has moved, with his family, to Mill Hill, Cabarrus County, where he supplies two churches. Mr. Shaw has a fine reputation as a teacher, and his forte is the training of small children.

THE YOUNG LADIES of Peace Institute were given a most delightful picnic by Professor Dinwiddie at Millbrook on Easter Monday. The school had an elegant private car for their use during the day, and the weather was all that could be desired for a picnic occasion. As one of the few special friends who were honored by an invitation, we have such charming memories of the day as will linger for a life-time.

THERE WILL BE more *teachers* at the Teachers' Assembly this summer than ever before. From every county in every section of North Carolina comes the glad report, "We all expect to be at the Assembly in June." The County Superintendents are urging their teachers to attend, well knowing the advantage which a teacher who attends the Assembly has over all others in the confidence of the people and in securing a good position in the schools. Attendance upon the Assembly is worth to a teacher, in many ways, ten times the slight expense of going to Morehead City.

CUPID AMONG OUR TEACHERS.

'Tis said that "figures never lie,"
That one and one are always TWO;
But Cupid proves, with 'work so sly,
Some wondrous things that figures do.
And when he claims a teacher's hand
All rules of figures then are done,
Though TWO before the preacher stand
This one and one are ALWAYS ONE.

MR. ANDREW L. BETTS, Associate Principal of Leaksville High School, married MISS LUCY HASTINGS BROOKS, of Reidsville, on Easter Monday. Rev. J. R. Brooks, D. D., performed the ceremony.

MR. JAMES M. BENSON, of Lake Comfort, Hyde County, Principal of Juniper Bay High School, married MISS ANNIE WILLIAMS, his assistant teacher, on the 6th of April, 1892. The ceremony was performed in the school-room by Rev. G. D. Langston.

NEW SCHOLARS.

ALICE NOBLE, daughter of Mr. M. C. S. Noble, Superintendent of the Wilmington Graded Schools, was born August 11, 1891.

A little daughter of Mr. E. P. Moses, Superintendent of the Raleigh Graded Schools, was born in Raleigh on March 30, 1892. The stranger has not yet been named.

EUGENE HALL BARKER, son of Mr. B. D. Barker, Principal of Apex High School, was born March 14, 1892. [We wish for our little namesake the greatest happiness and prosperity in life.—EDITOR.]

AT RECESS.

The books and slates now put away,
And let us laugh a little while;
For those who work there should be play,
The leisure moments to beguile.

HERE'S A BOY'S composition on physiology: "The body of a person is made up of the hed, thorax and the abdomen. The hed contains the brains, if ther is any; the thorax contains the hart and lungs; the abdomen contains the bowels, of which ther are five: a, e, i, o, u, and sometimes w and y."

Hon. JOHN C. SCARBOROUGH,
DEMOCRATIC NOMINEE FOR STATE SUPERINTENDENT OF PUBLIC
INSTRUCTION

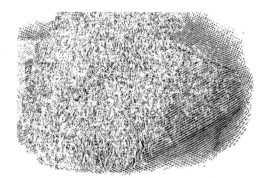

HON. JOHN C. SCARBOROUGH,

THE NORTH CAROLINA TEACHER.

| Vol. IX.. | Raleigh, May, 1892. | No. 9. |

EUGENE G. HARRELL,   = = = =   Editor.

BE TRUE TO NORTH CAROLINA.

BY THE EDITOR.

Tune: *Bonnie Blue Flag.*

To North Carolina here's my hand, my strongest faith and love,
For it is the noblest land beneath the Heavens above;
Then may my trust in Carolina never, never cease—
The bravest of the States in war—the grandest one in peace.

Chorus:

Hurrah! hurrah! for the Old North State, hurrah!
Which in the Nation's galaxy shines forth the brightest star!

Nature's riches of the soil throughout the State abound,
And in her cloud-land springs of life can everywhere be found;
While peace and plenty reign supreme in cot and palace home,
And joy abides from mountain peaks to ocean's snowy foam.—*Cho.*

In education, North Carolina takes the highest stand
Of all the States united in America's proud land;
May Heaven's blessings ever rest on Carolina's name,
While coming ages only add new luster to her fame.—*Cho.*

And when declining years shall bring me trembling to the grave,
As some vessel, tempest-tossed, goes down beneath the wave,
Here may my weary body end its pilgrimage on earth,
And mingle with the genial soil that gave it honored birth.—*Cho.*

North Carolina Teachers Abroad:

A SUMMER JAUNT

IN

ENGLAND, SCOTLAND, IRELAND AND FRANCE.

CHAPTER XXIX.

HOMEWARD BOUND.

"ALL ABOARD FOR NEW YORK—THE LAST DAY IN GLASGOW—POWER OF IMAGINATION—BELFAST, THE COMMERCIAL CITY OF IRELAND—THE JAUNTING CAR—THE IRISH AT HOME—LARNE, THE COMICAL CITY—AGAIN ON THE ATLANTIC—A HAPPY VOYAGE—A RUSH FOR NEWS—A JOYOUS RETURN—UNCLE SAM'S TARIFF OFFICERS—SAILING UP NEW YORK HARBOR—"THE TEACHERS' VISIT TO THE QUEEN"—HAPPY GREETINGS ON THE SHORE—THE END OF OUR HAPPY AND SUCCESSFUL JAUNT IN FOREIGN LANDS.

"ALL ABOARD for New York," exclaimed Professor Winston, as he entered the dining room on the next morning after our arrival in Glasgow.

"Surely you don't mean to say that we are to leave right now, Professor?" was asked by the girls with considerable interest.

"No. Not quite so suddenly as that," he replied, "but our stay on this side of the Atlantic is now only a matter of a few hours. And oh, my! the agony of crossing the ocean again!"

And we all gave a sympathetic groan.

It was expected that our steamer would sail for New York at 10 o'clock on the morning of August 9th, but, owing to some delays incident to stowing away the cargo, we were informed that our departure would be twelve hours later.

We were pleased at this information as it gave us one day more in Glasgow, and there were many things about this pleasant Scotch city of which we desired to know more. Our state-rooms had all been secured and assigned to the occupants soon after our arrival, therefore we had nothing to do but enjoy the day in the manner that best suited us.

Our esteemed friend Mr. John Morison again most kindly offered his valuable services to our party in visiting the many places of interest in and around this famous Scotch city; and with his kind assistance the day was spent both pleasantly and profitably. The girls purchased many pretty souvenirs of Scotland, our favorite country of the Old World, and numbers of them were wearing the beautiful Scotch stone, the "Cairngorm."

It is said that all strangers who purchase and wear this stone in Scotland are certain to visit that country again within ten years. If this legend has any foundation of truth, we will know just where to find a majority of the North Carolina party in 1899.

At 6 o'clock P. M. we all went on board our steamer, and as we were enjoying a condition of thorough fatigue most of the party immediately retired for the night. The departure of the steamer was again delayed, owing to an unusually large cargo, until far into the night.

As the Secretary was standing on the deck about midnight looking at the last preparations for departure, a lady slowly climbed out of the saloon clad in her *robe du chambre* and dropped almost exhausted into a steamer chair near him, groaning excruciatingly.

His sympathies were aroused, and approaching the sufferer as gently as he could he said, "You seem to be suffering, Madam, can I be of any assistance to you?"

"Oh, sir," she faintly replied, "I've had such a terrible night with this terrible sea-sickness. The rolling and pitching of the steamer has been awful, and my suffering is more than I can bear. I am afraid that I shall not live to reach the land. Oh, Lord!"

"My sympathies are with you, my dear madam, in your agony," replied the Secretary, "but, in my opinion, your suffering has been somewhat premature, for our steamer has not yet left the wharf, and is still receiving cargo in Glasgow."

The lady sprang from the seat and exclaimed, "Is that really true; are we yet lying fast at the wharf in Glasgow?"

"It is really true, Madam," answered the Secretary, "the ship has not yet left the wharf, and a calmer night I have never seen. You thought that the steamer would sail at 8 o'clock, and all your suffering has been wholly imaginary. It will be yet two days before we are on the ocean, and the agony that you say you have endured for the past six hours has been wholly in your brilliant imagination!"

The woman looked around to see if the Secretary had told the truth, then, becoming satisfied upon this point, she disappeared in the cabin much more suddenly than she had come on deck, and after her departure there lingered in the air the gentle refrain, "What a goose I have made of myself," while the Secretary meditated upon "The power of the imagination."

The lady was not a member of the North Carolina party.

After a smooth sail down the Clyde and across the Irish Sea our ship was made fast to the pier at Larne, Ireland, just as we arose from breakfast next morning. Captain Richie then informed us that the vessel would remain in that port during the day receiving cargo, whereupon we at once boarded the train for Belfast so that we might spend the day in the principal commercial city of Ireland.

Ireland is as beautiful a country as it is interesting. The railroad runs along the shores of Belfast Loch and through a fine section of farming land.   These "farms," as they are known in Ireland, are exceedingly diminutive in size, covering from three to ten acres, which are surrounded by a thick hedgerow of stone or orange shrubbery.

The Irish farmer is very much limited in his ideas of farming.   His entire crop, in most cases, consists of a patch of Irish potatoes about one acre in size, and half an acre in cabbage.   This "farm" is generally tilled by one woman, about a dozen tousley-headed children, three or four raw-boned goats and two mangy dogs.   In the meantime, the "master of the household" spends his time at the neighborhood inn discussing the beauties of home-rule and the corruptions of English royalty.

It may be well just here to state to our friends who contemplate a visit to the "Old Country" the brief agricultural fact that there is only one breed of potatoes in Ireland, and we hope you will not disgrace yourselves in a foreign restaurant by asking for a "sweet potato" or an "Irish potato" as we do in North Carolina.   The "sweet" potato, as we have it at home, is unknown on the eastern side of the Atlantic.

But these little farms are exceedingly well tilled.   As we pass them on the railway train they seem to be squares on a vast checker-board, distinguished only by the different shades of green as we have it from the potato or the cabbage patch.

Upon our arrival in Belfast we were besieged by hackmen just the same as we are in the United States; but we effectually resisted every temptation to ride until we spied the famous "Irish Jaunting Car."   When this fascinating vehicle was seen for the first time our girls became suddenly seized by physical exhaustion, and therefore we were compelled to ride.

The "jaunting car" is unknown everywhere else on earth except in Ireland.   And it is a vehicle unlike anything ever seen before. The car holds four persons besides the driver. They sit in pairs, back to back, and the only successful way to stay in the car when in motion is to put your arm around your companion, while the companion in turn hugs the driver.

The jaunting car is the most popular vehicle within our knowledge. Ireland cannot be properly inspected except from a jaunting car.

Belfast is a typical Irish city. Every kind of excitement that has ever occurred in Ireland has given Belfast a liberal share. It is a favorite city for strikes, riots and "free fights." The man who drove our jaunting car took special pleasure in pointing out to us the localities where the rioters delighted to gather and discuss the situation with that strongest of all arguments—the shelaleh. We were told that in the riots the women do as much fighting as the men.

There are a number of very interesting places in Belfast, and we made the best possible use of the four hours that we spent in the city. Among the special points of our visitation were the celebrated Printing and Illuminating Works of Marcus Ward & Co. We there saw the "Belfast Linen" paper in every stage of its manufacture, and the process by which the lovely Christmas and Easter cards are made.

One of the curiosities of Belfast is the Andrews' Flax Mill. You can follow the bale of flax from the time that it enters the mill until it is turned out made into linen jackets ready for market. Several of our girls bought handkerchiefs of fine linen just from the loom at prices ranging from five to twenty-five cents, and again we "blessed" that iniquitous United States tariff which makes us pay about one hundred per cent. more for these articles in America.

Just as the bells and whistles announced the hour of noon the great doors of the factories were thrown open and thousands of men, women and children thronged the streets on their way to lunch. We noticed that nearly all the women and grown girls were bare-headed and bare-footed, and otherwise very scantily clad. We were informed that many hundreds of those women received but twenty-five cents a week as wages for their work in the factories! This meagre sum was to furnish food and raiment and provide for all other expenses of living.

It is no wonder that Ireland is gradually emigrating to America.

We spent an hour in the vast Botanical Garden, the most beautiful that we had seen except the Kew Gardens in London. We had been in the Garden only a short while before each American heart was throbbing its patriotism beneath a sprig of Irish shamrock which had been proudly and gracefully presented by the gardener.

Our train returned to Larne about 5 o'clock P. M., whereupon we at once chartered every jaunting car within sight, having fallen desperately in love with that fascinating and coquettish vehicle. Of course, Larne was to be "done up" in proper style.

This is such an insignificant little village that "doing the town," is fully accomplished by jolting through its narrow and irregular streets in the jaunting car and buying a lot of Irish walking-sticks at the rickety old harness shop at the head of the principal street. And our clever old friend, the walking-stick maker, said that it was the biggest business boom that had ever struck his shop.

We often wondered how those girls disposed of all the walking-sticks which they bought in Larne, until we began to see them wherever we went in North Carolina proudly handled and flourished by handsome and appreciative young gentlemen who had been thus rewarded by their pet friends.

At 9 o'clock, just as the long twilight began to give place to the deeper shadows of evening, our good ship left her moorings and steamed out of the harbor. In a very short time all land had disappeared from view, and we were again upon the great Atlantic with nothing but the broad ocean around us.

As the ship was making a few ominous rolls and pitches, most of our party decided that they were going to be awfully sea-sick, then we retired early to our staterooms and patiently awaited developments.

But the "developments" never came.

The next day was bright and beautiful. The warm sunshine which flooded the world enticed everybody early upon deck, and what a surprise it was to find that nobody was sick! The sea was yet quite rough, and it was with considerable difficulty that we could move about the deck, and the steamer frequently "shipped a sea" which deluged everything forward.

But not a single person was sea-sick! And those few who had determined to suffer "a thousand deaths" during the voyage were specially free from even that "uncomfortable feeling" which is so familiar to all who travel upon the seas. It was a happy, jolly company, fully prepared to enjoy any little "devilment" which should chance to suggest itself. Long before we had safely gotten upon our "sea legs," the girls were romping over the deck and making even the mighty ocean to resound with the melody of their merry voices.

Even the Professor was most agreeably disappointed in being entirely free from his chronic ailment when out of sight of land, and he, too, enjoyed the ocean with "the children." His dry wit and brilliant humor afforded us many a hearty laugh during that memorable voyage, and we have unanimously voted Professor Winston to be the "prince of good fellows."

We enjoyed that homeward voyage. Every mile of the journey was pleasant and interesting. Our party, being largely in the majority, controlled the affairs of the trip. All the entertainments and amusements were in our hands, and well did we use them to our general enjoyment and that of all the passengers. The days were spent in games incident to ship life, and in the evenings there were concerts in the saloon in which every talent participated.

Many pranks were played upon our boys by the girls of the party, the favorite one being to fill the pillows in their staterooms with flour, which painted them white immediately upon retiring for the night. The merry songs were heard upon the deck and in the saloon until far into the evening, and the genial Captain Richie said that never before did he have such a jolly lot of passengers.

The voyage was somewhat rough throughout. A strong headwind prevailed, which kept the sea lashed into foam, while the heavy swells tossed the steamer about as a plaything. This restless condition of the sea afforded a member of the party an opportunity of dedicating the following lines to certain members who had previously enjoyed the terrible "malady of the sea":

The swells! the swells! these ruthless swells!
　Which now around us roar!
They bring to us most doleful yells
　From every cabin door.

The swells! the swells! triumphant swells!
　Oh! how they toss the ship!
They've got us, so their surging tells,
　In their relentless grip.

The swells! the swells! these horrid swells!
　Which shake the mighty earth!
They make our North Carolina belles
　Keep groaning in their berth.

The swells! the swells! these cruel swells!
　　How they vex poor sinners!
They are the monster who compels
　　Us to give up our dinners.

The swells! the swells! gigantic swells!
　　Which lift us to the sky!
While inward Nature so rebels
　　That we think we'll surely die.

Early in the morning of the 20th of August we sighted a number of pilot boats, some three hundred miles from shore. We then realized that we were drawing near the end of our journey, and that our happy family of tourists was soon to be widely separated, as each member would depart for distant homes.

We were sorry that the tour was ending.

Several of the pilot boats attempted to make their way to our ship, but "there was a great calm upon the waters," and the boats could only lie motionless with their sails idly flapping the masts. Therefore Captain Richie selected the boat which was nearest to our course, and in a very short time we were "hove to" and the pilot was climbing over the rail of the steamer.

Then there was a rush for New York papers. Everybody wanted to know the news. Of course the pilot had no papers under three or four days old, but we didn't care for that provided they told us what the world had been doing since we sailed from Larne ten days ago. No newspaper was ever before more eagerly read than was that much-worn copy of *The New York World* which we received from the pilot.

On the next morning we saw the first outlines of the land—OUR HOME LAND—and we all felt a thrill of excitement such as we had not before experienced. The barren wastes of Sandy Hook, over which the glorious "Stars and Stripes" proudly waved, were far dearer to us than all the rich landscapes, ancient castles, lofty towers and splendid palaces of Europe; and as we again looked upon our own dear, free America, our hearts swelled with tenderest emotions of pride, and somebody in our company softly sang a strain of that grand old melody, "Home, Sweet Home," in which sentiment we all most devoutly and heartily joined.

The ocean was now as peaceful as a lake. The wind had ceased and there was a dead calm. The mellow autumn sunshine subdued the waves and softened the air into balmy summer. The great ocean about us seemed to be a vast mirror, which reflected the full outline of our noble steamer with scarcely a ripple to mar that wonderfully serene and tranquil picture. The great engines seemed to realize that we were almost home, and each mighty throb proclaimed the joy of the safe return. The gulls drew nearer to us, and as they poised upon their broad, white wings just in the wake of the ship, our imagination interpreted the nodding and turning of their heads and their uncouth crying into a song of "Welcome home."

And all Nature welcomed our return; the earth, the air, the sea and the skies gave us their brightest smiles, while the sunbeams danced a minuet of joy upon the placid waters. The porpoise lazily coquetted upon the liquid mirror, while the petrel indulged in a most luxurious saline bath as it gracefully skimmed the glassy surface of the peaceful Atlantic. From these joyous scenes and this happy reverie of home we were ruthlessly aroused by the rattle of the steam derrick which was bringing our trunks from the hold of the vessel to the deck, where they were to await the pleasure of Uncle Sam's Customs officers.

This performance considerably excited the members of our party who had made many purchases abroad. Speculations were indulged in as to the probable fate of some silk dress, seal-skin sack, or bundle of kid gloves which had been bought in London and Paris. It was interesting to notice how our baggage had grown during our tour. The hand-satchel had become a valise, while in turn the valise had been replaced by a trunk; and the girl who left New York with only one trunk now possessed two in order to hold her property, and our worthy President had been obliged to purchase a trunk expressly to hold the toys and novelties which he had collected for his children.

Soon after we entered the harbor of New York the revenue boat came alongside the ship, and then came our first experience with Uncle Sam's tariff. The Customs officers sat at the tables in the saloon, and we all were required to form a long line so as to appear before them in turn and make written oath as to our baggage and contents. It is said by experienced persons that you can swear to anything you please before a Customs officer or tax assessor without the slightest violation of religion or conscience. Our faith in this tradition is somewhat stronger now than it was several years ago.

Having completed our "official swearing," there was nothing for us to do but remain on deck and enjoy the sail up that most magnificent harbor. This was not an uninteresting occupation, for, besides the matchless view which was spread out before us on either side, we were further entertained by listening to the comments upon the scene made by six hundred foreign emigrants who were standing on the deck below us.

Every nationality on earth was represented in that uncouth mass of humanity, and not one of them had ever before touched foot upon the shores of free America. It was evident that they did not have the slightest conception of the land in which they were seeking a home, and many remarks made by them convinced us that they had been given most distorted impressions of America. One dejected looking female pointed out to a companion the beautiful grounds of the navy yard and said, "There is the place where all emigrants are taken care of and fed until they get a good place to work." And her companion joyfully replied, "But we don't have to do much work in this country where wages are so high." We have often wondered since that day what became of those poor girls upon awakening from their happy dreams of the new land.

As we passed the Statue of Liberty an enthusiastic Italian rapturously exclaimed "Colombo!" "Colombo!" and he proudly pointed it out to his people about him as a monument to the great Christopher Columbus! The celebrated statue needs to be reconstructed by Monsieur Bartholdi.

Our next visit, as we slowly steamed up the harbor, was from the "Doctor's Boat," to see that there were no epidemic or contagious diseases on board. This examination was simply a perfunctory affair, and most of the passengers never even knew that "the Doctor was aboard."

But the Doctor's boat brought several of our friends from North Carolina to give us a cordial welcome home. There were many anxious inquiries as to "news from home," and one of our friends, in reply, informed us that "the whole State is talking about your visit to the Queen."

"Our visit to the Queen?" the Secretary replied, "Why, what do you mean?"

Our friend looked puzzled, and he said in explanation: "A letter appeared in the Raleigh papers from Professor Winston, stating that all your party had made a formal visit to Queen Victoria."

The Secretary smiled and said: "That is the hoax of the season. We have not been at any time within twenty-five miles of the Queen. The letter was written by the Professor when thoroughly sea-sick, in mid-ocean, a thousand miles from land, as a huge joke. He made many ridiculous statements in order that no one should for a moment believe anything in the letter. The letter was mailed immediately upon our arrival in Glasgow, and for the special purpose of letting our friends in the United States know that we had crossed the ocean in safety. I am surprised that any person should have believed the statements made in that letter."

We enjoyed many a laugh at the expense of that fictitious "Visit to the Queen," which had so excited our friends at home.

Owing to the fact that another steamer of the State Line was lying at the dock preparing to sail, our ship came to anchor in the stream. In a very short time thereafter a lighter came alongside to take all the passengers ashore to be handed over to the tender mercies of the Customs officers.

As we left the *Indiana* we gave the noble ship a last lingering look of love, and our hearts swelled with gratitude to her for bringing us safely on so long a voyage across the stormy Atlantic. The old ship seemed to realize and appreciate our thoughts, and the deep, hoarse salute to our departure by the engineer's whistle almost appeared to really come from the heart of the vessel. Within a very few minutes the lighter had reached the wharf, and with a thrill of delight we realized that our feet again rested upon beloved America, our own dear home-land.

There were many joyous greetings with kindred and friends, and our large and congenial tourist-family was gradually disappearing in these happy reunions of home circles. Many eyes glistened with tears as the strong clasping of hands in friendship's fondest farewell were given, while earnest pledges of life-long remembrance were uttered.

It was a touching scene on the wharf that day, and even now as we write of it, nearly three years afterwards, we pause to brush away a mist which suddenly dims our eyes.

The Secretary experienced, on that memorable occasion, sensations which were peculiar to no other member of the party. As he saw that all were again safely and happily at home, there was suddenly lifted from his heart and mind the exceedingly heavy anxiety and responsibility which had rested upon him during the past six weeks; and his heart was filled with profoundest gratitude to Him who had so safely guided our steps, and so carefully protected our health and our lives throughout our journeyings.

And we had ample reason to be thankful, for it was indeed one of the most successful and satisfactory trips ever made by a party of tourists. There were one hundred persons in our company and we had traveled over eleven thousand miles by land and by water, twice crossing the ocean; we had experienced every variety of climate, water and diet, and many peculiar social customs of the people of strange lands; and from the time of our departure from Morehead City, July 4th, until our return to New York on August 21st, there had not been a serious accident or case of sickness, nor had we lost a single piece of baggage or anything else of consequence, or missed any day of sight-seeing on account of inclement weather. Every member of the party had continued in good health, good spirits and good humor, thus fully prepared to enjoy every event of the trip. Truly it was a tour phenomenal by reason of its success, safety and pleasure.

The United States officials in the Custom House were exceedingly courteous, kind and accommodating to our people, and thus our obligations to Uncle Sam's tariff laws were soon complied with without the slightest trouble or delay. Every outgoing train then carried some members of the party to cheerful homes, where open doors and warm hearts awaited them; and as we waved a farewell to the last departing "tourist," we painfully realized that the memorable vacation jaunt in Europe by "The North Carolina Teachers' Assembly Party" had become indeed a thing of the past, save in our happy recollections of the journey.

THE "SNOW FLOWER" MYTH.

You would never think of looking for flowers in an arctic snow-drift, would you? Yet there is a flower that grows abundantly in the snows of Siberia. It is the shape of a star, about four inches in diameter, and has petals of great length. It springs up to the height of three feet in three days, and has only three snow-white leaves. The flower buds, blooms and fades in twenty-four hours. It is faintly scented. If touched with the warm hand, both it, the stock on which it rests and the leaves melt into a kind of snow. It produces seeds which, when sown in the snow, readily come to maturity and produce flowers. It was Anthnoskoff, the great Russian botanist, who in 1870 discovered this beautiful flower in Siberia. He took some of the seeds to St. Petersburg and had the satisfaction of seeing one of the plants flower in December, 1872, in the presence of the imperial family.—*Southern Educator, April, 1892.*

[The above purports to be a reply to an imaginary "Interrogation Point." An *educator* who professes to give information ought to be reasonably sure that he is telling the truth. The "Snow Flower" story is a newspaper hoax and was copied into the old book of "Queries," from which the *Southern Educator* reprinted it. There is no such flower as the "Snow Flower," nor was there ever a botanist by the name of "Anthnoskoff," and there is no truth whatever in the statement above quoted. Perhaps the *Southern Educator* will kindly give his "Interrogation Point" a brief biographical sketch of this "great Russian botanist!" It is not always wise to try to *appear* wise. As an educational journal THE NORTH CAROLINA TEACHER feels it a duty to correct errors wherever found which in any way affect our teachers and schools.— EDITOR.]

DO NOT DELAY too long in preparing your exhibit for the Educational Exposition at Morehead City during the session of the Teachers' Assembly. Get the articles ready, pack them carefully and ship them at once to Morehead.

"CAROLINA."

A new interest has recently been awakened in efforts to ascertain the true origin of the name of our State. Captain S. A. Ashe, editor of the *News and Observer*, Raleigh, says:

"Bancroft the historian, and some of the earliest writers about the settlements in Carolina, trace the name to the French lodgment made about Port Royal, in 1562. They indicate that the name Florida was applied to the country occupied by the Spaniards, and that the region northward was called Carolina by the French until Virginia was reached.

"When in 1606 King Charles made grants for the settlement of Virginia, which extended, we believe, as far up as Canada, he limited the northern settlement to certain bounds, left the centre open, and limited the London Company to the region between Cape Fear and the Maryland line.

"That territory continued to be called Virginia, as it had been designated from the time it was first named in honor of the Virgin Queen. Some twenty years later King Charles granted the territory from 36 degrees to 31 degrees (from Albemarle Sound down to the present Florida line), to Sir Robert Heath, and erected it into a province, and he said in the grant, 'we name the same Carolina.'

"After that the people of Virginia apparently called that region Carolina, and a Virginian going to Roanoke Island spoke of going to Carolina.

"Hon. Kemp P. Battle, LL. D., Professor of History in our University, contends that the origin of the name is this grant, and that it did not spring from the French lodgment at Port Royal, and he says he is sustained by Justin Winsor, a recent writer who has made special investigations

2

as to whether the French called the country 'Carolina,' and finds that they did not, but did call it Nova Francia.

"For our part we think that Charles probably called the 'province' he erected after himself, just as Elizabeth named Virginia in her own honor.

"The name 'Carolina' has been borne by this region ever since 1629, and we suppose that Dr. Battle is right, that it was so called in honor of the English King and not because of the French settlement sixty years before."

[It is evident that all the land from Albemarle Sound to Florida was originally named "Carolina," however much we may differ as to the source from whence the name came. In 1697 Carolina was divided into two colonies known as "Carolina" and "South Carolina," and these should now be the names of these two States. South Carolina was cut off from Carolina and took a new name, just as did West Virginia when it was separated from Virginia. There is no *East* Virginia, nor should there be any *North* Carolina; we should have only Virginia and West Virginia, and Carolina and South Carolina.

Of course we would be unwilling to give up the name "North Carolina" since our people have made the name so famous and so highly honored at home and abroad, but it is true, nevertheless, that we are really the "Carolinians." If the people beyond the Blue Ridge should form a new State it would be "Western Carolina." It may be proper for the children to take new names, but the mother State should remain the same.—EDITOR.]

———

THE TEACHER will, in future, spell the name of our charming Elm City as follows, "New Berne," as this is by request of the mayor of the city and is the desire of all the citizens except, perhaps, about some half-a-dozen people.

THE COLLEGE ASSOCIATION OF NORTH CAROLINA.

ORGANIZATION FOR 1891–'92.

GEO. T. WINSTON. LL.D., President, University of North Carolina.
CHAS. E. TAYLOR, LL.D., 1st Vice President, Wake Forest College.
N. C. ENGLISH, A. M., 2d Vice President, Trinity College.
W. S. CURRELL, PH. D., 3d Vice President, Davidson College.
W. A. WITHERS, A. M., Secretary, Col. of Ag. and Mech. Arts.

PROCEEDINGS OF THE FIRST ANNUAL SESSION HELD AT GREENSBORO, MARCH 22, 1892.

EDITED BY THE SECRETARY.

The Association was called to order at 11 o'clock in the Court-House by the President. The following members and visitors from the following Institutions were found to be present:

Davidson College—President J. B. Shearer.

Elon College—President W. S. Long.

Girls Normal and Industrial School—President C. D. McIver and Prof. E. A. Alderman.

Greensboro Female College—President B. F. Dixon and Prof. Dred Peacock.

Guilford College—President L. L. Hobbs, Prof. John W. Woody and Prof. R. C. Root.

North Carolina College of Agriculture and Mechanic Arts—Prof. W. A. Withers.

Rutherford College—Prof. W. E. Abernathy.

Trinity College—President John F. Crowell, Prof. J. M. Bandy, Prof. N. C. English, Prof. J. L. Armstrong, Prof.

J. M. Steadman, Prof. B. C. Hinde, Prof. H. Austin Aikins, Prof. L. W. Crawford.

University of North Carolina—President Geo. T. Winston and Prof. Karl P. Harrington.

Wake Forest College—President Chas. E. Taylor.

Hon. S. M. Finger, Supt. of Public Instruction.

Col. E. G. Harrell, Editor NORTH CAROLINA TEACHER and Sec'y N. C. Teachers' Assembly.

Supt. John J. Blair, Winston Graded Schools.

Supt. G. A. Grimsley, Greensboro Graded Schools.

Mr. J. R. Wharton, Supt. of Pub. Instruction of Guilford County.

Expressions of regret at not being able to be present were conveyed from President Alex. Q. Holladay, A. and M. College; Prof. W. S. Currell, Davidson College; Mr. Hugh Morson, President N. C. Teachers' Assembly; President R. L. Abernathy, Rutherford College, and Mr. E. S. Sheppe, Editor *The Southern Educator.*

The address of welcome was delivered by Mr. B. F. Dixon, who congratulated the State on the progress made in the cause of education in recent years. He considered it a pleasure to look into the faces of those who had more to do with the shaping of the education of the State than any other class of people. He extended a warm welcome.

In responding to the address of welcome, Mr. W. E. Abernathy said:

MR. PRESIDENT, LADIES AND GENTLEMEN: In behalf of the Association of College Professors of North Carolina, I desire to express our appreciation of the very graceful and cordial welcome tendered by the President of Greensboro Female College. I desire to congratulate the Executive Committee on the selection, for this our first meeting, of your beautiful city, renowned for the chivalry of her men, the beauty of her women, the classic culture of her citizens, and her wealth of historic name. This is holy ground. This is the birthplace of American freedom. It was here that the patriot warrior—whose name your city wears and will wear forever—marshalled his bruised and battered columns, and with the daring of despair threw them across the march of an everywhere triumphant foe. It was here arose the herald-star ushering in the sun which silvered the bayonets and banners of Yorktown. With pleasure and with pride we greet you in this historic city. But the greatest military genius of the world and of the ages, beneath the bending of whose eyelids the earth reeled and rocked, Napoleon Bonaparte, said: "The true victories, the only ones which we need never lament, are those won over the dominion of ignorance." Under its dismal covert crouch all crimes, lurk all lies, shelter all sins and suffering, hide all hurtful influences. The alphabet is the ally of liberty, the school-house is our Palladium. Plant it where you will—in pine woods or populous cities, build it of rude slab or polished marble, fill it with the young of rich or ragged, prince or pauper—you have erected a bulwark better than a cordon of bristling bayonets or stoutest soldiery.

We gather here to-day from all parts of North Carolina, from our separate fields of labor, to take counsel of each other, to read the rich pages of each other's experience, to feel the electric touch of elbows, to broaden our mental horizon, to learn more of the divinity of our divine art—the art of man-building. We are king makers. It is terribly true that we hold in our hands the distaff of the fates. Year by year the State calls upon us for our tribute of troops to fight on her fields, of brave men to bear her burdens. They are what we make them. The old Greeks, in the days of Euripides, when they punished a criminal punished his school-master with him; it was right. The teacher lives again in his students. Our lives and precepts will be re-enacted in the histories of those who go out from under our care—crystalized in the characters, thrilling in the songs, living in the laws, enwoven in the destinies of the future.

May all our deliberations here recognize the dignity and divinity of our profession, and win the approval of the Great Teacher.

Again I thank you for our welcome to your city.

The annual address was delivered by the President of the Association, Mr. Geo. T. Winston. (This address will be inserted in the next number of THE TEACHER.)

On motion of Mr. Chas. E. Taylor, a vote of thanks was tendered to the President for his excellent address.

On motion of Mr. J. L. Armstrong, it was decided that the business session be held at the close of the afternoon session instead of Saturday morning.

HOW TO INCREASE THE EFFICIENCY OF PREPARATORY SCHOOLS.

PAPER BY MR. JNO. F. CROWELL.

The educational conditions in North Carolina are somewhat as follows:

The elementary schools are woefully unequal to the task of doing the educational work peculiar to that grade of schools.

The intermediate schools are comparatively more-nearly equal to the work belonging to them, but yet are far from meeting the needs of the population on the one hand, and of answering the requirements of the colleges on the other.

There are very few distinctly preparatory schools in North Carolina. A strict adherence to the letter of the subject would throw us out of touch with actual conditions in the midst of which we live, and of which we must treat if we wish to do any good to the interests concerned. This paper treats of the preparatory work done in all classes of schools, and then suggests plans for increasing the efficiency of this work.

The schools which stand between the elementary schools and the colleges of the higher grade are the schools which undertake nearly all the preparatory work that is really done, excepting that done in cities by private tutors, and the work of the graded schools, which includes both the elementary and the academic portions of the preparatory training.

These schools may be divided into three classes:

1. The academy—the oldest and in many respects the best feature in our entire preparatory system.

2. The collegiate institute—which prepares for advanced standing in college.

3. The smaller colleges—a larger portion of whose students are of preparatory grade, but which have a baccalaureate curriculum and grant degrees both honorary and for work.

To this may be added a fourth—the larger colleges which give preparatory instruction to students who are conditioned upon requirements for admission to college, being at the same time allowed to enter the college courses of instruction.

These being the phases of the problem before us, how shall we solve it?

As a remedy for this fourth phase of the difficulty, that is, to meet the case of conditioned students, of which we must take account as things now are, I suggest:

I. *Provide an academy of preparatory instruction at the seat and under the management of every college which holds entrance examinations for admission to the freshman class, to which academy conditioned students may go to make good such deficiencies.*

After a study of several experiments I am prepared to say that this is the best way I know to relieve the college of preparatory work, and at the same time to make that peculiar work more efficient in preparing boys for full admission to college courses.

The want of the clear differentiation of the college work from preparatory work is one of the greatest obstacles to the improvement of both.

Hence, colleges ought to provide a separate institution to do local preparatory work, not only to coach delinquent applicants, but to provide preparatory advantages to the boys of the college community.

This is a comparatively inexpensive remedy. Undergraduates could do most of the teaching, superintended by a principal.

The colleges must go into the business of preparatory education, or beg their way into a precarious patronage. Opposition from the preparatory schools need not be reckoned in this matter of meeting a local condition which the preparatory schools elsewhere cannot meet.

Of the other phase of the question, how to improve the efficiency of the preparatory agencies in the academies, the collegiate institutes and the minor colleges, I am unalterably opposed to anything that looks like compression, by way of reducing the grade of work done. These things will right themselves quicker by reason than by force aimed at the institutions concerned.

II. The thing for us as an Association to do is to *prepare a standard schedule of requirements for admission to the A. B. course in our colleges in a separate form for circulation among all the schools engaged in preparatory work.*

With the sanction of this Association this can be done with great effect.

This would furnish a standard by which schools could be guided in their work, as well as give the student an idea of what he must have to enter. The trouble is that too few know what the colleges want.

Many academies and private tutors do not publish a course of studies to be taken for admission to colleges.

III. A third incentive to improve preparatory work would be *the holding of entrance examinations by joint arrangement of the colleges at the leading centres, in the cities and in the country,* say, at central points to cover sections of the State,

IV. *Induce the preparatory schools to have a distinctly college preparatory curriculum for admission to the freshman class*—no longer or no shorter. This pertains especially to graded schools in cities, and to collegiate institutes, whose general courses cover more years than the distinctly preparatory course does.

V. *Let the preparatory schools undertake less and do better what they undertake* under the head of preparatory work.

Preparation for advanced standing is a failure, with proper exceptions. We find that the majority of students who enter upon advanced standing drop out of college for want of acquaintance with college methods of study.

VI. *Let the colleges pay more attention to the preparation of their graduates for the work of teaching in the preparatory schools.*

Teach the science and art of teaching. Have a teacher's class in all the main preparatory studies.   Teach them how to teach a class in preparatory Latin, Greek, mathematics, history, English.

VII. *Let the colleges cultivate a more personal interest in the preparatory schools, by visiting these institutions and lecturing on educational work.*

VIII. *Introduce more modern methods and text-books.*

No text-book ten years old has any right, as a rule, to be in any course.

The following course of preparatory study is proposed as a three years' college preparatory course, with

(1.) The same course for all the first year (at the age of 12 or 13).

(2.) Two courses, classical and normal, the second year.

(3.) Three courses, classical, normal and scientific, the third year.

JUNIOR YEAR.

PREPARATORY TO ALL COURSES.

Terms.	Subjects.	Periods per Week.	Terms.	Subjects.	Periods per Week.	Terms.	Subjects.	Periods per Week.
Fall Term.	Arithmetic	5	Winter Term.	Arithmetic	5	Spring Term.	Arithmetic	5
	Latin	5		Latin	5		Latin	5
	Greek History	3		Roman History	3		American History,	3
	English	5		English	5		English	5
	Readings	2		Letter-writing	2		Bookkeeping	2

MIDDLE YEAR.

Terms.	CLASSICAL. Subjects.	Periods.	Terms.	GENERAL. Subjects.	Periods.
Fall Term.	Algebra	5	Fall Term.	Algebra	5
	Latin	5		Latin	5
	Greek	5		French	5
	Literature and Composition	3		Literature and Composition	3
	Declamation	2		Declamation	2
Winter Term.	Algebra	5	Winter Term.	Algebra	5
	Latin	5		Latin	5
	Greek	5		French	5
	Literature and Composition	3		Literature and Composition	3
	Physiology	2		Physiology	2
Spring Term.	Algebra	5	Spring Term.	Algebra	5
	Latin	5		Latin	5
	Greek	5		French	5
	Literature and Composition	2		Literature and Composition	2
	Declamation	3		Declamation	3

SENIOR YEAR.

Terms.	CLASSICAL. Subjects.	Periods.	Terms.	GENERAL. Subjects.	Periods.	Terms.	SCIENTIFIC. Subjects.	Periods.
Fall Term.	Latin	5	Fall Term.	Botany	5	Fall Term.	Geometry	5
	Greek	5		French	4		French	4
	Latin Comp.	2		Drawing	3		Latin	5
	General History	3		General History	3		General History	3
	Lit. and Comp.	3		Lit. and Comp.	3		Drawing	3
	Elocution	2		Elocution	2			
Winter Term.	Latin	5	Winter Term.	Physics	5	Winter Term.	Physics	5
	Greek	5		French	4		French	4
	Greek Comp.	2		Modern History	3		Latin	5
	Arith. (Col. Rev.)	4		Commer. Arith.	4		Arith. (Col. Rev.)	4
	Lit. and Comp.	2		Lit. and Comp.	2		Lit. and Comp.	2
	Elocution	2		Ethics (Everett)	2			
Spring Term.	Latin	5	Spring Term.	Chemistry	5	Spring Term.	Chemistry	5
	Greek	5		French	4		French	4
	Algebra (Rev.)	5		Civics	5		Latin	5
	Lit. and Comp.	2		Lit. and Comp.	2		Algebra (Rev.)	5
	Am. Hist. (Rev.)	3		Ped'gy (Psy. & Eth.	4			

Letter from Prof. Hugh Morson:

RALEIGH, N. C., April 20, 1892.

To the Secretary of the College Association of N. C.

DEAR SIR:—I regret very much that my professional duties prevent me from attending the meeting of the College Association to be held at Greensboro on the 22d inst., and I beg that you will express such regret on my behalf to the meeting, with assurances of my appreciation of the courtesy extended in inviting me to take a part in the discussion of the subject, "How to increase the efficiency of our preparatory schools."

This is a question which I consider of great mutual importance to both the colleges and schools of the State, and I trust that some action in regard to it may be taken by you which will result in advantage to us all. I think I can safely say that the preparatory schools and academies of the State are anxious to have some arrangement which will bring all their work into a harmonious system conducing to the good of all parties, and would be glad if the colleges would state fully what changes they think would be desirable in order to bring secondary and collegiate work into harmony. The schools will be found ready, I think, to enter into any arrangements their circumstances will permit to bring about the desirable unification of our educational system. It may not be amiss for me to suggest that some plan be devised to provide for a conference between the teachers of the preparatory schools and the college professors as regards the requirements for admission to college similar to that which I believe exists in New York, and perhaps other of our States.

Wishing for you a full and enjoyable meeting, and with renewed assurances of regret and disappointment at not being able to accept your invitation, I am, Very truly yours,

HUGH MORSON.

BUSINESS SESSION.

On motion, a committee on nomination of officers was appointed, consisting of N. C. English, Chairman; W. S. Long, W. E. Abernathy, Jno. F. Woody, and W. A. Withers.

Mr. E. G. Harrell, Secretary of the North Carolina Teachers' Assembly, stated that it was the desire of the Assembly that the programme for College Day at Morehead City be arranged by the Association at as early a time as convenient.

On motion, a committee was appointed to arrange this programme, consisting of Chas. E. Taylor, Chairman; J. B. Shearer, Jno. F. Crowell, L. L. Hobbs, and Karl P. Harrington; and it was requested that the Committee report this afternoon.

Mr. Taylor requested that any question thought to be helpful to the Committee be handed to the Secretary.

AFTERNOON SESSION—3:15.

Discussion of the subject, "How to Increase the Efficiency of the Preparatory Schools."

MR. HOBBS: A better grade of teachers might be obtained if better salaries could be paid. There would be difficulty in doing this, however, till the people showed a greater appreciation of the value of the schools and the work done.

MR. BANDY: Taking the entrance examinations to college as a measure of the efficiency of the schools, there is certainly need of their improvement. Taking Trinity College as an example, out of more than fifty applying for admission to the Freshman class about twenty were conditioned in mathematics, and perhaps as many in Latin and Greek. This state of things holds back other members of the class who were well prepared, and thus prevents the teacher and pupil from doing the best work.

MR. SHEARER: Hoped to see the day when primary education should be put on a higher plane of efficiency, and the schools continue all the year. We should not despise small things. It is not the large school with a large number of teachers that furnishes the bulk of the college students. These come mostly from the small schools with only one and sometimes two teachers. They do not always come from the cities, as there the commercial spirit takes hold of the young men and draws them off into business, instead of into college. It is to be regretted that many of the schools of say one teacher which had been in existence an hundred years—as those around Davidson College—are closed. The colleges should work actively for themselves; their representatives should visit the schools and lecture to them when they get a chance, and furnish them better teachers.

MR. ARMSTRONG: One of the great difficulties the college contends with is the lack of preparation of students in English, due to the fact that the time which should be given to this subject in the schools is given to something else. We cannot get English Grammar by studying Latin Grammar, any more than we can learn the geography of the earth by studying the moon. The easy grammar for students of five or six years of age is not of any great value. The student studying grammar should be older. The lack of the preliminary English training shows itself in bad spelling, and in the student not knowing the meaning of

words which should be perfectly familiar on his entrance
to college.

MR. WINSTON: There are many defects in our schools,
some of which cannot be remedied. The colleges can
help the schools by furnishing them better teachers; by
teaching pedagogics to those students who expect to teach;
by not recommending one who is incompetent; by exerting
their influence on the public to pay larger fees; by stimulating the schools in publishing in the annual catalogues
the names of the schools furnishing the best pupils; by
aiding the schools in getting better books.

MR. CROWELL: Many pupils are at a disadvantage in
not knowing how to study. The city schools seem to be
well conducted, and it is the country schools that have
least means and are therefore at a greater disadvantage.

MR. ABERNATHY: The idea advanced of the imporance
of the small school is one of great concern. Here one
teacher makes the school, and it is of great importance
that he should be well equipped for his work. It is strange
that the people pay so little attention to this, when they are
so particular about the qualifications of one whose work is
in law or medicine.

MR. ALDERMAN: It would be a good thing for this Association to send to the different teachers a circular letter
of requirements. The teacher is very patient and diligent in
his work, and anxious to make himself more efficient in it.

MR. AIKINS: In Ontario the system is under the Minister of Education. All the colleges have the same entrance
examination, and this is the finishing examination of the
schools. These examinations are prepared by a committee
of college and preparatory school men, thus combining
the opinions of those who look at the matter from different standpoints.

MR. McIVER: The Association has about one hundred
members, and although it is of value to discuss the question

before the Association, much more benefit would be derived if the matter could be presented to the people of the State. It would pay the colleges to defray the expenses of good men to go out into the counties and speak on education.

MR. WOODY: Better results could be accomplished by not teaching so many things in the preparatory schools, and doing more thoroughly what is done. The pupil should realize that the study of language, is one thing, and of books about language another. The preparatory schools and colleges should be in closer touch with one another.

MR. CRAWFORD: The activity of college presidents is now very great, and we are realizing a revival in education. New life is being infused into the schools. It will be of great value for the college men to go out among the people in the interest of education.

MR. FINGER: This Association is beginning its work in the proper way, i. e., from the top downward. It is an omen of good. The main difficulty with the schools is the lack of money, and it is a struggle for a livelihood. We should plant good teachers here and there; money is needed for this, and we should see to it that the people are willing to pay more. This is an age of combination of effort. The public schools are a power, and it is so with the graded schools. The hope of better work for the colleges lies in combination of work with the public schools. We should properly educate the teacher for his work, and see to it also that his Christian education is not neglected. The normal school is a necessity, and normal instruction should be given in all the colleges of the State. The methods of teaching have improved in the last ten years, and those who teach should be familiar with these methods. All the schools of the State have felt the impulse given by the first normal school at the University of the State. We need more money for education, and we should have free tuition at all the institutions of the State.

MR. HARRINGTON: There are about four hundred preparatory schools in the State, a very large number. The
power of example is strong, and if the pupils from the
graded schools of the cities show in their subsequent college work that they are better prepared than other pupils,
this will have a good effect and be a stimulus to the other
schools.

BUSINESS SESSION.

On motion of Mr. Long, the question of considering the
desirability of discussing during the Teachers' Assembly
the arrangement of a course of study for preparatory schools
was referred to the Committee on the Morehead City programme.

Mr. Harrell, editor, tendered the columns of THE NORTH
CAROLINA TEACHER for the publication of the proceedings
of the Association.

Mr. Crowell, for Mr. Sheppe, editor, tendered the columns
of *The Southern Educator* for the same purpose.

On motion of Mr. English, the Association accepted
the offers of these gentlemen, and extended to them the
thanks of the Association for the courtesy.

Mr. English, Chairman of the Committee on Nomination of Officers for the Next Year, made the following report
of recommendations : President, Chas. E. Taylor ; First
Vice-President, Jno. F. Crowell ; Second Vice-President,
J. B. Shearer ; Third Vice-President, L. L. Hobbs ; Secretary and Treasurer, W. A. Withers.

On motion of Mr. McIver, the report of the committee
was adopted, and the officers declared elected.

The Executive Committee, by authority of the Constitution, levied an assessment of one dollar per member to pay
the cost of postage, stationery and printing.

Evening Session—8 o'clock.

THE REQUIREMENTS OF THE A. B. DEGREE.

PAPER BY MR. CHARLES E. TAYLOR.

Forty or fifty years ago this would have been considered an easy if not a useless question. The requirements were so stereotyped and were so well understood that to have raised the question at all would have caused surprise.

The degree was generally recognized throughout the United States as, a credential to at least four years of certain residence and probable study at a chartered college, and, as a trade-mark in the world of letters, was supposed to guarantee considerable knowledge of Latin, Greek, and mathematics, a general knowledge of physics and philosophy, some acquaintance with chemistry and history and English literature, and, occasionally, a weak infusion of a modern language.

A rigid curriculum system was in almost universal vogue. Upon it, as upon a procrustean bed, the student was mercilessly bound, regardless of his tastes, proclivities and intended occupation. Comparatively few colleges were thoroughly manned with instructors, especially in the scientific chairs. The lack of endowments, laboratories, apparatus, as well as long established custom, made it necessary to require that an overwhelmingly large portion of the work of the colleges should be given to ancient languages and pure mathematics.

Far be it that we should underrate the work of the colleges during the last generation. It is known by its fruit. Foundations were laid for the largest and ripest scholarship, and it may be questioned whether, on the merely disciplinary side, we are doing better work or give more intrinsic value to the Bachelor's degree than did our fathers.

But whatever may have been its real value, the A. B. degree had a definite significance which has gradually become greatly obscured. It has largely lost its old meaning. Its new meaning may be better, but it is not yet generally understood and recognized. Two reasons may be suggested for this uncertainty about the meaning and value of the degree—

First: In almost all the States infant colleges — hundreds in all — have been given the chartered privileges of conferring degrees. And young men who have spent two or three years at so-called colleges, which are less well equipped than many good academies, are authorized to write after their names the same title which is won by arduous labor for four years at Harvard, Johns Hopkins or Vanderbilt.

Second: The elective system has been almost universally adopted in greater or less degree. Unfortunately, however, almost every college is, in this respect a law unto itself, and the variations are endless. The

American Academy of Medicine, which has set itself to the investigation of college degrees, and whose published reports are probably the best authority at our command, seems almost to despair of anything like consensus of opinions or uniformity of practice. That the elective system is wise, and absolutely necessary to some extent, will hardly be debated. Just how far it should be allowed is still, and is long likely to be, an open question. The system appears to be unavoidable, simply because life is short and art is long—and getting longer every day. The student's college life is a constant quantity. The work desirable to be done by him has shown itself to be a variable one. The scientific studies have become more and more differentiated, and a strange stress is wisely required to be put on political economy, history, English and the modern languages. The writer, when a youth, was a student in an excellent college, of high reputation, and comparatively well equipped. But all the scientific instruction given was five hours a week for one year. At the college over which he now has the honor to preside, nineteen hours a week for one year are needed for lectures alone, while ten hours are required for laboratory work. And the same change has probably been witnessed by most of our older men.

The problem before us, briefly stated in different terms, is this: Given a young man of average academic preparation who is to remain four years in college. What can the college best do for him in that time?

It will be seen at once that this question is not absolute but relative. The answer will depend upon—

(1.) The advantage offered by the college that he selects. In some institutions a well prepared student can literally "go through college" in four years. In others he would need eight or ten years to complete all the courses of instruction offered.

(2.) Upon the capacities and proclivities of the man. There is no absolute "best" about it. The course that is most desirable for one student is certainly not necessarily the most desirable for all students.

(3.) Upon the occupation which the student expects to pursue.

It is true that it is the part of the college to teach a student something about everything, and of the university to teach everything about something. But this need not imply that it is the function of the college to teach an equal amount about everything to each student, regardless of the work he expects to do in after life. Just as a university, whose peculiar function is specialization, should aim also at general culture, so also may a college, whose peculiar function is general culture, begin the work of specialization. We often speak of the college as laying foundations for after-building. Surely it is not wrong to lay the foundation deeper than elsewhere at the point where the superstructure will rest most heavily hereafter.

In view of the above considerations, the writer may be allowed to express the opinion that the student, while allowed to engross no branch of study, scientific or literary, should be permitted in working for the A. B. degree to lay more stress upon some than upon others. While, however, there is a growing belief that there should be some modification in the direction suggested of a rigid curriculum, there are wide variances of view as to the extent and manner of the change. Indeed, anything like perfect conformity is hardly to be hoped for. And yet it is very desirable that the whole matter be studied and debated, and that, at least, some general principles and standards be agreed to.

Amid the almost innumerable opinions held there is, among those who have discarded the unyielding curriculum system, a practical unanimity in one belief, a belief which the writer holds, that is that there should be presented to the student several courses, the successful pursuit of any one of which would secure for him the A. B. degree. Of course the number of these courses leading to A. B. should not be needlessly increased. All should be, so far as possible, of the same average difficulty and length, so that the student in making his option between them could be controlled entirely by considerations of relative utility. It seems desirable that there should be at least five of these courses, one making Ancient Languages prominent; another Pure and Applied Mathematics and Physics; another Chemistry and Natural History; another Political Economy and History, and another English, French and German. But in each of the groups those studies which are less prominent should never be subordinated in such a way as to make them appear unimportant. The student who chooses, for instance, the Ancient Language group must be made to understand that he must be as proficient in the Mathematics and Natural History required in that group as in Latin or Greek. Something of this sort, while requiring no less labor and time on the part of the student, seems to be a clear gain over the older system of requirements for A. B. If it really be so, is it not desirable that there should be a general adoption of it in American colleges?

The subject was continued in the following paper by Mr. Karl P. Harrington:

REQUIREMENTS FOR THE A. B. DEGREE.

It is a somewhat curious freak of nature that, in this new land of liberty, whose government is based upon the declaration that all men are free and equal, and whose history proves that neither wealth, nor family name, nor titled honors are necessary for a man to reach the highest position in commercial, political, ecclesiastical or scholastic circles, there should have been developed such a mania for degrees and titles as

3

to place Americans in a most unenviable position in this respect before the other great nations of the world.

The American girl who is to inherit the millions of some lard merchant, or oil manipulator, or railroad magnate, lays herself with all her wealth at the feet of any worthless European younger son of a once noble house in order to become, forsooth, "the Countess." A clergyman reaches the age of forty-five, and forthwith through his friends and relatives besieges some university faculty in order to take by force of fear of loss of patronage, or other possible vague disaster, the Doctorate of Divinity. The young teacher of the present day, knowing that the German degree of Doctor of Philosophy is the key most likely to open for him the door to high honors and lucrative salaries, seeks far and wide for the institution which will append the coveted letters "Ph. D." to his name for the smallest amount of time and effort spent on his part, or perhaps even accepts unblushingly the gift of the honorary title from some second-rate American college   It is hard to say whether the sight of this struggle after the name rather than the thing is more comical or pitiful. Our English cousins, strange as it may seem, are, for the most part, well content with plain "Mr.", even though they hold positions of eminence in the great Universities of Oxford and Cambridge; while among us every man who has ever been in a regiment is a "Major" or a "Colonel"; and the negro, seeing what suits the prevailing temper of his Caucasian neighbors, salutes every male white that walks the earth with the title of "Boss."

It was the inevitable result of this haste to obtain titles that all our university degrees should suffer more or less degradation. The newer the community the faster must be the life in order to overtake the older civilization; and, accordingly, in some sections boys have become "Bachelors of Arts" after doing an amount of work no greater than that completed during the first year of a respectable university. It is not a very uncommon thing in some colleges for boys to enter the Freshman Class that have already obtained the degree of "A. B." elsewhere.

"D. D." and "LL. D." have long been conferred regardless of the idea of expecting any exact correspondence between the original meanings of the titles and the attainments of the persons receiving them. Even Ph. D. was on the verge of ruin as the one remaining name-handle that a learned man might hold without its melting away in his grasp.

But the work of rescue has begun.   "Ph. D." has been "snatched as a brand from the burning," and men are refusing either to give or receive it as an honorary degree.   A very general movement is on foot to restrict within exceedingly narrow limits the number of Doctorates of Divinity and of Laws to be dispensed in the future.   "A. M.", which has for many years been generally given away to almost every college graduate of three years standing, is now being awarded more and more only upon rigid examinations in advanced studies. When, however, we turn to the A. B. degree, the most widely sought and given, and the most important of all, we are confronted with a remarkable phenomenon. A powerful under-tow seems to have set in at this point, which threatens to carry all definiteness of meaning away from under the title, "Bachelor of Arts," and scatter it at random over the whole vast sea of knowledge in unrecognizable disintegrating particles. From the oldest university in the land down to the youngest college of all, there is a bewildering haziness enwrapping the whole question of what should be required for the degree, and most radical differences of opinion concerning it are frequently expressed. One set of educators are for dropping Greek from the list of the requirements. Another class would banish Latin, too. Still others propose to throw open the gates to all comers, giving the degree for a certain amount of work done in any line, according to the whim of the individual student. A large majority of the respectable institutions refuse the degree to any except those who have completed a "Classical Course"; but many young and weak colleges still selfishly persist in awarding it, though aware that the work done by their students has been comparatively insignificant in amount and inferior in quality.

If the degree of A. B. is to carry any significance peculiar to itself, not only some definite amount, but some definite character of work must be understood to be implied by it; otherwise it will sink into disrepute, and be sought for by none. The elective system, like everything else based on a principle inherently sound, is liable to be carried to extremes, and the original purposes overreached. The theory that our academic students should have absolutely free choice of studies during the whole period of their residence in college halls, is based on a confusion of the German, the English, and the American ideas and methods in higher education. In Germany the university student has, at his entrance upon his work, passed through a strict required course of nine years in the secondary schools, and is, in some respects, better fitted for the degree of A. B. than our own average college graduate. He is prepared to specialize, and accordingly sets out upon some particular line of work, preparatory to a professional degree. The English University man has likewise in the great preparatory schools, like Eton or Rugby, received advanced training of a high grade; but enters upon his course with the degree of B. A., and a possible later M. A., as the goal of his ambition. The American boy who enters college has rarely spent over four years in the preparatory course, often much less; and his pate commonly contains "small Latin and less Greek"; and he is fortunate indeed if the possessor of a good knowledge of Algebra and plane Geometry, and the ability to write clearly and correctly a page of his native language. Yet, in four years he expects to obtain the same degree as his better trained English cousin; and not content with that, he begins to plead for the same absolute freedom in election of studies as the German university student. But our freshmen and sophomores cannot be put on a par with the foreign university students in this way. The plain fact is that the American boy at that stage of his intellectual career doesn't yet know enough facts, and hasn't yet acquired sufficient mental grasp and discriminating judgment, to be left entirely free, henceforth, to decide what he shall study in order to secure, as he believes, a liberal education. He has taken a larger part of his youth for amusement and idleness than the average studious boy of any other highly civilized nation on the globe; and the result is what ought to be expected. If the time ever comes, as perhaps it will, when our colleges shall do only college work, and our universities university work, then we may expect a required course in college, and an entirely elective course in the University; and maybe then the degrees will be adapted to the work done. Meanwhile, however, unsystematizing all system necessarily leads to a chaotic state of education; it is an anacronism in this systematic age.

Moreover, whatever demand there is for breaking down all barriers as regards the character of the work done for the degree of A. B. really arises out of sordid, time-serving and ignoble motives. At home and abroad the American people is recognized as the nation that makes haste to be rich. The money value of everything is immediately considered as soon as it is proposed. Let this principle be once applied to an academic degree, and forthwith the question becomes prominent, What degree is easiest obtained and soonest gained? And what studies will produce in practical life the most rapid accumulation of wealth? If these be the questions that are to decide the work done for the degree, the studies of the preparatory school must, of course, be those that can be soonest completed, and that are in themselves most directly practical for money-making; and likewise the college course must be throughout planned with a view to the same ends. In short, it is, too often, the cash value of the degree, and the comfortable feeling in its possessor and his parents which comes from having it, that are really sought for. The old question rises again to view, whether a man's life consisteth in the things that he possesseth, or in what the man is. The cry for the go-as-you-please degree means inevitable superficiality; and, if heard, it cannot but result in making men all the more mere utilitarian devotees of "the almighty dollar." .

It must be added that by having some definite standards for the degree and thus restricting it within certain limits, no injustice is done to any aspiring youth. The day when A. B. was practically the only academic degree that the average American boy could hope to achieve by honest effort, though not beyond our memories, is certainly now forever past. Ph. B., B. S., and B. L., are very generally given, and increasingly so; and the mind with literary, scientific or practical bias, can be accommodated with the course adapted to its individual want, and crowned with a degree equally honorable with that of A. B. Why, then, should there be any desire to take from the work done for any of these degrees its individual honor and distinctive mark, and make A. B. the catch-all, the meaningless appellation that gives no hint of the kind of mental attainments that its possessor may claim? Is there a lingering suspicion that "arts" are better than "sciences," or than "philosophy," or than "letters"? If so, let him who has such an opinion honestly choose the course that will by its distinctive work bring him the degree of A. B.; but let him not attempt to climb up some other way into the coveted position in the A. B. fold!

If, then, we decide that there should be some definite requirements for the degree of A. B., what ought these to be? Speaking comprehensively, they should be along the same general lines as the requirements for the same degree in the best institutions during the past centuries, modified incidentally by the demands of the latest and best general culture. For the degree of A. B. has universally been held to imply the completion of a course of study that would furnish the best foundation of general culture, upon which to build a superstructure in any department of advanced education that might be preferred, or with which a man, denied the privilege of special further study, might be reasonably grounded in the knowledge of the most important facts, and in the principles which are recognized as sound in the main divisions of current human thought. To those wishing to give any other especial bias to their training and mental industry, other courses are open, leading to other degrees. The course leading to the degree of A. B., however, is not, never has been, and never should be a specializing course.

General culture for an American youth in the present day ought to include a practical knowledge of his country's language and the literature of that language. It should also embrace the mathematical principles necessary to enable him to take up successfully any line of technical study or business. To these subjects must be added a fair working knowledge of the principles of all the most general and useful modern sciences. A knowledge of one's own physical and mental organism and processes is essential. The ethical theories, on which should be based the life of States and of individuals, must be pondered, with as wide a range of historical illustration as is feasible. Familiarity with at least one modern language cannot be omitted, and neither French nor German ought really to be a stranger (in these days) to any well educated man. No less indispensable than any of the foregoing subjects is a thorough acquaintance with the ancient classic languages and the most celebrated specimens of their literatures.

It is at this point that the modern hue and cry is raised that by giving so much attention to the classics the old course for the degree of A. B. becomes a specializing course. Even if this were admitted, it should still be claimed that this degree ought to have as fair a chance to preserve its own distinctive individuality among its equals as the degrees of B. S., or Ph. B., or B. L. The proposition referred to, however, is not here granted. What we are endeavoring to obtain for our young men is fundamental general culture. If the day has long since passed when a man who knew well Latin and Greek, and not necessarily much of anything else, was well educated, the day is not yet in sight when he who desires the best preparation for mingling confidently in the world of culture can afford to omit from his curriculum these classic languages. All our law, medicine, mathematics, aitronomy, linguistic science, philosophy, history, we trace back to Greece and Rome. In all departments of literature, in epic or lyric poetry, oratory, satire, the drama, we still find our models of style in Greece and Rome. The greatest scholars of to-day, our literary men, even most of our greatest scientists, have been thoroughly trained in their Latin and Greek, and most of them believe in it heartily. Can the man who has never read Homer, or Virgil, or Cicero, or Horace, be perfectly at home in the best educated circles of Rome, or Paris, or Berlin, or London, or Oxford, or Cambridge, or in any other one of a half-hundred cities and University communities in our own land? Perhaps so, occasionally. Likewise, of course, some will. desire to point out examples of good lawyers, physicians, poets and orators who have no acquaintance with Latin or Greek. Certainly! In a neighboring town one of the most successful business men cannot write his own name! "A word to the wise is sufficient."

The college requirements for the degree of A. B. should be such as presuppose the successful completion of a school course lasting through a number of years. There are abundant indications of a coming movement for radical improvements in grammar school and high school education that will make it quite possible for much more of the work that is now done in many colleges to be relegated to the preparatory schools. English grammar, for instance, will be taught in a common-sense way, and will be taught in one-half the time now devoted to it with so little result. Arithmetic, too, instead of being spread over a half-dozen years, will be well taught in less than half that time, and other mathematical studies may take part of the time thus left free.

Some of the subjects that the candidate for the degree of A. B. should have mastered when he enters college are the following: Algebra, plane geometry, practical use of the English language for both writing and speaking, and the main facts of Latin and Greek grammar, and of Greek, Roman and American history. He should be able to read easy Latin at sight, and the same might well be said of either French or German. He should have studied Latin not less than four years—five would be better—beginning at an earlier age than is usual, and Greek not less than three. He should, moreover, have been so trained by the elementary study of some scientific subject—say botany, or physics, or geology—as to stimulate and develop his power and habit of observation. All this can be easily accomplished under the instruction of competent teachers before the average boy reaches the age of sixteen, and no boy should enter a college or university at an earlier age.

The young man who has entered college thus prepared in knowledge, in power of observation, in grasp of linguistic and mathematical principles, can immediately derive benefit from all his instruction under the best instructors, and his course for the degree of A. B. will naturally be worthy of the name of college work. This course should include—

1. Enough advanced reading in the best Greek and Latin classics to lay their treasures open forever to the student, the courses lasting, perhaps, during the first two years.

2. Theoretical and practical rhetoric.

3. Solid and analytical geometry and trigonometry.

4. Logic and psychology.

5. A course in English Literature.

6. At least either French or German; both would be far better.

7. A fair knowledge of physics, chemistry, physiology, geology and astronomy.

8. Ethics and political economy; to which may be added some knowledge of civil government, and the United States Constitution in particular, unless all that is necessary on this line can be obtained in the preparatory schools.

To these subjects, which should be required for the degree, a somewhat wide list of elective courses should be added, out of which, particularly in the later years of his course, the student may choose enough to fill up his quota of work during the academic four years. His elective opportunities ought to be rich in literary and historical lines, for his previous study has fitted him well for such subjects. No less numerous should be the courses offered in scientific lines, in order that there may be no room for the charge that the sciences are discriminated against in the training of a Bachelor of Arts; but that rather, as ever, it may be possible for the brightest lights in the world of science to arise naturally from the number of those who take the regular classical courses in our best colleges. In all the required courses technical instruction and specializing tendencies should be avoided as much as is consistent with the best teaching; while in the classes which have been elected by students desiring to fit themselves for special work every opportunity should be afforded such men to investigate to the minutest detail any line of facts or phenomena in which they may severally take particular interest.

Finally, let it be urged that the requirements for the degree of A. B. should be essentially uniform in all colleges and universities. For this there are many reasons. Only three will be named here. In the first place they should be uniform to protect and promote sound scholarship. As long as young men can obtain for one-half the effort at some inferior institution the same degree that the best work at any first-class college will hardly yield them, many of them may be expected to fail to see why they should not take the easy course to reach the same nominal result. That means superficiality for the student and comparative contentment with low ideals for the instructor. It means a great body of half-educated youth annually turned loose upon our people, imagining themselves to have a fair chance among their more fortunate comrades who have had more complete training, and doomed to early or later disappointment. It means that the people pay dearly for this disappointment in poorly educated physicians, with whom to trust their lives; in poorly trained lawyers, with whom to trust their property; in stunted teachers, to whom in turn is committed the education of the coming generation. It means that throughout this country the suspicion will increase that always is felt by Europeans concerning the value of any American's A. B. degree; and the necessity will arise for every man to state in connection with his degree where he received it, a thing already in favor with us in some quarters. A. B. ought to be an honorable degree, and every possessor of it ought to be able to assert confidently that he has done as much and as good work to obtain it as any other man. Nothing shrivels up the intellectual courage of a man worse than the consciousness that he has been cheated into believing that he knows more than he really does.

Secondly, the requirements in the under-graduate courses should be uniform in order to facilitate the post-graduate study. The professor who undertakes to direct advanced work in any especial line must assume a certain amount of knowledge on the part of his class; and the work which they can unitedly accomplish will be vastly more and better, if they can begin at the same point in their deeper investigations. Too often at present a man who goes to one of our best institutions for post-graduate study finds himself obliged either to spend some time first in under-graduate study, or to enter upon his chosen work ill-prepared to get the most benefit from his instruction.

Lastly, uniformity of requirements is demanded for the permanent prosperity and success of individual colleges. "Honesty is the best policy." In the long run the American people in general, and the inhabitants of any section in particular, will recognize and honor high standards and honest work. The college that persistently continues to advertise itself as giving as much in its course for A. B. as the best institutions in the country, when everyone that knows anything about it knows the claim to be disingenuous, will sooner or later inevitably find its just fate under the law of the survival of the fittest. We hear a great deal said all over these United States about the too rapid multiplication of colleges, and much concern is expressed with regard to the probable result. Let it be understood that the ultimate solution of the problem of existence for every one of these hundreds of colleges depends entirely upon their ability in each individual case to prove themselves able to furnish as good an education as any other of their kind. When A. B. means just as much in one institution as in another the choice of an *Alma Mater* will be determined by local or denominational or other considerations, and by such only. But when that desirable result shall have been attained, there will be no place for the sham college, the would-be college, the college that is such only in ambition, and the sham A. B. will likewise vanish from the land.

DISCUSSION.

MR. HOBBS: This is a difficult question to solve. It is closely connected with the question of the requirements for admission. If these requirements for admission were settled, then it would mean four years work beyond this. The degree should indicate a capacity for work. If the question were divided into others, as how much Latin should be required, the answer could be given only in general terms. One should certainly know enough Latin to be able to read it easily, to be interested in it, and have a sufficient fondness to be able to continue the subject by himself or in a higher institution. The other questions to arise would be, "How much science?" "How much history?" "How much philosophy?" etc. The habit of study should certainly be formed, and it is hard to say just when this point is reached. Should like to put Bible study into the course. Should put in the observational studies. It might be possible to do this to a larger extent by beginning Greek later in the course and finishing it in a shorter time.

MR. TAYLOR: Stated that his paper had been prepared in haste, and he should like to hear from others present and have a full criticism of the subject.

MR. SHEARER: There is great difficulty in making the degree one of a high standard if there are fixed requirements. The tendency in this case is for students to get the degree who are not very far advanced in any one subject. On the other hand, licentious selections should not be allowed if such selections lead to a degree. We should try to make the degree mean more to those who have gone over the necessary course. The course should not be too flexible or too fixed, and in the course should be required a knowledge of the Bible.

MR. CROWELL: The A. B. course has remained about the same through the ages. Shall we shorten it? The custom has also been to have only one time in the twelve months at which a student could apply for the degree. Might we not allow it to be taken in four and a half years and then have an examination at Christmas. It seems that any A. B. course should include Latin, Greek, and Mathematics, and we should stand by this. Just because Harvard throws out Greek from its requirements for the degree, is no reason that we should do so. It is true that this may allow it to be taken by fewer candidates, but this will add to its value.

The time will come when the colleges will answer for the three months lost in the summer time.

MR. CRAWFORD: Was strongly of the opinion that some biblical instruction should be given to candidates for the A. B. degree.

MR. WINSTON: Wished to give his hearty approbation as to the study of the Holy Scriptures. No book is so full of human wisdom as well as of Divine wisdom. Yet there are difficulties in the way of requiring it to be taught in college. Two classes of institutions confer the A. B. degree. One of these gives a wider range of election, as Harvard, which requires no Latin or Greek, but which requires enough for admission to cover all the requirements in those subjects for graduation in many colleges. The same is true at the University of Virginia, and at other institutions. The colleges, as a rule, which give the most courses give the fewest degrees.

BUSINESS SESSION.

On motion, the following were elected members of the Association: Messrs. H. Austin Aikins, E. A. Alderman, W. E. Abernathy, L. W. Crawford, B. F. Dixon, Karl P. Harrington, B. C. Hinde, C. D. McIver, Dred Peacock, R. C. Root, John F. Woody.

A lengthy discussion followed as to uniform requirements for admission to college and graduation, and also as to the tabulation of the present requirements for this in the different institutions of the State.

Mr. Shearer stated that he was of the opinion that Article 7 of the Constitution should be stricken out, or in time it might cause trouble. He would not at present, however, offer an amendment to that effect.

Mr. Crowell, for the Committee on the Programme for College Day at Morehead City, made the following report of subjects recommended:

For the morning session, the subject of College Life—

(1) Athletics.

(2) The Social Side of College Life.

(3) Character Building in College.

For the evening session—

An open discussion of the subject, "Why I went to College, and what I got there."

On motion, the report was adopted, and the Executive Committee was asked to select the speakers.

The Executive Committee decided to hold the next annual meeting in Raleigh on February 24, 1893.

Adjourned.

GEORGE T. WINSTON, *President.*

W. A. WITHERS, *Secretary.*

North Carolina Teachers' Assembly.

ORGANIZATION FOR 1892·

OFFICERS:

HUGH MORSON (Raleigh Male Academy), President, . . Raleigh.
EUGENE G. HARRELL (Editor TEACHER), Sec. and Treas., . Raleigh.

VICE-PRESIDENTS:

1. J. J. Blair (Supt. Graded Schools), ... Winston.
2. J. E. Kelly (Model Male School), ... Charlotte.
3. Miss Catherine Fulghum (Graded School), . . Goldsboro.
4. W. J. Ferrell (Wakefield Academy), . . . Wakefield.
5. Miss Lizzie Lindsay (Graded School), . . . Greensboro.
6. P. M. Pearsall (County Superintendent), . . Trenton.
7. Miss Lina McDonald (Graded School), . . . Winston.
8. T. J. Drewry (Horner Military School), . . . Oxford
9. Mrs. S. Montgomery Funk (Chowan Bap. Fem. Inst.), Murfreesboro.

EXECUTIVE COMMITTEE:

Hugh Morson, *ex officio*, President, ... Raleigh.
Eugene G. Harrell, *ex officio*, Secretary, . . . Raleigh.
Eben Alexander (University of North Carolina), . . Chapel Hill.
W. L. Poteat (Wake Forest College), ... Wake Forest.
James Dinwiddie (President Peace Institute), . . . Raleigh.
Charles D. McIver (Pres't Normal and Industrial School
    for Women), ... Greensboro.
J. Y. Joyner (Superintendent Graded School), . . Goldsboro.
A. C. Davis (Superintendent Military School), . . Winston.
E. E. Britton (Principal High School), ... Roxboro.

NINTH ANNUAL SESSION, MOREHEAD CITY, JUNE 21 TO JULY 4, 1892.

ASSEMBLY NOTES.

EXAMINE CAREFULLY the programme of the Assembly, and be prepared to discuss any question that may be under consideration.

EVERY AMBITIOUS TEACHER SHOULD BE AT MOREHEAD CITY ON JUNE 21.

"EVERYBODY WILL be at the Assembly this summer," and you will have the pleasure of meeting more of your friends and acquaintances than ever before.

THE EDUCATIONAL EXPOSITION will fill every room in the Teachers' Building this summer, and the display will be of the greatest possible value and interest to our teachers.

ISN'T THE Assembly programme for the session a grand educational feast of good things? You can well afford to make any reasonable sacrifice in order to attend the Assembly this summer.

MR. ADOLPH COHN, of New Berne, dealer in pianos and organs, will furnish the Assembly with an elegant baby-grand piano and a very fine imitation pipe organ for use of the teachers during the coming session.

IF YOU want a good school, a position in a school, or a teacher for your school, don't fail to be present at the Assembly at Morehead City in June. The Assembly is going to do more work than ever before for the teachers and the schools.

THE INTEREST in the Assembly is far greater this year than ever before. From every section of North Carolina comes the glad news, "We are all going to the Assembly this summer." We think the teachers will enjoy the great meeting such as they have enjoyed no other meeting in the State.

THE TEACHERS' ASSEMBLY tickets will be on sale June 18, so that persons who desire to do so may go to Morehead City several days in advance of the session. Rooms may be engaged in advance by writing to Mr. John O. Plank, manager of the Atlantic Hotel. The trains reach the hotel on a quick schedule before night.

DON'T FAIL to be at the Assembly; yes, be sure to attend the session at Morehead City in June.

·REMEMBER THAT you do not send the annual fees for certificate of membership to the Secretary this year as heretofore. Your railroad agent will collect the annual dues when you buy your ticket to Morehead City. This plan has been adopted by the railroads at our solicitation, in order to save trouble to all persons who want to attend the Assembly.

DO YOU know that more good positions as teachers have been secured at the Assembly than by any other means known to North Carolina teachers? If you want a position as a teacher don't fail to be at Morehead City in June, and we think you will be supplied. There are already in hand numbers of desirable applications, both for teachers and for schools.

THIS SESSION of the Assembly is going to be the grandest *representative* body of North Carolina teachers ever seen in the State. There will be present more college presidents and faculties, more principals of high schools and academies, more superintendents and teachers of graded schools, more teachers of public and private schools in the country, and more "friends of education" than ever before.

WE BELIEVE that this is going to be the most successful and enjoyable session of the Assembly ever held. The outlook is unusually bright for a very large attendance. Teachers are realizing more each year that they cannot afford to be absent from this great gathering of the brotherhood at Morehead City, and "the people" also know that the most enjoyable outing of all the year is a visit to the Teachers' Assembly.

THE LITERARY SOCIETIES of Wake Forest College have elected the following speakers to represent them in the

Intercollegiate Oratorical Contest at the Assembly June 29: Mr. John A. Wray (Euzelian), of Knoxville, Tenn., and Mr. J. P. Spence (Philomathesian), of Elizabeth City, N. C. There will also be representatives from Trinity, Davidson and the University, and the oratorical contest promises to be one of the most interesting features of the Assembly.

YOU WILL meet at the Assembly this summer the faculties of all the colleges, the superintendents and teachers of all the principal graded schools, and the teachers of all the regular high schools and academies, and of many other private and public schools in North Carolina. It will be the grandest meeting of representative educators ever held in our State. If you want to find a North Carolina teacher between June 21 and July 4, you will have only to run down to Morehead City.

NO EDUCATIONAL organization in America has a better programme for this summer than our Teachers' Assembly. In many respects the programme of the Assembly will be of more interest and value to teachers than will be the work of any other association in the country. North Carolina is beginning to appreciate more than ever before the work and worth of North Carolina teachers, and at no place can the benefits of that appreciation be more liberally realized than at the Teachers' Assembly.

THE INSTRUMENTAL MUSIC CONTEST for the Assembly Gold Medal will be held on June 30. The rules, as made by the Committee, require that at least five persons shall enter, and no name will be received later than June 15. The contest is open to every school for girls in North Carolina, and there are already several names entered. All who desire to compete are requested to forward their names at once to the Secretary. No person will be admitted to the contest after the Assembly has convened at Morehead City.

MANY PLEASANT surprises will greet you at the Assembly this session.   The Atlantic Hotel has been so improved and repaired that you will scarcely recognize it; the Teachers' Building is thoroughly repaired and repainted; several steam yachts, row-boats and picnic boats are on the sound; a railroad will be across the beach; boat-houses are in excellent condition; a swimming master will teach the girls the absolutely necessary art of swimming; while pleasure, comfort and instruction will abound in a greater degree than ever before.

THE NUMBER of North Carolina teachers who go to the Northern summer schools of methods is growing smaller every year.   The thoughtful teachers are realizing that the practical work of our Assembly is of more value to them than all the theories and speculations of the inexperienced enthusiasts who are employed to do a certain amount of work in the various Northern "summer schools of methods" (so-called) for a certain price.   North Carolina schools are different from any other schools in this country, and the Teachers' Assembly tells the young teachers how the work may be best performed in the interest of the children of our State.

OUTLINE PROGRAMME

OF THE

NORTH CAROLINA TEACHERS' ASSEMBLY.

NINTH ANNUAL SESSION.

MOREHEAD CITY, N. C.

Tuesday, June 21, 1892.

Teachers and their friends will leave for the Assembly.   All trains in the State make connection at Goldsboro with the Atlantic and North Carolina Railroad for Morehead City.

Wednesday, June 22.

10:30 A. M.

OPENING ADDRESS, ... COL. A. M. WADDELL, Wilmington.

ANNUAL ADDRESS. By the President.

Appointment of special committees.

8:30 P. M.

"HINTS FROM NATURE" (Chalk Talk). MR. FRANK BEARD, Chicago.

Thursday, June 23.

10:30 A. M.

"THE TRUE TEACHER." Mrs. Idalia G. Meyers, Washington, D. C.

"DRAWING IN THE SCHOOL ROOM." MR. FRANK BEARD.

8:30 P. M.

"WHAT BUSINESS MEN EXPECT OF THE PUBLIC SCHOOLS." Col. J. S. Carr, Durham.

Friday, June 24.

11 A. M.

"WHAT IS SCIENTIFIC TEMPERANCE?" Mrs. Mary M. Hobbs, Guilford College.

Discussion by prominent citizens of North Carolina.

"NORTH CAROLINA AND THE SOUTHERN EDUCATIONAL ASSOCIATION." Capt. C. B. Denson, Raleigh.

Discussion by Dr. Geo. T. Winston, Prof. James Dinwiddie, Dr. R. H. Lewis, Professors Henry Louis Smith, M. C. S. Noble, F. P. Hobgood, Dr. B. F. Dixon and others.

8:30 P. M.

"STORIES IN PICTURES" (Chalk Talks). MR. FRANK BEARD.

Saturday, June 25.

11 A. M.

"MANUAL TRAINING OF BOYS AND GIRLS." Prof. C. E. Vawter, Miller Training School, Va.

General discussion.

"BIOLOGY." Prof. J. M. Stedman, Trinity College.

8:30 A. M.

"NORTH CAROLINA AT THE WORLD'S FAIR." Hon. S. M. Finger, Raleigh.

Sunday, June 26.

11 A. M.

Religious exercises in Assembly Hall.

4:30 P. M.

DEMOREST MEDAL CONTEST.

There will be speakers from Beaufort, Morehead City, New Berne, Kinston and Fremont.

4

8.30 P. M.

SERMON in the Assembly Hall.

Monday, June 27.

11 A. M.

MODERN LANGUAGE AND ENGLISH LITERATURE ASSÓCIATION.

"THE GERMAN UNIVERSITY SYSTEM." Prof. W. D. Toy, University of North Carolina.

"MODERN LANGUAGES IN SCHOOL AND COLLEGE." A discussion by Profs. Toy, Sledd and Hume.

"ENGLISH LITERATURE." Prof. H. J. Stockard, of Graham College.

"THE SCIENCE ÓF FAIRY TALES." Prof. B. F. Sledd, of Wake Forest College.

"HISTORICAL PAPER." Dr. S. B. Weeks, of Trinity College.

"THE PASSION-PLAY OF OBER-AMMERGAU: A Development of the Old Miracle-Play." Mr. Howard A. Banks, of Asheville, Late Fellow of the University of North Carolina.

8:30 P. M.

"HOW TO STUDY HAMLET." Dr. Thos. Hume, of the University.

Business Meeting of the Modern Language and English Literature Association.

Tuesday, June 2S.

"POPULAR EDUCATION DAY."

Special Programme arranged by State Superintendents' Association.

11 A. M.

ADDRESSES by Mr. N. B. Broughton, of Raleigh; Hon. H. A. Gudger, of Asheville, and Hon. M. W. Robbins, of Statesville.

3:30 P. M.

ANNUAL MEETING of County Superintendents.

8:30 P. M.

"OUR NEEDS." Prof. E. A. Alderman, Greensboro.

Wednesday, June 29.

INTER-COLLEGIATE ORATORICAL CONTEST.

The University, and Wake Forest, Trinity and Davidson Colleges will each send two representatives. The successful competitor will be awarded the Assembly Orator's Gold Medal.

3:30 P. M.

INSTRUMENTAL MUSIC CONTEST.

Open to pupils in any school for girls in North Carolina. A gold medal will be awarded to the successful competitor.

8:30 P. M.

CONCERT by the Glee Club of the University of North Carolina.

Wednesday, June 30.

"CLASSICAL DAY."

11:30 A. M.

"THE MENTAL, MORAL AND MONEY VALUE OF LATIN." Prof. J. B. Carlyle, Wake Forest.

"MYTHOLOGY." Miss Nannie Y. Burke, Peace Institute.

"LATIN IN THE PUBLIC SCHOOLS." Supt. G. A. Grimsley, Greensboro.

"THE CLASSICS IN ENGLAND." Mr. Ronald MacDonald, Ravenscroft School.

"THE INDUCTION METHOD OF TEACHING LATIN." Supt. Logan D. Howell, Tarboro.

"WHY TEACHERS SHOULD READ THE POEMS OF HOMER." Prof. J. M. Horner, Horner's School.

"GREEK AND LATIN IN SECONDARY SCHOOLS." Prof. F. E. Welch, Trinity.

8:30 P. M.

"CLASSICAL TRAINING." Dr. E. Alexander, Chapel Hill.

Friday, July 1.

11:30 A. M.

MEETING OF COLLEGE ASSOCIATION.

8:30 P. M.

"A NORMAL BIBLE LESSON." Conducted by PROF. H. M. HAMILL, Chicago.

Saturday, July 2.

11:30 A. M.

"A NORMAL TRAINING LESSON." PROF. H. M. HAMILL. General discussion.

8:30 P. M.

LECTURE. REV. THOS. DIXON, New York.

Sunday, July 3.

11 A. M.

SERMON. REV. THOS. DIXON.

The music of the Sunday services will be conducted by Miss Bessie Worthing, and the singing will be led by Whiting's celebrated Orchestra.

5 P. M.

SUNDAY-SCHOOL MASS-MEETING.

ADDRESSES by Prof. Hamill and other prominent Sunday-School workers.

8:30 P. M.

"SUNDAY-SCHOOL OPPORTUNITIES." PROF. H. M. HAMILL.

Monday, July 4.

Excursion to Atlanta, Ga., to attend the meeting of the Southern Educational Association. A special low rate for the round trip, and no change of cars from Morehead City to Atlanta.

Adjournment of the Assembly.

In addition to the regular programme, there will be exercises in physical culture conducted by MISS CLECHLEY, of Tarboro; lectures by Prof. FRANK M. SMITH, University of Tennessee; Hon. JOSIÁH H. SHINN, Superintendent of Public Education of Arkansas; and MR. T. F. DONNELLY, New York; an illustrated lecture, "What to see in London," by Rev. J. J. HALL, Raleigh. Addresses are expected by Gov. THOS. M. HOLT, Hon. ELIAS CARR, Hon. JOHN C. SCARBOROUGH, Hon. MARION BUTLER, President of Farmers' Alliance, Gov. T. J. JARVIS, Senator Z. B. VANCE, Capt. OCTAVIUS COKE, Hon. R. M. FURMAN, Hon. D. W. BAIN, and other prominent North Carolinians.

The "Educational Exposition" will be the largest and best display of school work ever seen in North Carolina. The exhibit will fill the ten large rooms in the Assembly Building, including articles from nearly every leading educational institution in North Carolina. This exhibit will be of special help and value to progressive teachers.

The "Assembly Teachers' Bureau" has secured good school positions for over three hundred members of the Assembly. The Bureau will be in session every day during the Assembly, and will extend its valuable aid freely to any teacher, committee, or school officer.

Miss BESSIE WORTHINGTON, teacher of music in the State Normal and Industrial School for Young Women, will have charge of all the music during the session. MR. ADOLPH COHN, dealer in pianos and organs, New Berne, N. C., will supply the Assemby Hall with an elegant Baby Grand Piano and a Pipe Organ for use in all the musical exercises and entertainment.

On the regular programme all papers and speeches, by order of the Executive Committee, are limited to twenty minutes, evening lectures to forty minutes, and speeches in general discussion will be limited to ten minutes. This rule will be strictly enforced. Every subject considered by the Association is open for full and free discussion, and teachers are urged to express their views without hesitation. The Assembly is not a meeting for "cut and dried" papers upon antiquated subjects, but it is a council of live teachers upon live topics, and it is specially desired that every view upon every subject shall be freely expressed; and it is expected that every teacher, from the "old-field school" to the president of the University, will feel free to speak upon any subject that may be under consideration.

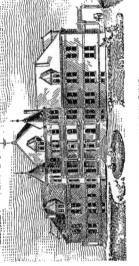

DORMITORY BUILDING.

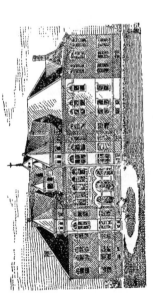

SCHOOL BUILDING.

STATE NORMAL AND INDUSTRIAL SCHOOL FOR YOUNG WOMEN,

GREENSBORO, N. C.

This institution is the crowning pride of North Carolina. It was established and has been built by the State during the administration of Hon. S. M. Finger, our present faithful and energetic State Superintendent of Public Instruction, and it is

EDITORIAL.

"Carolina! Carolina! Heaven's blessings attend her,
  While we live we will cherish, protect and defend her;
  Though the scorner may sneer at and witlings defame her,
  Our hearts swell with gladness whenever we name her."

THE NORMAL AND INDUSTRIAL SCHOOL FOR GIRLS.

We notice that some anonymous correspondents in the newspapers have erroneously given credit for the establishment of the State Normal and Industrial School for Young Women to various people who were simply "acting under orders." We desire to have this matter set right in the beginning of the history of the institution, and, therefore, will state for the information of everybody that the North Carolina Teachers' Assembly is the originator of this institution, and the moving agency by which its establishment was secured. The idea was first discussed by the Assembly in its organization session at Waynesville, in 1884; and the young lady who introduced the first resolution concerning the establishment of a State Educational Institution for the training of women is now living in Raleigh. At the following sessions, at Black Mountain and Morehead City, committees were appointed to bring the matter before the Legislatures. At every session of the Teachers' Assembly since that time the matter has been discussed and new committees have been appointed to memorialize the Legislatures in behalf of the school. After several previous failures the Legislature of 1890 voted to establish the college in response to the appeals of the Teachers' Assembly through its committees. The Assembly has paid every expense incurred in bringing the matter before the Legislature, including the printing of the various bills and memorials up to the session of 1890, and then paid over sixty dollars for the expenses of its committee which submitted the matter to the Legislature of 1890. To the Teachers' Assembly, therefore, belongs the whole credit for the establishment of the Normal and Industrial School for Girls. The committee which submitted the plan to the Legislature was simply doing what it had been appointed to do, and the Teachers' Assembly paid for the service. THE TEACHER is determined that educational honors shall be worn by those who have earned them, and we will always be very prompt to give credit where credit is due.

EDITORIAL NOTES.

THE ENTIRE edition of the April number of THE TEACHER was exhausted within less than a week after coming from press, although we printed three hundred extra copies. We had on file nearly enough new subscribers to use most of the extra copies.

THE JUNE number of THE TEACHER will not be issued until after the session of the Teachers' Assembly. This is our usual custom, and is done in order that the next number may contain full proceedings of the Assembly, which will close the current volume of THE TEACHER.

THE LATE Hon. William D. Kelly, State Senator from Pennsylvania, in a public speech said, "North Carolina is the most beautiful portion of God's earth upon which my feet have ever rested." The people of North Carolina and Senator Kelly have the same opinion upon this subject.

WE WANT to carry a party of about a thousand North Carolina teachers to the World's Fair at Chicago in July, 1893. Don't make any final arrangements for the trip until you see what THE NORTH CAROLINA TEACHER will be able to do for you as to plans, details and expenses of the trip.

THE TEACHER offered to the College Association, while in session at Greensboro, its pages for the publication of full proceedings of the session of the Association, and the offer was accepted. The journal of proceedings, as given to our readers in this number, is prepared and furnished by the Secretary, Professor W. A. Withers, of Raleigh.

AS A MATTER of justice to the preparatory schools of North Carolina, each college president in the State should publicly announce at the commencement this summer the number of students that each school has sent to the college, and which students were best prepared to enter. This will stimulate all the preparatory schools to better work and thus the object desired will be accomplished.

WILL NOT some prominent North Carolina school for girls confer a special favor upon the public and its patrons for one time by arranging a programme for the commencement concert to consist entirely of popular and familiar airs and songs? The people are thoroughly tired of the unmusical foreign music, which, to the average person, has precisely the same sound at every school concert. We want to enjoy, at least once, a genuine American concert in an American school.

AS A SPECIAL gift to music teachers and pupils for the new volume, we will send *twelve copies of sheet music*, vocal and instrumental, free to each one who sends a dollar for a subscription to THE TEACHER for this year. The music is full size and regular style and all the pieces are popular. The former prices of the music were from thirty cents to one dollar a copy. Make your orders early for the music as we have only a limited supply. The pieces sent you will be our own selection, but we will try to please you.

WE HAVE been searching for a long while for a thoroughly practical and reliable Encyclopedia for the use of teachers and schools which could be sold at a low price. We think that we have found just what we wanted in the "Americanized Encyclopedia Britannica." The work comprises ten large volumes, and is far more valuable to the American reader than the English edition, as it brings its work down to this year and contains over two thousand subjects not in the English or reprint editions, while it treats of every subject, great or small, that is mentioned in the Encyclopedia Britannica. We will supply teachers at the *wholesale* price, and will send circulars upon application.

ONE OF THE most pleasant and profitable educational meetings ever held in the State was the second annual session of "The Association of College Men" which convened at Greensboro on April 29. Dr. Geo. T. Winston was President, and Prof. W. A. Withers was Secretary. The attendance was good and every college for boys in the State was represented, and the programme of subjects was an excellent one, and there was a spirit of refreshing enthusiasm and culture prevailing in the meeting from beginning to end. The occasion was truly an inspiration to the workers in higher education, and it was thoroughly enjoyed by every person in attendance. The Secretary has prepared full proceedings of the session, which we give to our readers in place of the brief notes which we had made at the meeting. The colleges and private high schools of North Carolina have always held a very high place in the estimation of our people for their conservatism, thoroughness and efficiency, and that popularity is greatly increasing in this age of such wide-spread machine education. You will find both entertainment and profit in carefully reading the proceedings of the meeting.

NORTH CAROLINA teachers do not do enough general reading. We believe that our teachers are the best in the United States, and therefore we have the right to suggest lines of improvement. The teachers should keep well posted in matters of current history, literature, arts, sciences, and education. It has been stated that teachers read less than any other class of professional people. We have been investigating this matter, and must confess that we have not yet obtained sufficient evidence upon which we may deny the assertion. Teachers ought to be the best read people in a community. All teachers should be regular subscribers to their county papers, to some first-class New York weekly, a standard monthly magazine, and to one or more good educational journals. No person can do proper work without proper tools, and these are the necessary tools for every teacher who desires to do the best work. The teacher who does not take at least one reliable journal of education is as poorly equipped for good work as is the captain of a ship who goes to sea without a chart or compass. This ship *may* safely reach its port, and this teacher *may* educate a child—both by accident.

A NEW "History of the United States," by Robert Reid Howison, has just been published by Everett Waddy Company, of Richmond, Va. The book comprises 936 pages, is well printed and bound, and would be satisfactory to North Carolinians if it was not so intensely *Virginian*. We dislike "Montgomery's Leading Facts (so-called) in American History," because it is so blindly *Bostonian* (or sectional), and Howison's work is likewise objectionable. Among the many strange statements it is claimed that *Virginia* "made the earliest approach to a Declaration of Independence at Fredericksburg, April 29, 1775." In describing the third day's fight at Gettysburg in 1865, the old Virginia claim that to Pickett belongs all the glory is vigorously asserted, and the author endeavors to perpetuate

the old foreign slander of North Carolina by saying that
" Pickett had been impatiently waiting for the order to
advance. * * * General Pickett waited no longer but
galloped off to lead his Virginians to the assault. Never
was an advance more gallantly made. General Pettigrew's
division aided in it, and the statements so frequently made
that they faltered and gave way are untrue." This style
of writing is as false as it is misleading and slanderous. If
somebody has told a lie about General Pettigrew's matchless
charge at Gettysburg why shall the lie be again brought
forward in a school book? The text-books on English
history do not trump up all the historical lies of that nation
to keep the people from forgetting them so that they may
know the truth. Nor should a writer of United States
history for schools be guilty of such deplorable foolishness.

THE AIR IS full of complaints from college men that
students from the high schools, academies and public
graded schools, who apply for entrance into college, are not
properly prepared in grammar, spelling and arithmetic.
Too much time is given to the dead languages (too dead
to be ever again spoken) and not enough to the subjects of
practical use in life. The man or woman who cannot spell
correctly, and speak and write good English, is not educated, however much may be known of Latin, Greek,
Choctaw, Sanscrit, music and other ornamental branches
of learning. The colleges do not teach spelling, arithmetic and grammar, and this work is expected of the
preparatory schools. The " bad speller " is absolutely
useless in business or in the professions. At the recent
meeting of the College Association at Greensboro, many
of the speakers mentioned the fact that in the entrance
examinations of students many of them were found to be
sadly deficient in their knowledge of English, and it was
urged that all preparatory teachers give more time to
English grammar and the spelling-book. This condition

of affairs gives THE TEACHER a fine opportunity for saying "I told you so," because when some of our schools
(particularly the public graded schools) began a few years
ago to discard technical grammar and the spelling-book
we protested against the act and prophesied just the evil
result of which the college men now complain. It is far
more important that men and women shall be able to
spell and write their mother-tongue correctly, than that
they may know how to conjugate any or all of the dead
languages.

ABOUT OUR TEACHERS AND SCHOOLS.

THE UNIVERSITY has two hundred and fifty-four students, the largest
number since the institution was reopened after the War for Southern
Independence.

GREENSBORO FEMALE COLLEGE has an enrollment of two hundred
and forty-four pupils. Dr. Dixon, the President, is truly a most energetic and popular executive officer.

MR. D. L. ELLIS, President of Fair View College, has resigned to
accept the Superintendency of a Graded School at Kissimee, in Florida.
We wish our friend great success in his new line of educational work.

MISS IDA CELESTE SNELL, of Boston Conservatory of Music, is the
accomplished teacher of Music in Catawba College, at Newton. She was
one of the charming representatives of North Carolina at the launching
of the United States Cruiser *Raleigh*, at Norfolk, April 31st.

THE UNIVERSITY GLEE CLUB gave one of their delightful and unique
entertainments at Wilmington on the 6th inst. to an overflowing house.
These Glee Club concerts are about the most enjoyable occasions that
we know of which are offered to North Carolina people. The Teachers'
Assembly will be pleased with the Glee Club in June at Morehead City.

ST. MARY'S SCHOOL, at Raleigh, is going to celebrate its semi-centen-
nial this summer in grand style. Dr. Smedes is arranging a most
elaborate programme of exercises for the occasion, and thousands of
St. Mary's friends will be present to enjoy the celebration and add their
very best wishes for the continued prosperity of the noble old Institution.

BERTIE COUNTY has a fine Teachers' Council. The meetings are well attended and the work is proving of great interest and value to all the teachers. The next meeting will be held at Aulander on the 23d of July.

A PARTY OF students of Wake Forest College will, in a boat, explore Neuse River to its mouth during the vacation, reaching Morehead City in time to attend the session of the Assembly. They will be provided with a tent and all necessary equipments for camping during the trip, and they will also occupy the tent while at Morehead City. We wish the young gentlemen a most pleasant voyage.

THE COMMENCEMENT programme of the University is truly a tempting display of good things, and will attract the largest number of visitors which has been seen at Chapel Hill since the re-opening of the University in 1875. Dr. Winston is proving to the Trustees, and to all the friends of the University, the wisdom of their selection of a President, and we take special pleasure in again saying "I told you so."

WE HOPE TO meet every reader of THE TEACHER at Morehead City during the session of the Assembly in June, and it will afford us pleasure to be of any possible service to you towards making your visit in the greatest degree profitable and pleasant to you. The editor of THE TEACHER specially delights in rendering a service to North Carolina teachers, and you need not hesitate to call upon him for any assistance which it may be in his power to give.

THE TRUSTEES of the Normal and Industrial School for Young Women have elected the following teachers for the institution : Mathematics, Miss Gertrude W. Mendenhall, B. S.; Natural Sciences, Miss Dixie Lee Bryant, B. S.; Ancient Languages, Miss Viola Boddie, L. I.; Physical Training, Miss Miriam Bitting, M. D.; Vocal Music, Miss Bessie Worthington; Industrial Art, Miss Melle Fort; Domestic Economy, Miss· Edith A. McIntyre. Other chairs will be filled at a later date. All selected are Southern-born women except Miss McIntyre, who is from New York State ; and Misses Mendenhall, Boddie and Worthington are North Carolina women.

THE TRUSTEES of the Graded School at Wilson have decided to add a high school course to the school. We are sorry for this, as we have been greatly interested in the success of the school at Wilson, and our friends will find that the high grade is the first step towards the downfall of the school. The people of North Carolina are not willing to be taxed to pay for teaching in the public schools languages which are too dead ever to be spoken, and sciences which are absolutely useless to the average boy and girl in earning a living. It is vain to try to force upon the people what they do not want, and they do not want to have a very few boys prepared for college at public expense.

IN MEMORIAM.

" Death hath made no breach
In love and sympathy, in hope and trust.
No outward sign or sound our ears can reach,
But there's an inward, spiritual speech
That greets us still, though mortal tongues be dust.
It bids us do the work that they laid down—
Take up the song where they broke off the strain ;
So, journeying till we reach the heavenly town,
Where are laid up our treasure and our crown,
And our lost loved ones will be found again."

MISS LIZZIE I. CLARK, a member of the Teachers' Assembly European Party, and a teacher in the Bertie School, died at her father's residence, Dr. Wm. M. Clark, in Franklin County, May 11, 1892.

CUPID AMONG OUR TEACHERS.

'Tis said that " figures never lie,"
That one and one are always TWO ;
But Cupid proves, with work so sly,
Some wondrous things that figures do.
And when he claims a teacher's hand
All rules of figures then are done,
Though TWO before the preacher stand
This one and one are ALWAYS ONE.

MISS FANNIE JOHNSTON, one of Pitt County's fair teachers, was married near Greenville on April 20th, to Mr. D. S. SPAIN, of Greenville. Rev. James Winfield, editor of the *Watch Tower*, officiated.

AT THE bride's residence at Trinity College on April 20th, 1892, Rev. R. L. WHITE, a student from Northampton County, married Mrs. CARSON KEARNS, of High Point. Prof. W. H. Pegram performed the ceremony.

AT RECESS.

The books and slates now put away,
And let us laugh a little while ;
For those who work there should be play,
The leisure moments to beguile.

TEACHER.—"Now what kind of an animal is it, my dear, that furnishes you with shoes to wear and meat to eat?" Little girl—"My father, ma'am."

"HAVE you learned much German, Tommie, with your new governess?" "No, but the fraulein's learned lot's of English."

ON BEING ASKED what a nephew is, a little Boston school-girl replied : "It is when your niece is a boy," a statement which it would be hard to controvert.

FARMER CLOVER.—"I guess we'll have to elect Nathan Meddergrass school superintendent." Farmer Sassafras—"Why, he don't know nothin' 'bout eddication." Farmer Clover—"No, but his big punkin tuk the prize at the county fair."

SUNDAY-SCHOOL SUPERINTENDENT.—"Who led the Children of Israel into Canaan? Will some of the small boys answer?" [No reply.] Superintendent (somewhat sternly)—"Can no one tell? Little boy on that seat next to the aisle, who led the Children of Israel into Canaan?" Little Boy (badly frightened)—"It wasn't me. I—I jist moved yere last week f'm Mizzoury."

AN INQUIRING MIND.—"Mamma, who is Tunkantel?" "I'm sure I don't know, child. I never heard of such a person." "Does he love papa?" "I don't know." "Does teacher love him?" "Love who?" "Tunkantel?" "What are you talking about, my child?" "Well, I don't care. Anyway, I saw papa hugging teacher on the stairs yesterday, and teacher say she love papa better than Tunkantel."

SHE CHANGED HER MIND.—Pretty Teacher (severely).—"Did your mother write this excuse?" Bad Boy—"Yes'm." Pretty Teacher—"Humph! It looks very much like one of your scrawls." Bad Boy.—"Mamma wrote it, but, please ma'am, she had sister Jennie on one arm, crying with a bumped head, and brother Willie in the other, with a cut finger, and a lot of sewing on her lap, and she was rocking the cradle with her knees, and she had to write with her toes." Pretty Teacher (in the evening)—"I am very sorry, Mr. Poorchapp, but I have changed my mind. I shall never marry."

AND LINDLEY MURRAY WEPT.—To a Park Row waiter belongs the proud distinction of uttering what is probably the most ungrammatical sentence ever evolved from the brain of illiterate man. Saturday afternoon an old man took his seat at the table and gave his usual order to a new and rather case-hardened plate tosser. "Waiter," he piped, as the dishes were slammed down before him, "this beef isn't sufficiently underdone." With a smile of contempt the servitor bore the viands back to the kitchen window and returned a moment later without having changed them. "Say, old gent," he hissed through his clenched teeth, "we ain't got no beef what's no underdoner!"

THE NORTH CAROLINA TEACHER.

VOL. IX.   RALEIGH, JUNE, 1892.   NO. 10.

EUGENE G. HARRELL,   =   =   =   =   Editor.

THE TEACHER.

BY WILLIAM OLAND BOURNE.

I saw a teacher building slow,
   Day after day as passed the years,
And saw a spirit temple grow,
   With fear and hope, and often tears;
A mystic palace of the soul,
   Where reigned a monarch half-divine,
And love and light illumed the whole,
   And made its hall with radiance shine.

I saw a teacher take a child,
   Friendless and weak, and all alone,
With tender years, but passions wild,
   And work as on a priceless stone;
Out of the rude and shapeless thing,
   With love and toil and patient care,
I saw her blest ideal spring —
   An image pure and passing fair.

Upon a canvas ne'er to fade,
   I saw her paint with matchless art,
Pictures that angels might have made
   Upon a young and tender heart;
And growing deeper for the years,
   And flowing brighter for the day,
They ripened for the radiant spheres,
   Where beauty ne'er shall pass away.

THE RELATION OF THE UNIVERSITY TO PUBLIC EDUCATION.

——

BY HON. S. M. FINGER, STATE SUPERINTENDENT PUBLIC INSTRUCTION.

——

THE NECESSITY FOR INTELLIGENCE RECOGNIZED BY THE FOUNDERS OF THE REPUBLIC.

While our forefathers in the thirteen American Colonies, about 1750 A. D., and later, contended with England for abatement of the hard conditions imposed by monarchical government, the state of affairs in France was something like this: There was a king and about thirty thousand nobles whose main business it was to enjoy themselves at the expense of the people in all sorts of ways, many if not most of which were forbidden by the moral law, and to tell the great body of the people *what to do;* there were one hundred and thirty thousand priests and other church dignitaries whose main business it was to tell the people *what to believe;* and there were twenty-six millions of people, the third estate, whose condition was that of intellectual and bodily bondage. When Louis the XVI was compelled to call the States-General in 1788, the great body of the people were allowed to vote for the first time in one hundred and seventy-three years. They elected delegates who took charge of the government, and soon an ignorant mob took charge of the legislative assembly and the king, and the bloodiest revolution and civil war in the annals of time was the result. Conservative intelligence could not control the ignorant people, who had real grievances and were led by bold, cruel and designing men, such as Denton, Marat and Robespierre.

The necessity of intelligence among the people, even in despotic governments, was understood by the founders of our republic more than one hundred years ago.   They knew that it was even more necessary in republics, and they dreaded to cut loose from the mother country and from the monarchical form of government and place all power in the hands of the people.   Washington continually spoke of the necessity of promoting intelligence among the people, saying that it was the more necessary in republics in which all power resided in the people.   So, too, Jefferson, perhaps wiser than any of his contemporaries, devised for Virginia, and pleaded for it to his dying day, a system of public schools in regular succession from the lowest primary up to and through the University.   He died before much was effected, except the establishment of the University of Virginia, in which he so much prided himself, and of which he was the real father and founder.   It was much easier to establish a University than a great system of public schools— the cost was so much less ; and besides, it seemed a natural process to set at work the head of the system first.

It is too tedious to cite the names of the very many great men who feared for the stability of the republic for want of sufficient intelligence among the people, and who urged the establishment of schools supported by public funds.

CAUTION OF THE CONVENTION OF 1776.

It was this feeling of intense anxiety that caused our own wise North Carolina statesmen, who met at Halifax in 1776, to place in our State Constitution that oft quoted section, "a school or schools shall be established by the Legislature for the convenient instruction of youth, with such salaries to the masters paid by the public as may enable them to instruct at low prices; and all useful learning shall be duly encouraged and promoted in one or more Universities."

The caution and anxiety of the members of this Convention about trusting too much to an unintelligent people, may be appreciated by considering the limitation they put upon suffrage and the great power they gave to the Legislature.   No man could, under that Constitution, vote for State Senator unless he owned fifty acres of land and had paid his taxes; nor could any man vote for the members of the House of Commons unless he had paid his taxes.   The election of Governor was given to the Senate and House of Commons, as was also the election of all the Judges, Council of State, all general militia officers, State Treasurer, Secretary of State, the Attorney General, and all the Justices of the Peace.   Indeed, the people did not vote for any of their officers, State or county, except the members of the Legislature.

These men of the Convention of 1776, though hold to establish an independent government and pledge in its defense their lives, their fortunes, and their sacred honor, dreaded to launch the ship of state on the ocean of popular suffrage.   At times all through the successive decades down to the present, little by little has more power been given to the people, to be exercised by their direct vote for their officers ; and just in proportion as suffrage has thus been extended, has it also been insisted upon that educational effort must be extended, and it has been extended until we now have in North Carolina about seven thousand public schools annually in session.

IDEAS ABOUT PUBLIC EDUCATION BY THE FOUNDERS OF THE UNIVERSITY.

In the light of these facts, what must we think were the ideas of the founders of the University as to its relation to public education?   They evidently wanted education for everybody, but they began with the University, not with the country primary school.   Did they not think that it was first necessary to have a head, from which would shine out into the mental darkness rays of intellectual light?

Did they not think that it was first necessary to have a heart, from which would flow out into a system of public education great streams of morality and religion?

As a matter of fact, is not this just what has taken place? Was it not the sons of our University who were the most active in the establishment of the public school system which now furnishes a school-house on almost every hill-top? Go and read the earnest appeals of Judge Murphey and many others, who in times long gone by had the privilege of instruction in these classic halls.

I know full well that many of the alumni of this institution do not heartily, if at all, advocate the general system of public education ; and I know that there are some of the alumni now who, while ardent friends of their *Alma Mater*, and desirous of seeing her prosper, are either opponents of the general system, or at least not helpers. The fact remains, however, that in the establishment of the general system of public schools very much is due to the sons of the University.

THE UNIVERSITY COMPARED TO THE HUMAN ANATOMY.

In the human anatomy the head controls the members of the body, but the hands and the feet and all parts of the body send back through the nervous system messages to the brain. From the head there go out to all members of the body commands for action, and from the remotest finger tips answers are sent back. From the heart of the human body there is sent out to every part of the body a stream of pure blood, which keeps it alive and healthy, and from every part of the body is sent back this same blood, not so pure it is true in part of its journey, but still purified before it reaches the heart, and ready not only for the support of that organ, but to be sent out again for the support of all the organs of the body.

This picture of the human anatomy is the best illustration I can give as to what I conceive the relation of the University to public education ought to be. The intellectual, moral and religious life of the University should flow out into every remote part of society—into every occupation of the people. All the learned professions should be made more effective because of this life, and farming and all kinds of manual labor should be better done because of this life. Just as this life is made effective among the people, will they respond and send back to the source of this better life their greeting, their material support, and their sons, who having already felt at a distance the good influence of the University, desire to sit in her halls at the feet of her learned President and Professors.

THE STATE WELCOMES PRIVATE AID, BUT CANNOT DEPEND UPON IT.

Whatever may be said of private effort to educate the people in primary schools, in high schools and in colleges, there are perhaps but few people now who do not see that a system of public education is necessary, and that it is becoming more and more necessary as suffrage is extended. Few men will now be found to say that private effort can be made sufficient to provide the education necessary for good government. Most men are free to admit that not only should all the people be educated, at least to some extent, but that it is necessary in order to secure this education that the State must take the matter in hand. While the State undertakes this great work, she gladly welcomes all private aid that can be called to her assistance. The State cannot, however, depend upon private effort for any grade of this work. As she cannot depend upon private effort for her University work, or for her primary or secondary work, so she cannot entirely depend upon it for her high school work.

In the city schools, and in all public schools where it is possible, there should be established high school departments, in which there should at least be an optional course leading to the doors of the University and to the colleges; and at the University there must be such facilities for post-graduate work as will provide for the wants of all the graduates of all of our colleges.

MORAL AND RELIGIOUS TEACHING.

If the University is in fact intended to be the head and heart of the intellectual, moral and religious life of the State, what fearful responsibility rests upon her Trustees, Professors and her students. Perhaps it may be questioned whether or not, inasmuch as the State and Church are necessarily separate in our form of government, I am not going too far when I include religious training as a part of the University's duty. I quote Article 9, Section 1 of our State Constitution, the article that specially provides public schools, including the University : "Religion, morality and knowledge being necessary to good government and happiness of mankind, schools and the means of education shall forever be encouraged." Here we have a clear recognition of the necessity of teaching religion and morality, as well as of imparting secular knowledge, in our public schools. Of course it goes without saying that all sectarian teaching is excluded.

Our State Constitution, our statutes, and our Court proceedings. recognize God in His Word, and the morality which we inculcate is the Christian morality. The great principles of Christian morality prevail in this country. It is impossible to separate morality from religion, for the highest morality of any people is the highest religion of that people. This is the religion we are required to teach. But besides such teaching by precept, example is far more effective. The Sermon on the Mount was a great blessing to humanity, but perhaps not a greater blessing than were the three years of illustration of its beneficent precepts by the Saviour of mankind.

HOW THE UNIVERSITY'S INFLUENCE IS TO BE EXTENDED.

The responsibility of extending the University's influence is discharged only in part within the walls of the buildings and in the every-day social intercourse between the Faculty and the students. I hold that the President and all the Professors should go out among the people of the State and approve themselves to the people by personal acquaintance, by lectures on the University Extension plan, or otherwise. Every one connected with the institution should be a hearty friend of public education, not alone in the University, but he should also be an active friend of the whole system of public education, from the lowest primary and secondary schools up through the high schools to the doors of the University and the colleges. If the President and Professors exercise this spirit, no student will be able to take a course there without becoming an active worker in the public school cause. The whole institution—President, Faculty and students—should be thoroughly alive to the necessity of the education of all the people, and should be active workers to that end. It is a cause of great gratification that so much of this spirit now prevails there. It augurs well, not only for the lower public schools, but also for the safety of the University itself.

COURSE OF STUDY AND SCOPE OF WORK.

What the courses of study there should be, how much higher they should go, or how much lower, I have not time fully to discuss now, even if I were competent to discuss it. I may be allowed to suggest that the old classical and mathematical curriculum must not be insisted upon as a *sine qua non* for admission. However important it is for that curriculum to stand out prominently, entrance upon a course at the University should no more be dependent upon a definite amount of Latin and Greek and mathematics, than an A. B. course should be required for admission to the law school or medical school. I submit that entrance should be made to depend upon actual antecedent training received by the applicant, and his ability successfully to pursue such special studies as will prepare him for his chosen life work.

Our high schools aim at giving practical education, rather than at fitting young men for college ; and many young men, after having much training without reference to college life, change their minds and desire to take a higher course. I am glad that the different courses laid down in our University catalogue recognize these facts and provide a place for such young men. Our curriculum must conform to the ever-changing demand of the times, and the institution must become more and more a University in fact.

While the highest culture must not be neglected, it must not be forgotten that the times and circumstances demand intense practicability. The bread and meat question is, after all, the question which presses hardest now for solution. Labor-saving machines, and the great advance made in science and art in every direction, make it necessary for every State and every community to look sharply after the development of its material resources. Competition between the States and between individual citizens is sharper perhaps than it has ever been before, and our education system must take note of this fact. The science of political economy must have due consideration and emphasis. We should make as much as possible out of our soil, our mines, our forests, and our water-powers. This University should be the great leader of thought to accomplish this end, while at the same time she should give the broadest and highest culture for every kind of professional life. There is room for all the professors, each in his own particular chair, to exercise ingenuity. And last, but not least, the University should rescue from oblivion and set before the world to the fullest possible extent, our history as a colony and as a State. Our worthy Professor of History should set at work the whole student body, for the purpose of bringing to light every relic and document to be found in all the counties that will throw light upon our history, a history than which there is none more worthy in the sisterhood of States.

NORMAL DEPARTMENT.

Section 14, Article 9 of our State Constitution requires, as soon as practicable, the establishment in connection with the University of a department of agriculture, of mechanics, of mining, and of normal instruction. The State has seen proper to establish the three former, not in connection with the University, it is true; but she has not done anything for normal instruction at the University.

Through the liberal gift of $30,000 by the people of Greensboro, a normal college is soon to be opened in that city for young women. But the State has made no provision for normal instruction for her young men. While we hope eventually the doors of the college at Greensboro will be thrown open to young men also, and that more ample provisions will be made for normal instruction at other points than the University, yet I submit that something should be done in this direction all the time at the University.

A large proportion of her students are teachers during their stay at the institution in some capacity or other, and many of them become professional teachers after their graduation, or at least engage in the business of teaching for a year or two more, pending their preparation for some other vocation. From this practice much good comes to them, because teaching affords a splendid opportunity for the review of former studies, and for becoming thoroughly and practically grounded in them. I heartily commend this course to young men for their own benefit. But why should they not have opportunity here to study the science and art of teaching? Could not at least a model school be established here which would be an object lesson at all times for the benefit of young men? Could not all the children of Chapel Hill be brought together in some way in a permanent public school, and could not the services of some competent professor be secured to superintend them, and at the same time give a course of lectures at the University?

It seems to me that something can be done on some such plan as this that would not only comply with the Constitution, but that will also still further extend the University's influence, and that, too, in a most valuable relation to public education.

All the graduates of this institution should not only be hearty friends of public education, but whether they teach or not, I submit that they should have, as far as possible, instilled into them the great fundamental principles that underlie successful and practical teaching.

SYMPATHY OF THE PEOPLE REQUIRED.

But if the University is to accomplish such results, she must have the sympathy of the people of the State and their support. It is right and proper that the Christian denominations shall have their colleges to meet any special wants they may have as denominations, and the wants and wishes that any individual members may have in reference to the education of their children.

I heartily wish that all the denominational colleges in the State were richly endowed, not only to enable them to further Christianity, but also to enable them the more effectively to help in the work of making all the people intelligent. I take it for granted that as time rolls along, more and more will the people who have the highest education, whether educated at a college or at the University, favor the general public school system.

As the whole educated force of the State becomes more heartily in favor of public education, and sees it as a necessity, so will there be a growing demand for the highest and most varied University work. The time will come when the success of an institution will not be estimated so much by the number of students enrolled and graduated as by the actual work done, and when the people of all denominations will look more to their University as a place of special training, suited for every highest want of their sons. Let the denominations pursue their work, but let the University at the same time have their sympathy and support.

IDEAS OF CASTE TO BE ABANDONED, AND THE DIGNITY OF LABOR INCULCATED.

We still hear now and then an echo of a dying creed that taught that the education of the working people would make them dissatisfied, and unfit them for the state and condition in which God has been pleased to place them. This creed comes down the ages, and has had its followers principally among those people who believe in caste in society, and that God has made some classes of people specially to govern other people. It has no proper place in a republic, in which the abolition of all titles and caste is fundamental, in which equalities of rights and individual manhood are emphasized, and in which there is held out in the very fabric of our government the possibility to every man of doing great good to his fellow-men, and of rising to eminence among them by the due cultivation of his whole intellectual and moral being.

Among the students there should be no caste; no idea that one class of people is better than another inherently, but that one man is superior to another only as he may prove himself so to be by his individual manhood. The doctrine on this point that should go out from this University is, that proper education does not unfit any man for any kind of labor which his hands may find to do; that if an educated man is unfitted for doing anything that God has made it necessary to be done, this is not the result of the fact that he has had his intellectual and moral powers cultivated, but the rather of his having adopted wrong notions about labor. The old idea that labor is degrading, and is a badge of servitude, must be everywhere discarded, and we must recognize the truth of what Carlyle said: "Modern majesty consists in work; what a man can do is now considered his greatest ornament."

In this address I have outlined the spirit that should go out from the University. All the public school workers in the country and city, and all the private school workers, should catch it up, and with harmonious effort, touching elbows all along the line, from the lowest primary school up to the colleges and the University, it should be proclaimed that the State is to be saved from revolution and anarchy; that Christian civilization is to be advanced, and that the happiness and prosperity of all the people is to be promoted by the education of all the people, mentally and morally, and by inculcating proper ideas about labor.

If our civilization is to be preserved and advanced, this result will be attained, not so much by doctrinal teaching, however important that may be, as by works. What the world now specially needs is works, as an exemplification of Christian faith. I think the time will come when men will vie with each other in doing something for humanity with their own hands, rather than in giving money, which many now think is the fulfillment of their whole duty.

This will be an unusual spectacle, and yet it will be in accord with Christ's teaching and practice. In speaking of the final judgment, He drew the test of acceptance in the following language: "For I was an hungered, and ye gave me meat; I was thirsty, and ye gave me drink; I was a stranger, and ye took me in; naked, and ye clothed me; I was sick, and ye visited me; I was in prison, and ye came unto me." Here is the fullest inculcation of work of all kinds as a necessity to raise humanity. It was exemplified by the Great Teacher in His carpenter shop, and in every other way as He walked up and down in Palestine.

GIRLS WHO WANT TO WORK.

Almost all earnest girls nowadays come into maturity with a real longing for work. There are reposeful, middle-aged people, to be sure, who firmly believe that this is a mischievous and misplaced activity, and that it is going to work out all kinds of destruction if the race of women take to other things than domestic and polite accomplishments. Be that as it will, it doesn't pay to argue about what we shall never live to prove. Here you are, hundreds of you girls who honestly want to work, and who are honestly averse to house-work. It also happens to be true that women, like men, work for wages, and that the wages a girl gets for house-work, even in her father's house, are not such as encourage you to adopt house-work as a profession. And so it happens that you are thinking to-day about a wage-earning business outside your home more than you are thinking about a husband.

The first thing you've got to know is what you can do best. To find that out, consult your taste. If you think it would be beautiful to trim hats or make gowns, say so and stick to it. Then go to the best milliner or dressmaker in your town and ask her to let you come into her shop and learn. She won't pay you at first, but your father has fed you for several years, and can probably discharge that paternal duty for a few months longer. If you are bookish, and the law or medicine attracts you, go to the office of your father's lawyer or physician and borrow his simplest book and study it. In any case don't disdain the modest beginning that lies nearest your hand; you are not ready for wider fields yet. And when you've settled upon a work don't play with it; learn to treat it just as seriously as your big brother or your father treats his.

And so, as your diligence and knowledge grow together, you will perhaps come to a point where you must leave your father's roof in order to finish your preparation for your work or to widen your competence and so increase your wages. You must leave your small town for a city, or the small city for a larger one. Before this can be considered for a moment, one of two things is imperative : either you must have the certainty—not the mere possibility—of something to work at that will give you a modest living, or you must have money enough in reserve to pay your way for a year ahead. There is no compromising with this. Never leave your father's home on any other conditions. The number of young women who leave their homes each year and come to New York without definite provision for work is simply appalling, and out of this spring the awful tragedies of want and discouragement that drive women to death or worse.

With this provision made, go into your work with the whole of you. Take care of your health, and, for the rest, give your mind and body to your duties. You will get discouraged in every fiber of your tired body, but it will only do you good. The man or woman who doesn't get discouraged often and often, seeing his ultimate reach beyond his daily grasp, doesn't see far enough ahead ever to succeed. So be sure that you will get discouraged, and getting discouraged, encourage yourself because of that very thing.

You will probably be thrown much among men. Learn not to expect parlor etiquette in business places. You are not there to interpret the amenities of life to a lot of busy men, but to do your work competently and go your way sensibly. They may be as kindly intentioned as your own brothers, but they are too busy to assure you of their distinguished consideration. If they treat you brusquely, directly, and frankly, they're paying you the compliment of treating you like a sensible woman.

Above all, don't always be looking for things to hurt your feelings. They'll come sometimes, and bruise you in every fiber till you'll want to put your head down in your mother's lap and cry like a little girl. But you must learn to distinguish between wounded feelings and wounded vanity. A woman cries nine times out of wounded vanity, and once out of the wounded soul that calls for divinest soothing to heal. Let your vanity smart all it will; it's good for most of us.

Another thing you will have to learn, is to keep your word; to go where you say you'll go, and come when you say you'll come, and let the heavens drop if they will. But they won't—except in blessings on your head.

Last of all, you may be the daughter of rich parents, and you may not. If you are the former, behave yourself as if you were the latter. Don't preface your first request for work with the information that you are going to work because you want to and not because you have to; it's bad business policy and worse taste, and none of your employer's business anyway.—*Exchange.*

POSITION WHILE TEACHING.

The teacher who would do her best work will disregard the dogmatic dictum which says, "Keep out of your chair." To be not merely a school-keeper, but a teacher—to be a mother to the spirit of children—to bear children in the sense of inspiring them to noble ideals, requires care of self as much as physical motherhood. That the nervous energy be concentrated upon the brain—not expended in maintaining an erect position—that the mind be serene and composed, the teacher must be left free to find the attitude best suited for that result. Say to young teachers, "Be careful not to stand too much; you dissipate force that ought to be held as a reserve; you tire yourself. The best teaching requires a restful spirit"—Jesus sat in the boat to teach. He called his disciples around him and sat down to teach them. Because some phlegmatic teachers find it necessary to stand or stir about to keep awake, is no reason why they should assert that such a position is the only one to keep awake and interested, and that lazy people sit.

A great many people who have given the world literary work that will endure have testified that they could not do their best thinking while standing. The orator needs to stand in order to make gestures. He wants his audience to be merely receptive. The lecturer stands, in order to demonstrate or illustrate his meaning by diagrams. But the teacher aims to inspire activity in others. He needs to hold his own power in check and use it as a lever to lift others into activity. To educate—to draw out, the teacher needs to concentrate all the nerve energy of his organism upon his brain.

The teacher should be generally a teacher rather than an orator or lecturer, hence he should sit more than he should stand. But the teacher combines all of these characters,

2

and hence he should stand *when* there is a *purpose* in standing, and *sit* when he teaches.

I have noticed the emphasis placed upon standing as the only true position for the teacher. This is an erroneous notion, which may do harm to young teachers, who are inclined to accept the dictum of the *Journal* as "Law and Gospel" on all points essential to success; hence I ask it as a favor that "the other side" of this *standing* business be shown for their benefit.—*Missouri School Journal.*

MEN AND WOMEN.

A man chews or twists his moustache when he is nervous, and a woman bites her nails. Under momentary excitement a man scratches his head for an idea and a woman bites her lips. Men compose themselves by revolving their thumbs and woman by tapping their feet.

A man in trouble walks the floor and a woman gets on her back and has a good cry. A man in a temper swears and a woman breaks the crockery. In a rage a man squares his elbows and clenches his fists, a woman "draws herself up," as a story book puts it, and walks off with a war-horse kind of carriage.

A man flies into passion and flies out again, but women are generally calculating; they nurse their wrong and pout long after reparation has been made.

Men are naturally cruel; women are born naggers. Men have more decency than women; women have more modesty than men. Men praise the truth; women, peace. Men seldom hate without cause, women can invent cause for the slightest offence. Men are sustained by principle; women by religion.

A man will defend the reputation of a friend in an argument, and a woman will stand up for the reputation of her sex.—*Exchange.*

TEACHING PRIMARY SPELLING.

BY CLARA J. MAHONEY, CHICAGO, ILL.

One certainly learns to spell by spelling, as it depends wholly upon observation and memory. I doubt the humanity in making life a burden to the poor speller. A good speller is one by inheritance, or it is a gift from nature. Faithful drill will improve the defect, but if occasion requires much use of pen, the dictionary must be the companion through life.

Our methods and devices are few. First, the alphabet must be *learned;* then if the district is foreign the child must know both *name* and *sound;* so that if he leaves school at the end of the second year he can write a note that can be read, though it may delight the heart of the phonetic speller. As soon as he has learned *at,* he can at once build words of which that is the root as fast as they can be given, whether he knows the meaning or not.

Before a child reads a sentence, the words of that sentence are pronounced, spelled orally, and written on the board by the child. They should be perfectly written on the board by the teacher for the child to copy, once, on going to his seat; then erased and pronounced by the teacher for the class to write on their slates.

For busy work the child, with an envelope or box of letters, forms those same words on his desk, accustoming his eye to the different style of alphabets. In the second grade he commences to learn how to study. The teacher having written some words on the board with care, has them spelled by syllables, calls their attention to certain syllables, silent letters, etc.; *sees* that they are well written on the slates. They are spelled orally before reading, and short and long vowels are given. Pupils find for study and busy work, how many times the words occur in a reading lesson. For an occasional memory exercise the children may each spell a word of the lesson without any dictation from the teacher.

It is better that more attention be paid to common words, those in daily use, than a drill on words that are feats of memory. Words like *such, they, some, said, who,* and *where,* etc., should be put into simple sentences, so that by different grouping and frequent correction they will finally spell the common words according to Webster.—*School Journal.*

CANNOT AFFORD TO READ.

BY CHARLES M. HARGER.

Said a teacher in our hearing a few days ago :

"I am so lonesome for want of reading matter. The family with whom I board have no books and take but one paper. That is a monthly flash advertising sheet."

"But do you take no papers yourself?"

"No, I can't afford it. My wages are small and the school term is so short I cannot afford to spend a cent for such things."

Out upon such teachers! America has no use for them. The teacher, of all persons, must be abreast with the times. He should come before his school enthused with the world-life that is throbbing on, outside his little domain. And in these days of cheap newspapers, cheap magazines, correspondence, and agencies, he has no excuse for saying he cannot afford it.

Does the teacher not know that the surest way for him to stagnate in some backwoods country neighborhood is for him to attempt living and teaching outside the world? Does he not know that the most certain way to preferment and honor is through broad-minded culture? There lies the way, and he is indeed short-sighted who will be penny-wise in view of the possibilities before him.

CONSULTING THE DICTIONARY.

"Lobelia, is the dictionary handy?"

Sitting in his cushioned armchair, with his feet comfortably resting on another chair and a newspaper lying across his lap, Mr. Billiger McSwat addressed this question to his wife, who sat near the bookcase.

"Yes," replied Mrs. McSwat.

"If it isn't too much trouble I wish you would look for the pronunciation of the word 'mirage.'"

Mrs. McSwat took down the dictionary, opened the bulky volume, consulted it a few minutes and said:

"I always thought the word 'lichen' was pronounced 'litchen.' 'Liken,' with the 'i' long, has the preference."

"I knew that already. How about 'mirage?'"

Mrs. McSwat turned another leaf or two.

"In a minute," said she. "While I am about it I'd like to find out the meaning of the word 'linoleum.'"

"Hurry up, Lobelia."

"I am hurrying. Let—me—see. 'Link,' 'linnet,' 'linseed,' 'lint,' 'lion'—why, it isn't in the dictionary at all, Billiger. Isn't that queer?"

"Yes, yes. How much longer are you"——

"Just a minute. I'm coming to it."

Turning forty or fifty of the pages at once she ran her eye rapidly down one of the columns, stopped, put her finger on the place, looked up and observed:

"I didn't know there was such a word as 'mathemeg,' did you?"

"Never mind whether I did or not. I want to know"——

"It means a fish something like the cod, and it inhabits"——

"Who cares what it inhabits? If you're not going to find that word 'mirage,' madam, just say so, and I'll hunt it up myself."

"Just a second," said Mrs. McSwat, turning a few more

leaves. "'Mispickel!' First time I ever saw that word, anyhow."

"You've turned too far over. Go back a few pages."

"It means an ore of a silver or grayish white"——

"You're too far over, I tell you! Turn back a leaf or two!"

"I have. 'Misconstrue.' Accented on the second syllable. I never knew that before. Did you? I always thought it was"——

"Never mind what you thought it was! The word I want to know about is"——

"Yes, I know; I'll find it in about a —— there, I've turned too far back. 'Mezza voce.' Pronounced 'medza vocha.' Why don't they spell it that way, I'd like to know? Ah, here's a word I've always wanted to know the meaning of. 'Meter.'"

Mr. McSwat kicked over the chair his feet were resting on.

"It's a French measure of length, Billiger, equal to 39,370 English inches, or"——

Mr. McSwat crumpled up the paper he had been reading and threw it at the cat with all his might.

"Or 39,368 American inches," continued Lobelia, serenely unconscious of her husband's fidgets. "It is intended to be the ten millionth part of the distance from the equator to the"——

"Good gracious, Lobelia! Are you ever going to"——

"North pole, as ascertained by actual measurement of an arc of the meridian. What was the word you wanted me to find, dear?"

Then Mr. Billiger McSwat gave it up. He threw off his dressing gown, jerked on his coat, growled out something to the effect that it was just like a woman and he didn't care the ten millionth part of a continental ding ding whether she looked it up or not; and then he kicked the cat clear across the room and went out into the back yard to cool off.—*Chicago Tribune.*

IN THE SCHOOL-ROOM.

[FOR RECITATION.]

A TRIBUTE TO THE SOUTH AND HER PEOPLE.

BY W. B. HARRELL, DUNN, N. C.

> " My country, 'tis of thee,
> Sweet land of Liberty,
>   Of thee I sing.
> Land where my fathers died,
> Land of the pilgrim's pride,
> From every mountain side
>   Let Freedom ring."

Thus, in the exuberance of his love for home and birth-place, sang the patriotic Southern poet, soon after the days of our Revolutionary sires in which that grand and glorious struggle for National Independence, through which the thirteen American Colonies had so recently and success-fully passed, was the brilliant theme and burden of many a song, and pean of praise, on every tongue throughout the wide domain of this vast country which we happily style to-day, "The United States of America"—"The land of the free—The home of the brave."

I, therefore, on this occasion, with feelings of love and gratitude no less sincere and intense towards the now silent heroes of the days of '76, who lie buried and slumbering in quiet glory on the distant battlefields of the far remote past, would still call to mind the more recent fame and record of heroes and patriots who poured out the crimson tide of their life's blood to achieve (though unsuccessful) the, *to them*, so much desired independence and freedom of this bright and happy Southern land, then styled the "Southern Con-federacy."

Heroes, whose fame and deeds of noble daring will never be fully sung, nor their names or prowess be handed down to posterity as they should and richly deserve to be, still *heroes*, *nevertheless*, because they offered their lives in cheerful sacrifice for the defence of a *principle*, a most glorious *principle*, dear to every heart that throbs with affection and devotion for the country of which that heart can say, "This is my own, my native land."

God bless this happy South-land; and may our hearts respond ever in loving tributes of praise and honor when the names of Lee and Jackson, and Morgan and Pettigrew, and a host of others of our own State, and many farther South of us, equally brave and worthy, are brought to our minds in the histories that recount their brilliant fame in the times of their deepest despondency and defeat—a defeat made glorious and honorable because they deserved, and should have had, complete success.

But the days of that great Southern trial have passed away, and to-day behold the land in all her bloom and beauty—no "New South," as foes have vainly attempted to force upon us, but the same lovely clime of the warmest beams of the sun of light and health—the same home of the brave, the true, the hospitable and the kind—the same blest land of open hands and warm hearts for the stranger and the oppressed of all countries—the same God-favored and God-honored South-land of "the olden time," when every man's home was his palace, and his heart full of "the milk of human kindness," the same "happy land of freedom," from the mountains of our own western borders, to the far-away shores of the Mexican Gulf—the same ever-to-be-praised and honored *noble South ;* and North Carolina, the chief, and highest, and noblest, and grandest of them all forever; the land that has *no equal*— the people that have *no superiors* in all the broad realm of the universe ; and the homes whose latch-strings hang always on the outside for the weary and worn, both day and night.

Therefore, Hurrah! for the old North State forever! And "Ho! for Carolina," till our latest breath, say we; and we know your own hearts will warmly respond to the glad

"Hurrah! hurrah! for the old North State, hurrah!
Which in the Nation's galaxy shines forth the brightest star."

GEOGRAPHICAL TEST CARD.

PRIMARY GRADE.

Which is the south wall of your school-room?

How do you know it is the south wall?

In what part of the heavens is the sun at 12 o'clock?

Name that part of the sky where the sun rises.

What do you mean by the sun *rising*?

At what time of day is the sun highest in the sky?

How do you know which part of the sky is the west?

When does the sun set?

What is meant by the sun *setting*?

Where was the sun when you got up this morning?

Where is the sun in the middle of the night?

How is it you never see the sun in the north?

At what time of the year does the sun rise earliest?

What time did the sun rise to-day?

At what time of the year does the sun rise late and set early?

If you were in the middle of a large field at 12 o'clock, and the sun was shining, how could you tell which was north and south and east and west?

What do you call the four points?

Why are they called *cardinal* points?

Make up a word from the letters N E S W.—*Moderator*.

DELSARTEANISM.

She bendeth low!
She kicketh high!
She swayeth gently to and fro,
She treadeth only on her toe;
And when I asked the reason why,
The lissome maiden doth reply:
"Dear Edmund Russell doeth so."

"And who may Edmund Russell be?"
'Tis thus I catechise her.
She looketh in amaze on me:
She saith, "In truth I pity thee!"
She crieth, "Shame to thee; why, sir,
The high priest of Delsarte is he;
A type of wan flaccidity,
Our dear devitalizer!"

She fluttereth her wrists
Just like that matchless man·
She battereth her fists,
She doeth wondrous twists,
Though I don't see how she can.
She whirls and spins; insists
She likes it, till vague mists
Swim round her, and she's wan:
Just like that prince of priests,
The pale Delsartean.
—*Buffalo Courier.*

Bad luck is simply a man with his hands in his pockets and a pipe in his mouth, looking on to see how it will come out. Good luck is a man of pluck to meet difficulties, his sleeves rolled up, working to make it come out right.

QUESTIONS ABOUT A PENNY.

——

(The following questions may be used for a five-minute diversion. It will take a keen observer to detect every-thing :)

What fruit do you see?   A date.

.What is used in débate?   (Ayes and noes.)   Eyes and nose.

What flowers?   Tulips.   (Two lips.)

What animal?   Hare.   (Hair.)

What place of worship?   Temple.

What piece of furniture?   Sofa.

What do all seek after and few attain?   Fame.

What ten large buildings do you see?   Ten mills.

What vegetables?   Ear—of corn?

What did the Spartan mother give her son?   Shield.

What articles of Indian warfare?   Bows.

What root do you see?   Arrow-root.

Why is the cent like a prophet?   One sent.   (One cent.)

—*School Journal* (*N. Y.*).

THE CALF THAT WENT TO SCHOOL.

——

A dozen little boys and girls,
With sun-browned cheeks and flaxen curls,
Stood in a row, one day, at school,
And each obeyed the teacher's rule.
Bright eyes were on their open books.
Outside, the sunny orchard nooks
Sent fragrant breezes through the room,
To whisper of the summer's bloom.

A busy hum of voices rose,
The morning lesson neared its close,
When "tap, tap, tap," upon the floor,
Made every eye turn to the door.
A little calf that wandered by
Had chanced the children there to spy,
And trotted in to join the class,
Much to the joy of lad and lass.

Their A B, ab, and B A, ba,
It heard, and solemnly did say
"Baa! Baa!" then scampered to the green,
And never since in school has been.
Those girls and boys soon learned to spell
And read and write; but who can tell
How great that little calf became?
It may be, now, a cow of fame!
Or was that "Baa!" all that it knew?
I think it must have been.   Don't you?

—*George Cooper.*

ALL THE "DICTATION EXERCISES" in the new "North Carolina Practical Spelling-Book" are from the speeches and writings of North Carolina men and women, and this is a specially popular feature of the book. The list of woods, timbers, shrubs, and minerals, with correct spelling and pronunciation, are exceedingly valuable to North Carolina children. All prominet family names connected with the geography and history of the State are also given correctly, and the many new features of the North Carolina Spelling-Book will be very popular with teachers.

EDITORIAL.

"Carolina! Carolina! Heaven's blessings attend her,
While we live we will cherish, protect and defend her;
Though the scorner may sneer at and witlings defame her,
Our hearts swell with gladness whenever we name her."

THE TEACHERS AND THEIR ASSEMBLY.

The work of the ninth session of the Teachers' Assembly, held in June at Morehead City, was by far the best of all the sessions. The work was of a very superior order, the entertaining features were more numerous and interesting, and it was the largest attendance of actual teachers and the most representative class that we have ever seen at the Assembly. All the colleges and prominent schools were largely represented, and there prevailed the very best of professional fellowship throughout the entire session. The full proceedings of the meeting were excellently and carefully reported in shorthand by our stenographer, Miss Gertrude Jenkins, of Salem, who is one of the best shorthand reporters in the State, and thus the published journal will be of far more interest and value to the teachers than ever before. An evidence of the large attendance upon the session is the gratifying fact that the Secretary and Treasurer received near $1,700 in membership fees. The receipts were sufficient to pay all expenses of the session, and also to make the last payment due upon the Teachers' Assembly Building. The teachers of North Carolina now have a superb summer home, costing over $8,000, with not a single dollar of indebtedness upon the property. It almost seems impossible that this handsome and costly building could have been erected and paid for in full by the teachers within less than four years, but it is, nevertheless, a fact ; and that splendid structure will stand as a perpetual tribute to the educational enterprise and progress of North Carolina, which is greater than that of any other State of this Union.

EDITORIAL NOTES.

THIS NUMBER of THE TEACHER is very hurriedly prepared and many excellent articles have necessarily been omitted, but we assure our readers that we intend to make the coming volume even better than all preceding ones, both in quantity and quality of material.

NORTH CAROLINA has a new State song which is just published by Messrs. Alfred Williams & Co. It has the taking title, "True to North Carolina," and its spirit is in conformity to the urgent demand of the times, that the children of North Carolina shall be true to the State. The words were written by the editor of THE NORTH CAROLINA TEACHER, and the music is a popular Southern air adapted. Send twenty-five cents for a sample copy of the song.

THE "North Carolina Practical Spelling Book" is now ready for delivery. It is going to be the most successful book ever published in this State. The large first edition of five thousand copies is almost entirely sold by advance orders from teachers. The book contains so many new features of special value to North Carolina schools that it has received the heartiest approval of every teacher who has examined it. The Speller is carefully and thoroughly graded to meet the requirements of both public and private schools; it was prepared by a successful teacher, the work is well done, and the book is an honor to North Carolina.

IF YOU are a child of North Carolina never be afraid, ashamed or backward to raise your voice in defense of our beloved State. If some of the sons of our State are weak enough to become *Yankeeized* to the extent that they no longer have any conception of that noblest of all human sentiments—State pride—we must "deal gently with the erring ones," but promptly and emphatically reject all their feeble efforts to detract in any way from the glorious record of our Old North State. One of the highest ambitions of every teacher in this State should be to make his pupils true *North Carolinians*, for that embodies every principle of the perfect citizen.

YES, we know that the June number of THE TEACHER is far behind its date of issue, and hundreds of letters have been received by the editor asking "Why do I not get THE TEACHER for June?" As has been our custom for several years, that number has not been published until after the session of the Teachers' Assembly, in order that it might contain full proceedings of the meeting to conclude the volume of THE TEACHER and close the work of the school year. We have the proceedings of the Assembly in full, with the exception of two or three excellent papers, and now, after waiting for several weeks for them in vain, we have to go to press without them, therefore we must defer publishing the proceedings of the Assembly for a short while until all the papers are in hand.

THE RECORD of the memorable tour of our teachers in Europe is now published in handsome book form, containing many illustrations specially prepared for the book. The volume comprises about four hundred pages, and the jaunt is described in a lively, chatty and entertaining style quite different from the ordinary book of travels. The book is entitled "NORTH CAROLINA TEACHERS ABROAD," is beautifully bound in cloth and will be sent postpaid for $1.50. It is a valuable souvenir of the most famous trip to Europe ever made by the teachers of any State of the Union, and the story will be interesting and instructive to every reader. Only a small edition of the book is published, and most of the copies are already sold to members of the European party; therefore orders for the book should be sent at once to the editor of THE TEACHER for copies that may be desired.

WE HAVE about completed all arrangements by which our teachers may visit the World's Fair next year for very small expense. It is our intention to take several hundred teachers and their friends to Chicago on a twelve-day trip— allowing five days *en route* and seven days at the Exposition—and all necessary expenses of railroad fare and board, while in Chicago, will be only $35. Of course those who use berths in sleeping cars will expect to pay extra. We have no personal interest whatever in the trip, except to have our teachers visit the World's Fair at the smallest possible expense, and we intend to carry them at about one-half the cost of all so-called "Excursion parties" to the Exposition. The World's Fair of 1893 will be the biggest thing of the kind in the history of the world up to this time, and there will be no other exposition to equal it within our day and time, and therefore every teacher ought, by all means, to visit the great exhibit. The Fair opens on the 1st of May, and our party will go to Chicago about July 15, as the exhibit will not be fully arranged before that time, and we want you to see the grand show at its very best. Our party will have rooms at the new "Harvey House," which has capacity for three thousand guests and is beautifully located on the street car line in the suburbs of Chicago.

CUPID AMONG OUR TEACHERS.

'Tis said that "figures never lie,"
That one and one are always TWO;
But Cupid proves, with work so sly,
Some wondrous things that figures do.
And when he claims a teacher's hand
All rules of figures then are done,
Though TWO before the preacher stand
This one and one are ALWAYS ONE.

Mr. GEO. L. PATRICK, of Athens, Ga., and Miss KATHERINE LEWIS, daughter of Dr. R. H. Lewis, were married on June 8, 1892, at Hendersonville, at the residence of the bride's parents.

Prof. CHARLES B. PARK, of the North Carolina College of Agriculture and Mechanic Arts, married Miss EFFIE L. BROUGHTON, at Raleigh, on Wednesday, June 15, 1892.

IN MEMORIAM.

" Death hath made no breach
In love and sympathy, in hope and trust.
No outward sign or sound our ears can reach,
But there's an inward, spiritual speech
That greets us still, though mortal tongues be dust.
It bids us do the work that they laid down—
Take up the song where they broke off the strain;
So, journeying till we reach the heavenly town,
Where are laid up our treasure and our crown,
And our lost loved ones will be found again."

Prof. J. H. HORNER, of Oxford, founder and Superintendent of the celebrated Horner Military School, died at his home on June 13, 1892. Professor Horner was one of North Carolina's most eminent educators, and his death is greatly deplored.

CPSIA information can be obtained
at www.ICGtesting.com
Printed in the USA
BVHW04*1136011018
528939BV00008B/252/P